IMAGE, KNIFE, AND GLUEPOT

Image, Knife, and Gluepot

Early Assemblage in Manuscript and Print

Kathryn M. Rudy

https://www.openbookpublishers.com

© 2019 Kathryn M. Rudy

This work is licensed under a Creative Commons Attribution 4.0 International license (CC BY 4.0). This license allows you to share, copy, distribute and transmit the work; to adapt the work and to make commercial use of the work providing attribution is made to the author (but not in any way that suggests that she endorses you or your use of the work).

Attribution should include the following information:
Kathryn M. Rudy, *Image, Knife, and Gluepot: Early Assemblage in Manuscript and Print*. Cambridge, UK: Open Book Publishers, 2019, https://doi.org/10.11647/OBP.0145

Copyright and permissions for the reuse of many of the images included in this publication differ from the above. Copyright and permissions information for images is provided separately in the List of Illustrations.
Every effort has been made to identify and contact copyright holders and any omission or error will be corrected if notification is made to the publisher.
Further details about CC BY licenses are available at http://creativecommons.org/licenses/by/4.0/

In order to access detailed and updated information on the license, please visit https:// https://doi.org/10.11647/OBP.0145#copyright
All external links were active at the time of publication unless otherwise stated and have been archived via the Internet Archive Wayback Machine at https://archive.org/web
Digital material and resources associated with this volume are available at https://doi.org/10.11647/OBP.0145#resources

This work was supported by The Royal Society of Edinburgh.

ISBN Paperback: 978-1-78374-516-6
ISBN Hardback: 978-1-78374-517-3
ISBN Digital (PDF): 978-1-78374-518-0
ISBN Digital ebook (epub): 978-1-78374-519-7
ISBN Digital ebook (mobi): 978-1-78374-520-3
ISBN Digital (XML): 978-1-78374-725-2
DOI 10.11647/OBP.0145

Cover image: Folio from the beghards' book of hours, with a pen drawing of a kneeling cleric, beneath an initial that probably once contained a print depicting St Clare. London, British Library, Add. Ms. 41338, fol. 9v
Cover design: Anna Gatti

All paper used by Open Book Publishers is sourced from SFI (Sustainable Forestry Initiative) accredited mills and the waste is disposed of in an environmentally-friendly way.

Contents

Abbreviations	ix
Acknowledgments	xi
Bibliographical Note	xiii
A Note on Images	xv

0. Introduction: 1
Hybrid Books in Flux

1. Cut, Pasted, and Cut Again: 11
The Fate of 140 German and Netherlandish Single-Leaf Prints at the Hands of a Limburg Franciscan and a Modern Connoisseur

The Beghards of Maastricht and their Commercial Pursuits	25
Israhel's Roundels	39
The Logic of Accession Numbers	47
The Knife as a Tool for Creativity	54
Silhouettes and Doubles	59
The Thin Red Line	65
Split Personalities	71
Foliation	77
A Group of Woodcuts, Possibly Netherlandish	83
Appropriating German Engravings	89
Painted Prints from the Circle of Israhel van Meckenem	91

	Monogrammist A	96
	Attributions	99
	Recapitulation	102
	Book Production	108
	A Sheaf of Drawings	110
	Revolutionary Upheavals and the Dispersal of the Prints	132
	The Missing Images: In Paris?	140
	Rothschild	148
	Tross, Again	155
	Holes and Patterns	159
	Conclusions	162
2.	**A Novel Function for the Calendar in Add. Ms. 24332**	**167**
	Calendars and the Principle of Interchangeable Parts	168
	Book Technologies and Social Networks	174
	A Book for Children	186
	Jan van Emmerick	189
	Conclusions	194
3.	**The Beghards in the Sixteenth Century**	**197**
	Another Hoard of Prints From Maastricht	198
	The Calendar of Add. 31002	205
	Similarities Between Add. 24332 and Add. 31002	212
	25 Years Later	218
	Dating the Later Manuscript	223
	Israhel van Meckenem	226
	Conclusion: Changes Over Three Decades	239
4.	**Manuscripts with Prints:** A Sticky Idea	**245**
	Patterns	247
	Hiding in Plain Sight: Prints from Another Drugulin Manuscript	253
	The Dregs in Paris	263

Berlin	267
Bleeding into a Chalice	273
Manuscripts Still Intact	284
Israhel van Meckenem as a Master of Self-Promotion	293
Conclusions: Some Assembly Required	300
List of Illustrations	307
E-figures	321
Bibliography	337
General Index	349
Index of Manuscripts and Prints	355

Abbreviations

Amsterdam, UB	Amsterdam, Universiteitsbibliotheek
Berlin, KK	Berlin, Kupferstichkabinett
BM P&D	London, British Museum, Department of Prints and Drawings
BnF	Paris, Bibliothèque national de France
The Hague, KB	The Hague, Koninklijke Bibliotheek — The National Library of the Netherlands
Maastricht, RHCL	Maastricht, Regionaal Historisch Centrum Limburg
L	Lehrs, Max. *Geschichte und Kritischer Katalog des Deutschen, Niederländischen und Französischen Kupferstichs im XV. Jahrhundert.* 9 vols. (Vienna: Gesellschaft für vervielfältigende Kunst, 1908).
London, BL	London, British Library
London, BM	London, British Museum
P&D	Prints & Drawings
S	Schreiber, Wilhelm Ludwig. *Manuel de l'Amateur de la Gravure sur Bois et sur Métal au XVe Siècle.* 8 vols. (Berlin: A. Cohn, 1891-1911).
Vienna, ÖNB	Vienna, Österreichische Nationalbibliothek
Weert, GM	Weert, Gemeentemuseum Jacob van Horne

Acknowledgments

This book could not have been written without several important studies that preceded it. In addition to the great cataloguers of the nineteenth century, whose work I both loathe and cherish, my contemporaries have not only contributed to knowledge, but have also convinced me that this topic is worthy of pursuit. I am fortunate that many of those scholars have become friends: Hanno Wijsman, Ursula Weekes, James Marrow, Peter Schmidt, David Areford, Peter Parshall, Giulia Bartrum, Sheila O'Connell, Séverine Lepape, Huigen Leeflang, Erik Geleijns, Todor Petev, Eamon Duffy, Elizabeth Savage, and Ad Stijnman: thank you. I also thank Paul Taylor at the Warburg Institute for telling me where I could find the images whose photographs were neatly organised in the image library, Kathleen Doyle, Scot McKendrick, Julian Harrison, Clarck Drieshen, and Amy Jeffs at the British Library, Joris Van Grieken at the Koninklijke Bibliotheek van België — the Bibliothèque Royale de Belgique. James Marrow, Emily Rose, and Stephanie Azzarello provided nourishing hospitality and more. Jamie Harper suggested the book's title. And I thank Jeffrey Hamburger and Maria Theisen for inviting me to Vienna to discuss some of these ideas at a conference in 2015.

In 2011 and 2017 this project received grants from the Neil Ker Foundation, administered by the British Academy, for which I am truly grateful. In 2011 the Foundation granted me £1000 toward the cost of travelling to Paris to use the collections in the BnF; and in 2017 they granted me £1981.45 to partially offset the costs of images. The University of St Andrew's Open Access fund kindly contributed towards the cost of the book's publication by Open Book Publishers; the School of Art History also made a generous donation in exchange for my putting in 175 hours of work as chair of the Athena SWAN/Equality and Diversity

Committee in 2017. Andrew Demetrius of the School of Art History at St Andrews kindly prepared the digital images for publication.

I am grateful to Katharine Ridler, who read the text and suggested useful improvements, and to Emily Savage, who made perspicacious editorial suggestions. Lisa Regan helped me to find the unconventional scholarly voice in these pages, and I am deeply indebted to her insights. I thank the anonymous peer reviewers who did not pull any punches in their reports. One of them found it unsavoury that I discuss such topics as academic salaries, the costs of images, funding models, and the personal financial hardships that the academic marketplace foists upon us. However, at the risk of irritating this person further, I have not only decided to leave these sections in the final draft, but to develop them, as I believe that a more open discussion about such matters is urgent.

Bibliographical Note

Some of the ideas in this book first appeared in my previous books and articles:

Kathryn M. Rudy, 'How to Prepare the Bedroom for the Bridegroom', in *Frauen-kloster-kunst: Neue Forschungen zur Kulturgeschichte des Mittelalters*, ed. by Carola Jaeggi, Hedwig Roeckelein and Jeffrey F. Hamburger (Turnhout: Brepols, 2007), pp. 369–75.

—, *Virtual Pilgrimages in the Convent: Imagining Jerusalem in the Late Middle Ages*, ed. by Isabelle Cochelin and Susan Boynton, Disciplina Monastica, vol. 8 (Turnhout: Brepols, 2011), pp. 175–92; and 399–410.

—, *Postcards on Parchment: The Social Lives of Medieval Books* (Yale University Press, 2015), pp. 86–91.

—, 'Reconstructing the Delbecq-Schreiber Passion (as part of the St Godeleva manuscript)', *Unter Druck. Mitteleuropäische Buchmalerei im 15. Jahrhundert. Akten der Tagung, Wien, Österreichische Akademie der Wissenschaften*, 13.1.–17.1.2016, herausgegeben von Jeffrey F. Hamburger und Maria Theisen. Buchmalerei des 15. Jahrhunderts in Mitteleuropa Herausgeben von Jeffrey F. Hamburger, Band 15 (Petersberg: Michael Imhoff Verlag, 2018), pp. 156–67.

A Note on Images

As with *Piety in Pieces* (2016),[1] my previous book with Open Book Publishers, I am committed to making this book free and available to all. Placing images in text is time-consuming and drives up production costs. In order to minimize expenses, my publisher and I have decided not to reproduce images that are easily available on the internet, but rather to link to them using permanent URLs. There are therefore two sets of illustrations: figures that are reproduced in the book (fig.), and linked images, which I refer to as e-figures (e-fig.). These are numbered separately in the text and listed separately at the end of the book for clarity of reference. For the most part therefore, the material from the British Museum and several items in the Netherlands will appear here as linked images. If you read this book in one of its electronic formats, you can click on these links; those using a printed version may find it convenient to scan the QR codes. Related to the connectivity that this book implies, I have decided not to burden footnotes with the bibliographies of the prints that are in the British Museum, since these details can be accessed via the links and duplicating them would therefore be redundant. Images in the digital editions of this book will also feature a 'click to enlarge' function that enables the reader to view them in greater detail.

In the process of my research for this book, I created an Excel spreadsheet to keep track of the original composition of the manuscript, its nineteenth-century alterations, and the whereabouts of each element

---

1 *Piety in Pieces: How Medieval Readers Customized Their Manuscripts* (Cambridge: Open Book Publishers, 2016), can be accessed freely here: https://doi.org/10.11647/OBP.0094

today (if known). As the project grew in complexity, the table grew into one containing 14 x 646 squares, including some dynamic self-generating fields which added up how many folios, lost folios, and prints the original manuscript had. It is as simple as it can be, but no simpler. I have therefore decided to make this resource available to readers as an online Appendix, which can be accessed via this link: https://doi.org/10.11647/OBP.0145#resources

As with all Open Book Publishers books, *Image, Knife and Gluepot* exists in Open Access online (PDF, HTML and XML) editions, and in paperback, hardback, and digital (epub and mobi) editions.[2] In view of the number and quality of the images in this book, my publishers and I have decided to provide the option of a more expensive hardback edition (the paperback version is kept at the same low price as OBP's other paperbacks). The more expensive hardback edition is printed on the best quality paper available, in order to present the images as clearly and beautifully as possible. We hope that this range of options — the freely available PDF, HTML and XML editions; the economically priced epub, mobi and paperback editions; and the more expensively printed hardback — will satisfy all readers.

---

2   All editions can be accessed or purchased from the book's home page: https://doi.org/10.11647/OBP.0145

0. Introduction:
Hybrid Books in Flux

Pablo Picasso and Georges Braque are credited with having invented Synthetic Cubism when they pasted newspaper, wallpaper, and rope to the surfaces of images. They then wrote words, or parts of words, painted, and made marks on the surfaces of their multi-media objects. Marks they made united the various layers. The scraps of newspaper were of course cheaply printed and contained black-and-white texts and images, which the artists trimmed into various shapes, thereby adjusting the meanings of the scraps. To some degree, the newsprint functioned as texture or shading. Although their Synthetic Cubism is anthologised in art history books as being avant-garde and crossing borders by introducing printed paper into a high-culture form of production, in fact these features were already present in the fifteenth century, when book makers were cutting and pasting printed images into new arrangements, applying paint and ink that would connect the various pasted layers, and creating fictive frames around physical scraps. Fifteenth-century monastics inscribed text in various styles, some of which were meant to imitate printed letters. They then stitched their creations together with threads and bound them in leather. These book makers were in effect assembling new multi-media objects, whose elements crossed boundaries between high and low.[1] The new medium

---

1   Amy Knight Powell, *Depositions*: *Scenes from the Late Medieval Church and the Modern Museum* (New York: Zone Books, 2012); and Alexander Nagel, *Medieval Modern*: *Art out of Time* (London: Thames & Hudson, 2012) further articulate other relationships between modern and medieval art/objects. The affinities between the fifteenth- and

© Kathryn M. Rudy, CC BY 4.0

of print had connotations of being cheap even in the fifteenth century for, after all, some of the earliest printed objects in the West were playing cards, the ultimate secular gambling objects, flimsy adult toys.[2] Just like Picasso and Braque, certain book makers brought this black-and-white mass medium together with a firmly established art form that had exclusive connotations. Whereas the Cubists combined newspaper with easel painting, the people I consider here brought the cheap print into the midst of the manuscript, a medium charged with carrying the word of God, and which was traditionally commissioned by the upper social echelons.

This study is essentially about two media brought together: small images printed in the fifteenth century that were trimmed and then pasted to manuscript pages to adorn and embellish them. As Picasso and Braque would do in the twentieth century, book makers used the knife and gluepot as tools for creation. They probably thought of themselves not as avant-garde or edgy, but merely pragmatic. They used the new technology of printmaking to bring numerous images into the previously exclusive realm of manuscripts.[3]

---

twentieth-century products do not diminish the originality of the later artists, but rather illuminate the experimentality of both eras and force us to question our periodization.

2   In the early 1990s, Sheila Edmunds invited me to her house in the Finger Lakes, where we discussed the ideas she and Anne H. van Buren had published two decades earlier in: 'Playing Cards and Manuscripts: Some Widely Disseminated Fifteenth-Century Model Sheets', *The Art Bulletin* 56:1 (1974), pp. 12–30. This ignited my interest in the topics of this study.

3   Other studies that address the marriage of print and manuscript include: Frizt Oskar Schuppisser, 'Copper Engravings of the "Mass Production" Illustration Netherlandish Prayer Manuscripts', in *Masters and Miniatures: Proceedings of the Congress on Medieval Manuscript Illumination in the Northern Netherlands (Utrecht, 10–13 December 1989)*, ed. K. van der Horst and Johann-Christian Klamt, Studies and Facsimiles of Netherlandish Illuminated Manuscripts; 3 (Doornspijk: Davaco, 1991), pp. 389–400; *The Woodcut in Fifteenth-Century Europe*, ed. by Peter W. Parshall (Washington, D.C.: National Gallery of Art, 2009); Hanno Wijsman, with the collaboration of Ann Kelders and Susie Speakman Sutch, eds. *Books in Transition at the Time of Philip the Fair: Manuscripts and Printed Books in the Late Fifteenth and Early Sixteenth Century Low Countries*. Burgundica, 15 (Turnhout: Brepols, 2010); Todor Petev, 'A Group of Hybrid Books of Hours Illustrated with Woodcuts', in *Books of Hours Reconsidered*, ed. Sandra Hindman and James H. Marrow (London: Harvey Miller Publishers, 2013), pp. 391–408; Evelien Hauwaerts, Evelien de Wilde, and Ludo Vandamme, *Colard Mansion: Incunabula, Prints and Manuscripts in Medieval Bruges*. Exh. Cat., Groeningemuseum, Brugge (Ghent: Snoeck Publishers, 2018). All these studies treat prints made north of the Alps. Roberto Cobianchi, 'Printing a New Saint: Woodcut Production and the Canonization of Saints in Late Medieval

These tools — knife and gluepot — cut metaphorically both ways, as much later they also became the tools of the archivist, who separated complicated objects into their component parts so that they would fit into the categories of the archive. In an inversion of history, the archivists of the nineteenth century used a knife to cut up manuscripts that had prints in them, and then pasted those prints onto archival mattes for protection and storage. In this way prints would be classified and sorted, arrayed like butterflies on a lepidopterist's pin board.

However, the organisational aim of the nineteenth-century collection — to assemble and arrange every print by Albrecht Dürer, the Master ES, or other recognisable figures, to be complete — has little to do with what intrigues me about early printing; rather, I am pursuing the original functions of early print and charting the circuitous shift in technology from script to print.[4] For these goals, I am at cross-purposes with my nineteenth-century predecessors. When they cut prints out of manuscripts, they removed the prints from their original contexts, and made my job much more difficult. To understand the early functions of prints (who used them? how?), I will have to undo (virtually) the actions of knife-wielding nineteenth-century collectors. My goal here is to reconstruct books in order to reconstruct their contexts.[5] I am going to turn back the clock of the nineteenth century.

Terms such as 'printing revolution' make it sound as if the process of moving from script to print happened quickly and violently.[6] Instead,

---

Italy', in *The Saint between Manuscript and Print: Italy 1400–1600*, ed. Alison Knowles Frazier (Toronto: Centre for Reformation and Renaissance Studies, 2015), pp. 73–98, has begun identifying Italian prints that were pasted into manuscripts.

4   In this approach, I am inspired by Suzanne Kathleen Karr Schmidt and Kimberly Nichols, *Altered and Adorned: Using Renaissance Prints in Daily Life* (Chicago: Art Institute of Chicago; New Haven: Distributed by Yale University Press, 2011).

5   This study joins others that have endeavoured to reconstruct manuscripts broken up in the nineteenth century. See, for example, Judith Oliver, 'Medieval Alphabet Soup: Reconstruction of a Mosan Psalter-Hours in Philadelphia and Oxford and the Cult of St. Catherine', *Gesta* 24:2 (1985), pp. 129–40; and Aden Kumler, 'Canonizing a Catastrophe: The Curious Case of the Carmelite Missal', lecture at the conference *Canons & Contingence: Art Histories of the Book in England and America*, University of Massachusetts, Amherst, 2017 (unpublished). The missal Kumler discussed was clipped, disassembled, and its parts pasted into scrapbooks, now London, BL, Add. Mss 29704 & 29705.

6   The term comes from Elizabeth L. Eisenstein, *The Printing Revolution in Early Modern Europe* (Cambridge: Cambridge University Press, 1983). See the response by Herman Pleij, 'Printing as a Long-Term Revolution', in *Books in Transition at the Time of Philip the Fair: Manuscripts and Printed Books in the Late Fifteenth and Early*

the transition occurred over a period of seventy years or more and was not unidirectional: Einblattdrucke (single-leaf woodcuts, metalcuts, and engravings) often formed the models for painted miniatures, and incunables formed the exemplars for manuscripts.[7] In fact, the process of adopting print over handwriting in the Gutenberg age had several false starts, failed experiments, and blind alleys. Moreover, printing words and printing images did not share the same history. Manuscripts endured well into the 'printed age', with many books, pamphlets, and ephemera being made with a hybrid of techniques, specifically print and manuscript.

As we live in a world with multiple medialities, manuscripts still persist today: notes on the backs of cocktail napkins, the best kinds of love letters, Quaker marriage certificates, signatures on paper cheques, marginalia in books, some lecture notes, most angry notes on mis-parked cars, and the vast majority of graffiti are handwritten. The West Reading Room in the Cambridge University Library still has a fountain pen station, where those with fine writing instruments can fill their bladders with blue-black ink. These examples are some of the last outposts of handwriting. While working on this book I renewed my car's tax disc for the last time; by the time this book comes out, cars in Britain will no longer have to display physical, printed round cards indicating that their owners have paid the road tax, and this information will exist in electronic form only. Written culture is, once again, at the shoreline between dominant forms, with printed items growing dusty on shelves while new libraries are designed with large banks of computers, or simply larger cafés. As a result of this move away from the printed, the tangible, and the handwritten, people's handwriting has been declining lately. The book you are currently reading was written on a computer,

---

    Sixteenth Century Low Countries, ed. by Hanno Wijsman, with the collaboration of Ann Kelders and Susie Speakman Sutch. Burgundica, 15 (Turnhout: Brepols, 2010), pp. 287–307.

7   Sandra Hindman, and James Douglas Farquhar, *Pen to Press: Illustrated Manuscripts and Printed Books in the First Century of Printing* (College Park: Art Dept., University of Maryland, 1977); James Marrow, 'A Book of Hours from the Circle of the Master of the Berlin Passion: Notes on the Relationship between Fifteenth-Century Manuscript Illumination and Printmaking in the Rhenish Lowlands', *The Art Bulletin* 60:4 (1978), pp. 590–616; and Klara Broekhuijsen, 'The Bezborodko Masters and the use of prints', in *Masters and Miniatures: Proceedings of the Congress on Medieval Manuscript Illumination in the Northern Netherlands (Utrecht, 10–13 December 1989)*, ed. Koert van der Horst and Johann-Christian Klamt (Studies and Facsimiles of Netherlandish Illuminated Manuscripts, 3: Doornspijk, 1991), pp. 403–12.

and you may be reading it on a screen; its existence as a paper object may have been brief or unnecessary.

The late fifteenth and early sixteenth centuries, like our own era, also entertained multiple medialities, which enjoyed shifting levels of dominance across time and in various contexts.[8] The period of the handwritten codex roughly corresponds to the period of Roman Christian hegemony: the codex (as opposed to the roll) was the form of the big, bulky bible and its components. Encased as it was between two strong covers, the codex was self-protecting. Moreover, it was blatantly differentiated from the roll, which was associated with antiquity and with Judaism, although the roll persisted alongside the codex.[9] The manuscript codex would prevail as the chief bearer of Christianity and its texts from the early fourth century until the mid-fifteenth. Its stepchild, the printed book, would survive another 600 years (of heterodoxy, science, and waxing atheism) before the screen would wear it down, and along with it, sustained, absorbed reading.[10] This study is about early experiments in book construction, as the handwritten and illuminated book was giving way to the mechanically reproduced book, representing the beginnings of widespread reading and access to images on a personal, hand-held, and ownable scale. When the printed image met the handwritten word, the two had a brief and sultry affair on the page.

This research started with an image of St Barbara — a printed roundel pasted onto a handwritten page — which I found while I was looking for something else. Chasing down this roundel has involved a twelve-year hunt to reconnect prints with the manuscripts from which they

---

8   Those interested in pursuing further theoretical aspects of multiple modalities will benefit from Katherine Hayles and Jessica Pressman, eds., *Comparative Textual Media. Transforming the Humanities in the Postprint Era* (Minneapolis: University of Minnesota Press, 2013).

9   As J. P. Gumbert writes in 'Fifty Years of Codicology', *Archiv für Diplomatik: Schriftgeschichte, Siegel- und Wappenkunde* 50 (2004), pp. 505–26, at p. 519, 'rolls are not oddities, they are a valid and normal Medieval book type'. Rolls were ideal for certain functions, including providing supports for amulets, genealogical tables and other diagrammatic forms. Their poor survival rates reflect the fact that modern and early-modern storage systems privileged the codex.

10 Of course, the printed book and the manuscript codex and the manuscript roll all coexisted into the modern period, so these divisions were by no means absolute. The recent and vast literature addressing how reading on screens affects cognition changes constantly and is beyond the scope of this project.

were cut, to think about whole objects so that I can better understand their original functions. In the process, I have thought about the nature of collecting and classifying, the transformative properties of archives and the procedures of research in the humanities, the shifting meaning of value, the need to identify proper names in history. Rather than write a catalogue of manuscripts and the prints they formerly harboured, I have written a narrative about the process of discovering fragments and reuniting them with their former substrates. This is therefore a book about the institutions that collected prints in the fifteenth and early sixteenth centuries and about the institutions that decided to keep them for posterity, and how I interacted with those institutions for a decade. The categories formed in the nineteenth century have had a great impact on how one might do research on these objects, on which institutions hold them, on how they are classified, and which institutions will fund a study to reconnect them. While fifteenth-century writing and imaging technologies form the meat of this study, it is also about how research is done in the current shifting landscape. As I go to press, a new journal called *Fragmentology: A Journal for the Study of Medieval Manuscript Fragments* has published its first volume. Its editors, Christoph Flüeler and William Duba (Fribourg), are ushering in a body of studies made possible by European and American digitization efforts, which have also facilitated my project, to a degree.

I have invented a methodology that is intended to cope with a particular problem: manuscripts were cut up for their contents, which were then re-catalogued in ways that made it incredibly difficult to reconstitute them; I managed to reconstruct them (virtually), because I was able to develop my own organizational systems. My work therefore mirrors some of the work of the original scribes, who were also developing organizational systems within the manuscripts themselves. For the material under consideration here, scribes and book makers invented and imposed a primary system of organisation. Museums (and along with them, dealers and markets) imposed a second organizational system on the physical material. But a third system is my own. Much as the manuscripts existed in an institutional world that shaped them — of the monastery and then the museum — I too am operating in an institutional world of the university and the library/museum and the funding system that imposes constraints as well. Our labour is shaped by institutions, and these institutions themselves impose methods. They are part of the story I want to tell.

I have written this book in the first person because it is about my process of research as much as it is about the content of what I learned. Each step of the process demanded an innovative approach and taught me something distinct. By writing it in this way, I hope to convey something of that process and not just its outcomes. The resulting book is a methodological self-portrait; it is intended to explore how I have approached solving the problem of the gap between the manuscript as it was assembled in the fifteenth century and disassembled in the nineteenth. This is also a story of organizational systems, not only of the fifteenth-century manuscript, in all their complexity, and the nineteenth-century museum, in its hierarchies, but of the art historian who would attempt to look across this sea of raw visual and physical data and form patterns. In many ways, this methodology is *sui generis* — as it must be, since intuition plays an enormous role. But at the same time, in describing my own labour, I hope to reveal the contemporary institutional and organizational boundaries that continue to make it difficult to reconstruct lost books, even in the age of the digital and the database. My methodological story is personal; since it is my life it is chronological, but it is not linear. I do not present it as a *fait accompli*, but as a set of realizations and strategies that unfolded across the experience of the manuscripts themselves, most of which were viewed in parts and all of which were points in a vast constellation of books and images that I sifted through in pursuit of connections.

This study is intended to place art historical methods in the current moment as a third assembly of the book, one that needs to be exposed to view in order to have its institutional fault lines interrogated and its challenges discussed, and in particular, to have the art historical work that is done revealed, as that of the book maker and the curator is revealed. The copyist, the collector/curator, and the art historian are all labourers who toil within their respective institutions. And, like those earlier cultural workers, I too am facing institutional constraints. In adopting this first-person voice, I am revealing the labour of the art historian. Like that of the copyist and the curator, the (art) historian's labour is usually is presented as a polished final product, with the errors, blind alleys, and frustrations erased. The historian is usually the hero and master of the material.

Although few are in a position to disclose this art historical labour, I chose to do so at some risk, as it reveals my fumbling but also exposes the ways in which our research is affected by our personal lives (and funding). As I show in this book, that labour *is* the method — it is the way the work is done; and moreover, the hindrances that labour faces are themselves methodological challenges. Institutional limitations are methodological ones, for me as much as for the nineteenth-century curator. This book sets out to describe that in a way that we rarely do, an omission that obscures the true limitations of our research, and that circumscribes (secretly, invisibly) the kinds of projects we can take on unless we are willing, as here, to make vast personal sacrifices.

Chapter 1 reconstructs a manuscript by beghards in Maastricht. (Beghards were men who followed St Francis, considered themselves to be Franciscans, and who lived in community in towns and cities. They did not beg but made their living through their trade and labour.[11]) By reconstructing this book, I can show how the beghards learned to integrate the new technology of printed images into the making of their manuscript. That book straddles the two technological moments and sees the creators adapting midstream. A short Chapter 2 discusses the significance of the unusual calendar the beghards constructed, which goes some distance to help us understand how they thought in terms of fungible categories: these innovators in the realm of print technology were also inventing new ways of organising information. They experimented with how the book could be reordered to accommodate prints. These ideas speak to a larger concern in the era, one of reducing labour by using fungibility. What is surprising is that the beghards applied this idea to several different endeavours. This chapter will appeal to those who are interested in the history of organisational and indexing systems. I have given the subject a separate chapter because it is more technical than the other material. Chapter 3 analyses a second book that the beghards made, several decades later. The snapshot it

---

11 On Franciscans in the Netherlands, see Hildo van Engen, *De derde orde van Sint-Franciscus in het middeleeuwse bisdom Utrecht* (Hilversum: Verloren, 2006); and three studies by Bert Roest: *A History of Franciscan Education (c. 1210–1517)* (Leiden; Boston: Brill, 2000); *Franciscan Literature of Religious Instruction before the Council of Trent* (Leiden: Brill, 2004); *Franciscan Learning, Preaching and Mission c. 1220–1650: Cum Scientia Sit Donum Dei, Armatura ad Defendendam Sanctam Fidem Catholicam* (Leiden: Brill, 2015).

provides reveals how the beghards changed over the turbulent early sixteenth century, how much the print market had shifted in 25 years, and how the book makers increasingly absorbed and normalised the new technology of single-leaf prints. Chapter 4 departs from the beghards to consider many other manuscripts and the prints they formerly held, and assesses the extent of this practice of pasting prints in the fifteenth and early sixteenth centuries, as the archives have destroyed most of the examples and given us a diminished sense of the importance of this development in book history.

In the nineteenth century, the collecting process split woodcuts from engravings, although they were part of the same kinds of projects in the fifteenth century. Studying them provides some insight into the degree to which fifteenth-century book makers embraced the new technology and the extent to which nineteenth-century collectors dismantled it. One quality differentiating the two main printing techniques in the fifteenth century is that copper engraving lent itself to artists' signatures and monograms, whereas woodcuts generally did not (although Albrecht Dürer managed to sign his woodblocks). Israhel van Meckenem excelled in this realm, carving his name into hundreds of copper plates, many designs for which he co-opted from other engravers. He multiplied his name with every impression. David Landau and Peter Parshall even call Israhel an 'entrepreneurial printmaker and pirate'.[12] Whereas rulers had duplicated their images on coins for more than a millennium, Israhel was the first common person to use the mass media to grow his career, often by copying others' designs. He was also inventing new functions for prints and doing so faster than people could consume them; they also used them in ways that had not been intended. Israhel spread his name hither and yon in the fifteenth century and became a collector's must-have in the nineteenth: consequently, he bookends the chapters in this study.

Israhel not only visualized new ways to combine print and manuscript, but he also produced the components for scribes to realize his vision. And he not only signed his works in the fifteenth century, but he fed the market in the nineteenth century for collectors who desired objects (and complete series of objects) connected to proper names. The

---

12   David Landau and Peter W. Parshall, *The Renaissance Print: 1470–1550* (New Haven, CT, and London: Yale University Press, 1994), pp. 56–65.

book-making techniques of the fifteenth century are therefore reflected in the collecting practices of the nineteenth, and in both periods, books were assembled and prints disassembled, or vice versa. Both of these activities employed sharp blades and spatulas of glue.

1. Cut, Pasted, and Cut Again:
The Fate of 140 German and Netherlandish Single-Leaf Prints at the Hands of a Limburg Franciscan and a Modern Connoisseur

This chapter is about beghards in Maastricht who, around 1500, collected more than 150 single-leaf woodcut prints and engravings and glued them into an elaborate book of hours, the hulk of which is now in London, British Library Add. Ms. 24332. This is also the story of a curator who, in 1861, cut the prints out of the manuscript in order to mount them, according to their style or 'school', thereby giving them a completely different function. It is a case study of a larger group of books that straddled the old and new technologies, books made the old-fashioned way (by writing by hand) that nevertheless used the new technology (of printmaking) to introduce images. These books were waypoints along the transition from the handwritten to the printed book, a transition that was anything but smooth.[1] Finally, it is a study is about innovation,

---

1   Studies that have addressed this transition include: Curt F. Bühler, *The Fifteenth-Century Book: The Scribes, the Printers, the Decorators* (Philadelphia, PA: University of Pennsylvania Press, 2016, originally published 1960), esp. pp. 84–87; Mary Erler, 'Pasted-in Embellishments in English Manuscripts and Printed Books c. 1480–1533', *The Library*, 6:14 (1992), pp. 185–206 (who is primarily concerned with English material); Gerd Dicke, and Klaus Grubmüller, eds. *Die Gleichzeitigkeit von Handschrift und Buchdruck*, Wolfenbütteler Mittelalter-Studien, vol. 16 (Wiesbaden: Harrassowitz, 2003); Herman Pleij and J. Reynaert, eds., *Geschreven en Gedrukt: Boekproductie van Handschrift naar Druk in de Overgang van Middeleeuwen naar Moderne Tijd* (Ghent: Academia Press, 2004); Jan Willem Klein, 'Pragmatische Procesveranderingen in de Boekverluchting', in *Manuscripten en Miniaturen: Studies Aangeboden aan Anne S. Korteweg bij haar Afscheid van de Koninklijke Bibliotheek*, ed. J. A. A. M. Biemans, Klaas van der Hoek, Kathryn Rudy and Ed van der Vlist (Zutphen: Walburg Pers, 2007), pp. 217–29.

© Kathryn M. Rudy, CC BY 4.0   https://doi.org/10.11647/OBP.0145.01

new organisational systems, failed experiments, and about individuals responding to new technologies and integrating multiple fields of craft production. By telling this story in this first person, I am revealing my own organisational systems, failed experiments, and stumbling forays into integrating fields of craft.

Exploratory innovation took place with the book in the fifteenth century: mills sprang up to produce paper to feed the cottage industries that produced copper engravings, woodcut prints, blockbooks, handwritten and printed books, and all the hybrids and halflings in between. Transitioning from the handwritten book to the printed one was not swift, but involved bumps and false starts and abandoned experiments, resulting in books that had one foot in the old manual camp and the other in the new mechanical camp.[2] Important recent studies by Peter Schmidt, David Areford, and Ursula Weekes have investigated these transitions by analysing the social function of prints in the manuscript era.[3] They have rightly pointed out that prints can travel long distances before ending up in particular books. Furthermore, they have emphasized the functions of the prints over their style and have considered their afterlives, and they have asked how various early prints have acted in hybrids. The current

---

2   As James Douglas Farquhar states in 'The Manuscript as a Book', in *Pen to Press: Illustrated Manuscripts and Printed Books in the First Century of Printing*, ed. Sandra Hindman and James Douglas Farquhar (College Park, MD: Art Dept., University of Maryland, 1977): 'In this vast middle ground between the manuscript which copies a printed book and the printed book which simulates its manuscript model there is much material which relates to both media while conforming to neither. Book makers produced manuscripts with woodcut or engraved prints, printed books with miniatures, single leaves with and without script or block lettering, and the blockbook. Such experiments, among others, suggest that contemporary with the inception of printing with movable type — although not necessarily caused by it — there were a great many solutions for the illustrated book attempted in the book market' (p. 104).

3   Peter Schmidt, *Gedruckte Bilder in Handgeschriebenen Büchern: zum Gebrauch von Druckgraphik im 15. Jahrhundert*, Pictura et Poesis: Interdisziplinäre Studien zum Verhältnis von Literatur und Kunst (Cologne: Böhlau, 2003); Ursula Weekes, *Early Engravers and Their Public: The Master of the Berlin Passion and Manuscripts from Convents in the Rhine-Maas Region, ca. 1450–1500* (London: Harvey Miller, 2004); Peter Schmidt, 'The Early Print and the Origins of the Picture Postcard', and Ursula Weekes, 'Convents as Patrons and Producers of Woodcuts in the Low Countries around 1500', both in *The Woodcut in Fifteenth-Century Europe*, ed. Peter W. Parshall, Studies in the History of Art (Washington, D.C.: National Gallery of Art, 2009); David S. Areford, *The Viewer and the Printed Image in Late Medieval Europe*, Visual Culture in Early Modernity (Farnham, England; Burlington, VT: Ashgate, 2010).

study likewise concerns itself with one of those hybrids, containing handwritten text and mechanically reproduced images, all pasted together into a unity. With an estimated 156 prints originally pasted into it, the beghards' first manuscript contains (or rather, contained) more early prints than any other surviving manuscript, and as such, deserves a concentrated study. Unlike the objects of study of other recent analyses of such hybrids, my object was divided and dispersed, meaning that tracing its parts forms the first operation. This in turn necessitates analysing habits of nineteenth-century collecting, which precipitated the dispersal in the first place. What had started as an attempt to illustrate a manuscript book of hours without having to master draughtsmanship soon became a nearly obsessional project in integrating the many prints flowing through Maastricht. Other chapters in this book each address other manuscripts with their original prints, although most of those prints have now been cut out and stored separately.

How the prints came to be loosed from their manuscripts is a nineteenth-century story. If the decades flanking 1500 can be characterised by experiments in book making, the mid-nineteenth century was the era for categorising and cataloguing: the great *catalogues raisonnés* were written then. In the field of the history of printing, Wilhelm Ludwig Schreiber (1855–1932) and Max Lehrs (1855–1938) separated woodcuts from engravings and built the great corpus of fifteenth-century woodcuts and engravings that form the basis for modern understanding of the subject.[4] Creating knowledge depended on classifying the physical objects, but the modern pastimes of organising, labelling, and collecting came at a price. According to the Cartesian plan of the nineteenth-century museum, prints belonged to one department and manuscripts to another. Because a manuscript with prints did not fit this scheme, the Cartesians had to separate the prints from the manuscripts.[5] This scene recalls the story

---

4   Wilhelm Ludwig Schreiber, *Manuel de l'Amateur de la Gravure sur Bois et sur Métal au XVe Siècle*, 8 vols. (Berlin: A. Cohn, 1891–1911); and Max Lehrs, Geschichte und Kritischer Katalog des Deutschen, Niederländischen und Französischen Kupferstichs im XV. Jahrhundert, 9 vols. (Vienna: Gesellschaft für vervielfältigende Kunst, 1908).

5   Defining knowledge also led to the physical deconstruction of drawing collections, for which see Kristel Smentek, 'The Collector's Cut: Why Pierre-Jean Mariette Tore

of Procrustes, the son of Poseidon from Greek mythology. A smith with an iron bed, Procrustes invited every passerby to spend the night in his cruel lodge. He would stretch the guests who were too short for his bed, and sever the legs of those who were too tall. Likewise, print curators of the nineteenth century wrenched items out of books and into print collections, which demanded flat objects attached to mattes and stored in standard-sized boxes. Like Procrustes' long-legged guests, large prints were trimmed (or folded) to fit the mattes. For small prints that would have been dwarfed by the matte, curators pasted on several related examples, usually in elaborate symmetrical arrangements. These cataloguing activities of harvesting prints from manuscripts occurred all over Europe and America, to make the prints fit into the conceptual and physical category of 'individual printed sheets of paper'. At the moment of museum accession, all record of the original home of the prints was usually lost, and they became self-sufficient objects. And since, as I will show, prints and manuscripts might have widely different geographic origins, there was no obvious way to reconnect them even if one wanted to, which, until recently, no one did.

Reversing the work of the nineteenth-century curators meant employing their Cartesian methods beyond anything they had deemed possible: I made an Excel spreadsheet, which started as a simple grid. As the project grew in complexity, the table grew into one containing 14 x 646 squares, including some dynamic self-generating fields which added up how many folios, lost folios, and prints the original manuscript had. The Appendix is as simple as it can be, but no simpler.6 The spreadsheet allowed me to conclude that London, British Library Add. Ms. 24332, a manuscript book of hours and prayerbook, originally contained more than 541 paper folios, 2 parchment folios, and at least 156 prints and a handful of drawings in several styles.[7] At least two

---

    up His Drawings and Put Them Back Together Again', *Master Drawings* 46:1 (2008), pp. 36–60.

6 The Appendix can be viewed here: https://www.openbookpublishers.com/product/806#resources

7 Robert Priebsch, Deutsche Handschriften in England, 2 vols. (Erlangen: Fr. Junge, 1896–1901), vol. II, no. 251; Karel de Flou and Edward Gailliard, Beschrijving van Middelnederlandsche en Andere Handschriften, die in Engeland Bewaard Worden: Verslag Ingediend bij het Belgisch Staatsbestuur en de Koninklijke Vlaamsche Academie, 2 vols. (Ghent: Siffer, 1895–1897), vol. II (1897), pp. 103–06.

scribes at the monastery of beghards dedicated to St Matthew and St Bartholomew in Maastricht wrote this manuscript around 1500 (more about that date later). One of the scribes was Jan van Emmerick, who was probably the corrector, and probably furnished the manuscript with a table of contents and foliated it, thereby experimenting with new media and new ways of organising ideas.

Add. 24332 contained an enormous collection of prints made before 1500. These prints originated from several sources, and not just from one geographical region but from the Middle Rhine as well as from Dutch-speaking lands. Moreover, the prints were hand-painted in a variety of styles, a fact that reveals aspects of the colouring of prints and their distribution. Assembling all the prints, the leaves on which they are pasted, and the gutted hulk of the manuscript from which they were taken (Add. 24332 as the mothership) allows a multiplication of individual observations, which lends the entire project a historical context. Only by 'reassembling' the manuscript, at least in a spreadsheet and through electronic images, can one answer basic questions about it: what did the finished work look like? To what purpose was it put? Who used it? The task of reconstructing the manuscript was linked to the question of how the beghards assembled the book, and with what component parts. Did those parts come pre-assembled (painted and trimmed)? What, exactly, did the beghards have to do in order to get these components into shape to use them in Add. 24332? But let me tell the story in the order that the clues revealed themselves to me.

I began putting the pieces together in the 2005–2006 academic year while I was the Kress Fellow at the Warburg Institute in London. Looking for images representing the martyrdom of St Barbara in a landscape with a continuous narrative for a new hypothesis I was developing, I marched up to the vast photograph archive at the Warburg and began digging around to gather ideas.[8] There I encountered an image of the saint that was not relevant to my project but nevertheless caught my attention (fig. 1). It had a number of provocative features. First of all, the photograph captured an entire manuscript leaf, on which there was an image depicting St Barbara, but not a miniature. Rather, the image was

---

8   The resulting article appeared as Kathryn Rudy, 'A Play Built for One: The Passion of St. Barbara', in *The Sides of the North: An Anthology in Honor of Professor Yona Pinson*, ed. Tamar Cholcman and Assaf Pinkus (Newcastle: Cambridge Scholars, 2015), pp. 56–82.

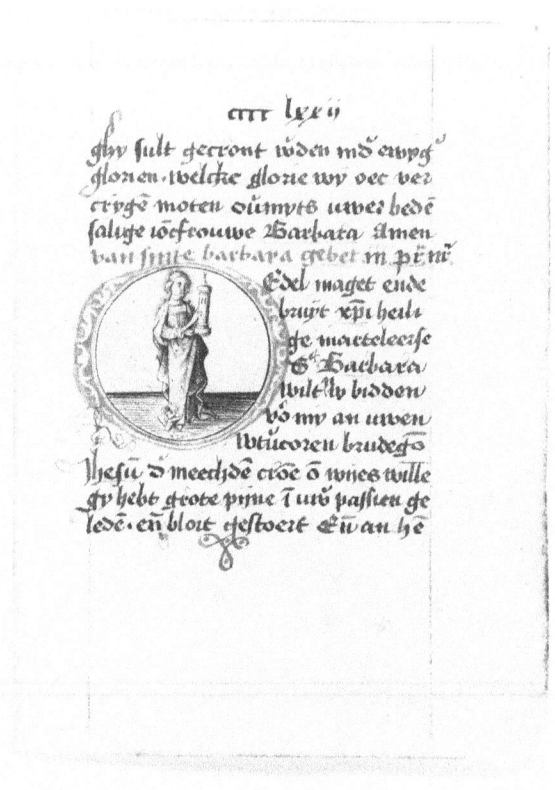

Fig. 1
Manuscript leaf written in Middle Dutch, with an engraved roundel by Israhel van Meckenem representing St Barbara, standing with her attribute. Unlabelled documentary photograph housed at the Warburg Institute, London.

an engraved roundel, which had later been trimmed and pasted into the leaf of a prayerbook. This roundel was recognisable as one printed by Israhel van Meckenem, a prodigious Rhineland engraver active from ca. 1465–1500.

Secondly, I noted that the manuscript leaf was not copied in a German dialect of the Lower/Middle Rhine, but rather in Middle Dutch, which meant that the print had travelled some distance westward before landing in a Dutch manuscript. Thirdly, the script was ornate. Written in a florid style, the letters have ascenders on the top line, and the descenders on the bottom line had been extended into festive curlicues. These features made the leaf memorable. Its most remarkable feature, however, was the number at the top, the Roman numeral *cccc lxxij*, written in a fifteenth-century hand. This was, in other words, original foliation, which is highly unusual for a prayerbook. Since the

Figs. 2a and 2b
Manuscript binding, binding front and back, blind stamped leather over boards, made by the beghards of Maastricht c. 1500 (rebacked after 1861). London, British Library, Add. Ms. 24332.

foliation had reached the number 472, I was apparently looking at a leaf from a very thick prayerbook. Unfortunately, the photograph gave no indication of what manuscript the folio belonged to or where the object was housed: the source of the photograph was not given on its reverse. In those days I lugged an A4-sized flatbed scanner around with me, so I scanned the photograph. I filed away these observations and carried on with my task of finding narrative images depicting St Barbara.

Meanwhile, since 2002 I had been working through all the Middle Dutch manuscripts in the British Library, looking at one or two manuscripts each time I had a few spare hours in London. On 6 April 2006 I called up Add. 24332 for the first time. This manuscript is a Netherlandish book of hours written on paper and preserved in its original binding (although its spine had been repaired, a detail that later proved important) (fig. 2). Its unusual script with the exuberant but amateurish ascenders was familiar from the photograph I had seen. I turned to folio *cccc lxxij*, expecting to find the image of St Barbara from the photograph, but that folio was not there. Instead, the manuscript had a blank leaf, a dummy, made of modern paper of the same weight and pale yellow colour as the inscribed leaves. It was now clear that the unlabelled Warburg photograph documented a detached leaf, one that had gone astray but was captured in a picture: a frustratingly unlabelled, untraceable documentary photograph.

Further inspection of the manuscript revealed not just one but many missing folios. This was immediately obvious because of the many gaps in the manuscript's original foliation and the many inserted modern blanks. In some cases an entire leaf had been removed and in others a leaf had patches of discolouration, indicating that something had been glued down and later re-lifted. Folio *ccc xlv* (modern foliation 312, fig. 3), for example, has an area of discolouration in an oval form. What had been lifted must have been a print, for areas at the top and left remained adhered to the page. I could make out the jagged crenulations often found around images depicting the Virgin of the Sun, which was probably the print originally glued to this leaf. A print of that subject would have enhanced the devotions written on that folio, since the print would have fallen on the same folio with a prayer to be read in front of 'an image of the Virgin in the sun' ('voer onser vrouwen bielde inder sonnen'), according to the accompanying rubric.

1. Cut, Pasted, and Cut Again

Fig. 3 Opening from the beghards' book of hours, Maastricht, c. 1500. London, British Library, Add. Ms. 24332, fols 311v–312r (modern foliation) or *ccc xlv* (original foliation).

Moreover, on the previous folio, opposite the leaf with the shadowy remains of the Virgin of the Sun, was a rectangular hole in the lower border where someone had cut out a section, presumably because it had contained a print. With the object excised completely, it was difficult to determine what its subject would have been. This was also the case for folio 283, where another rectangular hole pointed to a cut-out print (fig. 4). This time, however, the knife-bearer had cut straight through another image, the top part of it still glued to the verso side of the folio. That fragmentary image is a woodcut representing the Annunciation, carefully hand-coloured in washes of warm tones. Whatever the image on the reverse of this sheet was, it must have been even more spectacular than the woodcut, which was sacrificed in the process of removing it.

Fig. 4
Folio from the beghards' book of hours with part of a hand-painted woodcut depicting the Annunciation, Maastricht, c. 1500. London, British Library, Add. Ms. 24332, fol. 283v (modern foliation).

Besides the fragment of the Annunciation, only two other prints were left in the manuscript: a printed flower pasted into an initial on folio 254r (fig. 5), and an engraving representing St John supporting the swooning Mary on folio 307v (fig. 6). After it had been painted with delicate washes on the Virgin's halo and John's hair, the engraving had then been cut out, or 'silhouetted', and pasted near the gutter so that the figures would face the text. Script flowed around the contours of the Virgin's body, suggesting that the print had been pasted down before the time of writing and was not a later afterthought.[9]

---

9   One could compare the silhouetting of prints with the more vigorous trimming and reorganisation that they undergo in the sixteenth and seventeenth centuries, as described by Adam Smyth, *Material Texts in Early Modern England* (Cambridge: Cambridge University Press, 2018), esp. Ch. 1.

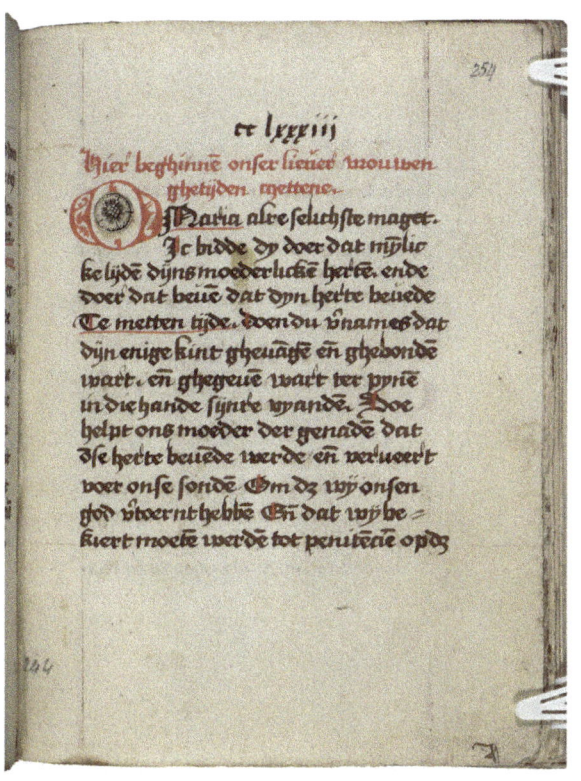

Fig. 5
Folio from the beghards' book of hours with a printed rosette pasted into the initial. London, British Library, Add. Ms. 24332, fol. 254r (modern foliation).

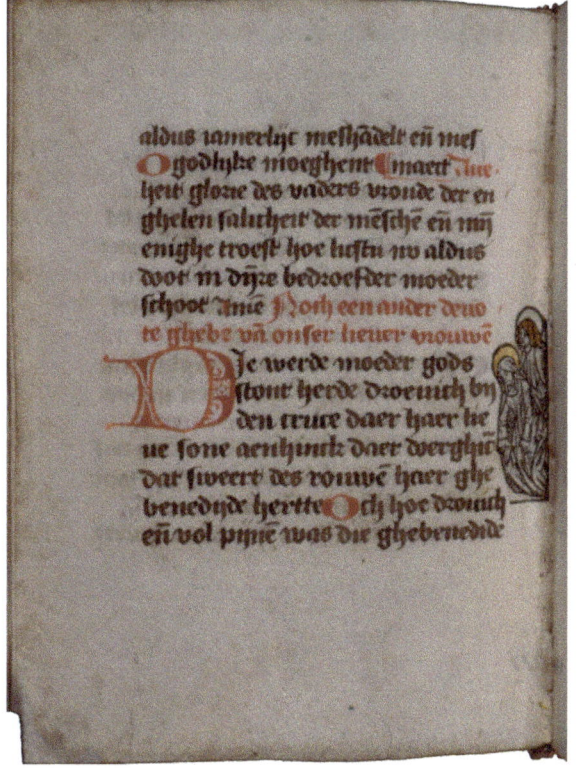

Fig. 6
Folio from the beghards' book of hours with a silhouetted engraving depicting Mary and John, Maastricht, c. 1500. London, British Library, Add. Ms. 24332, fol. 307v (modern foliation).

I spent the rest of the afternoon at the British Library listing all the missing folios in Add. 24332 and transcribing its calendar, which enabled me to localise the manuscript. Feasts in red included St Servatius (13 May; fig. 7), the Translation of St Servatius (7 June), and St Hubert (3 November). St Hubert's pilgrimage shrine is in his eponymous town in the Ardennes, and his presence therefore pointed to the Diocese of Luik (Liège), where the Ardennes are located. That St Servatius, the patron of the church in Maastricht, had two feast days in red not only confirmed that the manuscript was made in the diocese of Liège, but further suggested that it might have come from Maastricht, the site of the imposing Romanesque church housing the relics of and dedicated to St Servatius.

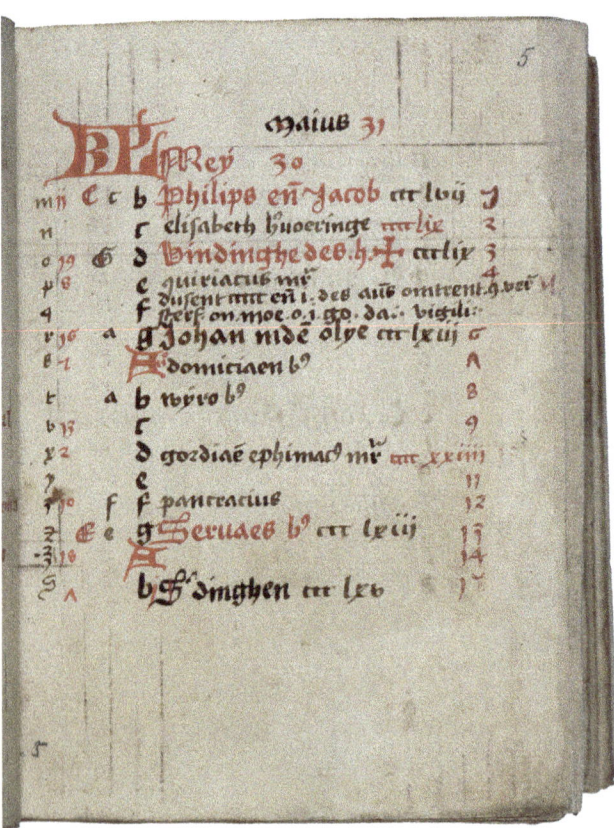

Fig. 7
Calendar page for the first half of May. London, British Library, Add. Ms. 24332, fol. 5r (modern foliation).

The many Franciscan saints strongly suggested that the manuscript was made in a Franciscan milieu. Their feasts included those of St Francis (4 October), St Anthony (17 January), the Translation of St Francis (25 May), and the Five Wounds of St Francis (17 September). Moreover, Francis was listed first among the confessors in the litany, and the names 'Jhesus, Maria, Anna, Franciscus, Clara' are used as a space filler after one of the rubrics that ends near the bottom of the page (fig. 8). Because of the masculine pronouns in the manuscript, as well as some particularities about a list of indulgences that I shall discuss later, I suspected that the manuscript came from a men's Franciscan monastery, even though the related vernacular devotional books embellished with prints, as shown in Ursula Weekes's important book, *Early Engravers and their Public*, were made in women's monasteries.[10] It appears that men were doing it, too.

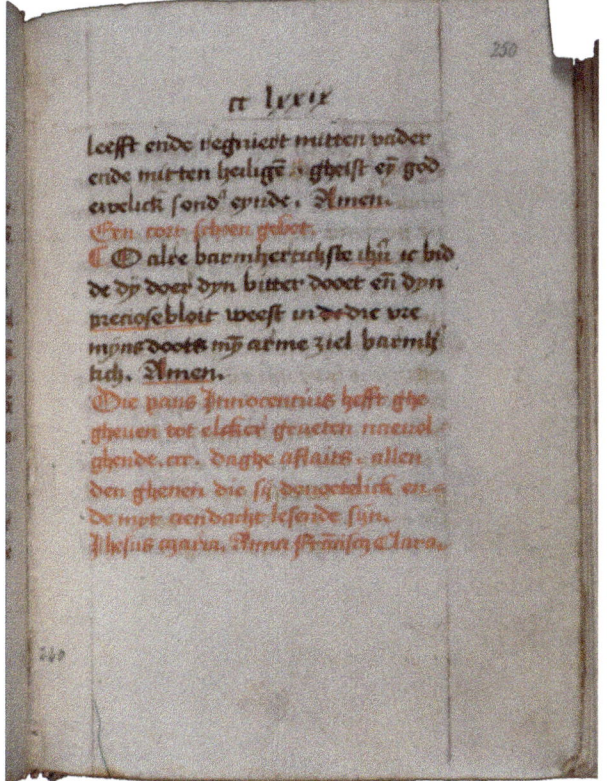

Fig. 8
Rubric revealing Franciscan affinities. London, British Library, Add. Ms. 24332, fol. 250r (modern foliation).

---

10   Weekes, *Early Engravers and Their Public*.

Other saints in the calendar further helped to narrow the provenance to a particular monastery in Maastricht. It included entries in red for St Bartholomew (24 August), as well as for the translation of his relics on 25 October, whereas most other calendars list the martyrs Crispin and Crispiaen on that day. In the litany, the Archangel Michael is underlined in red (folio 118v). These details made it possible to pin the manuscript to a particular monastery. In the early 2000s, while working on the Koninklijke Bibliotheek's website Medieval Manuscripts in Dutch Collections,[11] my friend Saskia van Bergen had assembled a list of every monastic and semi-monastic institution in the Dutch-speaking areas of what is now Belgium, Germany and the Netherlands. They are organised by town, dedicatory saint(s), gender, and confession. According to this list, only one monastery fitted the particular saints in Add. 24332: the house of beghards in Maastricht, dedicated to St Bartholomew and St Michael. Because St Bartholomew was an apostle, and St Michael an archangel, their feast days are written in red in many calendars, but the fact that the translation of St Bartholomew's relics is also given in red in Add. 24332 signals the extra attention that the users gave this saint. These features also suggest that the manuscript was made for the beghards' own use. This attribution concurred with that listed in Karl Stooker and Theo Verbeij's monumental study of manuscripts from the Low Countries with a monastic provenance.[12] Furthermore, the great historian of Netherlandish manuscripts, Jan Deschamps, had identified one of the three scribes who wrote 24332 as Jan van Emmerick, who was a beghard in Maastricht.[13]

Not only did the calendar confirm that the manuscript had come from the beghards in Maastricht, but it also helped with dating. A note in the calendar entered for 5 May provides a date (folio 5): 'dusent ccccc ende i des avonts omtrent .9. verssterf on. moe. o. i. go. da. Vigili' (1501

---

11 http://www.mmdc.nl/static/site/
12 Karl Stooker and Theo Verbeij, *Collecties op Orde: Middelnederlandse Handschriften uit Kloosters en Semi-Religieuze Gemeenschappen in De Nederlanden*, 2 vols, Miscellanea Neerlandica (Leuven: Peeters, 1997), vol. II, no. 878. The entries in vol. II, pp. 288–96 list the manuscripts known to have been in the beghards' possession.
13 Jan Deschamps, 'De Herkomst van het Leidse Handschrift van de Sint-Servatiuslegende van Hendrik van Veldeke', *Handelingen van de Koninklijke Zuidnederlandse Maatschappij voor Taal- en Letterkunde en Geschiedenis* 12 (1958), pp. 65–66, no. 9.

in the evening around nine o'clock 'on. moe. o. i. go. da.' died).[14] This note gives the date and time of death of someone important, but the exact identity of that someone remains a mystery, as it is obscured in a highly personal abbreviation. What is clear, however, is that this note was written in the same hand as one of those in the calendar, which suggests that the whole book was completed in or shortly before 1501. Other highly unusual aspects of the calendar, however, formed puzzles that I eventually cracked, and that gave me insight into the makers' minds. In short, they turned the calendar into a table of contents (which I will discuss in Chapter 2).

The Beghards of Maastricht and their Commercial Pursuits

Evidence in the calendar, as well as the identification of one of the scribes in the manuscript as Jan van Emmerick, revealed that the manuscript was written and constructed by the beghards of Maastricht around 1500. Why were these beghards so experimental in their use of prints and indexing systems? One answer is perhaps that they ran a binding operation, so they saw many kinds of new books in their studio and therefore were exposed to all the latest developments in book making. The unusual calendar and the pasted print are new technologies that they could have seen this way. A brief history of their house reveals a group of extraordinary men who were at the forefront of teaching, book making, weaving, trade, and commerce.

Franciscan spirituality came quite early to the Netherlands. St Francis of Assisi (1182–1226) was declared a saint two years after his death. Born into a rich family, Francis shed his possessions and preached extreme poverty. Along with the Dominicans, the Franciscans formed the mendicant preaching orders, and their rise also follows the formation of urbanisation in Europe. Unlike earlier orders, such as the Benedictines, the Franciscans did not seek remote, secluded terrain, but lived in the new cities and preached to their inhabitants. Franciscan preaching focussed on the Passion. For the many followers whom he

---

14 The note may refer to 'onze moeder' (our mother). I owe this suggestion to Hanno Wijsman.

attracted during his life, Francis wrote a Rule, which was approved orally in 1210 by Pope Innocent III (1198–1216), then ratified in a signed document in 1223 by Pope Honorius III (1216–1227). Although founded in Italy, the Franciscan movement spread quickly across the Alps. Within the Custody of Brabant, Franciscan male houses were founded in the following places:

- St Truiden (Sanctus Trudo): established in 1226–1231
- Tienen (Tenis): established as early as 1226; definitive buildings from 1266 onwards
- Diest (Deriste): established in 1228
- Leuven (Lovania): established in 1228
- Brussels (Bruxella): established c. 1228/31
- Mechelen (Machilinia): established in 1231
- Maastricht (Trajectum super Mosam): established in 1234

With a Franciscan presence established in the Netherlands immediately after St Francis died, the areas quickly had numerous Franciscan installations. Of these foundations, the earliest were built in St Truiden and in Tienen by 1226. St Truiden was therefore an important saint for Netherlandish Franciscans, and his feast day on 24 November and the translation of his relics on 11 August are listed in the calendar of Add. 24332. In Maastricht a monastery for the Minderbroeders, or Friars Minor, was built on St Pieterstraat, following its approval in 1234.

How did the beghards differ from other Franciscans who lived in Maastricht at the same time? Answering this meant delving into the voluminous literature written about the monasteries of the amateur scholars of Maastricht in the late nineteenth century. In the publications of the archives of Limburg, they mentioned the beghards' school, loom room, and bindery. Unlike other branches of Franciscans, the beghards did not beg for alms: instead, their various business activities — weaving, binding, and teaching — supported them financially. It is difficult to assess just how wealthy the beghards were in the fifteenth century. Although their spiritual ideal was poverty, they owned expensive things. One of their most precious objects was an image of Christ carved in ivory, which disappeared during the Napoleonic takeover of the monasteries.[15] An ivory image suggests that they were not utterly impoverished. Drawings made in 1746 also paint a lavish picture of the beghards' possessions: the brotherhood of the Trinity, which was formed in 1646 when the Turks released Christian prisoners, celebrated its hundredth anniversary at the altar of the beghards in Maastricht, on which occasion three drawings were made. They show a richly decorated baroque altar, and ample, well-appointed rooms.[16] Even in the fifteenth century the brothers were well off. Far from the Franciscan ideal of begging for their meals, these brothers engaged in several commercial pursuits.

It is difficult to know how lucrative their bindery was, but it is clear from examining their extant bindings that they exercised their trade with a practiced degree of craft using high-quality materials. For example, they bound a manuscript for the female Franciscans in Maastricht with blind-stamped leather over oak boards (Maastricht, Regionaal Historisch Centrum Limburg, 22.001A Handschriften GAM, inv. no. 462; fig. 9). Into the leather they stamped an image of St Servatius under a gothic canopy. Flanked by two angels, Servatius holds a bishop's staff in one hand and an enormous key in the other, which suggests that he has the 'keys' to the city of Maastricht. Underfoot are two flailing beasts, which represent the Jews he converted. (In this way, his iconography is connected to that of St Lambert.) His name, Servatius, appears in gothic script in the frame above and below the saint. In other words, the beghards used stamping technology to brand their wares, and to connect the book with a particular place. Inside is an experiment in that the book contains a design that had probably been imported from Delft and then worked into the calendar (fig. 10). That design is a clock face, with the finger of God as the ticker and the numbers 1–12 in Roman numerals sliding around the dial.

---

15   For a lively account of Napoleon's art pillaging, see Cecil Hilton Monk Gould, *Trophy of Conquest: The Musée Napoléon and the Creation of the Louvre* (London: Faber & Faber, 1965).

16   A. D. Welters, 'De Kloosterkerk der Begaarden te Maastricht', *Nedermaas* 1927/8, pp. 33–35. The drawings are preserved in 21.210B, inv. no. 1982.

Fig. 9 Manuscript binding, blind stamped leather over boards, made by the beghards of Maastricht c. 1500. Maastricht, Regionaal Historisch Centrum Limburg, 22.001A Handschriften GAM, inv.nr. 462.

Fig. 10 Clock folio, facing January calendar page. Opening folios in a prayerbook made in Maastricht c. 1500. Maastricht, Regionaal Historisch Centrum Limburg, 22.001A Handschriften GAM, inv.nr. 462.

To spend some time in Maastricht was a logical next step, but it was not until 2008 that I had the opportunity to go there while working on the website Medieval Manuscripts in Dutch Collections. Joan Blaeu's map from 1650 (e-fig. 1), one of the Netherlandish city views he made when not mapping Scotland or the Far East, shows the city and its intimate relationship with the river Maas (Meuse).

Joan Blaeu's map (e-fig. 1)

 Joan Blaeu, Map of Maastricht, from the *Toonneel der Steeden* (Views of Netherlandish Cities), 1650.

https://hdl.handle.net/20.500.12434/6f08104e

The medieval city walls lie within the bounds of the expanded seventeenth-century ramparts. Among the medieval buildings depicted is the *lakenhal*, or cloth hall, the centre for trade among the city's weavers (including the beghards). Nowadays, aside from the occasional bus that comes barrelling across the square, the old centre is mostly a pedestrian zone. The Church of Our Lady greets the viewer with a Westwerk like a fortified castle, which protects a fourteenth-century wooden painted pietà inside. Men in suits now visit her during their lunch hours and rub their pain into the surface, burnished by thousands of hands.[17]

Maastricht's major Franciscan church, which, along with its adjacent cloister and monastic buildings, now functions as the city archive, was in the centre of the city and close to the river, but with some luck and persistence they were able to acquire the neighbouring lots. The church has a nave and two side aisles and is wholly made of local Limburg marlstone (fig. 11). It originally had extensive wall paintings, only small fragments of which are now left. A cult image depicting the Virgin as the Star of the Sea (*de Sterre der Zee*) once occupied the chapel of the Holy Virgin at the right side of the choir; that image, which still draws immense crowds, has now been moved to the nearby Church of Our Lady, when she is not being processed through the streets of the city.

---

17 Kathryn M. Rudy, *Rubrics, Images and Indulgences in Late Medieval Netherlandish Manuscripts*, Library of the Written World, vol. 55 (Leiden: Brill, 2017), pp. 3–4.

Fig. 11
Franciscan church,
Sint Pieterstraat,
Maastricht (now the
Regionaal Historisch
Centrum Limburg).
Photo: Kathryn M. Rudy.

On Witmakersstraat, a stone's throw from the Minderbroeders' monastery and church on Pieterstraat, was the house of the beghards (*begaarden*). The beghard movement was founded during St Francis' lifetime, when the saint saw that large numbers of lay people wanted to follow him. Francis responded to this by writing the rule for the 'third order' in 1221, which laymen and laywomen could follow if they cared to turn their backs on the world, which meant living in poverty, renouncing worldliness and possessions. Some of these laypeople formed brotherhoods and lived communally, calling themselves beghards. (Beguines are not female beghards, although beguines were indeed laywomen who lived communally.[18] Beguines did not follow the

---

18   For beguines and their manuscripts, see: Judith Oliver, 'Je Pecherise Renc Grasces a Vos: Some French Devotional Texts in Beguine Psalters', in *Medieval Codicology, Iconography, Literature, and Translation: Studies for Keith Val Sinclair*, ed. by Peter Rolfe Monks and D. D. R. Owen. Litterae Textuales, pp. 248–66 (Leiden: E. J. Brill, 1994); Walter Simons, 'Reading a Saint's Body: Rapture and Bodily Movement in the

Third Rule of St Francis, and their history is only tangentially related to that of the beghards, despite the similarity of their names.)

The beghards were living in a house on Witmakersstraat by 1268, with a chapel dedicated to St Bartholomew.[19] That chapel was originally intended for the brotherhood to perform their prayers. A few years later, the beghards grew into a monastery, and some of the members became priests. They applied to the Chapter of Our Dear Lady for permission to build a larger chapel where the priests could perform Mass, along with a cemetery, a request that was granted in 1308. Their new chapel was dedicated to SS Michael and Bartholomew together. Later the beghards abandoned the Chapter of Our Dear Lady and joined the Chapter of Zepperen in 1450.[20] (These were ecclesiastical jurisdictions, distinct from the much better-known Capital of Windesheim.) It is possible that Zepperen was more closely connected to trade and therefore had better business dealings.

Whereas the *minderbroeders* (friars minor) occupied the large monastery and church complex on Pieterstraat, the beghards lived nearby in a convent on Witmakersstraat. Both communities followed the Third Rule of Francis. Witmakersstraat means 'bleachers' street', a name probably given because of the linen-weaving and bleaching industries that took place there. While the friars minor earned their living by preaching and begging, the beghards taught pupils and wove linen. As a company of weavers, the beghards joined the guild of weavers (*lakengilde*) in 1453, although it is not clear whether they did so by choice or force. While this meant that they became subject to the guild's regulations, inspections, and fees, at some level, guild membership must have been beneficial to their trade, for in 1484, they

---

"Vitae" of Thirteenth-Century Beguines', in *Framing Medieval Bodies*, ed. by Sarah Kay and Miri Rubin, pp. 10–23 (Manchester; New York: Manchester University Press, distributed by St. Martin's Press, 1994); Joanna E. Ziegler, *Sculpture of Compassion: The Pietà and the Beguines in the Southern Low Countries, c.1300-c.1600*. Etudes d'Histoire de l'Art, 6 (Brussels; Turnhout: Institut historique belge de Rome; Brepols, 1992).

19 For an overview of the beghards' origins and history, see M. Schoengen and P. C. Boeren, *Monasticon Batavum*, 3 vols. (Amsterdam: Noord-Hollandsche Uitg. Maatschappij, 1942), Franciscans, pp. 139–40.

20 Baron von Geusau, 'Korte Geschiedenis der Kloosters te Maastricht', Publications de la Société Historique et Archéologique dans le Duché de Limbourg = Jaarboek van Limburgs Geschied- en Oudheidkundig Genootschap XXXI, nouvelle série, no. tome XI (1894), here p. 41.

also expanded their weaving business by building a larger atelier. Shortly thereafter, however, the city council brought a formal complaint against them because the large number of looms they operated constituted burdensome competition for the city's other weavers. As a result of this complaint, the city limited the beghards' looms to eight. During most of their history, there were sixteen brothers living in the house; it is possible that they originally had sixteen looms — one for each brother — before they were forced to reduce them by half. Perhaps the beghards filled the empty space by constructing a book bindery, which would also bring in some additional money, thereby making up for the loss of income from the missing looms.

In their bindery the beghards made hand-tooled leather bindings, including the binding of Add. 24332. Panel-stamped leather over boards, the manuscript's binding displays the names 'Jhesus' and 'Maria' in banderols at top and bottom, a coat of arms that is no longer legible, and small circles with evangelist symbols. Apparently, the beghards bound not only their own manuscripts but also those for others. In this regard, the beghards of Maastricht must have had some dealings with the sisters of Maagdendriesch (a word that means 'tertiary virgins'), a neighbouring house for female tertiaries. Originally a group of laywomen who decided in 1200 to live together in religious community, the group adopted the Third Rule of St Francis in the fourteenth century, at which time their residence became a monastery where the sisters lived in enclosure.[21] In the fifteenth century the convent grew considerably, accommodating at least forty sisters in 1415. At the same time, their chapel, which until that time had been only for use by the sisters, was opened to the public as a church, and was dedicated to St Andreas by the Bishop of Liège, Erard van der Marck, in 1471. Maagdendriesch, thereafter known as the Convent of St Andreas, also had an active scriptorium. No fewer than sixteen manuscripts produced or owned by these sisters have survived.[22] The beghards bound at least two of these, including a prayerbook copied in part by sister Katrijn van Rade, a sister at Maagdendriesch (Amsterdam, UB, Ms. I G 12; fig. 12); and Maastricht, RHCL, 22.001A Handschriften

---

21 Ibid., here: pp. 44–45.
22 Stooker and Verbeij, vol. II, pp. 297–303.

GAM, inv. no. 462 (fig. 9). Like these two manuscripts, Add. 24332, has been bound in blind-stamped leather over a book block held together with four cords. The brass clasps of all three bindings are remarkably similar. It is possible that I G 12 was made for a layperson. If so, then the female and male Franciscans might have worked together as a team to create saleable manuscripts for the public.

Fig. 12
Manuscript binding, blind stamped leather over boards, made by the beghards of Maastricht c. 1500. Amsterdam University Library, Ms. I G 12.

In addition to binding books, the beghards of Maastricht, thanks to their relationship with the Capital of Zepperen, also took in students and provided education. The brothers ran a school. As the content of their books reveals, they taught reading and arithmetic and probably writing as well, possibly to create new scribes for their scriptorium. They allowed copyists to write with their own idiomatic scripts. This is significant, because women who made manuscripts in some convents — especially in the western part of the Netherlands — were taught a corporate style, so that their work was indistinguishable from their convent-mates'. In this way, multiple sisters could work on the same manuscript and yet produce a streamlined product that looked consistent through and through. In contrast, the beghards in Maastricht (and in other convents of both genders in the eastern Netherlands) were apparently allowed to keep their own distinctive handwriting. In their books the beghards did not hide the fact that book making was a collaborative process. It is therefore possible to see that Jan van Emmerick worked with several other scribes on various projects. For example, he and two other scribes from the same monastery copied the Pseudo-Bonaventure-Ludolphian Life of Christ (Weert, GM, Ms. CMW 41). Emmerick inscribed the text on folios 6r–111v and 148r–158v, Adam de Beecke inscribed the text on folios 112r–125r, 136r–147v, and 160r–188v, and the man known in the literature as the 'Servaas scribe' (because he partly copied a book about the life of St Servatius now in Leiden) inscribed the text on folios 125v–135v.[23] One of their innovations was to adapt manuscript production by incorporating even more hands, more forms of labour into the final product, without masking the individual qualities of the various contributors.

The beghards also collaborated with women. Not only did the beghards bind Maastricht, RHCL, 22.001A Handschriften GAM, inv. no. 462 for the female tertiaries in their city, but they also completed the manuscript. Two of the hands in Add. 24332 also appear in the front matter in the women's manuscript. Specifically, in Maastricht 462, fols 15v-16v contain a calendar and computational tables written by the beghards (fig. 13 and 14). They have traditionally been dated 1515 because of the inscription within the circles, but that number is ambiguous; the words 'Anno domini IVIV' may have been written later. There is a second number written to the left of each circle: mvc (=1500), which may be the date when this manuscript was inscribed. These Roman numerals are written in the same hand as the calendar

---

23 Many of the manuscripts made in this monastery are now in the Gemeentemuseum in Weert. For a discussion of the Servaas scribe and all the manuscripts he worked on, see Deschamps, 'De Herkomst van het Leidse Handschrift van de Sint-Servatiuslegende van Hendrik van Veldeke'.

hand and foliator of Add. 24332, that of Jan van Emmerick. Apparently the beghards provided the front matter before binding the sisters' manuscript. It is also possible that the beghards bound prints into the book, but these have now been removed.[24] The next table, for calculating the golden number, contains clues about now-missing components (fig. 15). Here an offset appears in the form of wet, red border decoration, as if the sisters painted the borders when the page was already in the book; they then closed the manuscript before the paint had fully dried, which resulted in an extensive and messy offset. It is possible that the beghards had placed an uncoloured print in the book, which prompted the owners to embellish it.

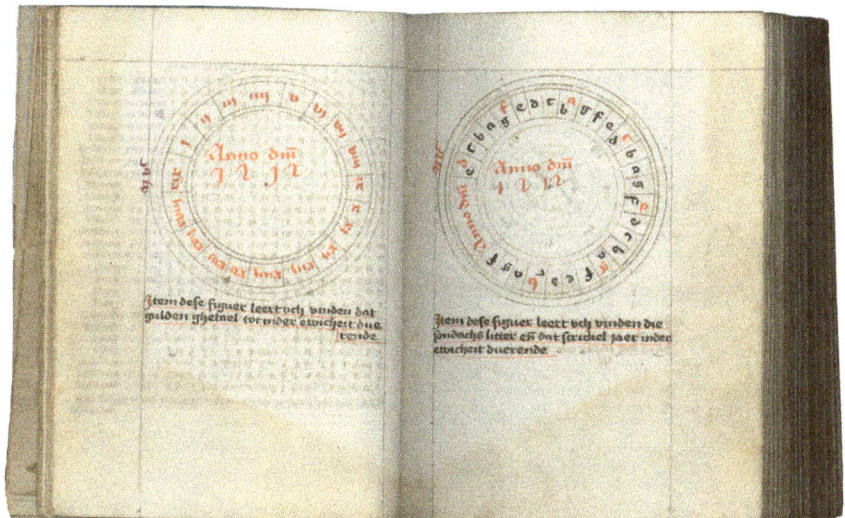

Fig. 13 Opening in a prayerbook made in Maastricht, with computational circles dated 1500. Maastricht, Regionaal Historisch Centrum Limburg, 22.001A Handschriften GAM, inv.nr. 462, fol. 15v-16r.

---

24   There are missing folios before 138 and 162.

Fig. 14 Diagram for calculating the length of Advent, copied by Jan van Emmerick. Maastricht, Regionaal Historisch Centrum Limburg, 22.001A Handschriften GAM, inv.nr. 462, fol. 16v-17r.

Fig. 15 Table with offset from now-missing leaf. Maastricht, Regionaal Historisch Centrum Limburg, 22.001A Handschriften GAM, inv.nr. 462, fol. 17v-18r.

While in Maastricht, I became more aware of the importance of its physical location: it lies on the River Maas, a wide navigable river (fig. 16). From Maastricht, the beghards had good water access to the Rhine, including the Lower Rhine, which was the cradle of printmaking, and to the entire Low Countries, including the entire Maas valley. The wide variety of prints, with xylographic and engraved text in dialects of Dutch and German, is testament to the wide systems of distribution that prints had by the late fifteenth century, and to the centrality of the beghards as traders. They had much to offer in return: book-binding services, woven cloth, reading lessons, prayers for your sorry soul. All these existed in a single economy, along with prints. That is what is fascinating about the beghards' book: it brings together such a large number of prints from different sources, with wide geographic origins, and testifies to the beghards' far-reaching network.

Fig. 16 The River Maas, photographed from the bridge, with a view of the medieval Marian church. Photo: Kathryn M. Rudy.

The archives in Maastricht hold the beghards' cartulary, that is, a transcription of foundational documents (Maastricht, RHCL, 14.D015, inv. no. 6). According to an entry on fol. 1v, the 'book is to contain all of the possessions and goods that belonged to the convent', including 'all of the books, rolls, and registers' written since the founding of the convent in 1343. In fact, only the first few pages comprise a cartulary, while further sections reveal facts about their business dealings. Where a late-fifteenth- or early-sixteenth-century scribe found some blank space on fol. 3v, he added a list of monetary values and exchange rates: how many grotes are there in a mark? This list would have served the brothers as they carried out various kinds of trade, with people from the German-speaking and Dutch-speaking lands.

Many of the prints that the Add. 24332 formerly held were from the German-speaking east, but several of them were from the Netherlandish-speaking west. For example, a full-page engraving, used as one of the manuscript leaves (fol. *ccc lxvii*) (e-fig. 2), has extensive engraved text around it in Dutch, a sure sign that it was made in the Dutch-speaking lands.

BM 1861,1109.645 — IHS monogram (e-fig. 2)

IHS monogram, as a full-page image. Netherlandish engraving. London, British Museum, Department of Prints & Drawings, inv. 1861,1109.645.

https://hdl.handle.net/20.500.12434/6d0f3ffb

The fluttering text consists of a prayer to the 'Sweet name Jesus and Mary' in the vernacular.[25] However, the beghard has not placed it in the book to accompany a prayer to the sacred monogram, but rather to preface a prayer to St Bernardino. Perhaps there simply were no prints available that represented that saint, so the beghard instead embellished his prayer with the symbol with which Bernardino was most closely associated, the sacred monogram in flames. This example not only attests to the wide geographical area from which the beghards were getting their prints, but it also underscored two other issues, which become themes in the current study. First, printmakers were often producing items at a distance from their customers, and as such they

---

25 It reads: 'Ghebenedijt moet sijn den soeten naem Ihs ende Maria synre ghebenedider moeder nu ende inder ewichheid. Amen'.

were not necessarily producing exactly what the recipients needed. The second point follows from the first: consumers often had to made subtle adjustments to items they received, or to use the imperfect subjects as the best available alternatives.

The beghards were innovative book makers interested in streamlining the traditional method of making manuscripts. They made books for their own use and perhaps for sale as well; either way, they were therefore interested in things like the affordability of the books and the ease of making them. They were early adopters of using paper for making books of hours, which had almost always been on parchment. They took their accumulated craft skills and applied them to various cultural products. Poised as they were on the River Maas, they had many more opportunities to trade than other (semi-)monastics would have had. Most important for their innovation, perhaps, was that as bookbinders, they saw their neighbours' books, and all the new innovations, pass under their noses. One of those innovations was taking sheaves of prints, cutting them apart, and pasting them into the pages of books. In that light, it is fitting that the attribute of the beghards' patron saint Bartholomew is the knife.

Israhel's Roundels

Now I knew that the beghards of Maastricht made Add. 24332 around 1501 and that the manuscript had had some quantity of prints removed from it. I possessed (a scan of) a photograph indicating that at least one of those prints had been made by Israhel van Meckenem, proof from a fragment left in the manuscript itself that it originally included woodcuts, as well as engravings, and an indication that at least some of the removed folios bearing prints might be preserved somewhere. But where? The photograph with the St Barbara documented a leaf that was no longer in the manuscript. Therefore, my biggest question remained: where was that leaf with the roundel of St Barbara? Would St Barbara lead me to the rest of the missing prints? I put this question to Paul Taylor at the Warburg photograph archive. He indicated that the St Barbara leaf had been photographed for a project to document the engravings of Israhel van Meckenem housed in the British Museum, and that the Warburg archive possessed two more related roundels, similarly mounted. One of these represented SS Peter and Paul, standing together with their attributes (fig. 17). I could see that it was folio *ccc lxxij*, one of the folios removed from Add. 24332. The photograph of the other Israhel print showed the roundel with a male saint pasted to what must have been the verso side of a folio, one without visible foliation at the top (fig. 18).

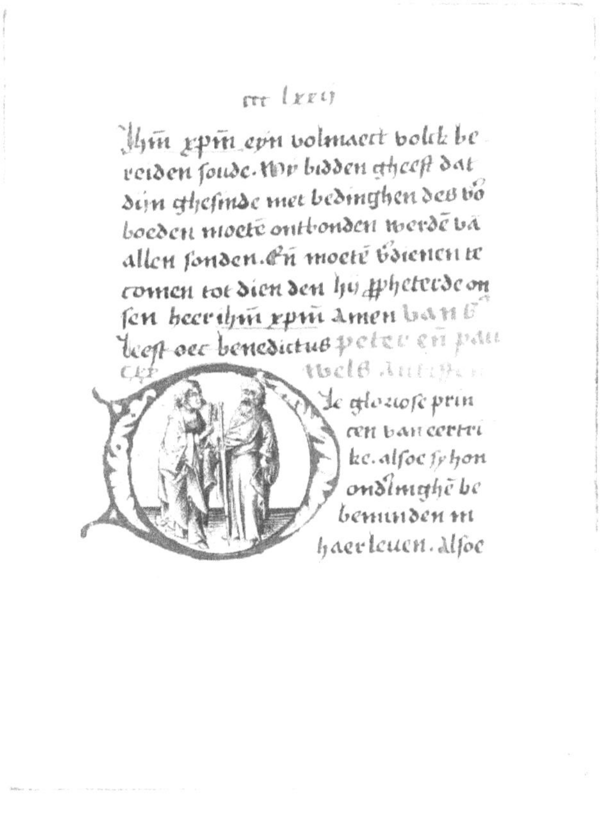

Fig. 17
Manuscript leaf written in Middle Dutch, with an engraved roundel by Israhel van Meckenem representing SS Peter and Paul, standing with their attributes. Unlabelled documentary photograph, housed at the Warburg Institute, London.

Other projects and a new job as a curator of manuscripts in The Netherlands, a post I held beginning in September 2006, prevented me from going to the British Museum right away to look for Barbara, Servatius, and Peter and Paul. My questions vexed me, and when I finally had the chance, I spent a day in the BM's Prints and Drawings Study Room on 13 December 2006. In my life as a manuscript historian so far I have visited dozens of museums and libraries to consult hundreds, if

Fig. 18
Manuscript leaf written in Middle Dutch, with an engraved roundel by Israhel van Meckenem representing St Wolfgang, who has been transformed into St Servatius. Unlabelled documentary photograph, housed at the Warburg Institute, London.

not thousands, of manuscripts and early prints, but I still get a nervous, excited feeling when I am going to see a special object that I have only read about or seen in a microfilm. Usually I cannot sleep the night before, especially if I am about to visit a library or collection I have never visited before. Having flown into London the previous evening and had a brief, excited sleep, I walked into the Prints and Drawings Study Room the next morning and thought I had stepped back in time. Whereas the rest of the building has been modernised, the Study Room retains its wooden desks, glass cases, and card catalogues from an earlier era (fig. 19). A sign on the wall near the entrance indicates that visitors have to declare their own property, meaning that people sometimes come into the collection to compare an impression of their own print with something in the collection. On any given day there is usually someone playing the part of a male nineteenth-century aesthete, complete with a monocle and a choice titbit from his collection.

Fig. 19 The interior of the Prints & Drawings Study Room at the British Museum, London.
Photo: Kathryn M. Rudy.

The room's interior reflected a past glory, a time when craftsmen were charged with the task of making hundreds of hardwood bookshelves, with dovetail joins and bevelled glass windows, with materials brought from British colonies. This room swelled with the loot of the empire. It housed items from the empire's far-flung territories and its deep-reaching past. As I later learned, in the mid-nineteenth century, the Museum was accessioning hundreds of objects a day, and therefore must have been employing a bevy of junior curators, clerks, and technical assistants to prepare the incoming items for storage. At the BM, the prints are affixed to cardboard mounts and stored in boxes, most of which were made in the nineteenth century during the collection's growth spurt. These boxes are lined with the same kind of marble paper used as paste-downs in bookbindings made in this period. It is astonishingly beautiful. The values of craft are everywhere in attendance.

Within a short time, the staff at the BM had located the print depicting St Barbara by Israhel. In three dimensions and in full colour, the manuscript folio emerged from the storage box, with a red penwork border framing the roundel that formed an extra, perceptible layer (e-fig. 3). Sure enough, two other folios from Add. 24332 that Paul Taylor had shown me in photographs were also mounted on the same board, both with printed roundels by Israhel: folio *ccc lxxij* (with SS Peter and Paul) (e-fig. 4) and the verso of folio *ccc lxiii*, with St Wolfgang (e-fig. 5). In the same box were other mattes with prints attributed to Israhel. In other words, the nineteenth-century cataloguers had grouped them together in this box in order to associate like with like. Imposing categories on them was part of oeuvre-creation. Museum assistants had removed the prints from their context as devotional objects in a religious manuscript and had put them instead in the context of a named artist and his oeuvre.

BM 1861,1109.660 — Manuscript leaf written in Middle Dutch (e-fig. 3)

Manuscript leaf written in Middle Dutch, with an engraved roundel by Israhel van Meckenem representing St Barbara, standing with her attribute, formerly part of Add. 24332. London, British Museum, Department of Prints & Drawings, inv. 1861,1109.660.

https://hdl.handle.net/20.500.12434/bfade03b

BM 1861,1109.679 — Manuscript leaf written in Middle Dutch (e-fig. 4)

Manuscript leaf written in Middle Dutch, with an engraved roundel by Israhel van Meckenem representing SS Peter and Paul, formerly part of Add. 24332. London, British Museum, Department of Prints & Drawings, inv. 1861,1109.679.

https://hdl.handle.net/20.500.12434/500265f2

BM 1861,1109.680 — Israhel van Meckenem (e-fig. 5)

Israhel van Meckenem, printed roundel with St Wolfgang, who has been transformed into St Servatius, pasted into the initial of manuscript folio, formerly fol. *ccc lxiii* of London, British Library, Add. Ms. 24332. London, British Museum, Department of Prints & Drawings, inv. 1861,1109.680.

https://hdl.handle.net/20.500.12434/1ac4bd1d

When Israhel produced his roundels, he made entire sheets with thematic unity that users could cut apart. Two of these sheets from the series of saints survive intact in the British Museum (e-fig. 6) and (e-fig. 7).

BM 1873,0809.642 — Israhel van Meckenem (e-fig. 6)

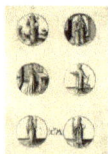

Israhel van Meckenem, sheet of six roundels depicting Christ as Salvator Mundi and five standing saints. London, British Museum, Department of Prints & Drawings, inv. 1873,0809.642.

https://hdl.handle.net/20.500.12434/db692147

BM 1873,0809.643 — Israhel van Meckenem (e-fig. 7)

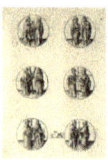

Israhel van Meckenem, sheet of six roundels depicting pairs of standing apostles. London, British Museum, Department of Prints & Drawings, inv. 1873,0809.643.

https://hdl.handle.net/20.500.12434/92140750

However, book makers also used them and incorporated these and other designs into a variety of projects (see Chapter 4). When the beghards used the prints, they cut them from the sheet and pasted them onto the beginnings of texts, where they created, as James Marrow has termed them, 'instant historiated initials'.[26] It is often repeated that these circular prints, each about 34 millimetres in diameter, were made as designs for goldsmiths. Whether that was their intended function or not, book makers soon found another use for them as designs for quickly producing historiated initials. The beghards pasted at least three of Israhel's roundels onto three different folios of Add. 24332. When those folios were cut out of the manuscript 360 years later, they were mounted on a board together (1861,1109.660; 1861,1109.679; and 1861,1109.680). Possibly copying designs by the Master ES, Israhel

---

26   Marrow, 'A Book of Hours from the Circle of the Master of the Berlin Passion: Notes on the Relationship between Fifteenth-Century Manuscript Illumination and Printmaking in the Rhenish Lowlands', p. 611. Mary Erler analyses the phenomenon of the printed roundel pasted into a manuscript in 'Pasted-in Embellishments in English Manuscripts and Printed Books c. 1480–1533', *The Library*, 6th ser., 14 (1992), pp. 185–206.

engraved these roundels in eight sheets of six roundels each, totalling 48 small prints. Most of the sheets have been cut apart, and a complete set of the 48 prints has not yet come to light.

The now detached folio *cccc lxxij* has an engraving depicting St Barbara made by Israhel (e-fig. 8), which was trimmed out of the seventh sheet in the series (e-fig. 9).

BM 1861,1109.660 — Detached folio *cccc lxxij* (e-fig. 8)

Detached folio *cccc lxxij* with an engraving depicting St Barbara made by Israhel van Meckenem. London, British Museum, Department of Prints & Drawings, inv. 1861,1109.660.

https://hdl.handle.net/20.500.12434/67d4934e

BM 1873,0809.642 — Israhel van Meckenem (e-fig. 9)

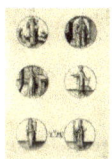

Israhel van Meckenem, sheet of six roundels depicting Christ as Salvator Mundi and five standing saints. London, British Museum, Department of Prints & Drawings, inv. 1873,0809.642.

https://hdl.handle.net/20.500.12434/8f0229e3

There is a tiny slip of the burin in the circle around her, so that the circle has a tiny black tail; the same mark also appears in the full sheet of Israhel's prints. Working quickly, Israhel was not a perfectionist. His round frames provided guidelines for their user, who has carefully cut just outside the frame in order to isolate Barbara's image within a roundel. This has been made to fill an initial O, which has then been painted with red decoration. Clearly, the scribe pasted in the image first, and then red paint was applied around it, so that the whole ensemble constructs a seven-line historiated initial. Whereas the rubricator's ink is more purple (cooler), the decorator's paint is more orange (warmer). This suggests that the process of constructing the multi-layered page took place in several stages.

The same sheet of roundels (1873,0809.642) divulged another image that the beghards used, one now glued to the verso side of folio *ccc lxiii* (e-fig. 10).

BM 1861,1109.680 — Detached folio *ccc lxiii* (e-fig. 10)

Detached folio *ccc lxiii*, verso side. London, British Museum, Department of Prints & Drawings, inv. 1861,1109.680.

https://hdl.handle.net/20.500.12434/64120d59

This roundel presents a case of transformed identities. Israhel had depicted St Wolfgang, whose attribute is an axe; he was especially venerated in Austria and Bavaria, where Israhel was apparently also marketing prints. However, St Wolfgang was not particularly venerated in Maastricht. As if the scribe of Add. 24332 were taking the advice he had inscribed on folio *ii* (14r), that if devotees could not find a devotion to the saint of their choice, they should find a similar saint and simply change the name, he has scratched out Wolfgang's axe, and added a gasping serpent below the figure, in order to rechristen him Servatius. Just to ensure that users would properly understand the saint's new identity, the scribe has added the words 'Sanctus Servatius' in the white space of the print.

Was it Jan van Emmerick who realised that the first word in this prayer was not going to be a *D* or *O*, but rather an *S*? Because an *S* does not easily accommodate an image inside it, the scribe has not cut out the print as a roundel, but as a square: it would not form a historiated initial, but a seven-line 'miniature'. The decorator (also Emmerick?) has then made a square border around the circular one, and added some decoration in the interstices. This fact demonstrates that the scribe had the whole sheet of roundels: they were not delivered to him already trimmed from their support. He was probably cutting them out as he progressed in his writing of the manuscript. If he had the entire sheets and was cutting them as he wrote, then he may well have used the rest of the roundels elsewhere in the project.

Scrutinising this page reveals, however, that Israhel's print could not have been the scribe's first solution for this space in the manuscript. There is some glue still showing at the top of this print, which suggests that a slightly larger print (or miniature) filled this space. Whatever was represented in that image must have been even less satisfactory than the prints of St Wolfgang-as-Servatius. One can imagine a scenario in which the scribe, nearly finished with his task of writing the manuscript, was left with a niggling feeling that he had not got St Servatius — the patron saint of his own city — quite right. He found the image depicting St

Wolfgang among the partially trimmed stacks of prints, and decided to doctor it. He then removed the previous print and put in the new Wolfgang/Servatius, which is slightly smaller. When he pasted it in, he covered — ever so slightly — the text on the line below. Specifically, this one covers the ascender of 'bidt' below the print, indicating that the print was applied after the writing was done.

None of the three engravings by Israhel van Meckenem has been painted but, rather, each was left in its raw printed form, with the fine engraved lines conveying rich drapery. Red and blue initials were painted in after the writing was completed and the prints were pasted in. Some of this decorative paint has splashed onto the prints (for example, onto the image of Peter and Paul) (e-fig. 11).

BM 1861,1109.679 — Manuscript leaf written in Middle Dutch (e-fig. 11)

Manuscript leaf written in Middle Dutch, with an engraved roundel by Israhel van Meckenem representing SS Peter and Paul, formerly part of Add. 24332. London, British Museum, Department of Prints & Drawings, inv. 1861,1109.679.
https://hdl.handle.net/20.500.12434/8d621959

This helps to clarify the order of operations in constructing the manuscript: write, leaving space for images; then paste them in, and continue writing below or next to the print; then embellish with red and blue paint. As I continued to study the manuscript, I would find further nuances in this process.

That was all I could accomplish in a day in the Prints and Drawings Study Room at the BM. The opening hours are constricted, and I was still trying to feel my way around the place. It usually takes me several visits to a library or archive to learn the ropes. The other missing folios could not be far, but I did not know how to get to them. I could not return to London to keep looking for the prints until 20 April 2007, when more clues revealed themselves.

The Logic of Accession Numbers

I was run ragged from my job as curator of manuscripts at the Koninklijke Bibliotheek of the Netherlands, and felt I had aged about ten years. Going to London and immersing myself in someone else's collection was a lovely escape. The curator Sheila O'Connell was on duty in the Study Room the next time I came in, in April 2007, and I explained that I wanted to find the rest of the prints that had been removed from Add. 24332. Immediately, she brought me the Register for 1861 and explained how the logic of the accession numbers at the BM could help solve my problem (fig. 20). Until a computerised system replaced it, new acquisitions were entered in a tall, lined ledger book, with one line for each incoming item. The curator would write a short description of each print in the Register, and at the same time assign it an accession number: the first four digits represent the year of acquisition, the next four are the month and day, and the final digits consist of a consecutive numbering of the prints entered on that date. These digits were stamped onto the back of the print with what must have been a rubber-stamper with moveable parts. Looking at the Register from the mid- to late nineteenth century, I was struck by the sheer quantity of acquisitions.

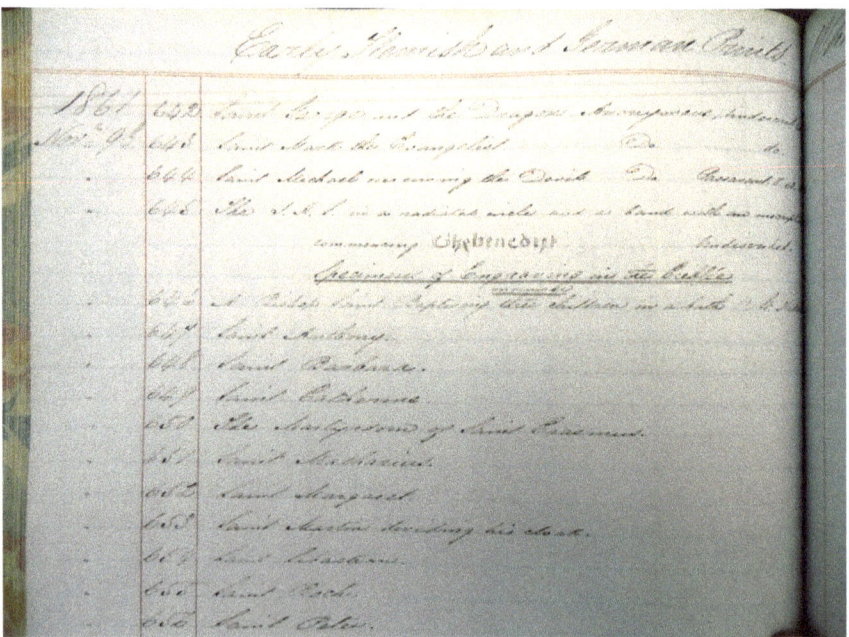

Fig. 20 Page from Register for 9 November 1861. London, British Museum, Department of Prints & Drawings. Photo: Kathryn M. Rudy.

Israhel van Meckenem's roundel depicting St Barbara which I had come to see had the accession number 1861,1109.660, which meant that it was the 660th print to be entered in the Register on 9 November 1861. As the British Empire was thriving and throbbing, the keepers of its culture accessioned objects into the national museum at breakneck speed. To deal with acquisitions efficiently enough, the curators wrote only the briefest description of new items. On that date, items 632–693 were listed as a group as having all come in a single batch from a Mr Tross. This was Edwin Tross (1822–1875), an art, book, and print dealer who lived at 5 rue Neuve des Petits Champs in Paris. When the curator registered the prints from the manuscript in 1861, he categorised them according to three major divisions: 'Early Flemish and German prints' (632–645); 'Specimens of Engravings in the Criblée' (646–656; I will delve into the meaning of Criblée later); 'Small Figures Cut from Prints' (657–693). Among these three categories, further divisions were made based on technique, style, and hand. Many of the prints formed series, and the curator-connoisseur reconstructed those series (which had been broken up when they were pasted into the manuscript) when the prints were distributed throughout its pages based on their subjects.

With the same bureaucracy that Britain was exporting to its colonies, the British Museum was keeping different kinds of records in different ledgers. Another book contained records of financial transactions. In one entry, dated 6 November 1861, Mr Carpenter, then Keeper of Prints, wrote to the Trustees to ask for funds, including £35 to purchase '20 early Flemish and German prints' (fig. 21). Although the details are slightly off, this entry probably refers to the prints now accessioned as 1861,1109. 632–693. The prints entered the collection three days later. Some staff at the British Museum suggest that this wording indicates that the prints were already separate from the manuscript in which they were pasted. I disagree. I think it is clear that the Museum bought the entire manuscript and then cut out the prints and accessioned them. The wording may indicate that they considered the manuscript a mere vehicle for transporting the small printed goods. Evidence includes that the manuscript itself was kept, perhaps because it was in an old binding. Later, when I returned to the British Library, I noticed that a note at the back of Add. 24332 proclaims that the manuscript was transferred from the Department of Prints and Drawings. (Until the British Library was formed in 1997, its book collections formed the library of the British Museum, so this would have meant transferring the object from one department to another.) This note demonstrates that the Museum purchased the entire manuscript. The Department of Prints and Drawings was in possession of that manuscript — its binding, paper folios, and pasted-on prints — but it passed on the elements that were not of interest, that is, the binding and the text pages lacking prints.

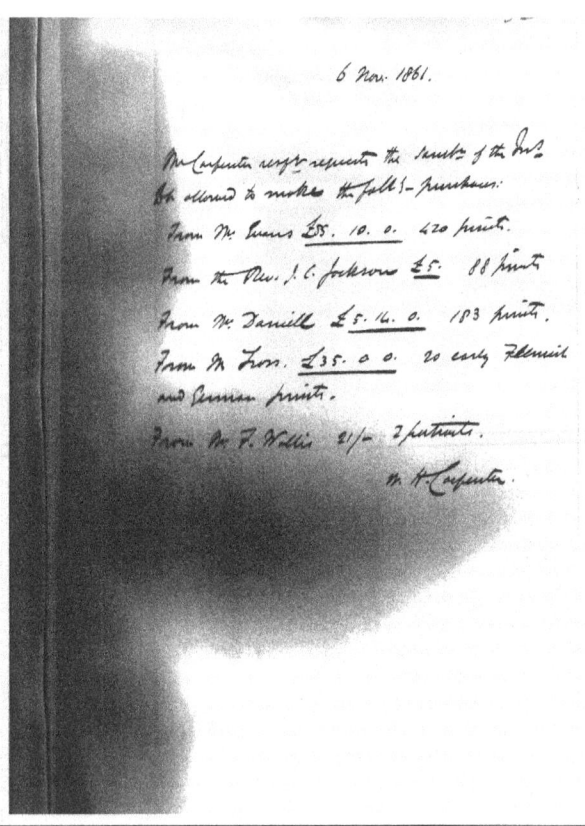

Fig. 21
Letter from Mr Carpenter, dated 6 November 1861. London, British Museum, Department of Prints & Drawings. Photo: Kathryn M. Rudy.

The prints in Add. 24332 must have been its most attractive feature, and the manuscript must have looked quite dishevelled when it arrived in November 1861, missing four quires and half its prints. The following month, December, the manuscript, now fully denuded of its prints, was transferred to the Museum's Department of Manuscripts. There the manuscript was given its accession number, Add. 24332. The accession number system at the British Museum (and later the British Library) works like this: manuscripts that entered the Library within a complete collection retained the name of that collection and received a sequential number.[27] For example, the Harley manuscripts formerly belonged to Robert Harley (1661–1724) and Edward Harley (1689–1741), earls of Oxford; their collection was purchased for Britain in 1753. Those manuscripts that did not enter the Library in a complete collection were added to the 'Additional' manuscripts, and assigned a number in chronological sequence according to date of entry. Add. 24332 is the penultimate manuscript to have entered the collection in 1861; thus, the Department of Manuscripts processed it in December that year, shortly after the Department of Prints had handed it over.

In the Department of Manuscripts, the newly christened Add. 24332 received an inscription on its eighth paper flyleaf, which reads: 'Received from the Department of Prints, 12 Dec. 1861 (Purch. of M. Tross of Paris)'. The note continues on the verso side of that same leaf: 'Mem. The missing leaves, initial letters etc had been cut out before this volume was transferred to my department. FM'. It required little digging to learn that FM is Frederic Madden (1801–1873), the Keeper of Manuscripts at the British Museum from 1837 to 1866, who was apparently aware that a misdeed had been carried out in the Prints and Drawings Department of his own institution. It may have been Madden who ordered that conservation work be performed on the mutilated manuscript. Someone in the book conservation laboratory added sixty-two blank folios to the manuscript to replace the missing leaves; the placement of these blank leaves is indicated in the Appendix.[28] The motivation for this infilling may have been structural: attaching a blank leaf to a half-bifolium whose partner had been excised would help to keep the singleton from falling out of the binding. The conservation staff rebound the manuscript in its original boards, which are covered with its panel-stamped leather, although they replaced the spine (see fig. 2). The 62 added leaves preserved the thickness of the book block so that it would still fit into its old binding. This detective work required my darting back and forth between the British Library and the British Museum, which are now about a mile apart. The next step was to study all the prints and figure out how they fitted into the book.

---

27 The Cotton Collection within the British Library is an exception to this pattern: Cotton items still have shelf numbers based on the busts of Roman emperors that Cotton used to identify the bookshelves in his elaborate collection.

28 As mentioned, the Appendix can be viewed here: https://www.openbookpublishers.com/product/806#resources

Back at the BM, I began requesting the 62 items, and they arrived in a haphazard order as the Study Room assistant brought them over. They were housed in more than a dozen archival boxes, so I made it through only a few items on the first day. In 2007, staff at the BM would deliver an entire box with prints mounted on mattes, plus a pair of white gloves, and going through the boxes took a deliciously long time, attenuated by the donning and doffing of gloves, synchronized with alternating gestures of shifting mattes and manipulating a track pad. Slow research also meant that I took notes for this project, plus what turned out to be notes for four further articles, based on the other prints that arrived unsolicited in the boxes. Now, ten years later, they only bring the matte containing the requested print, so the opportunities for serendipity have evaporated. This new efficiency kills many opportunities for knowledge generation. Between the morning and afternoon sessions at the Study Room on the fourth floor of the BM, one can run over to the Warburg and get a bit more work done, or go to the London Review Bookshop and keep typing, or even just sit on the benches in the fourth-floor galleries and keep working as long as the early-gen laptop battery holds out. Since it involved planes, trains, storage of what became terabytes of visual material, and running between institutions, this was slow research punctuated by fast movements. One has to move inchmeal in an archive to ensure that the prints are flat and safe, not curled or at risk of creasing, to note down the codes and numbers for each item that represent different approaches to cataloguing. Scrutinizing is hard work. This includes noticing features of the object itself — its substrate, ink, quality of line, the kind of colouring it received (freehand or with a template? Wash, gauche, or lake?), its offsets, the contours of its paper, notes and text (handwritten or printed? Original or later?) — as well as features of the object in its new context (How has it been trimmed? What else is on the matte?). For the sake of the archive, I wash my hands like a surgeon, take Vitamin D, and avoid people (especially children) who might have colds. I wouldn't want to risk sneezing on the fifteenth century.

That first day, the few boxes of prints I worked through were enough to accelerate my heartbeat and make me gasp in recognition and delight. I savoured the items in each box, perusing every item on every matte, taking notes in a burgeoning file, stopping to look things up in Lehrs or Schreiber, carefully lifting the prints on their hinges to look at the back, note down glue stains, and read the texts. I transcribed these texts partly in order to get to know the hands, hoping to store them in my memory to identify the same hand some time in the distant future. For the next two years, from spring 2007, on many of my free days, I would fly to London, go straight from Heathrow to the BM and call up some more boxes of prints. This project, I am afraid, was not ecological. I tried to assuage my elaborate energy expenditure by offsetting it slightly, bringing my organic waste from Holland to London in my suitcase, and feeding it to the inhabitants of our London wormery. Regularly flying banana peels across the English Channel made me feel a bit better.

Roundels attributed to Israhel were stored in boxes containing other works by the same engraver, and the rest of the prints were doled out into numerous boxes for anonymous Netherlandish and German artists. They were organised, in other words, first by named personalities, such as Israhel van Meckenem, and then the anonymous works were organised by medium and 'school', so that all the anonymous German woodcuts, for example, were housed together, and the anonymous Netherlandish engravings were housed together. Box after box disgorged the *membra disjecta* from the beghards' manuscript, each item now re-categorised according to a nineteenth-century connoisseur's classification system, all amid a sea of the *membra disjecta* from other manuscripts.

At the British Museum I pored over the prints and looked for patterns. I thought about the fifteenth-century process of acquiring prints, cutting them up, and pasting them into a manuscript. I thought about the reverse: the nineteenth-century process of acquiring manuscripts, cutting them up, and pasting them onto mattes.

As I waded through these bulky, unwieldy boxes, the leaves of Add. 24332 appeared, one after the other. These leaves allowed me to reconstruct one of the most fascinating manuscripts made in a monastic context around 1500. Sheila O'Connell let me have access to one of the department's computers, and gave me permission to download all the images of the fifteenth-century prints, which had recently been digitised, and also showed me how to search in the department's database. All this information was to go online shortly and is now available publicly; the links appear throughout this text. At the British Library I transcribed all the rubrics in Add. 24332 and collated the manuscript with the help of an elaborate diagram.

The Knife as a Tool for Creativity

After experiments by the Synthetic Cubists, Kurt Schwitters and other artists working in collage would harness the knife as a tool for creativity in the period between the First and Second World Wars. Schwitters worked alongside the Dada movement, along with fellow collage artist Hannah Höch, who used photomontage to comment on the absurd, which she 'cut with a kitchen knife', as one of her titles put it.[29] Long before, though, in the fifteenth century, book makers such as the beghards were using the knife to isolate bits of printed paper and bring them together into new arrangements. At times the beghards even seem to have been aware of the absurdity of some of their creations, since the medium of *papier collé* lends itself to impossible jumps in scale between pictorial elements. They played with this visual dissonance, for example on a page with an engraving depicting St Mark with his lion: it has been printed onto a full page that has been inserted as folio *ccc liii*, with the image on the verso (e-fig. 12).

BM 1861,1109.643 — Leaf from the beghards' manuscript (e-fig. 12)

Leaf from the beghards' manuscript with an engraving depicting St Mark, sometimes attributed to Israhel van Meckenem, and another smaller engraving depicting a winged lion. London, British Museum, Department of Prints & Drawings, inv. 1861,1109.643.

https://hdl.handle.net/20.500.12434/dcfa6c6d

But there was empty space in the image, and the beghards had some small prints lying around, so they pasted a tiny print of the winged lion onto the horizon line so that the two lions gaze at each other. In red ink the rubricator has built a small chapel around the added lion, as if to acknowledge that the two beasts are in different scales and separate ontological levels. The same red ink has been used to make a free-hand line around the frame, thereby presenting a printed line and a hand-drawn one moving in parallel around the image.

That the beghards deployed several roundels from Israhel suggests that they were obtaining entire sheets of roundels and cutting them apart.

---

29   See Maud Lavin, *Cut with the Kitchen Knife: The Weimar Photomontages of Hannah Höch* (New Haven, CT: Yale University Press, 1993).

One series depicts six female saints in half-length. Most of these have been deployed as instant historiated initials, in the same way that the roundels with Barbara, Peter and Paul, and Wolfgang/Servatius were pasted in as initials. These virgin roundels are attributed to a German engraver known as the Master of the Flower Borders (Meister der Blumenrahmen), after a series of prints he made with flower borders.[30] The series of six engravings are all about 22 millimetres in diameter, each one depicting a female saint seen in bust-length, with her attribute. The prints are:

BM, 1861,1109.659 — Apollonia (e-fig. 13)

St Apollonia roundel (engraving), pasted into initial before a prayer to that saint. London, British Museum, Department of Prints & Drawings, inv. 1861,1109.659.

https://hdl.handle.net/20.500.12434/8142772d

BM, 1861,1109.662 — Catherine (e-fig. 14)

St Catherine roundel (engraving), pasted into initial before a prayer to that saint. London, British Museum, Department of Prints & Drawings, inv. 1861,1109.662.

https://hdl.handle.net/20.500.12434/53765d41

BM, 1861,1109.663 — Cecilia (e-fig. 15)

St Cecilia? roundel (engraving), pasted into initial before a prayer to that saint. London, British Museum, Department of Prints & Drawings, inv. 1861,1109.663.

https://hdl.handle.net/20.500.12434/0d62a32c

BM, 1861,1109.664 — Columba (e-fig. 16)

St Columba? roundel (engraving), pasted into initial before a prayer to that saint. London, British Museum, Department of Prints & Drawings, inv. 1861,1109.664.

https://hdl.handle.net/20.500.12434/78e8d1bd

---

30 For a discussion of this engraver, see Weekes, *Early Engravers and Their Public*, pp. 60–64, 85–87, 169–73 and passim.

BM, 1861,1109.673 — Maria Magdalene (e-fig. 17)

Mary Magdalene roundel (engraving), pasted into initial before a prayer to that saint. London, British Museum, Department of Prints & Drawings, inv. 1861,1109.673.

https://hdl.handle.net/20.500.12434/6d0f15f6

BM, 1861,1109.674 — St Margaret, used here as Dymphna (e-fig. 18)

St Margaret roundel (engraving), pasted into initial before a prayer to St Dymphna. London, British Museum, Department of Prints & Drawings, inv. 1861,1109.674.

https://hdl.handle.net/20.500.12434/795948e7

Five of the six prints are hand-painted in a similar style, with bold solid colours for the saints' robes and backgrounds (fig. 22). A likely scenario is that the beghards were buying groups of prints, possibly as intact sheets that they could then cut apart and paste into manuscripts, and that the sheets of prints were already hand-painted (indeed, there are no other prints from the manuscript painted in this way). In fact, one can see that they were printed together on the same sheet, because they

Fig. 22 Engraved roundels representing virgins, some used as initials in the beghards' book of hours. London, British Museum, Department of Prints & Drawings, inv. 1861,1109.659, 662, 663, 664, 673, 674.

appear semi-intact in another manuscript prayerbook, Vienna, ÖNB, ser. Nova 12715.[31] This prayerbook was probably made by nuns, who added printed images, both large and small, to the pages. In some cases, they stitched the images to the pages with brightly coloured silk, as if turning the mechanics of attachment into a form of embellishment. Given that groups of small roundels appear together in this manuscript, it makes sense that the engraver who produced them sold them as a set. This scribe pasted the engraved roundels representing virgin martyrs (figs 23 and 24) on the recto and verso of a folio entirely given over to prints. The manuscript has become a scrapbook for devotional prints. Telling in the beghards' manuscript, however, is that the prints were clearly made as a sheet that could be cut up.

Fig. 23
Folio from a prayerbook with three engravings by the Master of the Flower Borders glued to it and one sewn to it. Vienna, Österreichische Nationalbibliothek, ser. Nova 12715, fol. 29r.

---

31 Ursula Weekes discusses this manuscript in *Early Engravers and Their Public*, pp. 167–85.

Fig. 24 Opening from a prayerbook with three engravings by the Master of the Flower Borders glued to it and one sewn to it. Vienna, Österreichische Nationalbibliothek, ser. Nova 12715, fols 29v-30r.

In Add. 24332, the roundels are carefully trimmed, and capital letters are often formed around them. Many suffrages begin with the exclamation of lament, 'O!', which is onomatopoeic with wailing in Dutch (and in English). This is handy for the scribe since it is a large, full, round letter — the perfect shape to historiate — as in the roundel depicting Mary Magdalene (e-fig. 17). The suffrage to this saint commences with a letter *O*, which the hand-coloured print fills. Likewise, the engraving depicting St Catherine used to historiate the letter G, for 'God gruet u', at the beginning of a prayer to St Catherine (e-fig. 14).

Things have gone slightly awry, however, in the prayer to St Dymphna or Dingen (e-fig. 18). It begins not with an *O* but an *I* ('Ic bid u, o alre heilichste joffrou ende mertelersse St Dympne') so there was no letter with a large empty centre into which to paste the roundel. Instead the scribe has pasted Dymphna's image into the first line of the text, not trimmed into a circle but cut so that it has a straight bottom edge, which then sits on the ruled line. The image interrupts the rubric, appearing between the word 'St' and the word 'Dingen'. This solution is interesting because it reveals something about the print trade: it confirms that the beghard bought an entire sheet with six female martyrs, untrimmed, and that he trimmed them himself according to his needs. I can imagine the beghard with his stack of prints, a plan for the order of the prayerbook sketched out, and writing along with trimming and glueing.

How the small prints were pasted in reveals the process by which the beghards wrote and assembled the manuscript. For example, the scribe planned that the prints depicting SS Catherine, Apollonia, and Cecilia (e-fig. 13) (e-fig. 15) should fill initials near the tops of their respective folios. In contrast, when the first initial in the prayer did not have an open letter, the scribe had to come up with a different strategy for affixing the print. In the case with the print representing a female figure with a small bear, whom the scribe has interpreted as St Columba (e-fig. 16), he has pushed her image to the end of the line.

Of course, all fifteenth-century printmakers used knives, burins, and other tools that cut and removed material in the service of image-making. Why should they not have used knives in the next stage of image-production as well?

Silhouettes and Doubles

Silhouetting was the ultimate in knife-wielding work — cutting around the main figure in a print and discarding its background. Whereas the roundels were designed to be cut out, the large figurative prints were not. Cutting these out required a more inventive act of creativity, rather than doing the expected thing. Some prints have been silhouetted so that the justification of the handwritten text flows around their outlines. For example, the scribe trimmed the image of St John holding the swooning Virgin, one of the prints still left in Add. 24332 (see fig. 6). These figures must have been cut from a larger Crucifixion image, but now the trimmed image of Mary is nestled up to a prayer to the Virgin's sorrows, which laments, 'The true mother of God stood sorrowing by the cross where her son hung' ('Die werde moeder gods stont herde droevich bij den cruce daer haer lieve sone aenhinck'). Thus, whereas in the original print, the image of Mary faced an image of the cross, now she faces a textual description of the cross. This *mise en page* demonstrates that the scribes who wrote the manuscript were also intimately involved with selecting, trimming, and pasting the images.

Trimming and pasting the print can change its meaning entirely, as with a small image pasted onto a page with a prayer to St Elzéar of Sabran (or Elzearius, Elchearius), whose name is underlined (fol. *cccc xxv*) (e-fig. 19).

BM 1861,1109.665 — Engraving depicting a generic figure (e-fig. 19)

Engraving depicting a generic figure, trimmed and used to represent St Elzéar. London, British Museum, Department of Prints & Drawings, inv. 1861,1109.665.

https://hdl.handle.net/20.500.12434/e378b127

Of course the small engraving had not originally been intended to depict St Elzéar, who is utterly obscure. Rather, the figure may have come from a Crucifixion group, where it would have represented St John at the foot of the cross; but here the scribe has silhouetted the male figure and thereby cut off any distinguishing features that he might have had. In its new context, the figure could serve as Elzéar, or any other (male) figure the user wanted to portray.

The grandest of these recontextualisations accompanies the prayer for the consecration of the church of St Francis in Maastricht. Unusually, this page has not one but two prints pasted to it (e-fig. 20).

BM 1861,1109.686 and 687 — Prayer for the consecration (e-fig. 20)

Prayer for the consecration of a Franciscan church with two prints, one representing a Franciscan, the other a church. London, British Museum, Department of Prints & Drawings, inv. 1861,1109.686 and 687.

https://hdl.handle.net/20.500.12434/86e3ffd8

After the beghard cropped the images of St Francis and the church closely, he arranged them on the page, pasted them down, and inscribed a prayer to the consecration of the church so that the text flows around the images. In other words, he has incorporated the silhouetted images into the fabric of the page. He has accomplished these acts of cutting and pasting so that they magnify the meaning of the prayer: the kneeling figure seems to be down below, directing the words of the prayer towards the represented church. The words separate the supplicant and his object of devotion, but they also form the ether in which these elements float. The consecration prayer is for a particular church, the Franciscan church in Maastricht. Although the beghards' house is now destroyed, their church, at the end of the same street, still stands.

Before the beghard silhouetted it, the image almost certainly formed part of a narrative scene showing St Francis receiving the stigmata, in a composition similar to the painting by Jan van Eyck (e-fig. 21).

Jan van Eyck (e-fig. 21)

Jan van Eyck, *St Francis receiving the Stigmata*, ca. 1430-32. Oil on parchment on panel. Philadelphia Museum of Art.

https://hdl.handle.net/20.500.12434/add8a667

As in the painting, St Francis appears in three-quarter view, kneeling. The beghard has cut out the figure of the saint, thereby excising Francis's narrative and attributes. In effect, the beghard has turned a specific man, St Francis, into a generic Franciscan male 'everyman', one who stands for each of the beghards using the book. Every male Franciscan is a copy — or print — of Francis.

A leaf with a pasted-on image of St Benedict offers another opportunity to understand how the scribe deployed silhouetting as a creative tool (e-fig. 22).

BM 1861,1109.641 — St Benedict (e-fig. 22)

St Benedict, engraving. London, British Museum, Department of Prints & Drawings, inv. 1861,1109.641.

https://hdl.handle.net/20.500.12434/9d67d830

This ruled leaf has a roman numeral (*ccc xvi*) on the other side, so it is clear that the print was pasted on a verso. It accompanies a rubric and prayer to St Benedict, which started on the recto and continued on this verso. The image was given a light wash, carefully silhouetted, and then pasted on so that the figure fills part of the text block, and forms its left boundary. St Benedict is integrated into the text, and he seems to gaze at it. In this case, the knife-wielder has taken the opportunity to trim away the background, frame, and landscape behind the saint in order to bring the figure closer to the text. Rather than standing alone on the page, St Benedict is nestled around a blanket of words. The scribe has even aligned the print so that the saint faces the prayer dedicated to him, and so that both the saint and the prayer seem to press down on the devil below his feet. This means that someone, probably the scribe, was using the knife as a creative tool, a tool for rethinking the *mise en page*.

Although I am interested in the role of the St Benedict engraving (641) in the manuscript and its relationship to the other prints in the book, previous scholarship has focused on the print's style and its relatively high level of technical accomplishment. According to Lehrs, Israhel van Meckenem made the print, but another engraver retouched the plate.[32] Lehrs also calls this an 'early work' of the artist, as an added form of apology, to explain the print's low quality.

Lehrs's description also conveys an element of German nationalism. He notes that the print has been silhouetted, partially coloured, and 'pasted to the leaf of a Lower German manuscript next to a prayer to St Benedict'.[33] The electronic Register for this item repeats this information. But the manuscript is not in fact Lower German; rather, it is written in Middle Dutch. (British cataloguers routinely refer to the entire language group as 'Flemish', which also reveals a cultural bias.) Lehrs, a German, viewed history through the lenses of his own nationality. Nearly every cataloguer wants to see signs of early innovation in his own culture.

The print of St Benedict was mounted to a matte at the BM with another, similar print also depicting St Benedict. Examining them together reveals something about how the team of beghards considered the aesthetics of prints (e-fig. 23).

---

32 Lehrs IX.268.320, where IX is the volume number, 268 is the page, and 320 is the catalogue number.
33 Lehrs IX.268.320.

BM 1861,1109.640 — St Benedict (e-fig. 23)

St Benedict, engraving. London, British Museum, Department of Prints & Drawings, inv. 1861,1109.640.

https://hdl.handle.net/20.500.12434/23281d22

They are not impressions of the same plate, but are comparable in terms of subject matter, layout, and size. Both are unique impressions. The other side of print 640 has been ruled and inscribed with the folio number *ccc lxxviii*, and the end of a prayer to St Paul and the beginning of one to St Dierick, a much less well-known saint. It seems that the beghard judged the relative quality of the two prints: he allowed the better of the two to represent Benedict himself (641), and chose the worse one to stand as a proxy for Dierick (640). As a consequence of this choice, the beghard treated the two prints differently. He trimmed the saint and the demon on which he stands from a larger sheet, and pasted the silhouetted print on the text page so that the left edge of the text follows the saint's head and shoulders. He left the other print of St Benedict intact, and treated it as a leaf of the manuscript by ruling on the back and writing on it. Lacking an image depicting St Dierick, the beghard found that the lower-quality image of St Benedict, who was also an abbot, was close enough.

In 1861 the British Museum curator saw a relationship between the two prints and placed them on the same mount. Lehrs had suggested that both prints were made by Israhel, but touched up by another engraver, and Friedrich Wilhelm Hollstein (1888–1957, a German print dealer who moved to Amsterdam in 1937), later questioned their relationship to Israhel altogether. Both the beghard and Lehrs saw in the prints what they wanted to see. The beghard turned an image of St Benedict into one of St Dierick, and Lehrs turned the prints into *objets d'art* by a famous, nameable artist. Both the beghard and connoisseur to read images through the lenses of their respective judgements.

Delving into the boxes, I realised that there were several cases in which the scribe had more than one image representing a particular saint, more than necessary. He therefore manipulated their identities. One pair of engraved duplicates depicts St Anne with the Virgin and Christ Child. For one of these (e-fig. 24), the expressionless, stiff figures (where are St Anne's knees?) sit in an unconvincing interior space (where is the organ-playing angel sitting?). The other engraving of the same subject is more fluid and expressive, and is signed by an engraver 'OV' or 'GV' (e-fig. 25).

BM 1861,1109.634 — St Anne with Virgin and Child (e-fig. 24)

St Anne with Virgin and Child, engraving. London, British Museum, Department of Prints & Drawings, inv. 1861,1109.634.

https://hdl.handle.net/20.500.12434/2efe8653

BM 1861,1109.635 — St Anne with Virgin and Child (e-fig. 25)

St Anne with Virgin and Child, engraving. London, British Museum, Department of Prints & Drawings, inv. 1861,1109.635.

https://hdl.handle.net/20.500.12434/b1721240

Although they have the same subject, the two prints fulfil different functions in the manuscript. On the back of 634 is the end of a prayer to Mary and the beginning of one to St Joest. Apparently, the scribe meant this image to enhance the prayer to Mary, who does indeed appear in the image. Print 635 originally accompanied a prayer to St Anne, which consists of a contrafact of the Ave Maria, to be said before an image of St Anne. By 'contrafact' I mean a non-humorous parody, a prayer that keeps the same rhythm and structure as a familiar tune (or prayer), but changes the words. As with many contrafacts, this one riffs on the Ave Maria, rewritten slightly so that it is relevant to St Anne instead of her daughter. In other words, he used this print, which has more expressive figures, a more convincing interior, and more ornate decoration, to represent St Anne. A third image depicting St Anne found a resting place at the beginning of the prayers to St Anne on folio *ccc xci*, but this has been cut out. From these placements, one can deduce a few rules: the scribe must have had several images of St Anne before him, and put some of them in the section of the prayerbook with prayers to her. There are so many prayers to the Virgin that he did not have enough images of her to furnish every prayer; therefore, he reached for a print in which Mary figures as a secondary character and applied it to a Marian prayer. As in the case of the two images of St Benedict, he made a quality judgement: that the best print (the most beautiful?) depicting St Anne would accompany a prayer to her, and the second-tier images, those of middling quality, would be distributed elsewhere. This evidence suggests that the beghards used their creativity to adapt to the new rigidity of print technology, where the printers were anticipating their needs but not quite getting it right.

The Thin Red Line

Placing the prints was intimately linked with writing the manuscript. That the scribe was silhouetting some prints suggests that he had a stack of images at his disposal, which he was applying as he wrote the book. Another way in which the scribe interacted with the images was to rubricate them. The scribe used the red rubricator's pen to make frames around many of the images, or to pick out details within the image by applying a thin red line. Just as black text is framed with red rubrics, monochrome prints are also framed in red boxes.

One idea that had occurred to me while thinking about the print depicting the female trinity, or Anna-te-drieën (e-fig. 25), was that the rubricator (who was also the scribe) had inscribed some of the areas of the otherwise monochrome print with red ink. That, it turned out, was a theme in a group of these prints. Specifically, the rubricator enhanced 635 by tracing the Gothic architecture and outlining the frame, giving the bottom of the frame a 'bevel' by triple-lining it. This feature — enhancing the images with red ink — appeared regularly: several mattes reveal page after page of the beghards' manuscript, most of which have been treated with red (figs 25, 26, 27). Earlier I showed that the silhouetted prints demonstrated that the scribe was responsible for pasting on the prints and writing around them. Now these folios, with prints framed in red, suggest that the scribe was not only the person gluing on the prints but was also the rubricator, and that the rubricator was also the person who 'framed' the prints in red ink.

Fig. 25
Matte with manuscript leaves from Add. 24332 glued to it, with engravings representing St Francis and others. London, British Museum, Department of Prints & Drawings.

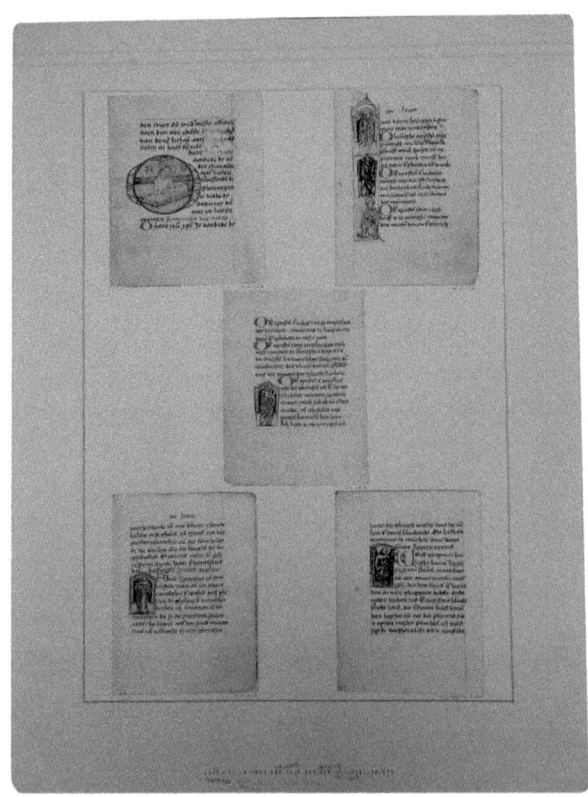

Fig. 26
Matte with manuscript leaves from Add. 24332 glued to it, with small engravings. London, British Museum, Department of Prints & Drawings.

1. Cut, Pasted, and Cut Again 67

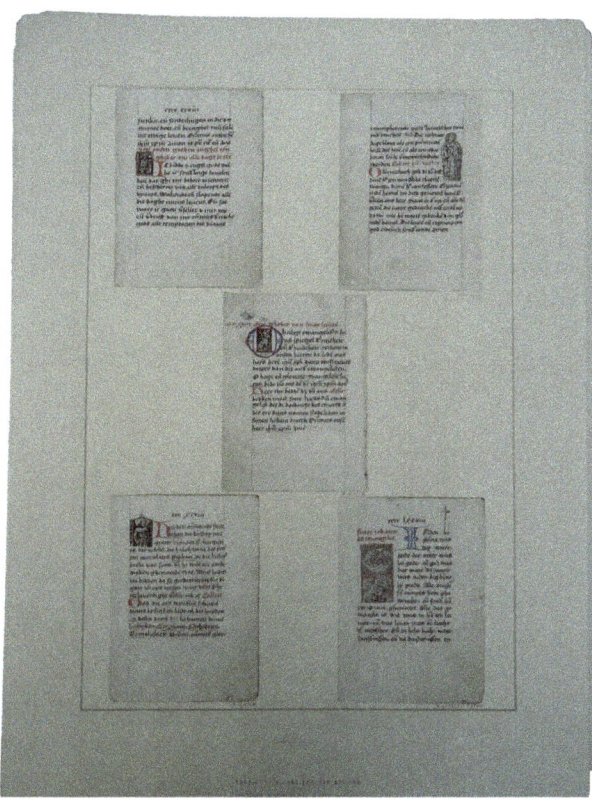

Fig. 27
Matte with manuscript leaves from Add. 24332 glued to it, with small engravings. London, British Museum, Department of Prints & Drawings.

At least in some sections of the book, the regular scribe was also rubricating the text. For example, on folio *ccc lxviij*, with a prayer to St Francis, the scribe's distinctive script reappears in the rubric (e-fig. 26).

BM 1861,1109.666 — Manuscript leaf with a prayer to St Francis (e-fig. 26)

 Manuscript leaf with a prayer to St Francis and an engraving. London, British Museum, Department of Prints & Drawings, inv. 1861,1109.666.

https://hdl.handle.net/20.500.12434/acbebc80

The same red ink was used to make a frame around the figure. Since the scribe would have to leave a space of the appropriate size and shape for this image, it is likely that he is the one who trimmed and pasted it on, before proceeding with the writing. Since he also rubricated the page, it is likely that he also framed the print in red in the same campaign of work. This page also proffers both thick and thin lines in red, indicating one pen for writing and one for underlining. The scribe has used the thin pen to frame St Quentin, who appears with the nails of his martyrdom driven into his shoulders (e-fig. 27).

BM 1861,1109.676 — Manuscript leaf (e-fig. 27)

Manuscript leaf with a prayer to St Quentin and an engraving. London, British Museum, Department of Prints & Drawings, inv. 1861,1109.676.

https://hdl.handle.net/20.500.12434/4d93048f

He has used a thicker nib for inscribing words. However, the rubricator has deployed the same logic when altering the image as he has when creating the prayer text: drawing attention to something that is essentially black and white by adding a bright colour to it. Because the same principle appears in both text and image, and because the ink around the image appears to be the same as the ink applied in the rubrics (albeit with a different pen or brush), I contend that the rubricator also decorated the prints with red designs.

Mid-sized rectangular German engravings must have come from several different sources and therefore had different styles, but the beghards integrated them with red lines. Two of these, representing St Peter (e-fig. 28) and St Matthias (e-fig. 29), probably arrived already coloured with pink, green, and yellow washes.

BM 1861,1109.692 — Manuscript leaf (e-fig. 28)

Manuscript leaf from Add. 24332 with a prayer to St Peter and an engraving. London, British Museum, Department of Prints & Drawings, inv. 1861,1109.692.

https://hdl.handle.net/20.500.12434/7c16bdd0

BM 1861,1109.691 — Manuscript leaf (e-fig. 29)

Manuscript leaf from Add. 24332 with an engraving depicting St Matthias. London, British Museum, Department of Prints & Drawings, inv. 1861,1109.691.

https://hdl.handle.net/20.500.12434/29a6855a

That they have been hand-coloured in a similar way reveals their common source. The rubricator stroked the architecture surrounding the St Matthias, trying to do so symmetrically. He had difficulty with this, because the painter had not applied the green symmetrically, painting all the left side but not all the right. As a result, the red additions at the bottom of the architecture do not match. The rubricator did not add red to the St Peter. This suggests that he was not going through the prints systematically and embellishing them but, rather, that he was selectively embellishing prints after they were already pasted down to the text pages. Red lines helped to integrate the images into the rubricated book.

Not all the small prints have been decorated in red. I looked for patterns. One was that the rubricator added red around the image on folios where he was already busy rubricating text. The image of St Quentin is a case in point. Two other rubricated engravings, which both show St Francis receiving the stigmata, also suggested this (666, see e-fig. 26), and (e-fig. 30).

BM 1861,1109.667 — Manuscript leaf with a prayer to St Francis (e-fig. 30)

Manuscript leaf with a prayer to St Francis and an engraving. London, British Museum, Department of Prints & Drawings, inv. 1861,1109.667.

https://hdl.handle.net/20.500.12434/72e479af

Because the beghards on the Witmakersstraat had Bartholomew and Francis as their patron saints, it is not surprising to find multiples of them in their book, especially Francis, who was apparently well-represented in the printed offerings that pedlars had on hand. These unassuming small images of St Francis appear in red frames, which, although simple, add emphasis to the image. Outlining the images in red might be akin to writing saints' names in red in the calendar. The frame around 667 serves another purpose: although the print is small and barely fills five text lines, the rubricator has aggrandised it: he has added a gothic roof to the print, as if the scene were taking place in a shrine.

Another function of the red framing is to unify disparate items. Folio *ccc lxxxv*, which presents three engravings depicting apostles, takes this red framing aesthetic to an extreme by placing the figures in a flimsy stack of niches in a Gothic church (e-fig. 31).

BM 1861,1109.668, 677, 678, and 669 — Leaf from the beghards' book of hours (e-fig. 31)

Leaf from the beghards' book of hours, with three engravings glued to it. London, British Museum, Department of Prints & Drawings, inv. 1861,1109.668, 677, 678, and 669

https://hdl.handle.net/20.500.12434/a11440fb

Strangely, the subjects of the prints (Peter, Paul, and Paul-turned-into-James) do not correspond exactly to the prayers next to them (to Paul, Andrew, and James). It is as if the scribe merely conceptualized the prayers as 'dedicated to apostles' and then proceeded to paste in an assortment of small relevant prints along the left edge. Rather than have two Pauls next to each other, he transformed the lower one by cutting off his sword and turning the handle of the sword into a shell. Although the apostles have approximately the same scale, they have been printed with different degrees of ink density, and the scribe must also have realised how jarring the prints were next to one another. The snaking red pen decoration is an attempt to unify them.

The rubricator was also at work on an engraving depicting St John having a vision of the beast of the Apocalypse while on the island of Patmos (e-fig. 32).

MB 1861,1109.670 — Leaf from the beghards' book of hours (e-fig. 32)

Leaf from the beghards' book of hours, with an engraving depicting St John on Patmos. London, British Museum, Department of Prints & Drawings, inv. 1861,1109.670.

https://hdl.handle.net/20.500.12434/31e5559d

Here, unusually, it marks the beginning of the Gospel according to John, rather than the Book of Revelation. This is because John the Evangelist was believed to be both the author of the Apocalypse and of the Gospel ('In the beginning was the word'). John appears below, and the beast with the head of a woman in a roundel above, as if it were in a thought bubble.[34] The delicate print contains thousands of minute strokes in a

---

34   Sixten Ringbom, 'Some Pictorial Conventions for the Recounting of Thoughts and Experiences in Late Medieval Art', in *Medieval Iconography and Narrative: A*

small (40 x 22 mm) area. However, the beghard apparently found the print wanting and therefore gave it a red frame. He then went back and forth with his red pen between the two tiers, as if to emphasise the seam between the earthly and visionary realms, between St John and the object of his vision.

I was not sure whether the rubricator was also the person applying the yellow wash to the dragon's wings and John's hair, but an engraving depicting the Christogram convinced me that it was. It shows the letters *ihs* standing out in white against a dark field of cross-hatching (e-fig. 2). This highlights the letters in the centre, which the rubricator further emphasizes by painting the ring around the letters yellow, as well as the flames reaching out from the disc, as if 'yellow' stood for radiance. If the roundel were a clock, then at the five o'clock position there is a red decoration within the yellow band, at the letters 'Ihs'. This red ink has run into the yellow, which indicates that the yellow was slightly wet when the red was applied. Therefore, the red and yellow were applied in the same campaign of work, by the rubricator who was also one of the scribes. Thus, this yellow decoration was supplied by the beghards.

Several operations therefore took place in the beghards' atelier (cutting, pasting, touching in yellow, rubricating), but they did not hand-colour the images they received, except in these circumscribed ways.

Split Personalities

In my exploration of the prints so far, I had seen that the beghards received prints of multiple sizes, made in various places by different printers, and brought them together into the book, sometimes using the knife, red ink, and a yellow wash to heighten and unify them. They were working with prints in large sizes that could fill an entire octavo leaf (or indeed, become an entire leaf), or prints in smaller sizes that could be glued to the page. For this project, the beghards worked as much with the knife as they did with pen, wash and glue to make and enhance meaning. One constant battle they waged was to make an existing stock

---

Symposium, ed. Flemming Gotthelf Andersen, Odense Universitet. Laboratorium for Folksproglig Middela litteratur (Odense: Odense University Press, 1980), pp. 38–69.

of images fit into a desired set of devotions, when the correspondence was not exact, whether in terms of iconography, size, or shape.

Occasionally, the beghard trimmed a larger, presumably rectangular, print into a round form to make a historiated initial out of it. An example is 657 (e-fig. 33), in which the print, depicting the Virgin of the Sun who stands on the moon, has been trimmed on all sides to fit into an O.

BM 1861,1109.657 — Top half of a leaf from the beghards' book of hours (e-fig. 33)

Top half of a leaf from the beghards' book of hours, with an engraving representing the Virgin of the Sun. London, British Museum, Department of Prints & Drawings, inv. 1861,1109.657.

https://hdl.handle.net/20.500.12434/6da68562

The trimmed print is as tall as three lines. A large white space around the print suggests that this was not the beghard's original solution but a makeshift one to plug a gap in the book. He found the closest appropriate image, (over)trimmed it, and pasted it on. Likewise, a rectangular winged ox engraving filled an oval letter before a prayer to St Luke (e-fig. 34). The scribe has worked the negative space of the resulting lobes into the letter's design.

BM 1861,1109.685 — Leaf from the beghards' book of hours (e-fig. 34)

Leaf from the beghards' book of hours, with an engraving depicting a winged ox. London, British Museum, Department of Prints & Drawings, inv. 1861,1109.685.

https://hdl.handle.net/20.500.12434/8e6d1ef9

Thinking about and assembling the small engravings representing standing male saints brought a curious phenomenon into focus. The scribe must have had three copies of a small engraving representing St Lawrence. One has been used to represent St Lawrence himself (e-fig. 35). A copy of the same image of St Lawrence has been used to represent St Vincent (e-fig. 36). From ink, the scribe has fashioned a rake over the saint's shoulder so that he casually displays his object of martyrdom. And finally, the scribe has taken a third copy of the print, trimmed off Lawrence's attribute, and drawn three rocks over the saint's head. St

Lawrence has become St Stephen (e-fig. 37). Alternating between the knife and the pen, the beghard was able to transform three identical prints to serve different needs of the book. The engravers' intended purpose for these little prints of saints is unclear. Did printmakers create them precisely for this use? Or so that people could simply own tiny prints and keep them in the home? Doubtless, they served multiple functions, but uncovering just what these were in the absence of clear contextual evidence is not possible. The reconstructed beghards' book provides but one example for a class of objects with flexible uses.

BM 1861,1109.672 — Leaf from the beghards' book of hours (e-fig. 35)

Leaf from the beghards' book of hours, with an engraving depicting St Lawrence. London, British Museum, Department of Prints & Drawings, inv. 1861,1109.672.

https://hdl.handle.net/20.500.12434/0e573e54

BM 1861,1109.682 — Partial leaf from the beghards' book of hours (e-fig. 36)

Partial leaf from the beghards' book of hours, with an engraving depicting St Lawrence used to represent St Vincent. London, British Museum, Department of Prints & Drawings, inv. 1861,1109.682.

https://hdl.handle.net/20.500.12434/79a323c9

BM 1861,1109.671 — Leaf from the beghards' book of hours (e-fig. 37)

Leaf from the beghards' book of hours, with an engraving depicting St Lawrence, used to represent St Stephen. London, British Museum, Department of Prints & Drawings, inv. 1861,1109.671.

https://hdl.handle.net/20.500.12434/fe140795

What I find particularly interesting is how the scribe continually intervened in the identity of the printed subjects. The beghards bought several more rectangular German engravings featuring single standing saints, but they did not always depict the desired saint. They pasted one of these to a folio which has on its recto the end of a prayer to Mary Magdalene and the beginning of one to St James (e-fig. 38).

BM 1861,1109.690 — Leaf from the beghards' book of hours (e-fig. 38)

Leaf from the beghards' book of hours, with an engraving depicting St Paul, used as St James. London, British Museum, Department of Prints & Drawings, inv. 1861,1109.690.

https://hdl.handle.net/20.500.12434/e9f19c47

But they apparently lacked an image of St James and had to make one out of an engraving of St Paul: with a finely trimmed nib, the scribed used the same dark brown ink that he used for the text to draw a pilgrim's hat on the figure's head, and added shells to the blank space on either side of his ears. Furthermore, the scribe has enhanced both text and image with a few strokes of red.

Another print was hand-coloured in a similar way, with a bit of yellow wash plus the rubricator's red lines on the architecture. This print represents St Agatha (e-fig. 39).

BM 1861,1109.693 — Leaf from the beghards' book of hours (e-fig. 39)

Leaf from the beghards' book of hours, with an engraving depicting St Agatha. London, British Museum, Department of Prints & Drawings, inv. 1861,1109.693.

https://hdl.handle.net/20.500.12434/a8cfa393

She holds a pair of pincers, carrying her breast aloft by its nipple, all under a clumsy arch. A letter *b* that may be a monogram appears top right in the image, but the identity of this engraver remains mysterious. The print has been affixed to a page in the middle of a prayer to Agatha. Because the print was a bit wider than the space, the copyist moved it a centimetre into the margin to leave more room for script. In other words, the scribe had to make concessions to accommodate the images. They are too small to serve as full-page 'miniatures' but large enough that they nearly push the text from the page. The rubricator, who added the word 'an[tiphon]' in the margin, stroked some of the capital letters in red, and underscored the name of the saint in the same colour; he also overscribed some of the printed lines in the architectural frame of the print. I find it strange that the rubricator did not pick out details of this martyr's breast, or her halo, or her palm — those elements that convey her martyrdom and sanctity — to 'underscore' her particular attributes, but chose neutral pieces of architecture to highlight.

An adjacent category of small images has a much clearer reason for existing: to fulfil an indulgence. For example, it contains the prayer 'O, Adoro te in cruce pendentem', the most richly indulgenced text in the pre-Reformation period (e-fig. 40).

BM 1861,1109.658 — Leaf from the beghards' book of hours (e-fig. 40)

Leaf from the beghards' book of hours, with an engraved roundel depicting Christ as Man of Sorrows used as a historiated initial. London, British Museum, Department of Prints & Drawings, inv. 1861,1109.658.

https://hdl.handle.net/20.500.12434/8ae40eb5

The beginning of the prayer, however, is missing. My explorations of the British Museum's collection did not unearth the previous folio, *ccccc xviii*, which probably had an image of the Mass of St Gregory on it, an image that was efficacious in activating the often enormous indulgences that accompanied recitation of this prayer. I suspected that the beghard had one large image of the Mass of St Gregory, which he used as a full-page 'miniature' that has now gone missing, and secondarily a small image depicting Christ as Man of Sorrows, which he applied to a secondary lower level in the hierarchy of decoration.

This roundel pasted onto fol. *ccccc xix*, 658, is highly derivative. It is a simplified copy of an image of Christ as Man of Sorrows by Israhel (fig. 28), which itself is probably a copy of a previous print, which is probably a copy of the miracle-working micro-mosaic image of Christ as Man of Sorrows made around 1300 in Sinai and kept at Sta Croce in Gerusalemme in Rome, where it was elaborated framed and put on display as a major pilgrimage attraction (figs 29 and 30).[35] Christ's head, strangely, leans towards the side of damnation, and the letters that fill the background are reversed. In other words, this print was probably made by a slapdash engraver, who copied an existing design without bothering to reverse it for the printing process.

---

35 Martina Bagnoli, ed. *Treasures of Heaven: Saints, Relics, and Devotion in Medieval Europe*, exh. cat, Cleveland Museum of Art, Walters Art Museum, British Museum (New Haven, CT: Yale University Press, 2010), pp. 203–04, with further references.

Fig. 28 Israhel van Meckenem, Christ as Man of Sorrows, engraving. Paris, BnF, Département des Estampes, Ea 48Res.

Fig. 29 Mosaic icon with the Akra Tapeinosis (Utmost Humiliation), or Man of Sorrows, in a series of frames. Mosaic icon, Byzantine, late 13th–early 14th century. Basilica di Sta Croce in Gerusalemme, Rome.

Fig. 30 Detail of the Mosaic icon from the previous figure.

Foliation

So far, the prints that had arrived (and the leaves to which they were stuck) fitted neatly into my spreadsheet. I was fortunate that the beghards who had assembled the manuscript had foliated it; they enabled my task of reconstruction. But then came a difficulty: a matte with two pages from the beghards' manuscript that were pasted down, thereby obscuring the foliation. (Most other prints are attached with hinges and can therefore be lifted.) One of these was an engraving showing the infant Christ seated on a cushion within a sacred heart (e-fig. 41); the other a full-page engraving by the Monogrammist F, which shows the dead Christ being supported by his standing mother, with the *Arma Christi* displayed as two coats of arms above (e-fig. 42).

F has engraved his initial into a miniature shield in the lower frame. One wonders whether he considered that his burin resembled an instrument of torture. If so, he might have felt implicated in creating Christ's pain.

BM 1861,1109.632 — Jesus as an infant holding the *Arma Christi* (e-fig. 41)

Jesus as an infant holding the *Arma Christi*, Netherlandish engraving. London, British Museum, Department of Prints & Drawings, inv. 1861,1109.632.

https://hdl.handle.net/20.500.12434/4389fc3b

BM 1861,1109.637 — Leaf from the beghards' book of hours (e-fig. 42)

Leaf from the beghards' book of hours, with an engraving depicting the dead Christ being supported by his standing mother, with the *Arma Christi* displayed as two coats of arms above. Netherlandish, engraving, attributed to Monogrammist F. London, British Museum, Department of Prints & Drawings, inv. 1861,1109.637.

https://hdl.handle.net/20.500.12434/a87353b9

How these two pages are mounted affects how they must be viewed, and how they may not be viewed. As curators accessioned them, they put the prints into 'schools', which is one of the reasons these two landed on the same matte, in a box with several other early engravings from the Netherlands. Because they are now glued next to one another, the two prints must be viewed together. Both artists constructed Christological imagery and found ways to fill the interstices with Passion iconography. In 632 the infant holds the cross with the Crown of Thorns as if to foreshadow his earthly demise, and the image could be read as a giant wounded heart framing an innocent Jesus, with his punctured arms and feet filling the corners (e-fig. 41).

A long, fluttering banderol has an inscription in Dutch. As it winds around the heart, it announces: 'O mynsch, drach my wonden in dyn herte van bitteren die ic ontfinc om dinre mynnen …' (O, loved one, carry my wounds in your heart from the pains that I endured out of love for you…). That the scroll winds around so that some of the text is upside-down implies that the print was meant to be loose, because it would have been unwieldy to turn the whole book to read it when the print formed a page.[36]

In the service of connoisseurship, both Lehrs and Hollstein described 632. While the print is clearly Netherlandish, they both saw the need to frame it as derivative of a German precedent: nationalism often informs scholarship. Hollstein thought that the engraving was a copy after the Master with the Banderols (L 81), while Lehrs thought that this engraving and another by the Master of the Martyrdom of the Ten Thousand (L 86) were based on a lost original. Although I could not get excited about chasing down a lost original, their thinking still bears on mine: the way in which these prints were originally collected, mounted, and stored has an enormous influence on how viewers see them now. Because of the way they are mounted, it is difficult to avoid seeing them in terms of style.

It also takes some effort to imagine them off their mattes and back into the book in which they were mounted in 1500. What role did they play in the unusual book of hours made by Franciscan men in 1500? Its original foliation should help to figure that out. Unfortunately, both these Netherlandish engravings were glued down to the mount, so that the back was illegible. A tantalising hint of the foliation came through the top of the paper of 632 and of 637, but neither was immediately legible. I needed to read the texts on the glued-down versos of the two Netherlandish prints in order to work out where they belonged in the manuscript, and to read the foliation that was leaking through. I explained my problem to the curators, but the Study Room was about to close, and I had to return to The Hague. Giulia Bartrum, the curator, promised to do what she could about having the prints that were pasted directly to their matte (rather than hinged) all lifted. The next few months were extraordinarily busy, and only when they had passed could I fly back to London and squeeze in a few hours' work in the Study Room. By that time, the staff of the BM had lifted these leaves from their mount so that I could read the backs, including the foliation. I was grateful.

---

36   Kathryn Rudy, *Postcards on Parchment: The Social Lives of Medieval Books* (New Haven, CT; London: Yale University Press, 2015) contains a discussion of single sheets that can be better read unencumbered by a book block.

To my surprise, neither 637 nor 632 had prayer text on the back or, even more remarkably, any foliation. I realised that the ink at the tops of these folios was not leaking through the back, but consisted of offsets of folios they had previously been adjacent to. This meant that the text was mirrored. Digitally flipping the top of 637 made it easily legible (fig. 31). Now the Roman numeral read *ccc xxxixj*, where the final character, *j*, had a strange loop. But this did not make sense as a Roman numeral. Studying the front of the Infant Christ (632) more closely (and mirrored), I read the faint stain at the top as the number *c xxxiii*, followed by the same loopy sign as the mystery stroke that occurred on 637: why was the foliation — plus the funny mark that looked like a loopy *j* — impressed in mirror-writing on the front?

Fig. 31 Detail of London, British Museum, Department of Prints & Drawings, inv. 1861,1109.637, flipped to reveal the offset inscription.

Reconsidering the problem, I realised that the loopy *j* was a sign for *bis*, a word used in Dutch to indicate an interpolation. For example, a sequence could read 1, 2, 2*bis*, 3.... meaning that an element had been added between 2 and 3. (I am collapsing time here. Now that I know the answer, the loopy *j* is no longer a mystery and seems obvious; however, it took me months to arrive at this solution.) A beghard, possibly Jan van Emmerick, must have interpolated the leaves into the book after it had already been foliated. That is why these leaves were blank on the back: they had not been ruled for use in the original production of the manuscript, but added later. In both 637 and 632, the ink stains I had read at the tops of the respective folios were offsets from adjacent folios, but those adjacent folios had also been interpolated. It was these adjacent leaves that the scribe had called *bis* (specifically, *c xxxiii bis* and *ccc xxxix bis*). From this one could deduce that first the book had been written and foliated. Then more prints were added and some of them were foliated with *bis*, and this ink bit into 632 and 637, which were added in a third round of additions. The ghostly offsets were caused by pages (presumably with prints) that were no longer extant. These leaves were missing in my spreadsheet, so I added them, noting that I had inferred their existence from the offsets on their respective following folios.

Moreover, the reason for the offset from the previous folio was that the beghard had added several prints after the book was finished and foliated, and at least two of them were bound next to one another when he went through the book and foliated the new leaves; one of these he foliated as *ccc xxxix bis*. When he closed the book, the wet ink was transferred to the front of the Pietà. The print that I had inferred from this evidence — with the handwritten folio number *ccc xxxix bis* — was not to be found in the manuscript nor in the boxes at the British Museum.

Another ramification of this discovery had to do with time: whereas the leaves with regular foliation had a *terminus post quem* of around 1501 (the date of the inscription in the calendar), these added leaves could be slightly later. It appeared that the beghards had come upon a small supply of Netherlandish engravings after the book was finished, but could not bear to omit them from the project. The beghards must have inserted 637, the print depicting Mary holding her dead son, at the end of an indulgenced prayer to the Virgin of Compassion, and before the *Stabat Mater* in Dutch (e-fig. 42). This imagery is multivalent, by which I mean that it could be appropriate contemplative material before any one of a number of texts about Christ and his Passion, or Mary and her Compassion.

The other print that was blank on the back, 632 with the Infant Christ, also spent time squeezed next to a leaf that had *bis* in its foliation: it was one of two extra folios placed into the manuscript so that they would face the incipit for the Seven Penitential Psalms, which begins on folio *c xxxiii*. Normally, one would expect to find an image of the Last Judgement to mark this text; perhaps the beghards did not have a print with that image and used two others instead, apparently as an afterthought.

The stratigraphy — that is, the order in which the parts of the book were assembled — reveals something important about the beghards' processes. It would seem that they began decorating the book with drawings only, and then introduced prints part-way through the making process. The opening of the Seven Penitential Psalms, for example, originally had a black and rubricated text, a drawing showing Christ with an orb in a decorated capital, as a digital reconstruction shows (fig. 32). In a second phase, the book maker inserted a folio, presumably a print that no longer survives. Its existence can be inferred from the faint offset of foliation on a second print that the book maker inserted: a Netherlandish engraving depicting the infant Christ on a pillow. A digital reconstruction of this proposed opening reveals further evidence that the infant Christ once faced the incipit: some of the yellow wash from the orb in the initial seems to have transferred to the print, just under Christ's disembodied left hand (fig. 33). This proposed reconstruction also explains why most of the prints are concentrated in the second half of the manuscript: the beghards only thought of using prints in this way after they had inscribed folios *i- cc lxvii*. For the folios before this point, they added some prints *ex post facto*, as they did with the infant at the Seven Penitential Psalms.

Fig. 32 Digital reconstruction to show the proposed original state of the opening of the Seven Penitential Psalms (Add. 24332, fol. 104v and Add. 41338, fol. 6r).

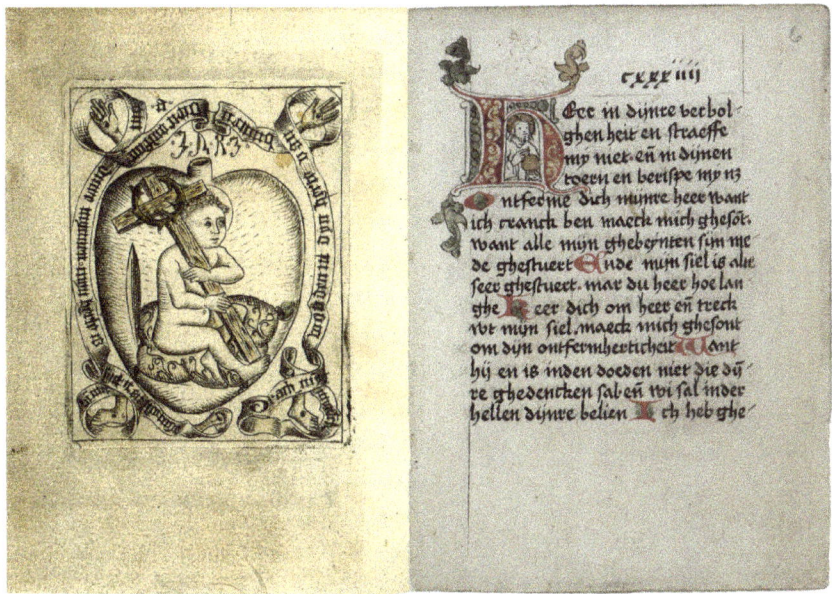

Fig. 33 Digital reconstruction to show the proposed third state of the opening of the Seven Penitential Psalms (London, British Museum, Department of Prints & Drawings, inv. 1861,1109.632 and Add. 41338, fol. 6r).

A Group of Woodcuts, Possibly Netherlandish

Whereas Lehrs and Hollstein catalogued the engravings, Schreiber catalogued the woodcuts and metalcuts. Having separate systems of classification for prints by media gives them a false sense of distinctiveness and separation, when it is clear that they were being used alongside one another and therefore shared many of the same functions and possibly the same methods of distribution. Because woodcuts seem to have been more closely associated with the woodworker's studio, and engravings with the goldsmith's studio, the resulting products have been assigned a concomitant value, with modern collectors more actively pursuing the items that bear a trace of the goldsmith's studio. Their relative value may also derive from their fifteenth-century supply: a single woodblock yielded even more prints than did a copper plate, and woodcut prints may have been even less expensive than prints made by copper engraving. However, the similarities in the finished products outweighed the differences in their production, and the beghards, at least, were incorporating them into the same project side by side. Users seem to have been more concerned with what was represented than with how it was represented and with what technique.

The way in which I have organised this material here results in part from the way the nineteenth-century cataloguers described it, and the way the nineteenth-century curators filed the physical objects. In this section I treat the woodcuts that the beghards also pasted in their book of hours. These woodcuts poured out of a different part of the British Museum's Study Room.

In 1861 the conservator had seen that various woodcut prints formed a series, and therefore grouped them as numbers 646–655 in the Register for 9 November 1861. They depict the following saints (with their Schreiber number in brackets):

St Nicholas (S2714; 1861,1109.646) (e-fig. 43)

Leaf from the beghards' book of hours, with a woodcut depicting St Nicholas. London, British Museum, Department of Prints & Drawings, inv. 1861,1109.646.

https://hdl.handle.net/20.500.12434/75a4b1c2

St Anthony (S2541; 647) (e-fig. 44)

Leaf from the beghards' book of hours, with a woodcut depicting St Anthony. London, British Museum, Department of Prints & Drawings, inv. 1861,1109.647.

https://hdl.handle.net/20.500.12434/761ffcf0

St Barbara (S2559; 648) (e-fig. 45)

Leaf from the beghards' book of hours, with a woodcut depicting St Barbara. London, British Museum, Department of Prints & Drawings, inv. 1861,1109.648.

https://hdl.handle.net/20.500.12434/8b52f262

St Catherine (S2582; 649) (e-fig. 46)

Leaf from the beghards' book of hours, with a woodcut depicting St Catherine. London, British Museum, Department of Prints & Drawings, inv. 1861,1109.649.

https://hdl.handle.net/20.500.12434/b75dc987

St Erasmus (S2622; 650) (e-fig. 47)

Leaf from the beghards' book of hours, with a woodcut depicting St Erasmus. London, British Museum, Department of Prints & Drawings, inv. 1861,1109.650.

https://hdl.handle.net/20.500.12434/dea0315d

St Macarius (S2691; 651) (e-fig. 48)

Leaf from the beghards' book of hours, with a woodcut depicting St Macarius, used as St Paul. London, British Museum, Department of Prints & Drawings, inv. 1861,1109.651.

https://hdl.handle.net/20.500.12434/a6f85a7f

St Margaret (652) (e-fig. 49)

Leaf from the beghards' book of hours, with a metalcut depicting St Margaret. London, British Museum, Department of Prints & Drawings, inv. 1861,1109.652.

https://hdl.handle.net/20.500.12434/528638af

St Martin (S2706; 653) (e-fig. 50)

Leaf from the beghards' book of hours, with a woodcut depicting St Martin. London, British Museum, Department of Prints & Drawings, inv. 1861,1109.653.

https://hdl.handle.net/20.500.12434/088e2934

St Sebastian (S2728; 654) (e-fig. 51)

Leaf from the beghards' book of hours, with a woodcut depicting St Sebastian. London, British Museum, Department of Prints & Drawings, inv. 1861,1109.654.

https://hdl.handle.net/20.500.12434/5292976a

St Roch (S2724; 655) (e-fig. 52)

Leaf from the beghards' book of hours, with a woodcut depicting St Roch. London, British Museum, Department of Prints & Drawings, inv. 1861,1109.655.

https://hdl.handle.net/20.500.12434/0cb2bc9d

According to Schreiber, these woodcuts were 'made around 1480–1490 in Ghent(?) and removed from a Flemish prayerbook'. Now we know that the manuscript they came from was Add. 24332, but Schreiber did not know that. He probably reasoned that this series was made in Ghent because it includes an image depicting St Macarius (e-fig. 48), Bishop of Antioch in Pisidia, who was especially venerated in Ghent: St Macarius had made a pilgrimage to Ghent to see St Bavo and, at the end of his visit, Macarius fortuitously died of the plague, leaving the denizens of Ghent with his relics. Macarius was therefore venerated as one of the plague saints and was also considered efficacious against other epidemic diseases. His name is often written in red in calendars made in West Flanders. The beghards of Maastricht, however, did not especially venerate Macarius, and while his name does indeed appear in the calendar under 15 January, it is not in red and lacks a Roman numeral. This means that the beghards made no special concession for Macarius, and did not recite extra prayers on his feast day. It follows, then, that they did not especially need an image of Macarius in their book. Because the scribe did not want the print to go to waste, he changed the saint's identity: he has pasted this print to folio *cc xcvii*, which initiates a prayer to St Paul the Hermit, thereby turning St Macarius into St Paul. In making this transformation, the beghard has crossed out the name St Macarius printed in xylographic text at the top of the image, by stroking it with red. Contrary to his intention, this stroking highlights the word rather than hiding it. It is curious that he did not simply trim off the inscription or silhouette the print to get rid of the label. What is clear is that the beghard lacked a print depicting St Paul, but had one depicting St Macarius, so made do with what he had.

Schreiber had included descriptions of these prints in the third volume of his great *Manuel de l'amateur de la gravure sur bois et sur métal au XV*^{e} *siècle*, the one dedicated to metal prints and paste prints. At that time he thought they were all metalcuts, but he realised that they differed from most other metalcuts. For this reason he added a note to most of the entries in this group: 'La gravure … a été réalisé à l'aide du couteau sans emploi de la manière criblée'.[37] Schreiber noted that the St Margaret (e-fig. 49) came from the same manuscript, but was part of a different series.[38] Later, all these prints (except for the St Margaret, which I will discuss next) were given different Schreiber numbers to reflect the fact that they were no longer thought to be metalcuts but, rather, woodcut prints.[39]

Campbell Dodgson (1867–1948, who was the Keeper of Prints and Drawings at the BM from 1912–1932) also pointed out that the print depicting St Margaret does not belong with the others.[40] Whereas the rest of the prints are indeed woodcuts, the print of St Margaret is a metalcut. One can easily see, however, why Schreiber, working quickly through thousands of prints, would have assigned the St Margaret to the group because the woodcuts look as if they derive from metalcut models: they have extensive surface patterns, and the woodcutter takes delight in representing brick walls and stippled surfaces. As with most metalcuts, the woodcuts in this series have a high ratio of black printed area to empty area.

Furthermore, a compositional difference separates the St Margaret from the others: whereas the woodcuts in this group are oriented to the right, this metalcut is oriented to the left; consequently, the book's designer pasted it so that it was justified with the right margin and the saint still faces the prayer text. It is clear from this example that the

---

37 S2691.
38 S2541 (St Antoine/Anthony, which is the first print in this group to appear in the catalogue).
39 The prints were transferred in 1935 to Schreiber, Woodcuts Vol. 4, S1230a.
40 S2699; Campbell Dodgson, *Catalogue of Early German and Flemish Woodcuts in the British Museum*, 2 vols, London, British Museum Trustees, 1903, cat. B.15(3), puts the prints in this group together and discusses them on p. 183, comparing at some length the woodcut technique with that of 'dotted' metalcuts.

scribe with the glue pot was evaluating each print as he deployed it and judging how best to place each item. Whereas the other prints in the series are painted carefully with thin washes, this image is painted rather sloppily with a semi-opaque green and a shiny lake red; because metalcuts leave so much black 'negative space' on the image, they can be painted quickly by brushing pigment across the surface.

Although the metalcut representing St Margaret must be removed from this group, another woodcut that does belong to it but was unknown to Schreiber is an Annunciation, a fragment of which has been left on folio 283v (*ccc xvii*; fig. 4). Like the rest of the woodcuts in this group, the backdrop of the image is highly worked and patterned; the woodcutter has taken special delight in rendering textures such as Gabriel's wings. Considering these woodcuts as a group reveals aspects of the production, marketing, and distribution of prints in the fifteenth century. All the woodcuts in this series are painted in light washes of warm tones, with an emphasis on red, orange, and a warm brown, and they have a double frame of yellow and black. They all measure 53 x 42 millimetres. It is possible that the nine woodcuts were printed on the same sheet, in three rows of three. The fact that the prints in this group have such similar hand-colouring suggests that the beghards bought them already hand-coloured, perhaps even intact on a sheet, which they subsequently cut apart.

Most of the prints in this series present a saint who is turned to the right in three-quarter profile. This orientation suggests that the artist had a function in mind for these prints, namely their current one of serving as illuminations in prayerbooks. With the saint oriented towards the right, the image can be glued so that it is justified with the left margin, and the saint will then face the incipit of the relevant prayer text.

Whereas all the female saints appear in three-quarter length with their respective attributes, a few of the male saints (Erasmus, Nicholas, Martin) are depicted at a moment of high dramatic tension. The image of St Nicholas, or *Sinterklaas*, for example, shows the saint calling three naked youths forth from the dead by raising his hands and gesturing at them in the tub (e-fig. 43). St Martin is depicted just as he is about to cut a piece of his ermine-trimmed garment to give it to a crawling beggar whose legs have been cut off by the frame (e-fig. 50). St Erasmus is not shown performing a miracle but undergoing his gory martyrdom, as short-legged and pig-faced men wind his intestines onto a windlass (e-fig. 47).

This evidence shows that the beghards assembled woodcut prints as well as metalcuts in the same book. They did not make the same distinctions between these categories that the nineteenth-century cataloguers would make. Moreover, given the number and diverse origins of the prints in the manuscript, it is possible that local wholesalers of prints bought them from various printmakers, including those in Germany and West Flanders. Finally — and this is a point that bears repeating because it occurs throughout the beghards' manuscript — the book's designers were interested in using every available image, even if some were inappropriate and had to stand in for other saints. They abided by a principle of fungibility.

Appropriating German Engravings

Many of the image-text couplings I have detailed reveal that the copyist hunted for the right print to paste with a desired prayer, and if no print was forthcoming, he adjusted an existing print by trimming off a printed attribute and adding a hand-drawn one instead. But in several cases I wondered whether the image had priority, and therefore the beghard searched for an appropriate prayer to copy alongside it. One example appears on folio *cc lxvii* (e-fig. 53).

BM 1861,1109.688 — Leaf from the beghards' book of hours (e-fig. 53)

Leaf from the beghards' book of hours, with an engraving depicting Bernard interacting with an image of Christ that comes alive. London, British Museum, Department of Prints & Drawings, inv. 1861,1109.688.

https://hdl.handle.net/20.500.12434/23d63d3e

The engraving depicts Jesus embracing St Bernard; it is pasted to a page whose recto has this rubric, underlined:

> Hier na volcht een ynnich gebet dat synte bernardus gemaict heefft [sic] om mede te bewenen die passie ons heren. Ende men leest hoe in eynre tijt st bernaert dit gebet las voer den heilige cruce. Ende het wart gesien hoe hem dat beelde vanden cruys loesde ende neich hem neder ende

omhelen [sic] Bernardum. Ende het is vanden stoel van romen mit aflait begaest ende gestediget als men leest mit werdiger devoecien II M III C ende LXX iaer ende LXX daghe aflaitz. Die syn die vijf grueten totten vijf wonden ons liefs heren ihesu xpi. Gebet.

[Here follows a devout prayer that St Bernard wrote to experience compassion with the suffering of Our Lord. One reads how once upon a time St Bernard read this prayer before the holy cross, and it was observed that the image loosened itself from the cross and bent down to embrace Bernard. The seat in Rome has granted and confirmed this with an indulgence, so that if someone reads it with true devotion [he will earn] 2370 years' and 70 days' indulgence. These are the five greetings to the five wounds of our dear lord Jesus Christ. Prayer.]

So strong and heartfelt are Bernard's prayers that they animate the image. That is what is happening in the image. It accompanies the 'Greeting to the Five Wounds of Christ', a prayer that occasionally, but not always, includes a version of this rubric. The beghard's possession of the print may have motivated him to include the long narrative rubric to explain the image.

Framed as it is with metallic brown, this print has been treated differently from the others. It appears to be the only occasion in the manuscript in which the beghards experimented with a metallic border; perhaps they were extending the size of the print so that it filled the entire ruled text-block area. The print has been made on much finer paper than the manuscript pages: even if the beghards had received it on a larger sheet, its thin paper would have been inappropriate as an unmounted folio in the manuscript. Moreover, its paper is thirsty and has drunk in the black ink, as well as the light washes in yellow and green. There are no other prints from this series surviving in the book, although the thin paper and the metallic border would be easy to recognise if other prints showed up in other collections. Such features would trace these prints to a common source.

Lehrs often notes the origins of the engravings he catalogues. For this image of St Bernard and Christ (688), Lehrs realised that the print had been preserved in a manuscript, and he even knew that Tross had sold the manuscript in Paris in 1861.[41] But it simply was not his project to reconstruct manuscripts. Rather, his project was to break them down, to

---

41   Lehrs vol. III, p. 398, no. 73 (St Bernard).

sort the prints into categories, to assign them to masters. In fact, a large portion of the prints he sifted through had come from manuscripts. To note them all would be to lose concentration on his purpose.

The BM mounted this print with another depicting St Christopher attributed to the same artist, the Master of the Martyrdom of the Ten Thousand (689) (e-fig. 54).

BM 1861,1109.689 — Leaf from the beghards' book of hours (e-fig. 54)

Leaf from the beghards' book of hours, with an engraving depicting St Christopher, attributed to the Master of the Martyrdom of the Ten Thousand. London, British Museum, Department of Prints & Drawings, inv. 1861,1109.689.

https://hdl.handle.net/20.500.12434/fb8fbeb0

It has been pasted so that it accompanies the beginning of a prayer to St Christopher. The beghard could not resist adding his own bit of colour to what I suspect came to the monastery already hand-coloured: a few red pen strokes on the cross that the infant Jesus carries make the print the beghard's own.

Assigning both the St Christopher and the St Bernard to the same engraver, the cataloguer mounted them side-by-side to the same matte. What is telling in this juxtaposition is that they look very different. That is partly due to the fact that they have been printed on different kinds of paper, and the St Christopher is painted in bold colours, while the St Bernard is crusty and brown. Even if the same master had made the plates (and I am not advocating this), they were printed and finished by two separate processes, possibly in separate locations.

Painted Prints from the Circle of Israhel van Meckenem

Two prints, classified as German, were pasted down to their mounts and were therefore difficult to place in the manuscript. One of these represents Christ at someone's bedside (636) (e-fig. 55), and the other represents the standing Virgin and Child in a niche (633) (fig. 34).

BM 1861,1109.636 — Leaf from the beghards' book of hours (e-fig. 55)

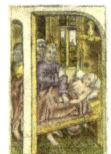

Leaf from the beghards' book of hours, with an engraving depicting Christ raising Jairus's Daughter, attributed to Israhel van Meckenem. London, British Museum, Department of Prints & Drawings, inv. 1861,1109.636.

https://hdl.handle.net/20.500.12434/c521155b

When 636 entered the collection in 1861, the subject was misunderstood, as the Register reads: 'One of the illustrations of the Ars Moriendi, representing the Saviour at the bedside of a dying man. Anonymous'. In fact, the print shows a rarely depicted moment from Christ's adult miracles: the Raising of Jairus's Daughter. This story, told in Mark V:35–43 and in Luke VIII:49–56, describes Jesus reanimating a twelve-year-old girl. In the image Christ stands next to the girl's bed; he holds her

Fig. 34
Leaf from the beghards' book of hours, with an engraving depicting the Virgin and Child, by Israhel van Meckenem. London, British Museum, Department of Prints & Drawings, inv. 1861,1109.633.

arm and gestures with his right hand as if to call her from the dead. An archway in the left-hand wall reveals a small sliver of a figure. Christ's impossibly placed feet appear under the bed. A thick support unevenly bisects the image vertically, thereby framing the back of the left-hand figure. Both in its subject matter and its treatment of space, the image is extraordinarily strange.

The Raising of Jairus's Daughter in the print is stylistically related to the Virgin and Child (633). They probably stemmed from the same campaign of work. Both prints comprehend several layers of space, including interior walls that are pierced to reveal a glimpse of the outside, and experimental framing techniques. In addition to this daring deployment of space, they were printed and hand-coloured in the same washes. In both prints, olive green, pink, and dark yellow transparent washes dominate the spectrum. The semi-opaque green wash has obscured the signature 'IM', which is clear on the uncoloured version of the Virgin and Child that is mounted on the same matte in the BM, even though they have different accession dates (e-fig. 56).

BM 1851,1213.864 — Engraving depicting the Virgin and Child (e-fig. 56)

Engraving depicting the Virgin and Child, by Israhel van Meckenem, signed 'IM'. Uncoloured version. London, British Museum, Department of Prints & Drawings, inv. 1851,1213.864.

https://hdl.handle.net/20.500.12434/7b9c7c52

This suggests that the original owners of 633 and 636 — the beghards — were not interested in the name Israhel van Meckenem. Their task was not to collect prints attached to named artists. Rather, their task was to amass and utilise numerous small prints, which were only valuable for their content, rather than for their authorship. Although both 633 and 636 share the same pigments, these pigments differ from anything else in the manuscript. This means that the beghards did not do the colouring themselves but received the prints already coloured. It also seems that uncoloured versions of the same prints were available in the market, but that the beghards chose the coloured ones.⁴² This would have added to the expense, making cheap images cost two or three times what they would have in their nude state. But they were still inexpensive. Years later I would realise what this obscuring of Israhel's sign meant for the dismemberment of the book and the collection of its parts (as I will show below).

I looked at 636 for the first time on 24 April 2007. It was pasted down to its archival mount, meaning that the text on the reverse was not readable. Consequently, it was unclear where this seldom represented scene would have fitted into the manuscript. The print fills the entire page and, like other prints of similar size, was not glued on but inserted directly into the quire. Possible clues hid in the foliation: the closely related Virgin and Child leaf (633) was foliated later very faintly with some kind of metal point, possibly lead, with the Roman numeral 'cc lxii j', once again with the curved j standing for *bis*. On another visit, in January 2008, Giulia told me she had lifted 636, but even after I could see the back, I could not tell where this print originally fit in the manuscript because the back of the leaf is blank, and neither the recto nor the verso is foliated. Jan van Emmerick (or one of his brethren) apparently had as much difficulty placing this image as I did.

Contrary to my expectations, 633 had also been inscribed. Although the print was probably inserted as an afterthought (given the *bis* foliation), its obverse is nevertheless inscribed with the end of a prayer to Mary, and a rubric that mentions Johannes XXII (1316–1334) for a prayer about indulgences that are 'given to all believing Christians' (fig. 35). Depicting the standing Virgin and Child, the image apparently belonged to the adjacent Marian prayer on fol. *cc lxii* (233), which prefaces a long text about indulgences. Thus, the beghard had matched the Marian image with the Marian prayer.

For the purposes of conveying this result in the present study, however, I had a problem: although the front of the sheet had been scanned, the person doing the scanning apparently cleaned up the digital image by trimming it down, thereby cropping away the Roman numeral at the top (e-fig. 57).

How can I make an argument about where the image sat in the manuscript without this evidence in the photograph? I cannot. Because

---

42 Susan Dackerman, *Painted Prints: The Revelation of Color in Northern Renaissance & Baroque Engravings, Etchings & Woodcuts* (University Park, PA: Pennsylvania State University Press, 2002), esp. pp. 9–47 and passim.

1. Cut, Pasted, and Cut Again

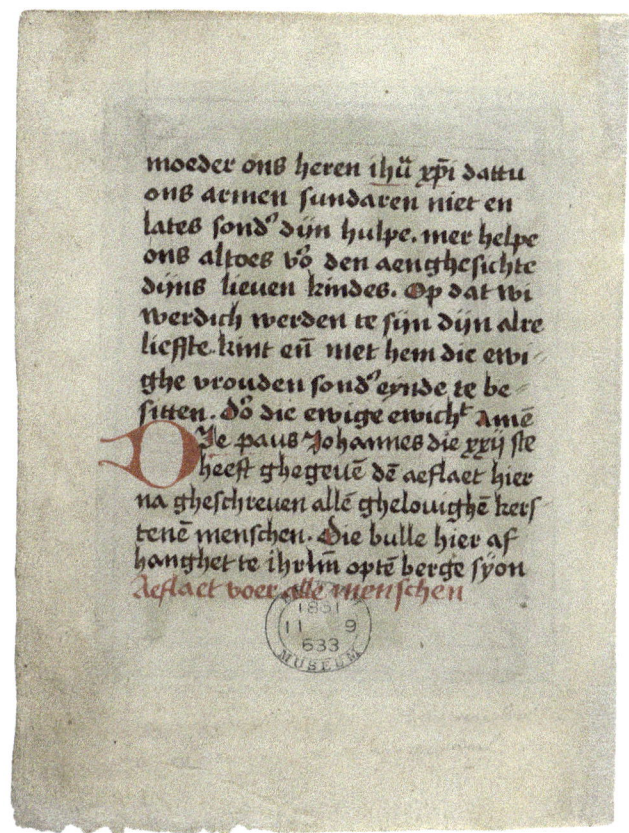

Fig. 35
Leaf from the beghards' book of hours, reverse of London, British Museum, Department of Prints & Drawings, inv. 1861,1109.633.

BM 1861,1109.633 — Leaf from the beghards' book of hours (e-fig. 57)

 Leaf from the beghards' book of hours, with an engraving depicting the Virgin and Child, by Israhel van Meckenem. London, British Museum, Department of Prints & Drawings, inv. 1861,1109.633.

https://hdl.handle.net/20.500.12434/a5c471dc

of the scanner operator's overzealous cropping, I had to pay for new photography, which at the British Museum costs £60 per shot, plus £35 per image for reproduction fees, for a total cost of £190 to make this point. It was not until 2017, with a grant from the British Academy, that I bought photographs of the front and reverse of 633.

Monogrammist A

On another trip to the British Museum's fourth-floor galleries, a box of fifteenth-century Netherlandish engravings disgorged two leaves from the manuscript, mounted on a single matte (fig. 36). One depicted St Cecilia and the other St Catherine as St Lucy. Lehrs attributed both to an engraver he called Monogrammist A after the ornate letter 'A' he inscribed in his plates. He was active in the Low Countries, probably in the final decade of the fifteenth century. His prints often include elaborate fluttering scrolls, sometimes with Middle Dutch text inscribed on them. One of the prints Lehrs attributed to Monogrammist A depicts St Cecilia, with a voluminous amount of fluttering scroll, which has not been filled in (638)[43] (e-fig. 58).

BM 1861,1109.638 — Leaf from the beghards' book of hours (e-fig. 58)

Leaf from the beghards' book of hours, with an engraving depicting St Cecilia. London, British Museum, Department of Prints & Drawings, inv. 1861,1109.638.

https://hdl.handle.net/20.500.12434/885dfcd7

Printed above to the left and right of her halo are the identifying words 'Sancta Cecilia'. The banderol and its inscription seem to fill otherwise empty space with objects, to make every space count. Perhaps the most interesting aspect of the St Cecilia is that she has been elaborately and intricately painted with a brush and transparent washes of red lake, green, yellow, and pale lilac. The person who added the pigmentation did not, however, inscribe the banderol. That is counter-intuitive, as one might think that the scribe who assembled the manuscript would have a hard time resisting the invitation that the banderol furnished. Its emptiness remains a mystery.

The other print pasted to the mount, which depicts St Catherine (639), similarly has a florid monogram *A* near the bottom, but its use of space is highly dissimilar to the other image (e-fig. 59).

---

43 Lehrs wondered about the dating of several prints treated in this study. About the St Cecilia (Lehrs VII, 14, p. 343, 1861.1109.638), he wrote: 'Auf der Rückweite 15 Zeilen Text. 1861. Aus demselben flämischen Gebetbuch wie Nr. 15. Nach den welligen Formen des Spruchbandes scheint es doch fraglich, ob der Stich noch dem XV. Jahrhundert angehört.'

1. Cut, Pasted, and Cut Again

Fig. 36
Two leaves mounted onto a single matte. London, British Museum, Department of Prints & Drawings, inv. 1861,1109.638 and 639.

BM 1861,1109.639 — Leaf from the beghards' book of hours (e-fig. 59)

 Leaf from the beghards' book of hours, with an engraving depicting St Catherine, used as Lucia. London, British Museum, Department of Prints & Drawings, inv. 1861,1109.639.

https://hdl.handle.net/20.500.12434/cc830276

Although Lehrs attributed this to the Monogrammist A, it has precious little to do with the image of St Cecilia, except that they are both standing female saints rendered in engraving. Lacking a printed label announcing the identity of the saint made the Catherine print more flexible. In fact, the beghards exploited the print's indeterminacy, for they did not need another image of St Catherine. Although Monogrammist A had intended the figure to represent this saint, with her sword of martyrdom at her hand and the wheel on which she was tortured at her feet, the beghard already had an image of St Catherine — the one made by the Master of the Flower Borders (e-fig. 14) — and he needed instead the much less popular St Lucy. Using some adept strokes of the pen, the beghard has turned the one into the other. He has disguised St Catherine's wheel of martyrdom, turning it into a basket, and has inscribed the name *Sancta Lucia* to frame the saint's head. Perhaps he was taking a clue from the image of St Cecilia and added the inscription in a similar florid script, so that the two words *Sancta* and *Lucia* flank the figure's head. Whoever wrote 'Sca Lucia' was not the same as the person who foliated the book. Finally, using the rubricator's pen, he has inscribed two vertical strokes of red on the saint's name and two more on her throat, to indicate Lucy's martyrdom by sword. This is further evidence that writing and assembling this manuscript was a group effort.

Earlier I showed how one of the beghards had transformed the image of St Wolfgang into St Servatius. These transformations underscore some of the problems of using prints: they were relatively brittle; they were produced at some distance from the people who used them; the producers could not anticipate the subjects that would be needed. Because the recipients were several steps away from the producers, they did not necessarily have a feedback mechanism to exercise control over the production. With all these constraints, the end-users developed a creative approach: to use a few strokes of the pen to create what they needed. Later I learned that at least one German printer made female saints with interchangeable attributes that could be swapped (see Chapter 2). But they did this in order to reduce the labour of the printer, rather than to supply the recipients with their desired subject. In both cases, makers and users pushed back against the fundamental rigidity of print.

That his full-page prints have been inserted directly into the binding, rather than glued onto blank pages, makes it likely that Monogrammist A was breaking into the market of prints that could be used as single-leaf 'miniatures', which were made and distributed for direct insertion into the bindings of manuscripts. The beghards turned several more large prints into pages in the book. This was a clever move, because it meant that the backs of the prints would not be wasted space. By using this space, they could contain the thickness of the book somewhat. Without using the backs, it would have far exceeded its 541+ original folios.

Attributions

It is the fortune of famous, nameable artists to have a large oeuvre attributed to them. Unknown works, according to nineteenth-century thinking, have to be attributed to someone, preferably someone with a name. Lehrs's project was to sort the known engravings into groups and assign them to particular makers. At the centre of such a practice lies an idea that a single genius was responsible for making each distinctive style. Then, works of the same style that were executed less well could be attributed to the 'workshop of the master'. In other cases Lehr found mechanisms for explaining varying quality within the work of a single genius. For example, he attributed a somewhat mediocre engraving depicting St George to the hand of Israhel van Meckenem, but suggested that another artist had reworked the plate (642)[44] (e-fig. 6). Hollstein, recognising that figure is devoid of emotional life and that the lance enters the dragon's neck and emerges from an impossible angle at the bottom of the throat, does not ascribe this unique impression to Israhel: he believed Israhel could not have made such a bad composition. Lehrs also attributed a much more dynamic full-page print depicting St Michael to Israhel, even though the print is not signed with the engraver's monogram (644) (e-fig. 60).

BM 1861,1109.644 — Leaf from the beghards' book of hours (e-fig. 60)

Leaf from the beghards' book of hours, with an engraving depicting St Michael, sometimes attributed to Israhel van Meckenem. London, British Museum, Department of Prints & Drawings, inv. 1861,1109.644.

https://hdl.handle.net/20.500.12434/6c739957

In fact, Israhel van Meckenem became a magnet for attributions of engravings, no doubt because he is one of the few named engravers. Engravings attributed to him include the full-page St Mark inserted as folio *ccc liii* (e-fig. 12), an attribution I strongly doubt. I considered whether the beghards themselves were producing these prints, but

---

44 References to all of the academic literature mentioned in this section appear on the BM website, alongside the images. Follow the links to find them.

the possibility is remote since they do not appear to have produced images of their patron saints, the obvious choice of subject matter for any religious house.[45] Hollstein again questions this attribution for good reason. Although at least here the engraver has employed a range of textures — cross-hatching, stippling, and parallel curvilinear lines — to achieve various surface effects, nevertheless the style is much duller than that of signed works by Israhel.

One might conclude that prints made after Israhel were made on the Middle or Lower Rhine, where Israhel himself worked, but that need not have been the case. As Peter Schmidt and others have shown, the rapid transmission of prints before 1500, coupled with the relative simplicity of replicating the bold lines of most woodcuts, meant that they were often quite easy to copy.[46] In fact, the entire output of some engravers consisted of copying other masters' works. There is no need to assume that a design originally engraved on the Middle Rhine could not have been copied hundreds of miles away. It is possible that some copies were even made in the Low Countries.

The game of attribution has only limited attraction for me. Two other aspects hold more interest: first, that someone, presumably a beghard, has pasted a lion into a red kiosk on the horizon line in the St Mark print (e-fig. 12) not satisfied with the print as it was, he glued a second attribute to the image, filling up the blank space on the horizon line. Secondly, that another print from the same plate survives, and it is mounted to the same matte (fig. 37). This was the same print but treated in a different way. And it did not come from the batch of prints that had entered the BM in 1861; rather, its accession number indicated that it had arrived in 1868. It was time to revisit the register and to poke around there for more clues about this second St Mark (e-fig. 61).

---

45 Cf. Weekes, 'Convents as Patrons and Producers of Woodcuts in the Low Countries around 1500'.
46 Schmidt, 'The Early Print and the Origins of the Picture Postcard'; Peter Schmidt, 'The Use of Prints in German Convents of the Fifteenth Century: The Example of Nuremberg', *Studies in Iconography* 24 (2003); Schmidt, *Gedruckte Bilder in handgeschriebenen Büchern: zum Gebrauch von Druckgraphik im 15. Jahrhundert*; Peter Schmidt, 'Bildgebrauch und Frömmigkeitspraxis: Bemerkungen zur Benutzung früher Druckgraphik', in *Spiegel der Seligkeit: Privates Bild und Frömmigkeit im Spätmittelalter*, ed. Frank Matthias Kammel and Andreas Curtius (Nürnberg: Verlag des Germanischen Nationalmuseums, 2000).

BM 1868,1114.114 — St Mark (e-fig. 61)

St Mark, engraving. London, British Museum, Department of Prints & Drawings, inv. 1868,1114.114.

https://hdl.handle.net/20.500.12434/d4915dff

The stunning results will be taken up in Chapter 3 but first the Register divulged some more clues about Add. 24332. As the investigative work continued, some dangling threads were tied up.

Fig. 37
Two impressions of an engraving depicting St Mark, mounted onto a single matte. London, British Museum, Department of Prints & Drawings, inv. 1861,1109.643 and 1868,1114.114.

Lehrs thought that 636 (Jairus's Daughter) was made by Israhel, who frequently copied existing prints then signed them with his monogram (e-fig. 55). Israhel, Lehrs contended, copied 636 after a lost original by the Master of the Berlin Passion, and it probably belonged to the same suite as L 24 (on the same mount) and L 29. Israhel may have made this print as early as 1465, although it is also possible that the plate could have been used for decades and inked and printed only later. Avoiding a discussion about hands and copying and lost originals, I note only that Lehrs and other nineteenth-century cataloguers were also collectors. These two activities were connected. Then as now, works of 'art' attributed to a famous artist commanded a much higher price than anonymous works. Cataloguers were motivated to attach prints to names for the benefit of their own collections, and for the benefit and ease of classifying them within museums.

Recapitulation

A spreadsheet helped me to organise all the information about each print and each folio in the manuscript (for a more worked-up version see the Appendix). But the spreadsheet had shortcomings. Adding all the images to the squares made the file too large, and it spread out the information too much. Sjoerd Levelt, an information manager at the Netherlandish Koninklijke Bibliotheek burned File Maker Pro onto my computer and gave me a quick lesson in its use. Girded with a flat text dump of the database that the BM had given me and a copy of *Databases for Dummies*, in no time I had built a database that became a much better tool for reconstructing the manuscript, with all the images necessary. I used the text dump as the raw material for my own database, but added fields that allowed me to match the prints with the manuscripts they had come from. (This eventually allowed me to start logging all the early prints I encountered, and all fifteenth-century Netherlandish manuscripts with prints removed from them — but I don't want to get ahead of my story.)

The spreadsheet revealed that most of the prints are concentrated near the end of the book, with only a few at the beginning. I think what happened was this: Jan van Emmerick wrote the beginning of the book before he came upon the idea of incorporating prints into it. That idea dawned on him in the act of writing. Perhaps he was exposed to the idea by encountering a multi-media experiment when the brotherhood received a manuscript with prints, which some early adopter had sent to the beghards' house for binding. It is possible that the quires at the beginning of the book, which have been lost, contained many prints (for example, an entire Marian cycle), but I doubt it, for there is no trace of them. Perhaps publishing this book will provide the spell to conjure these quires out of hiding.

In no particular order the prints arrived, with each archival box divulging one or two more folios. Progress was slow because each box contained many other distractions, and because I measured and described each print, and made a transcription of the text on each one, noted the Roman numeral foliation, and fitted each into the growing spreadsheet. For example, 634 was mounted on a matte with other prints which had clearly come out of a manuscript, but not the beghards' book of hours (fig. 38). Whoever had assembled and glued down the prints on this matte was demonstrating his or her tacit understanding that the two leaves in the middle had belonged to the same manuscript. And this person was also trying to create a *papier collé* assemblage on the matte that would have balance without symmetry: the two uncoloured full-page prints lie on the central axis in a pleasing design. This modern framer was acting like a beghard, pasting on prints in a pleasing

Fig. 38
London, British Museum, Department of Prints & Drawings, inv. 1861,1109.634 (St Anne, Mary, and Jesus) and three other manuscript leaves, including two from the St Godeleva manuscript.

manner, forging relationships, adding text. But whereas the beghard was adding prayer text to make the images worthy of worship, the framer was adding accession and bibliographic information in a highly abbreviated form, making them worthy of a museum. Both the framer and the beghard worked in a highly coded language, making marks around the glued-on prints for a particular in-crowd.

The boxes in the BM had yielded 63 prints, mounted on 54 folios. This was the largest horde of early prints that could be connected to their original contextual home. However, not all the prints originally pasted into the manuscript were now in the BM. By my calculation (summarised in the Appendix), 146 leaves, or partial leaves, had been removed from the original manuscript. Partially removed leaves included fol. 271 (fig. 39) and fol. 309 (fig. 40). Not all these 146 leaves originally had prints glued to them. For example, folios *xxxiv–lxxiv*, which are now missing, probably represent five quires that had been lost or removed before the manuscript came to London, since no prints from this section have survived in the British Museum. (I can speculate that this section consisted of five quires of 8 leaves each, plus one tipped-in full page representing a printed image, totalling 41 leaves, which would account for folios *xxxiv–lxxiv*. I cannot estimate how many pasted-on prints were included in this section. Because that section contained rosary devotions, it may have contained one or more of the popular prints featuring this devotion.) It is likely, however, that the remainder of the missing leaves — 105 of them — were expressly removed because they had valuable and collectable prints glued to them. The Department of Prints and Drawings now houses 54 of these leaves, containing 63 prints (several of the leaves contain more than one print). This meant that 51 single leaves, as well as a section of the manuscript comprising five quires, were still unaccounted for. Furthermore, I have counted 41 'holes' in the manuscript, or places where discolouration from glue indicates that a print has been removed. If I add it all up, I can estimate that the original manuscript had the following prints:

> five quires of 8 leaves, plus a singleton, where the singleton is probably a print, which are all missing
>
> 51 single leaves, which are still missing, containing approximately 51 prints (conservative estimate)

63 prints, which are now in the British Museum

41 'holes' are in the manuscript, which cannot be accounted for by the prints in the BM

2 (partial) prints, which are still in the manuscript

A conservative estimate for the number of prints in the original manuscript is therefore 158. Only 65 of those — or 41 per cent of them — are now accounted for. I suspect that the other 93 leaves and/or prints were removed after the manuscript was stolen from its monastery in Maastricht and before it was sold to the British Museum in London. In other words, after the French Revolution but before 1861, it is likely that 93 prints and leaves containing prints were removed from this manuscript and sold. Paris was the most likely place for these sales, as the revolutionary movements in Europe were like a maelstrom that funnelled choice bits of material culture to the French capital. They

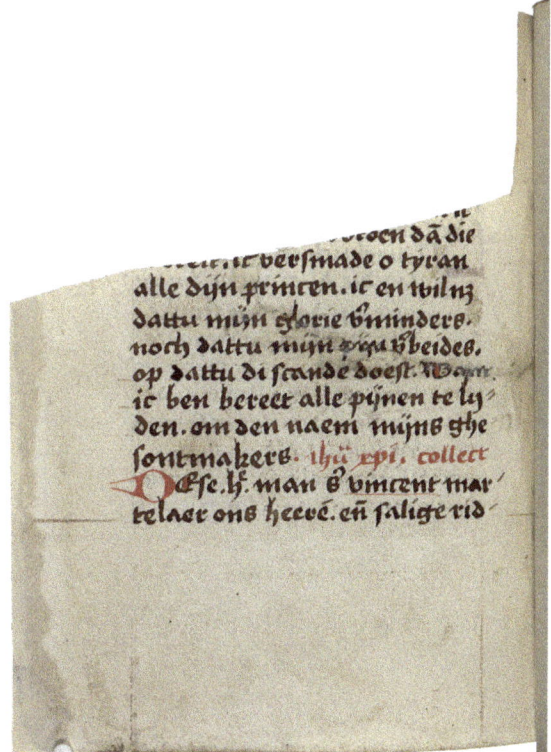

Fig. 39
Folio in the beghards' book of hours, which has been partially cut off. Maastricht, c. 1500. London, British Library, Add. Ms. 24332, fol. 271v (modern foliation).

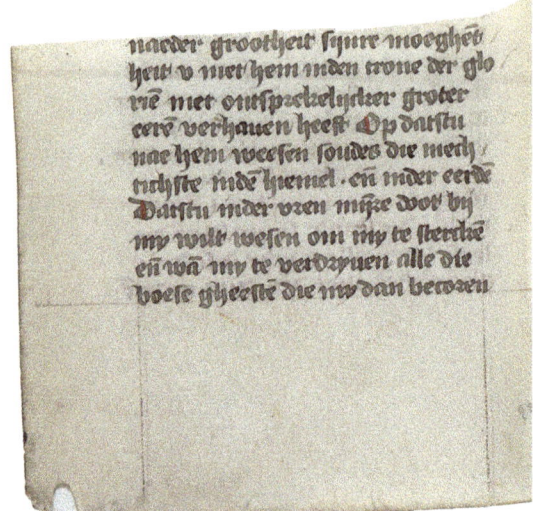

Fig. 40
Folio in the beghards' book of hours, which has been partially cut off. Maastricht, c. 1500. London, British Library, Add. Ms. 24332, fol. 309v (modern foliation).

might even still be there. It took me until summer 2012 to find the time and money to go to Paris to look for them. In the meantime, I thought about the prints in the BM with accession numbers 1861,1109.633-693 and figured out where they originally belonged in the manuscript.

Both Lehrs and Schreiber realised that the prints had come from a manuscript, but neither of them had an idea of how many prints were involved. For one thing, Schreiber was busying himself only with woodcuts and metalcuts, and Lehrs only with engravings, so their purviews were already each diminished by half. Secondly, their recognition of the source of the prints rarely went beyond the small group they were dealing with at the moment, and these groupings were almost always related to attributions. So, for example, Lehrs notes of the engraving representing St Cecilia (the one with the fluttering banderol; 638, see fig. 36), 'from the same Flemish prayerbook as no. 15'.[47] When discussing the small, hand-coloured roundels representing female martyrs (including 673, 674, 662), Lehrs puts the six roundels together in his discussion and notes that the prints 'come from a Lower German breviary acquired from Tross in Paris'.[48] However, he does not connect the 'Lower German breviary' with the 'Flemish prayerbook' that the St

---

47 'Aus demselben flämischen Gebetbuch wie Nr. 15'. Lehrs VII, p. 343.
48 'Aus dem 1861 von Tross in Paris erworbenen niederdeutschen Brevier'. Lehrs III, p. 221.

Cecilia and St Catherine/Lucy came from. About the St Peter (L 58), he notes that the print is a copy after the Master of the Flower Borders: 'Compare with II, no. 59 and II, no. 61, which come from the same Lower Rhenish breviary. It was full of attached prints of the fifteenth and sixteenth century'.[49] Likewise, he mentions that the St Bernard, comes from 'a Lower German manuscript acquired from Tross in Paris in 1861', but does not equate this manuscript with the one he mentioned previously.[50] He has moved from the definite article to the indefinite one, as if Tross sold dozens of manuscripts in Paris in 1861 (which he certainly did). About the St Christopher (L 69), he writes: 'partly painted with green and yellow and pasted to a page from a manuscript acquired in 1861 from Tross in Paris. On the front and back, each 15 lines of Flemish text'.[51] Of the St Agatha (e-fig. 39), Lehrs writes: 'coloured, from the Lower German prayerbook acquired by Tross in Paris in 1861'.[52] Sometimes he calls it the 'Lower German breviary' (Lehrs III, p. 221), other times a 'Lower Rhenish breviary', still others the 'Lower German prayerbook', and sometimes the 'manuscript with Flemish text'. He did not realise that he was referring to the same manuscript each time.

Even the BM workers who glued the prints to mattes realised that some came from the same prayerbook. Several of the mattes (figs 25–27) hold only pages from the beghards' manuscript. Yet no one had the overall vision to put all the pieces together, especially after the pages with drawings were removed, accessioned into the prints department, and then transferred to the manuscripts department.

This confusion was then absorbed into the web-based catalogue housed at the BM, because it depends on the research that preceded it. For this reason, the curator's note for 1861,1109.656, a woodcut depicting St Peter which had been folio *ccc lxxiii*, is somewhat misleading: 'The leaf is taken from a Flemish MS. book of prayers, which Schreiber dates

---

49 'Vergl. auch Nr. 59 II. und 61 II, die aus demselben niederrheinischen Brevier stammen. Es war mit Stichten des XV. und XVI. Jahrhunderts vollgeklebt'. Lehrs III, p. 320.
50 '1861 aus einem von Tross in Paris erworbenen niederdeutschen Manuskript', Lehrs III, p. 73.
51 'Teilweise mit Grün und Gelb bemalt und auf ein Blatt aus einem 1861 von Tross in Paris erworbenen Manuskript geklebt. Auf der Vorder- und Rückseite je 15 Zeilen flämischer Text'. Lehrs III, p. 396.
52 'Koloriert, aus dem 1861 von Troß in Paris erworbenen niederdeutschen Gebetbuch'. Lehrs IX, p. 252.

about 1480–1500. Dodgson thinks it probably had been written after 1500. Although the leaf had been acquired together with ten other leaves from a Flemish book of prayers (registered as 1861,1109.646–51 and 653–55), neither Schreiber nor Dodgson link these, and it is therefore not very likely that their provenance is the same'.[53] That was in 2012. Now that I have been working on this project for several years, the Museum staff has updated some of the records to reflect my work in progress so that the record for 692 reads: 'The engraving was inserted into a breviary, originating from the Lower Rhine region, acquired by Tross in 1861 in Paris'.[54] It is the nature of online databases to reflect only the latest version of understanding and not to provide a history of how that understanding came to be. It is also the nature of such databases to erase individual contributions of catalogues, to anonymize all knowledge. Some of the Museum's records for other items from this set recognised that the prints were attached to a manuscript that they date '1465' in some of the individual records. These records were not linked with each other, and no one had made the connection that all of the leaves had come from a single manuscript.

Book Production

Together with these fragments, the manuscript revealed experimentation with new methods of book production — including the use of prints not just from one source, but made using a variety of production techniques over a wide geographic range — and of organising information within the manuscript. Pre-fifteenth-century manuscript production involved a series of steps: the book's designer laid it out, worked out which images and text columns belonged together, ruled the folios accordingly, then orchestrated the production. This began with the scribe, who wrote in the text, leaving space for the initials and miniatures. The inscribed bifolia were then sent to a

---

53 See the 'Curator's comments' section in the British Museum online record for this print, www.britishmuseum.org/research/search_the_collection_database/search_object_details.aspx?objectId=1348312&partId=1
54 See the 'Curator's comments' section in the British Museum online record for this print, www.britishmuseum.org/research/collection_online/collection_object_details.aspx?objectId=1397519&partId=1&searchText=1861,1109.692&people=115186&page=1

gilder, who applied gold leaf as required, then to an illuminator and a decorator, who contributed imagery and painted border decoration. After 1390, this series of steps began to shift, at least for the middle of the market for books of hours: scribes wrote out the standard texts, making sure that major text divisions fell on a fresh recto folio.[55] Simultaneously, illuminators created loose, full-page miniatures that could be slotted into books of hours. Unlike in the earlier period, the illuminators did not need to have the textual parts of the book at hand in order to create these images. Illuminators made generic imagery that could be added to one of any number of books. A manager, or stationer, brought these components together and bound them. In this way, scribes and illuminators could concentrate on creating repeated units efficiently. They did not have to meet, and their wares could be stockpiled for later assembly. Pasting prints into manuscripts yields a further division between makers of images and makers of text. With printing, images were cheap enough that their makers could experiment with hundreds of new subjects, not just the Infancy and Passion of Christ and indulgenced subjects that became standard fare for the illuminators of loose sheets (such as the Masters of the Pink Canopies).[56] Image-makers did not have to anticipate exactly which images were needed for standard texts. Furthermore, they could live hundreds of miles from their end users. The beghards were collecting hundreds of prints, and pasting them and writing on the pages simultaneously. This would also considerably disrupt the hierarchy of decoration.

Add. Ms. 24332 challenges this conception of book making. Rather than starting with the script and leaving spaces in the text for

---

55 One can point to earlier instances of the physical separation of the work of scribes and illuminators, whose respective work was joined shortly before binding. For example, cycles of full-page images were often inserted at the beginning of Psalters. However, the efficiency of such production methods is stepped up around 1390, driven no doubt by demand for books of hours.

56 A full account of the Masters of the Pink Canopies and their workshop methods has yet to be written. Until then, see Maurits Smeyers, *Vlaamse Miniaturen voor van Eyck, ca. 1380-ca. 1420*. Catalogus: Cultureel Centrum Romaanse Poort, Leuven, 7 September-7 November 1993. Corpus of Illuminated Manuscripts = Corpus van Verluchte Handschriften, 6 (Leuven: Peeters, 1993), pp. 4–12; and Sandra Hindman, *The Robert Lehman Collection. IV: Illuminations* (New York and Princeton, NJ: Metropolitan Museum of Art in association with Princeton University Press, 1997), pp. 53–60.

miniatures, the book's maker must have pasted prints from a stack of mismatched engravings and woodcuts, and incorporated them into the book as he progressed with the writing. These prints were glued to the page first, and then the text written around them or on the backs of them. In other words, image was primary and text secondary as an organising principle of book construction. My spreadsheet suggests that the beginning of the book did not have many prints, and that in fact, the beghards began the tandem process of writing and gluing once they had started making the book. Even after the book was finished, the beghards continued to acquire prints and add them to the book. They struggled to place them in logical positions, where they would enhance the themes of the texts. Part of their *modus operandi* was to add more images to the beginning of the book, since that part had been neglected, as they had not come up with the idea of pasting in stacks of prints until the copying was already under way. In other words, this manuscript comprises the beghards' first attempt at combining manuscript with print. I was witnessing the beginnings of their thinking about combining the two technologies, and also witnessing their early response to printed images: once they started, they kept going, and kept stuffing images into the book, right up to the moment they bound it.

A Sheaf of Drawings

On 18 January 2008 I revisited the handwritten register Sheila had shown me on the first day in the BM's Study Room. It often happens that I need to visit primary and archival documents multiple times, because the first time I am so innocent of their contents that I do not fully understand what they are offering. Only after a period of considerable study and reflection can I perceive their messages. On my second visit, this register unlocked more secrets about the manuscript and its original images. Prints that had been taken from Add. 24332 were registered under numbers 632-693 for the date 9 November 1861. Now the ledger offered a piece of information I had missed the first time: at the end of the list there was also a group of drawings that the BM had purchased from Tross on the same date. These were a continuation of the prints that Tross had sold to the BM on that day.

Furthermore, a handwritten note stated: '694–706 transferred to Dept. of mss. 21 Dec 1926. CD'. Then in different ink, someone had added: '(Add. MS. 41338.)'. CD, as I would learn, was Campbell Dodgson (1867–1948), the great historian of early prints.[57] He was indicating that these items — all classified together as drawings — were transferred to the manuscripts department in 1926 where they became Add. Ms. 41338. Leaving the BM, I dashed to the British Library and called up Add. Ms. 41338.

While waiting for the manuscript to arrive, I read the notice for Ms. 41338 in the Catalogue of Additions. It describes 'Thirteen leaves from a book of hours, possibly from St Trond in Belgium, in Middle Dutch'.[58] B. Schofield, who catalogued this, was the Keeper of Manuscripts in the late 1950s, three decades after these folios had entered the Department of Manuscripts in 1926. No doubt he suggested St Trond as a place of origin for the thirteen leaves because of the presence — as I soon discovered — of St Trudo in the sheaf.

Schofield listed the contents as follows:

1. Computus tables, including

    'Homo signorum' diagram showing the influences of the Signs of the Zodiac, f. 1

    Table of the moon's place in the Signs, arranged on the 19-year cycle, f. 1b

    Wheel of Fortune, combined with the names of the months, f. 2

    Table, beginning at 1500, for finding the dominical letter according to the 19-year cycle, f. 2b

2. 'Die cruys ghetijden, Hours of the cross', first leaf only. A somewhat similar version is found in Add. 15267, fol. 78. f. 3

3. 'Hier beghint die metten van den heilighen gheest', first leaf only, f. 4

---

57 See Frances Carey, *Campbell Dodgson: Scholar and Collector, 1867–1948* (London: British Museum in association with the Parnassus Foundation, 1998).
58 *Catalogue of Additions*, vol. XXII, pp. 16–17.

4. Psalm vi. 2–11, beginning 'Heer in dijnre verbolghenheit en straeffe mij niet', the first of the seven Pen Ps, first leaf only, f. 6

5. 'Hier beghint die vigilie voer alle ghelovighe dooden', Vigils for the dead, first leaf only, f. 7.

6. Six leaves, not consecutive, containing miscellaneous prayers and devotions, which includes prayers to SS. Gertrude, Abbess of Nivelles (f. 8b); Trudo (Trond), Eucherius, B of Orleans, and Libertus, all patrons of St Tond (f. 12); memorials of SS. Gregory (f. 8), Francis of Assisi (f. 9), Clare (f.9b) Advent (f.13b).

When the thin manuscript arrived an hour later, I saw that Add. 41338 did indeed comprise thirteen leaves cut from the beghards' manuscript, mostly incipits of texts. The size of the pages, the script, and the foliation matched that of Add. 24332. It contained drawings in several styles, some on parchment, most on paper. Each sheet was glued to a stub and arranged in order of its original folio numbers (in Roman numerals), except for the first four, which were on parchment and had no original foliation. A note at the back of the manuscript indicated that it had been foliated in March 1934 (in Arabic numerals), eight years after the leaves entered the library and presumably were bound. It was clear that the nineteenth-century cataloguer at the British Museum had grouped the thirteen leaves together in the 1861 register because these leaves had drawings rather than prints. This was a continuation of the cataloguer's larger project, to organise the new acquisitions by medium, grouping the metalcuts, the woodcuts, the engravings, and finally the drawings.

Realising in 1926 that the thirteen leaves belonged together, Campbell Dodgson had decided that they fitted better in the manuscripts department than in the prints department, so he gathered them up, had them bound under a different signature, and sent them to the other department. Neither Dodgson in 1926 nor B. Schofield in the manuscripts department had noticed that the thirteen leaves had been cut from a manuscript in the British Museum's own collection. If they had, they might have integrated the leaves into Add. 24332 rather than binding them separately with no reference or concordance connecting the two.

This was a piece of detective work that would pay dividends. Within this sheaf, now bound as Add. 41338, the images contained much valuable information. These sheets firmly emphasise St Francis and St Clare, the premier male and female Franciscans, which also confirmed the manuscript's Franciscan origins. Two of the parchment folios present dated computational tables, and one of the drawings bears the name of a draughtsman. Connecting these pieces 147 years after they had been separated allowed me to have more information about the whole than each component allowed in isolation: clues in Add. 24332 allowed me to localise the thirteen fragments with drawings better than Schofield had (who had thought they were from St Trudo); and clues in Add. 41338 allowed me to date Add. 24332, as well as the items that had been removed from it, with greater accuracy. Only by viewing them together did the parts divulge enough information to piece together who made the manuscript, where, and when, and the unity provided a fuller picture of how early prints functioned than had been previously possible.

Tables and diagrams fill the first two folios in Add. 41338. These are on parchment rather than on paper. (It was a common practice in Eastern Netherlandish manuscripts to combine folios on paper with those on parchment. Often the parchment folios form the outer leaves of a quire, or occupy the beginning of the manuscript, because parchment can withstand more wear.) The first diagram shows 'Zodiac man', that is, a human figure with the signs of the zodiac inscribed on his body, indicating which signs have jurisdiction over which body part (fig. 41).[59] On the verso of the same leaf is a diagram indicating how the figure is to be used to determine good (*goed*) and evil (*quaet*) days for performing phlebotomy (bloodletting) to benefit the various body parts with their astrological jurisdictions (fig. 42). These diagrams suggest that the beghards were engaging in phlebotomy, which is not surprising, as it was the most widespread medical practice in the Middle Ages.

Diagrams filled the recto and verso of the next sheet (fig. 43 and 44). Three of these resemble volvelles, series of concentric circles with pointers that sweep around like a clock arm. However, these low-tech volvelles, which are simply inscribed on the page, have no moving parts,

---

59   For discussions of 'Zodiac man', see Harry Bober, 'The Zodiacal Miniature of the *Très Riches Heures* of the Duke of Berry-Its Sources and Meaning', *Journal of the Warburg and Courtauld Institutes* 11 (1948), pp. 1–34; Linda E. Voigts and Michael R. McVaugh, 'A Latin Technical Phlebotomy and Its Middle English Translation', *Transactions of the American Philosophical Society* 74:2 (1984), pp. 1–69.

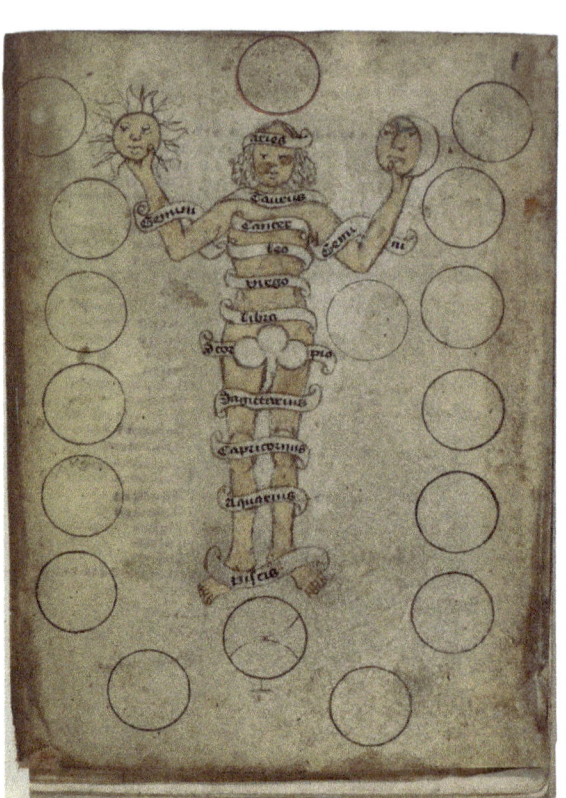

Fig. 41
Zodiac man, from the beghards' manuscript. London, British Library, Add. Ms. 41338, fol. 1r.

Fig. 42
Leaf formerly belonging to the beghards' manuscript. London, British Library, Add. Ms. 41338, fol. 1v.

and their pointers consist merely of rubricated lines. The verso presents a diagram for finding the dominical letter according to the nineteen-year cycle beginning with 1500, with a separate dial for leap years. The pointer — constructed of red lines not dissimilar from those framing prints elsewhere in the manuscript — indicates that the year 1500 was in the nineteenth year, and that it was a leap year. This type of diagram is useful for contextualising the manuscript, as it often provides the date in which the manuscript was made, because the scribe and user would have no need to calculate dates in the past. The pointer indicates the starting date, 1500, which is consistent with the date I had estimated for Add. 24332, based on the date *1501* inscribed in the calendar. The new, more precise year of production would become 1500.

Fig. 43
Unfoliated front matter, formerly belonging to the beghards' manuscript. London, British Library, Add. Ms. 41338, fol. 2r.

Fig. 44
Leaf from the beghards' manuscript. London, British Library, Add. Ms. 41338, fol. 2v.

A detail in the innermost circle reveals one way in which the scribe was straddling two worlds. The innermost circle lists the years, 1–19, in the metonic cycle. He has written the numbers i-xvii in Roman numerals, but has then switched to Arabic for the final two, 18 and 19, having realised that these were neater and more space efficient. Combining older systems with newer ones characterises the beghards of 1500.

The two diagrams that occupy the recto are more unusual. One of these lists various categories of saints, beginning with the four church fathers (Gregory, Jerome, Augustine, and Ambrose), followed by the four evangelists, the four marshals, and finally the saints whom one petitions in times of illness (John the Baptist, Cornelius, Hubert, Ghielis). As with the diagram on the verso, this one has the nineteen years of the Metonic cycle at its inner circle, again with a pointer labelled '1500' (m°v^c). This diagram, then, singles out individual saints in these categories for each year, beginning in 1500.

At the bottom of the recto is another stationary volvelle that deals with cyclical time. From the centre of the diagram emanate twelve spokes with the months inscribed on them. In the interstices are fates, such as life, death, rich, poor, honour, scandal. A red pointer at the centre can (virtually) sweep this circle, in an annual wheel of fortune. Stains on this folio match those on Add. 24332, fol. 17, which contains a table for calculating the date of Easter.

The front matter in the manuscript was not foliated in the fifteenth century. These diagrams probably were bound before fol. 19, but an offset on 19r (fig. 45) indicates that there had formerly been yet another circular diagram, but that diagram is not among the extant leaves. This missing diagram had a red round frame and yellow paint, purple penwork, and black printed lines that transferred to the facing page.

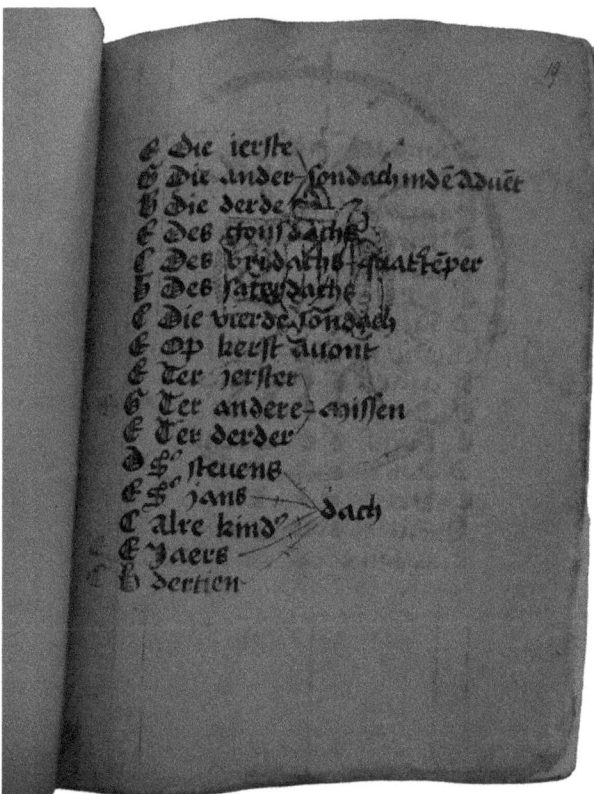

Fig. 45
Folio in the beghards' book of hours, showing the offset of a now-missing image. Maastricht, c. 1500. London, British Library, Add. Ms. 24332, fol. 19r (modern foliation).

Locating the original manuscript home for the prints that are now in the British Museum forces one to reconsider the dating of those prints; the manuscript, dated 1500, provides a *terminus ante quem* for all the prints (with the possible exception of the four or five that were added after the original foliation was carried out and are blank on the back). Because the BM's electronic catalogue is always in flux, I do not know what version you will find there.

So, dear Reader, please erase the statement that is not true:

Prints that had, until 2008, been dated to the sixteenth century and need to be re-dated are –
Or, prints that the British Museum has re-dated in the light of this evidence are –

635 — Virgin, Child, and St Anne, by the Master 'OV' (e-fig. 25).

645 — IHS monogram, made by an anonymous Netherlandish master (e-fig. 2).

657 — a fragment of an engraving depicting the Virgin and Child (e-fig. 33).

658 — Christ as Man of Sorrows, made by an anonymous Netherlandish master (e-fig. 40).

661 — a closely trimmed engraving representing St Bartholomew, standing (e-fig. 62)

665 — a male figure, silhouetted from a larger sheet, here representing St Elzéar of Sabran, a Franciscan tertiary (d. 1323) (e-fig. 19)

666 — St Francis, anonymous Netherlandish engraving (e-fig. 26)

667 — St Francis receiving the stigmata, anonymous Netherlandish engraving (e-fig. 27)

668 — St James the Greater, engraving (e-fig. 31)

669 — St John the Evangelist, engraving (e-fig. 31)

670 — Two-tiered engraving, with St John on Patmos below, and the Beast of the Apocalypse above. Netherlandish engraving (e-fig. 32).

672 — St Lawrence; 682 the same image of St Lawrence, used as St Vincent (e-fig. 36); 671 the same image of St Lawrence, used as St Stephen (e-fig. 37). All impressed from the same plate, but the impressions were trimmed differently.

676 — St Quentin, Netherlandish engraving (e-fig. 27)

677 — St Paul, engraving (e-fig. 31)

678 — St Andrew (?), engraving (e-fig. 31)

683 — Angel, Netherlandish engraving (e-fig. 63)

685 — a small rectangular engraving representing a winged ox for St Luke (e-fig. 34)

686 and 687 — Church and a kneeling monk, 2 trimmed Netherlandish engravings (e-fig. 20)

BM 1861,1109.661 — Leaf from the beghards' book of hours (e-fig. 62)

Leaf from the beghards' book of hours, with an engraving representing St Bartholomew. London, British Museum, Department of Prints & Drawings, inv. 1861,1109.661.

https://hdl.handle.net/20.500.12434/ed3dc20b

BM 1861,1109.683 — Manuscript leaf with a prayer to one's (e-fig. 63)

Manuscript leaf with a prayer to one's personal angel and an engraving representing an angel. London, British Museum, Department of Prints & Drawings, inv. 1861,1109.683.

https://hdl.handle.net/20.500.12434/219b6850

Several of the other folios gathered into Add. 41338 are the incipit folios for major texts. One is the incipit of the Hours of the Cross (formerly folio *lxxv*, fol. 3r, fig. 46). A draughtsman, possibly the scribe, has added a quick drawing to the initial, consisting of a crucifixion sticking out of the *H* (for *Heer*, Lord), so that the crucified figure seems to stand on the letter. A drawing of similar ilk appears at the incipit of the Hours of the Holy Spirit (formerly folio *xci*, fol. 4r, fig. 47). It is possible that the small drawing in the initial, depicting Christ as Salvator Mundi, may have been copied from a print. That may also be the case with a drawing — again depicting Christ with an orb — that marks the incipit of the Seven Penitential Psalms (fig. 48). And an initial with colour wash depicting a skeleton prefaces the Vigil of the Dead (formerly 1861,1109.703, and formerly folio *c lxxxiiij*, fig. 49). With an economy of means, the scribe has turned the letter into a sarcophagus that holds a decomposing body crawling with worms in its mouth, but painted in skin tones. One has the sense that the scribe made these drawings, that they are extensions of the simple embellishment of the initials. Perhaps the scribe would have filled these initials with prints if they had been available.

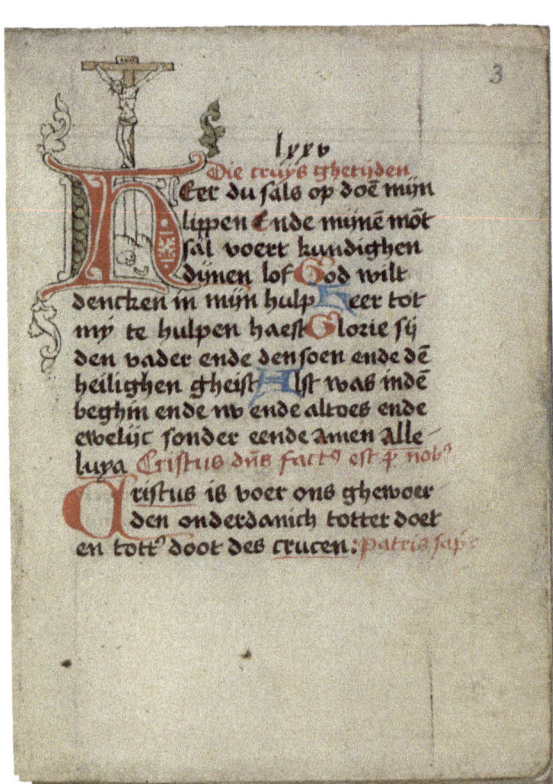

Fig. 46
Incipit of the Hours of the Cross, formerly belonging to the beghards' manuscript. London, British Library, Add. Ms. 41338, fol. 3r.

Fig. 47
Incipit of the Hours of the Holy Spirit, formerly fol. xci in the beghards' manuscript. London, British Library, Add. Ms. 41338, fol. 4r.

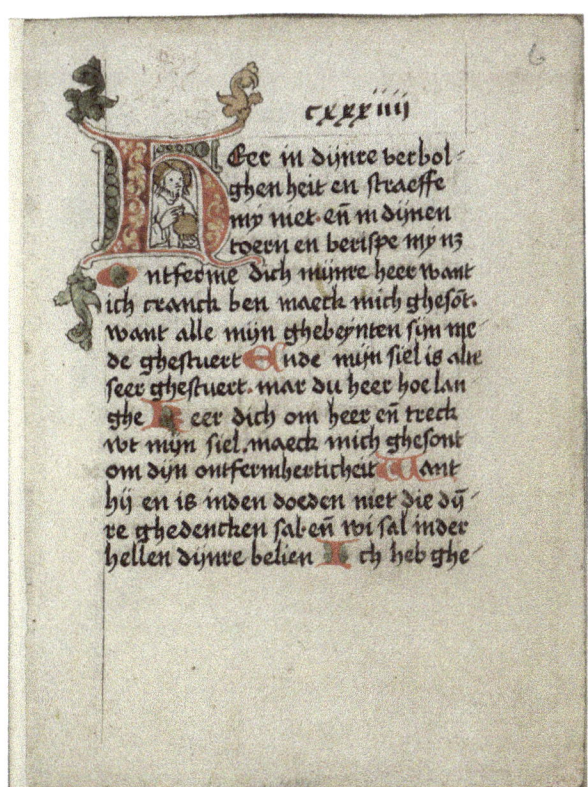

Fig. 48
Incipit of the Seven Penitential Psalms, formerly fol. cxxxiiij in the beghards' manuscript. London, British Library, Add. Ms. 41338, fol. 6r.

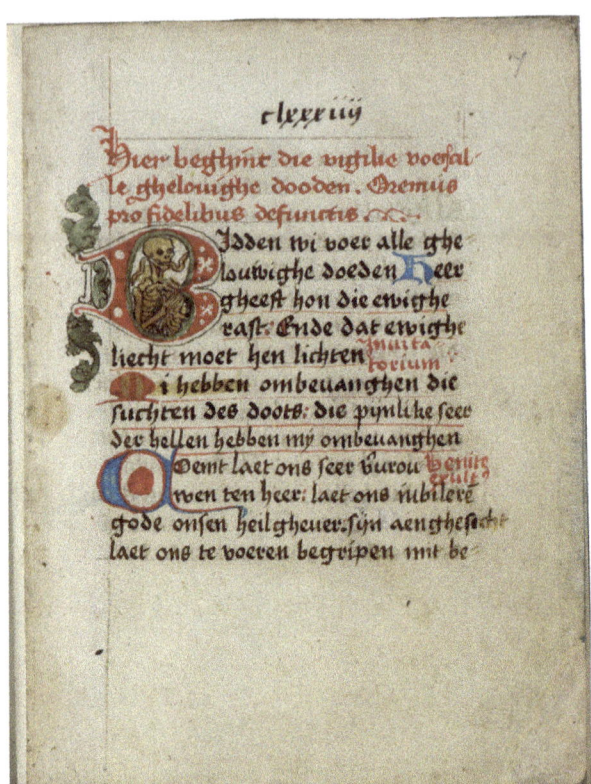

Fig. 49
Skeleton incipit prefacing the Vigil of the Dead, formerly fol. c lxxxiiij in the beghards' manuscript. London, British Library, Add. Ms. 41338, fol. 7r.

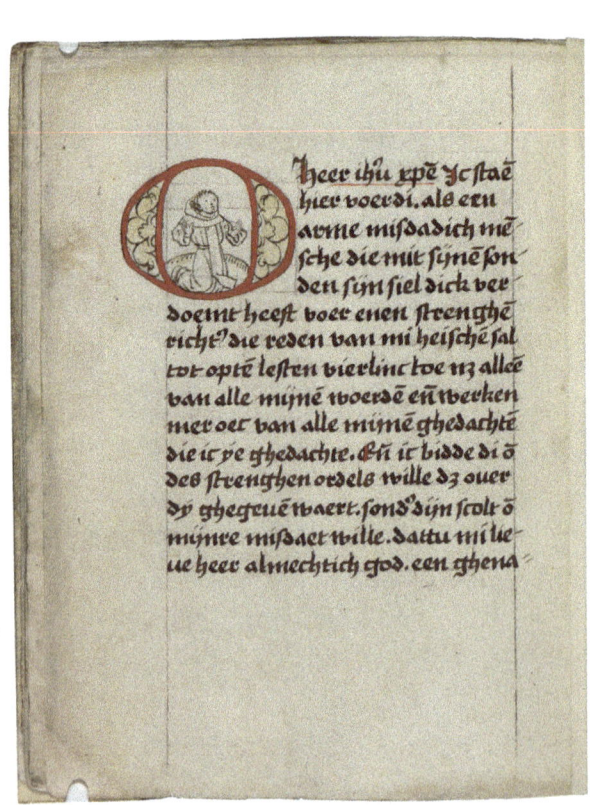

Fig. 50
London, British Library, Add. Ms. 41338, fol. 11v.

Someone, perhaps the scribe, has drawn a robed man kneeling in awe (one of several such drawings, in fact, among this group of folios) to fill an initial for a prayer that begins, 'O, Lord, I stand here before you as a poor sinner' (fig. 50). The draughtsman has responded to the prayer by depicting a male figure kneeling before God or, more accurately, before the prayer text that is a conduit to God. According to the P&D register for 1861,1109.700, this print depicts an 'O with a kneeling monk in ecstasy'.

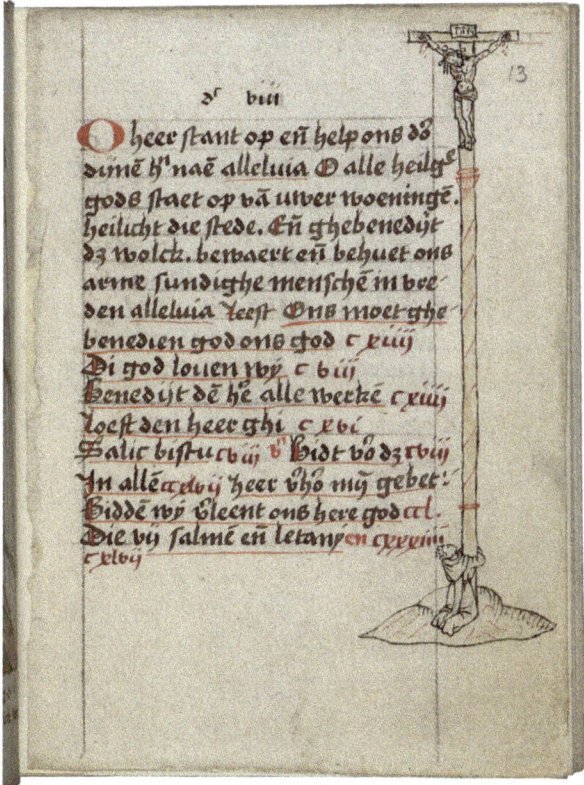

Fig. 51
Folio from the beghards' book of hours, with a marginal pen drawing depicting a kneeling cleric at the foot of the Cross. London, British Library, Add. Ms. 41338, fol. 13r.

A text that makes an impassioned plea for intervention is the most ebullient embellishment from this hand (fol. 13r, formerly folio d^c viii; fig. 51).[60] A kneeling man clutches the bottom of Cross, while Christ bleeds

---

60 In the sometimes quirky way in which the scribe writes Roman numerals, d with a superscript c denotes 500, not 600.

above him. The height of the cross extends beyond the height of the text block, while the shaft of the cross and the text physically connect the man to his object of devotion. These drawings, made in brown ink and with the rubricator's red with the yellow watercolour embellishment that marks some of the initials, most probably stem from the hand of the scribe, who had these materials at hand; he was apparently depicting himself in prayer in response to the text on the page. Close observation reveals that the shaft of the cross warbles and sputters to its height: the scribe did not make it with a ruler but freehand. It was a spontaneous interaction with the text, inscribed before a ruler could be found.

The text on folio *d^c viii* demonstrates another way in which the beghards used labour-saving techniques in book production: the bottom of the page contains a series of prayers listed only by their incipits along with the folio numbers where the reader could find the full edition. To complete the sequence of prayers mandated, the reader was to turn to folio *c xiiij* and read from it, then read from several other folios, before finishing with the Seven Penitential Psalms and Litany on folios *c xxxiiii* and *c xlvij*, respectively. Filling the outer margin, the image of the Franciscan embracing the cross would have helped the reader find this page again after turning to other parts of the book.

An unusual drawing depicting St Gertrude also appears to be constructed from the scribe's brown ink and yellow watercolour (fig. 52).[61] Gertrude founded the abbey at Nijvel/Nivelles (now in Belgium), where her relics are also kept; she was venerated all over the Southern Netherlands and Limburg. According to popular lore, she was efficacious against vermin, which is why she is represented with mice crawling over her. This drawing has been made directly onto the ruled paper, for the drawn lines go over the ruling. It may have been that the same scribe who made the drawing also inscribed the text, since the same brown ink has been used for both. He then wrote around the drawing, as if it were one of the silhouetted prints. However, the confidence of the lines in this drawing differs significantly from the less crafted strokes in the other drawings made directly on the page, most notably, the images of the praying and kneeling men in robes. Such confident work may have resulted from copying the figure from a print, possibly even by holding it up to the light and tracing it. Is it

---

61   The drawing measures 62 mm high, and 23 mm wide at the elbows.

possible that the scribe had only one copy of the print but wanted to duplicate the image manually so that it could appear in more than one book? Did the idea of printing itself open a universe of possible operations involving duplication? Or had the graphic form of the print itself, with its dark lines imprinted onto semi-translucent paper, inspired a form of image transfer and enabled amateurs to carry out manual reproduction?

Fig. 52
Folio from the beghards' book of hours, with a pen drawing depicting St Gertrude with mice. London, British Library, Add. Ms. 41338, fol. 8v = fol. ccc xiii.

This suggestion that some drawings were copied from prints is more intriguing in light of the image of the Virgin of the Sun (fol. 5r, fig. 53). This image departs sharply from the other drawings in the manuscript, and it was copied from a print that survives, an engraving by Master IAM of Zwolle; this engraver was active in the second half of the fifteenth century (e-fig. 64).

BM 1845,0809.95 — Virgin *in sole* (e-fig. 64)

 Master IAM of Zwolle, Virgin *in sole*, engraving. London, British Museum, Department of Prints & Drawings, inv. 1845,0809.95

https://hdl.handle.net/20.500.12434/b558356e

One of the differences between the printed prototype and the subsequent drawing is scale: the drawing is considerably smaller. Viewing the two images side-by-side reveals that the draughtsman who copied the image faithfully reproduced some parts but enhanced others. Instead of the simple rays of light that the engraver imposed with his burin perpendicular to the tangent of the Virgin's curving body, the draughtsman has added rays of light that look at if they were cut out of sheet metal and connected by a garland of roses. The draughtsman also added two angels who crown the Virgin. He has also made the dragon larger and fiercer, with even greater claws. Most significantly, he has added an image of a praying cleric, who may be meant to represent himself. He has inscribed the words 'O mater dei memento mei' rising from this monkish man, which further suggests that the writer/draughtsman associated himself with the figure. He has also made a frame of text around the image: above it reads: 'Pulchra es amica mea et macula non est in te' (Song of Solomon, IV:7); below: 'Ipsa conteret caput tuum' (Genesis III:15); left: 'Necdum errant abissi et ego iam concept eram: proverbiorum ultimo' (Proverbs VIII:24); right: 'ab originali peccato virginem Mariam…'. That he has added text to the image, and that he chose make a proxy of the print by hand, suggest that he was trained as a scribe.

Master IAM of Zwolle's engraving is significantly larger than the drawing, which causes a problem for my theory about transferring the design. Whereas the engraving measures 233 x 144 millimetres (the size of a trimmed copy in the British Museum), the manuscript folio only measures 143 x 101.6. Therefore, the draughtsman could not have traced the backlit engraving onto the paper directly. However, the Virgin's outline and her contours correspond directly when the two figures are superimposed. It is possible that the draughtsman scaled down the image himself, since he was drawing it freehand. A second possibility is that Master IAM of Zwolle made the engraving in two sizes, and

Fig. 53
Folio from the beghards' book of hours, with a pen drawing depicting the Virgin of the Sun, with a kneeling portrait of a male cleric and a frame filled with inscribed prayers. London, British Library, Add. Ms. 41338, fol. 5r.

the smaller size (which our draughtsman would have used) no longer survives. A third possibility is that another printmaker produced the image in a smaller size, but no copies survive. A fourth possibility is that our draughtsman found some other way of mechanically reproducing the image and at the same time shrinking it. Perhaps he used an apparatus such as the pantograph. Although this device is not recorded before the seventeenth century, perhaps a proto-model existed around 1500, at a time when there were new experiments in the mechanical reproduction of images. Whether relying on the pantograph or not, this image therefore stands at the boundary between mechanical and purely manual reproduction, a hybrid means of production within a hybrid manuscript.

Studying the drawing reveals its piecemeal production. Its artist has taken the basic form of the Virgin and Child from the engraving. He has invented some details, such as the scalloped edges of the Virgin's garment, which were not in the print. He has added the thick flames and rose garland, and the angels who crown Mary. Their faces are not as sensitive or as expressive as that of Mary herself but are similar in style to the face of the kneeling man, who has also been added freehand in the available space. Although the position of this figure is similar to that inscribed at the bottom of a leaf also bound in Add. 41338 with a prayer to St Clare (fol. 9v; fig. 77), this kneeling figure has been created with more interior modelling and less reliance on heavy outline. One might conclude that the drawing of the Virgin of the Sun was made by a different person from the beghard who depicted himself at the bottoms of several pages. However, the Virgin of the Sun artist might still have been a brother who was trained as a scribe.

Perhaps the Virgin of the Sun image was made outside the beghard's monastery and was never meant to form a page in a book of hours. Constituting a flexible autonomous image, the sheet is not dependent on a manuscript to give it meaning.[62] In fact, the inscriptions in the frame of the image give it a personal biblical context that is separate from that of a book of hours. This image may have been designed to hang on a wall or to sit in a shrine. There is no indication that it was designed for this or any other manuscript. The motif is similar to that found on certain parchment paintings, such as one that has been preserved in a prayerbook probably made nearby in Tongeren (fig. 54). Multiple layers of iconography would have made it appropriate for different kinds of devotion: simultaneously, it presents the Virgin of the Sun, the rosary, the coronation, and devotion to the words 'Ihesus' and 'Maria'. Works that were made as gifts, I hypothesised in *Postcards on Parchment*, often have multivalent imagery, so that they would be useful for the recipient for a variety of devotions and purposes, not a single fixed one. I proposed that the image may have constituted a gift, from one brother outside the beghards' monastery to someone within it. To preserve the leaf, Jan van Emmerick or one of his colleagues collected and bound it into the manuscript.

I tried to figure out where this drawing of the Virgin would have fitted in the manuscript. At first I thought that the leaf had the number

---

62   Rudy, *Postcards on Parchment*, pp. 103–04.

Fig. 54 Virgin of the Sun, parchment painting, inserted to face a prayer to the Body Parts of the Virgin. The Hague, Koninklijke Bibliotheek, Ms. 75 G 2, fol. 196v-197r.

xcviij at the top. However, folio *xcviij* was already accounted for near the beginning of the Hours of the Virgin. Eventually I realised that the final character in the Roman number is the sign meaning *bis*, which is the same sign I had encountered in the other hard-to-place print, 637 (see fig. 31). Now it made sense: the drawing with the Virgin of the Sun was folio *xcvii bis*, which followed the incipit of the Hours of the Virgin. Only after the scribe had foliated the entire manuscript did he insert this leaf near the beginning of the premier Marian text. This leaf, in other words, was added as an afterthought, inserted between folios *xcvii* and *xcviii*. That would also explain why this drawing is blank on the back, unlike the other full-page images in the manuscript: the book's maker had added these folios too late, after the manuscript had already been copied and foliated. This would also support my earlier hypothesis: Jan van Emmerick only began adding images to this book when he was part-way through copying. After he had finished, he added this image to the Hours of the Virgin, which he had not illustrated at first.

Two additional leaves may have been received as gifts before landing in the manuscript. These depict St Lambert (fig. 55) and St Trudo (fig. 56; formerly folio *cccc lxvi*, BM 697).[63] It seems that the same person made them, as they appear in a closely similar style and palette, both figures fully frontal and under a baldachin, as if they were filling a private chapel and receiving visitors. They are represented, in other words, as cult figures. At the bottom of the St Lambert image is an inscription: 'Sanctus Lambertus', written in a strange spiky script. Is this supposed to imitate engraved script? Or is it just the most ornate display script that the draughtsman could muster? Likewise, the image of St Trudo has an inscription: 'Sanctus Trudo Confessor: biddet voer den maelre broder Henrich van Venray' ('Pray for the painter, brother Henrich van Venray'). That Henrich van Venray calls himself 'brother' suggests that he is a Franciscan; that he calls himself *maelre* suggests that he is a painter, or was a painter, or considered himself a painter. What is significant here is that the figure of St Trudo holds a church. Trudo (Truiden in Dutch, Trond in French) is both a saint's name and a place name; the place was the site of the earliest Franciscan monastery in the Netherlands, established in 1226–1231. St Truiden was the headquarters, as it were, for Netherlandish Franciscans. One scenario that tallies with this evidence is: a young man named Henrich who came from the town of Venray joined the Franciscans, moved to St Truiden, and became the monastery's painter. He painted, among other images, two on paper, including one depicting his monastery's founder, St Trudo, to which he signed his name. He gathered up two of these paintings and sent them to his co-religionist brothers in nearby Maastricht, who honoured the gift by incorporating the images into the book of hours they were writing. If Henrich van Venray offered the images as a gift, then he demanded a counter-gift in the form of prayer: that the recipient of the image should pray for him and his patron saint, who literally holds the church to which the painter belongs.

The other sides of both leaves have also been ruled and inscribed (fig. 57 and 58), just as the large prints are ruled and inscribed. This demonstrates that the scribe/planner had the two coloured drawings and most of the other images available from the beginning and set out to make a book with them. A prayer to St Matthew is inscribed on the verso

---

63 I discuss these images in ibid., pp. 87–91.

Fig. 55
Folio from the beghards' book of hours, with a coloured drawing depicting St Lambert. The frame measures 123 x 68 mm. London, British Library, Add. Ms. 41338, fol. 10r, formerly folio cccc xxiii, BM 696.

Fig. 56
Folio from the beghards' book of hours, with a coloured drawing depicting St Trudo. The frame measures 114 x 62 mm. London, British Library, Add. Ms. 41338, fol. 12v.

of the St Lambert image. The scribe has pasted a small print depicting an angel, the evangelist's symbol. With a few flicks of the rubricator's red pen, he has made a small house for the printed figure. Using just the tools of the scribe, plus the print, the knife, and the gluepot, the beghard has become copyist, illuminator, and decorator.

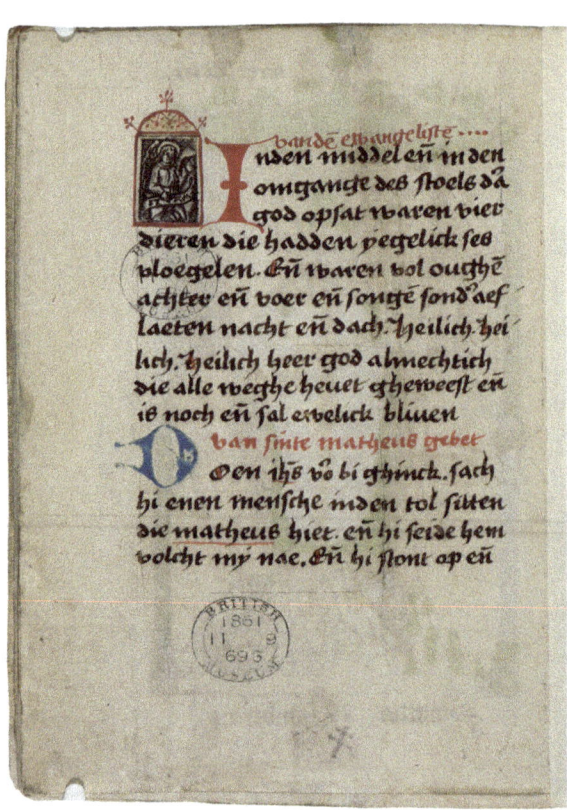

Fig. 57
Folio from the beghards' book of hours, with an engraving depicting St Matthew. London, British Library, Add. Ms. 41338, fol. 10v.

Revolutionary Upheavals and the Dispersal of the Prints

Just as a wall with a small amount of graffiti attracts more graffiti, a manuscript with one thing pasted to it often attracts many more things, and a book with items cut out of it also attracts further mutilations. For Add. 24332, the first wave of those mutilations probably occurred in France and the lands it occupied, as a result of the Revolution. A

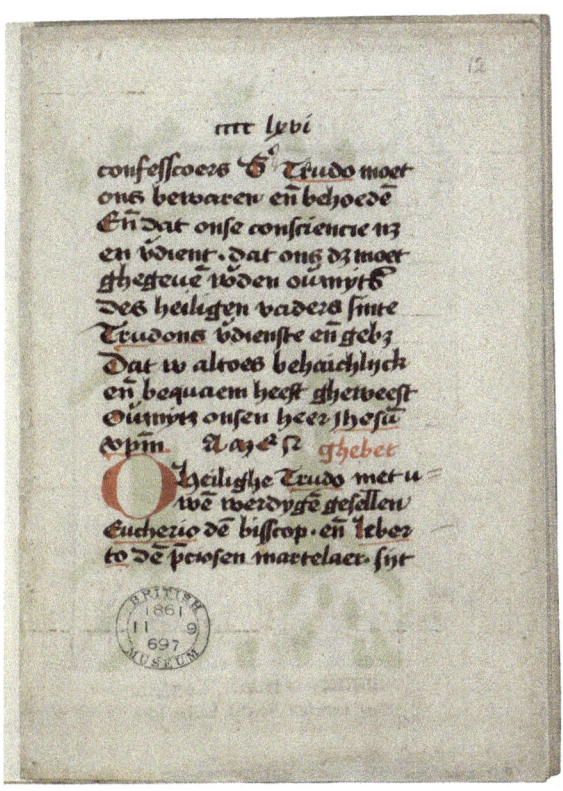

Fig. 58
Folio from the beghards' book of hours. London, British Library, Add. Ms. 41338, fol. 12r.

law of 1 September 1796 (or *15 fructidor an IV* according to the French Revolutionary calendar) forced all members of religious houses to quit their monasteries to abide by the 'stables et conformes à la justice et à l'humanité'. Under this rule, all religious orders, congregations, abbeys, priories, houses of canons and canonesses regular had to leave their institutions, with one small exception: women in religious institutions dedicated to teaching and caring for the sick, that is, teachers and nurses, were allowed to stay on. Men who had these functions, however, had to leave. Effectively this meant that, in Maastricht at least, the Sepulcrienen (the sisters of the Holy Sepulchre, who ran girls' schools) and the Penitenten (members of the penitent order, who worked in hospitals) stayed on, and all other religious were forced to find a new way of life, independent from the monastery. Just over a year later, on 26 November 1797 (*5 frimaire an VI*), a new law was issued, forcing even teachers and nurses to leave their compounds.⁶⁴ These laws caused tremendous upheaval in Maastricht, as all the religious houses were forced to close. Their property was confiscated and land sold. After the beghards had left their home in September 1796, their building on the Witmakersstraat was auctioned in 1798 for 21,150 francs.⁶⁵ It marked the end of an era.

At this point, I had pieced together Add. 24332, Add. 41338, and the objects that had entered the BM Prints Department on 9 November 1861 as having all come from the same manuscript. I had localised the manuscript to the beghards of Maastricht and dated it to 1500, and noted a few prints that were inserted into the book shortly thereafter that were foliated differently. I had built a database to work out which prints were originally pasted where. But this also told me that there were still more prints left unaccounted for. Looking for the missing prints would take me to France, where the manuscript may have been partially dismembered between 1796 and 1861.

Napoleon treated works of art from conquered neighbouring countries as trophies. First and foremost he sought paintings. He even made their transfer to the Louvre a stipulation in his armistice treaties, especially those with Italy. According to the 1797 Treaty of Tolentino with Pope Pius VI, 'The Pope will deliver to the French Republic one hundred pictures, busts, vases, or statues at the choice of the commissioners who will be sent to Rome, among which objects will specifically be included the bronze bust of Junius Brutus and that in marble of Marcus Brutus, both located in the Capitol, and five hundred manuscripts chosen by the commissioners'.⁶⁶ In July 1798 (*9-10 thermidor VI*), the Fête de la Liberté took place on the Champ-de-Mars in Paris. The French put the trophies of their conquests on display, in museums, in exhibitions, in processions.⁶⁷ In 1803 the Louvre was renamed the Musée

---

64 Baron von Geusau, 'Korte Geschiedenis der Kloosters te Maastricht', Publications de la Société Historique et Archéologique dans le Duché de Limbourg = Jaarboek van Limburgs Geschied- en Oudheidkundig Genootschap, XXXI, nouvelle série, tome XI (1894), pp. 3–131, esp. 5-6; Adam van Broeckhuysen, 'Het klooster der Bijgaarden in de Witmakersstraat gelegen', Publications de la Société Historique et Archéologique dans le Duché de Limbourg = Jaarboek van Limburgs Geschied- en Oudheidkundig Genootschap, XLII (1906), p. 38.

65 Ibid, esp. 'De Begaarden', pp. 41–43.

66 Quoted in Patricia Mainardi, 'Assuring the Empire of the Future: The 1798 Fête de la Liberté', *Art Journal* 48, no. 2 (1989), pp. 155–63 (p. 156).

67 See Martin Rosenberg, 'Raphael's Transfiguration and Napoleon's Cultural Politics', *Eighteenth-Century Studies* 19, no. 2 (1985), pp. 180–205. Most of these

Napoléon, with the history of Western art on display. As Cecil Gould, the former Keeper at the National Gallery of London, put it, 'The Musée Napoléon was born of three parents, republicanism, anti-clericalism and successful aggressive war'.[68]

As the French armies went through conquered territories, they closed monasteries and confiscated their possessions. Most of these they sold at auctions rather than sending them to Paris for accession into the Musée Napoléon. Thus, even the objects that the Napoleonic forces did not send to Paris still left their original surroundings, and swirled around in the art market for decades thereafter. Certain dealers bought and sold them, made collections and dispersed them, and organised the classification categories. Activities around this collecting included cataloguing, comparing, and building knowledge, making a narrative out of the detritus that was shaken loose by the Revolution.

When Napoleon's armies closed the monasteries of the occupied Netherlands in 1797, they confiscated the goods inside. From the Dutch-speaking lands, Napoleon confiscated objects from Averbode Abbey, and then blew some of the buildings up in 1810. Among the trophies was the great carved polyptych now in the Cluny museum in Paris. Carved by Jan de Molder in 1513, it depicts Christ's sacramental blood and related themes. It escaped destruction partly because it was not made out of metal and therefore could not be melted down.

Not all of the confiscated goods entered the French national collections; many items were released into the market. Cataloguing became a central activity for dealers, so that they could study and classify their objects, and add value to them by increasing knowledge about them. Aficionados such as Schreiber, Paul Heitz (1857–1943) and Theodor Oskar Weigel (1812–1881), who were both collectors and dealers, were immersed in the flow of goods that poured from the monasteries Napoleon had closed. Weigel collected choice bits, and then drew up sales catalogues that represented the sum of knowledge on early printing.[69] This system both created *amateurs* (in the French sense of the word) and funded them.

---

studies concentrate on the works taken from Italy, especially the Old Master paintings and sculptures from classical antiquity.
68 Gould, p. 13.
69 Theodor Oskar Weigel, *Katalog frühester Erzeugnisse der Druckerkunst der T. O. Weigel'schen Sammlung: Zeugdrucke, Metallschnitte, Holzschnitte ...Versteigerung 27.(-29.) Mai 1872* (Leipzig: Weigel, 1872).

Cataloguing the loot also took place at a national level: it constituted another aspect of legitimising it for the country, but this took longer than capturing it. Only under Napoleon III (1808–1873), the emperor of the Second French Empire (1852–1870) was a series of manuscript catalogues of the Bibliothèque Imperiale drawn up, 'by order of the Emperor' (fig. 59). They began, following national lines, with the manuscripts written in French, before moving on to manuscripts written in other languages. Dutch- and German-language manuscripts fell low on the list of priorities, especially after France lost the Franco-Prussian War in 1871. Manuscripts at the Bibliothèque nationale de France (BnF) are still catalogued according to principles laid out in this early era, with the language of the script determining the manuscript's shelf number. Thus, all the manuscripts written in French form a group, and an elevated one at that.

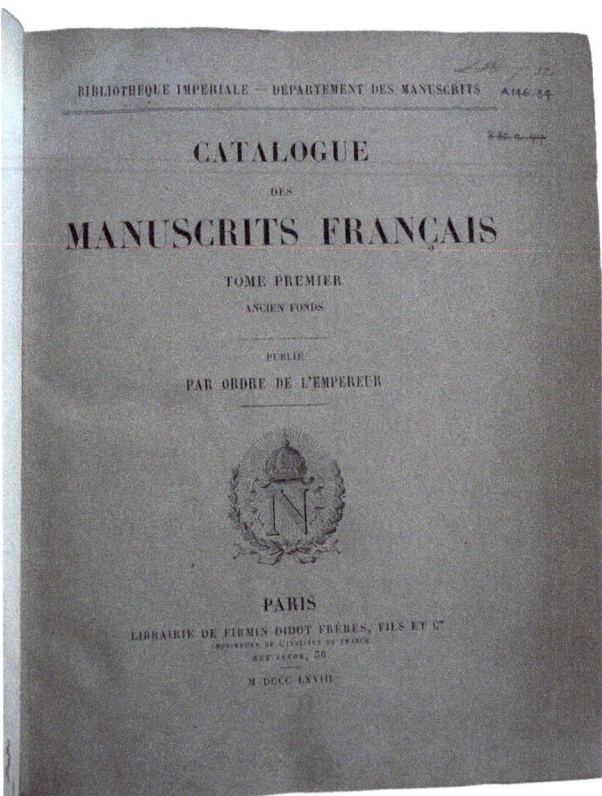

Fig. 59
Title page from 1868 catalogue of the Bibliothèque Imperiale.

Of the manuscripts that were confiscated from the monasteries of Belgium and the Netherlands, some were destroyed. Some were taken to Paris and either auctioned or accessioned. A large crate containing several hundred manuscripts was secreted in Maastricht and then discovered later in the nineteenth century. Called the Maastricht Collectie, these were distributed to four libraries in the Netherlands: the Koninklijke Bibliotheek in The Hague, and the University Libraries of Leiden, Utrecht, and Groningen.[70] All but twelve of these manuscripts are accounted for in these collections, but the book of hours from the beghards does not appear to be among the 'missing' twelve. Instead, Add. 24332 and many other manuscripts from the eastern Netherlands were swept up in a trail of goods whose vortex was Paris. Although the exact trajectory of each item cannot be determined with accuracy, it can be said that Napoleon's policy of closing down the monasteries in all the territories he occupied and confiscating their property had the effect of putting many monastic manuscripts — as well as liturgical and religious objects of all kinds — on the market. In the wake of this shake-up, dealers materialised who orchestrated the redistribution of works from religious to secular ownership. The beghards' manuscript was probably taken to Paris during this chaos.

At the British Museum, the Register for 1861 indicates that the prints were acquired by M. Tross, a member of a family of book dealers based in Paris. They must have done a swift trade in reselling books that had been confiscated by Napoleon's armies: their names appear often in the sales records of manuscripts and prints purchased by the BM in the nineteenth century, and they sold items to other institutions as well, including the BnF, as I later learned. When the dealers prepared manuscripts for sale, the objects often changed shape. A few items were allowed to remain intact, or relatively intact. Most of the manuscripts containing prints must have been cut apart at this time, in the early nineteenth century. The manuscripts themselves (largely written in Middle Dutch or German, and therefore unreadable and undesirable to the French) were discarded or liquidated. They yielded the engravings,

---

70 Jos M. M. Hermans, 'Elf Kisten Boeken uit het Gouvernementsgebouw te Maastricht: Lotgevallen van de Limburgse Handschriften en Oude Drukken, Gevonden in 1839', in *Miscellanea Neerlandica. Opstellen voor Dr. Jan Deschamps ter Gelegenheid van Zijn Zeventigste Verjaardag*, ed. Elly Cockx-Indestege and Frans Hendrickx (Leuven: Peeters, 1987), pp. 105–43.

woodcuts, and metalcuts, which now populate the print rooms of major national collections across Europe.[71] Although many of the paintings that Napoleon looted were subsequently repatriated after 1814, the monastic remains that had already been auctioned off, as well as the books that had been cut up, could not be.

I suspected that half the prints were removed in France, before the book was sold on to the British Museum. If the manuscript had been confiscated from its monastery by Napoleon, then the prints may have landed in a collection as a group, either directly or through the mediation of dealers. I looked for them by scouring the pages of *Einblattdrucke des fünfzehnten Jahrhunderts*. These constitute nearly a hundred large volumes about early single-leaf printing that were initially published by Paul Heitz (1923–1999), a scholar/collector based in Strasbourg.[72] Each volume covers one collection or a group of nearby collections, some public and others private. The volume numbers were not published in chronological order by volume number, and the upheaval of two world wars slowed and frustrated the process. Prints in Polish collections only appeared in 2016.[73] During the twentieth century, many prints changed hands or were destroyed, so the volumes capture a changing reality.

Although later editions present the images printed in black and white directly onto large pages, in early editions (such as a set in Brussels) the prints are hand-coloured to resemble the originals and reproduced as tipped-in sheets, pasted to the large album pages. In other words, this special edition of the series makes a *simulacrum* of the collector's album, rather than a catalogue of it. The collector's unit was the matte, either in an album or a box. The way in which Heitz published the prints was therefore guided by the principles of the collector, who sought to remove prints from their original contexts and place them instead in the context of the collection. Studying prints and

---

71 David S. Areford, *The Viewer and the Printed Image in Late Medieval Europe. Visual Culture in Early Modernity* (Farnham, England; Burlington, VT: Ashgate, 2010), pp. 105–63.

72 *Einblattdrucke des Fünfzehnten Jahrhunderts*, ed. by Paul Heitz and Wilhelm Ludwig Schreiber, 98 vols (Straßburg: Paul Heitz, 1899–2016).

73 Zofia Ameisenowa. *Einblattdrucke des Fünfzehnten Jahrhunderts in Polen: Holz- und Metallschnitte in den Bibliotheken zu Gołuchów, Krakau, Lemberg, Lublin, Płozk, Thorn und Warschau.* Einblattdrucke des Fünfzehnten Jahrhunderts (Strassburg: J.H. Ed. Heitz/Heidelberg: Universitätsbibliothek, 2016).

collecting them, breaking manuscripts apart and pasting prints and their doppelgängers into albums were all mirrored activities. These volumes occasionally revealed groups of prints or series that could have been removed *en masse* from a single manuscript, but I found no such sub-collections that corresponded to the prints removed from Add. 24332.

The Heitz volumes did not cover the BnF; for that, I scoured the pages of Bouchot's catalogue of '200 prints' in the BnF from 1903.[74] Bouchot was a nationalist, and as he selected 200 prints from the collection and wrote about them, he did his best to maximise the role of France in the history of early printing, and to minimise that of Germany and the Low Countries. He attributed many prints to France that were clearly made elsewhere. His nationalism obscures the historical facts, but what is useful about his book is that he recorded the method and date of acquisition, if known. Otherwise, this information was not recorded systematically for the other early prints in the BnF.

Michèle Hébert's 1982 catalogue of the northern European engravings in the BnF supplements Bouchot's work of 1902 and is complete rather than selective.[75] But this, alas, is one of the more useless catalogues ever produced, for it excises all context, does not report what is on the backs of the images, reproduces them in a jarring variety of scales while refraining from indicating the size of the prints, and fails even to hint at the provenance or date of acquisition. It is difficult to imagine any project for which this catalogue would be a useful aid. Achieving no satisfaction with Hébert, I wrote to the BnF's Cabinet des Estampes in January 2008 to ask about a cache of fifteenth-century Netherlandish and German prints that might have entered the collection around or before 1861. I never received a reply. To figure out whether the cache of prints from Add. 24332 had landed in Paris would require a trip there; however, I put off this trip for several years and finished a few other book projects instead.

---

74 Henri Bouchot. *Les Deux Cents Incunables Xylographiques du Département des Estampes: Origines de la Gravure sur Bois—Les Précurseurs—Les Papiers—Les Indulgences—Les 'Grandes Pièces' des Cabinets d'Europe—Catalogue Raisonné des Estampes sur Bois et sur Métal du Cabinet de Paris* (Paris: Librairie centrale des beaux-arts, 1903).

75 Michèle Hébert, Bibliothèque Nationale, Cabinet des Estampes. *Inventaire des Gravures des Écoles du Nord: 1440–1550*, 2 vols. (Paris: Bibliothèque nationale, 1982).

The Missing Images: In Paris?

By the time I resumed this project in 2010, I had left my job as the curator of manuscripts at the Koninklijke Bibliotheek in the Netherlands. In my free year, I walked the Camino de Santiago, wrote a film script, and wrote an article about 'Dirty Books' while holding a fellowship at the Courtauld; for this project, I measured the darkness of fingerprints and cumulative wear in medieval manuscripts to work out which sections had been most frequently read.[76] To fund the prints-in-manuscripts project, in the autumn of 2010 I applied for a grant from the Katharine F. Pantzer Junior Research Fellowship in the History of the Printed Book and was declined. In their boilerplate rejection letters, boards rarely justify their decisions. Perhaps they considered my project to be a manuscript, not a print, project. In January 2011 I drove to Scotland in an ice storm to take up a lectureship at St Andrews. I lived between a violent ocean that heaved dead aquatic mammals onto the shore, and a muddy field: between a stinking rock and a soft place. This strongly motivated me to redouble my efforts to escape to sunlit urban culture, and in the autumn of 2011, I applied for a fellowship from the Neil Ker fund — for the study of medieval manuscripts — administered by the British Academy, to go to Paris to look for the prints. The BA awarded me the fellowship but gave me only a third of the money I had requested. This put me in a bind: accepting the grant meant that I still had to go to Paris and do the work I had laid out, but do it on a third of the budget I had estimated, and make up the rest myself. I had already spent tens of thousands of dollars/euros/pounds on this project. I realised that a project such as this can only be completed by people with private funding. For their art history projects, the other 99% have to confine themselves to theoretical arguments about objects that have already been published or do web-based studies of digitised objects. To do original research on previously unknown manuscripts that are spread around Europe is a pricey sport.

I decided to make up the difference and accept the partial grant, which meant counting pennies. It was cheaper to rent a small apartment in Paris than to book a hotel for the entire period. Websites were

---

76 The article was a free, digital-born publication, which enabled a large and diverse audience of readers to find and download it. See Kathryn M. Rudy, 'Dirty Books: Quantifying Patterns of Use in Medieval Manuscripts Using a Densitometer', *Journal of Historians of Netherlandish Art* 2, no. 1 (2010).

beginning to appear that offered the kind of housing I sought. Various friends came to stay with me in my apartment, including someone I had met on the internet who was writing a novel involving time travel to the Middle Ages, in which my work on 'Dirty Books' provided some of the fodder: the hyper-masculine scientist-hero of the book scrapes some bacteria from a manuscript that is lurking under a layer of gold leaf, goes back in time, and cures the bubonic plague.[77] Days I spent in the BnF, evenings at art galleries, walking in Paris, bouncing ideas around with creative friends, and avoiding spending money.

One of the problems is that the Réserve print room within the BnF was open only two hours per week (although during the time I was working on this project, they expanded their hours to four per week, Tuesday and Thursday, 10–12). I braced myself for the traumatic experience of applying for a BnF reader's card, which is expensive and requires an interview, in French, about why you need to see Dutch and German prints and manuscripts. Back in 1999, when I visited the BnF for the first time, the man who interviewed me wore a pince-nez and lacked any wrinkles that might have suggested he had ever smiled. He sat across an imposing desk from me, asking me questions about my research and then wincing as I stammered out a vaguely French answer, he all the while wielding a long and shiny knife with which he cut open the virgin pages of a nineteenth-century book, still connected at the top edge. He plodded on with this task through a haze of palpable boredom, and when I made a particularly egregious grammatical error he would pause, wince in such a way that he burned calories in the process, and then use his hand to corral some of the fibres he had launched from the book's fold by the action of his flashing knife blade. I wondered whether he was going to hold me at knife-point and make me conjugate irregular French verbs, but he just grew bored of me and flung a reader's card at me by way of dismissal.

Everything was different, and better, when I returned to Paris in 2012. The BnF staff had become friendlier. They treated Americans more sympathetically under Obama than under a Bush. The man with the pince-nez had disappeared, to be replaced by buoyant staff members who were helpful in any language. Most importantly, there was a new curator of prints in the BnF, Séverine Lepape, who aided my research tremendously and made it much more efficient than it otherwise would have been. I was able to complete my necessary work in Paris in a week.

---

77   The novel was never completed.

I was in Paris for a week in summer 2012, bearing a spreadsheet with information about the size of the prints and their probable subjects. I was looking for approximately 124 prints of certain sizes and with particular subjects, as my spreadsheet indicated. (See the Appendix.) Rows in the spreadsheet I had coloured grey corresponded to missing prints and folios. In the archive mountains of dossiers and archival boxes were brought to me. Unlike the prints in London, those in Paris do not have identifying numbers that are related to their date of accession. While some prints were glued to mounts of standard size, as in London, most were mounted into albums, in which like were arranged with like in balanced compositions (fig. 60). I pored over the BnF's fifteenth-century print holdings. Measured them. Evaluated their subjects. Of the prints I was looking for, many were small and had been cut from the page; others presumably had been full-page images, which could therefore not be on pages higher than 144 millimetres. (Folios in the Add. 24332 are between 143 and 144 mm high.) For folios with a hole cut into them, the corresponding print must have been smaller than the hole. I was also looking for images with red penwork of the sort that the beghards applied

Fig. 60 Album from Paris, BnF, Département des Estampes, with three engravings by Israhel van Meckenem representing Christ as the Man of Sorrows. Published with kind permission from the Bibliothèque nationale de France.

Although many of the fifteenth-century prints in the BnF must have been excised from manuscripts, only a few still had bits of manuscript hanging from them, like flesh hanging from the bone. Prints still attached to a manuscript fragment could reveal their origins. In my first pass through all the fifteenth-century prints in the BnF, I found none with scraps of the Middle Dutch script from Add. 24332. If the BnF had purchased the prints, they had dispersed them onto various mounts, steamed them from their manuscript substrates, and thoroughly disguised and decontextualized them. That some of the prints still had some bits of manuscript attached to them demonstrated that part of the collection, at least, was harvested from manuscripts. For example, a small image of the Virgin of the Sun had been pasted into an initial (fig. 61). This, however came from a German, rather than from a Netherlandish, manuscript, to judge from the scrap of handwriting that still adheres to the print.

Fig. 61 Virgin of the Sun engraving, hand-coloured and pasted into the letter H in a German prayerbook. Paris, BnF, Département des Estampes, Ea20aRes. Published with kind permission from the Bibliothèque nationale de France.

My failure with these search methods forced me to begin looking at the problem in a different way. If a dealer/collector in or before 1861 obtained a manuscript full of prints and wanted to pluck just a few, which ones would he take? In my estimation, he would have mined the manuscript for its most collectable prints, those with the highest value, both cultural and monetary. I speculated that these would include prints with gold on them and those by named masters. My hypothetical dealer apparently did leave a few of the fine engravings by Israhel van Meckenem behind, and in particular the molested St Wolfgang. He wanted clean copies. Furthermore, the dealer or collector had been willing to cut through one of the Netherlandish woodcuts (with the Annunciation, on fol. 283v, see fig. 4) in order to capture whatever was on the other side. It is possible that he rated engravings more highly than woodcuts? Dozens of fifteenth-century engravings in the BnF became candidates, for example, one bearing the monogram of the

Fig. 62
Crucifixion, hand-coloured engraving, with a red penwork frame. Paris, BnF, Département des Estampes, Ea18cRes 28. Published with kind permission from the Bibliothèque nationale de France.

Master ES, depicting the Face of Christ held by SS Peter and Paul. This print, however, measures 155 millimetres, making it slightly too large to fit into Add. 24332. However, several prints in the BnF did meet my requirements.

An engraving representing the Crucifixion, now in the BnF, has the kind of red penwork frame associated with prints pasted into manuscripts (fig. 62). Furthermore, the paper substrate of this print appears to comprise a complete leaf, cut from a manuscript, but not trimmed. It still had the dirt from handling the book near the bottom outer (left) corner, and stains along the right edge that might be glue, from when the leaf was inserted into a book. But was that book Add. 24332? Although this leaf had red penwork, it was not the same as that in the beghards' book, and I concluded that the crucifixion did not come from the manuscript I was trying to reconstruct.

I was looking for a Mass of St Gregory or another image appropriate to the *Adoro te* for folio *ccccc xviii*. An engraving attributed to Israhel van Meckenem (Paris, BNEstampes, Ea48Res; fig. 63) was a possible candidate. This image had been trimmed into a rectangle exactly 102 millimetres wide, which is the width of Add. 24332. In general, nineteenth-century French curators did not trim printed material off, even if they sometimes trimmed the print down to the quick. Far more likely was that someone — such as a beghard — had cut this roundel so that it would fit into a small manuscript. Furthermore, the beghards clearly received prints made by Israhel van Meckenem: this printer had a geographic range that included Maastricht, and the beghards were already among his customers. One can imagine that the French dealer leafing through Add. 24332 when it was still intact would select the largest and best prints for his collection and eventually his sales room. The Christ as Man of Sorrows was 'signed' 'IvM', and therefore more valuable to a collector, a breed perpetually more interested in objects that can be attributed with some certainty. Like the others in Paris, this print has been pasted to its mount, so I could not check the reverse to see if it contained the beghards' distinctive scripts, and my hypothesis remains conjectural.

Another print that may have come from Add. 24332 is a painted metalcut depicting the Adoration of the Magi (fig. 64). This print is 109 millimetres high, and would be a good fit for folio *ccc xviii*, which should

Fig. 63 Israhel van Meckenem, Christ as Man of Sorrows, engraving. Paris, BnF, Département des Estampes, Ea48Res. Published with kind permission from the Bibliothèque nationale de France.

have imagery relevant to the Infancy of Christ. In fact, any one of dozens of prints depicting the Adoration of the Magi would be appropriate in this position, but this one caught my eye in the same way that it might have caught a nineteenth-century collector's eye — as something slightly unusual, colourful, and noteworthy for its technique. Perhaps these qualities made the collector decide to express his desire with a knife. In fact, the back of the print has traces of glue and script, as if someone had pasted this image over a text page (fig. 65). Overlapping script with an image would be inconsistent with the design principles of the beghards' manuscript, which suggested that this print had been pasted somewhere else, not in the beghards' broken book.

Fig. 64
Adoration of the Christ Child by the Magi, painted metalcut. Paris, BnF, Département des Estampes. Published with kind permission from the Bibliothèque nationale de France.

Fig. 65
Reverse of the previous image. Paris, BnF, Département des Estampes. Published with kind permission from the Bibliothèque nationale de France.

Rothschild

Séverine suggested that I look for the missing prints in the Rothschild collection at the Louvre. The famous family of bankers based in Paris in the nineteenth century were tremendous collectors of all kinds of exquisite objects, including manuscripts.[78] I had not realised that the Rothschilds' appetite also extended to early prints, nor that the Louvre now housed the family's print collection, because the collection had not been published. That day I wrote to the keepers of the print collection at the Louvre. They were able to accommodate my visit the next day; but they could give me just two hours with the collection, during which I would be allowed to photograph as much as I wanted. Armed with a couple of cameras, fully charged, extra batteries, pencils, papers, and ruler, I went to the Louvre and took 500 documentary photographs in the space of two hours.

In 2012 only one catalogue of the Rothschild prints existed, in typescript, with each sheet carefully tucked into an individual plastic sleeve.[79] This catalogue provided little information. Twentieth-century curators had mounted the prints onto standard-size mounts and stored them in giant folders, with a list of contents accompanying every box. They have been organised by medium and in chronological order, not in the order of accession. To see all the fifteenth-century prints, I called up the first fourteen boxes, and the early history of printing unfolded before me. It was clear that many of the early prints had been taken from manuscripts, and some may have even been taken from Add. 24332. Several prints had themes, approximate dates, and sizes that made them possible contenders for the beghards' project.

For example, an engraving depicting the Adoration of the Christ Child by the Magi, now Rothschild 57 (fig. 66) may have been one of the two full pages removed from the manuscript, either folio *ccc xviii* or *ccc xxxi*. Both these folios fell in a section about the birth of the Christ Child, which would have been enhanced by a variety of infancy images. While

---

78 Some of the manuscripts ended up in Waddesdon Manor in Buckinghamshire, and some form the Rothschild Collection in the BnF in Paris. See L. M. J. Delaissé, James H. Marrow, and John de Wit, *Illuminated Manuscripts* (Fribourg: Published for the National Trust by Office du livre, 1977); Christopher de Hamel, *The Rothschilds and Their Collections of Illuminated Manuscripts* (London: The British Library, 2005).

79 In 2014, Séverine Lepape became the curator of the Edmond de Rothschild collection in the Department of Graphic Arts at the Louvre and is preparing a catalogue of the collection.

Rothschild 57 has some stray lines, made in the plate when the burin slipped slightly (for example, one slip overlapping the top boundary line), and some attempts at three-dimensionality that fall flat (the kings' crowns), the print overall is sensitive and expressive. Its left edge has been trimmed, as if the print had been cut out of a bound volume, such as Add. 24332, but because it is now mounted to a board, it is impossible to know whether it is inscribed on the other side with the distinctive script of that manuscript.

Fig. 66
Adoration of the Christ Child by the Magi, engraving. Paris, Louvre, Rothschild.

The print adjacent to the Adoration in the Rothschild collection, no. 56, had some of the same features, which likewise made it a candidate. (Items in any collection with consecutive numbers sometimes share a common origin.) This print shows a little-known event, St Augustine at the beach (fig. 67). While strolling on the sand and contemplating the nature of the Trinity, Augustine encountered a small boy who was running between the water and a small hole in the sand, carrying a seashell. When Augustine asked the boy what he was doing, the boy replied that he was carrying the sea to the small hole, one shellful at a time, until the whole sea was contained in the hole. St Augustine exclaimed, 'That's impossible! The sea is great and the hole is small.' The boy agreed, but retorted, 'I will sooner empty the whole sea into that small pool than you will comprehend the mystery of the Trinity!' Then the boy disappeared. According to the Golden Legend, the boy was an angel, sent to the saint to teach him about the limits of human understanding of the mysteries of the faith.[80]

Fig. 67 St Augustine encountering the infant Jesus on a riverbank, engraving. Paris, Louvre, Rothschild 56. Paris, musée du Louvre, collection Rothschild Photo (C) RMN-Grand Palais (musée du Louvre)/Tony Querrec.

How might this have fitted into the manuscript? One can imagine that children would like this story, because of the role reversal between teacher and student. While I am far from certain that this print once

---

80 Jacobus de Voragine, *The Golden Legend: Readings on the Saints*, trans, William Granger Ryan, 2 vols. (Princeton, NJ: Princeton University Press, 1993), vol. II, pp. 116–32.

sat in Add. 24332, it might have functioned as did the other of the two full pages removed from the manuscript in the infancy section, either folio *ccc xviii* or *ccc xxxi*. I was proposing, in other words, that someone had removed two engravings from the manuscript that had been close together. That both landed adjacent to one another in the same nineteenth-century collection strengthened this hypothesis. Furthermore, a feature of no. 56 made it an attractive candidate for this role: a rubricator had touched the lips and cheeks of the saint and the boy with a red pen, as well as a quincunx of bosses on Augustine's book. Perhaps the rubricator was confused about the subject of the print, and therefore gave the child a red stigmata, turning the boy/angel into Jesus. This was in keeping with the activities of the rubricator elsewhere in the manuscript, where the red pen enhanced many of the otherwise black-and-white images.

Many other prints in the Rothschild collection were similarly tantalising as candidates for the beghards' manuscript, yet similarly inconclusive. For example, an engraving representing the Pentecost that was highly gilded may have been removed from folio *cccc xcvii*, a folio, I had suspected, originally with a full-page image of that subject (fig. 68). I could imagine a situation in which a French connoisseur, upon opening the beghards' book of hours shortly after it was confiscated around 1800, would have felt bedazzled by all the prints, and cut a few out to collect or to sell. He would have cut out the best and brightest, including those with gilding, such as the Pentecost, which would have originally formed a folio in the manuscript. A problem with this example relates to the professional photography provided by the Louvre: it flattens the shimmering gold and disables one from seeing the tooled burnished background. Professional photography from the Louvre costs, in 2019, €65 per shot, but my own hand-held photograph of the same object captures the texture of the surface and the cut left edge more effectively (fig. 69).

The Pentecost print clearly belonged with the next print in the Rothschild collection, no. 55, representing Christ in Judgement, an engraving gilded in a similar way to no. 54 (figs 70 and 71). Perhaps this Last Judgement once prefaced the Seven Penitential Psalms and had been foliated as *c xxxiii bis* and had caused an offset on 632. If so, then it was part of the second wave of prints added by the beghards. We shall never know with certainty, however, because an early collector trimmed it down to the quick, thereby removing any foliation or offsets.

Fig. 68
Pentecost, gilt engraving, formerly pasted to fol. cccc xcvii of the beghards' book of hours? Paris, Louvre, Rothschild 54. Paris, musée du Louvre, collection Rothschild Photo (C) RMN-Grand Palais (musée du Louvre)/ Tony Querrec.

Fig. 69
Pentecost, gilt engraving, formerly pasted to fol. cccc xcvii of the beghards' book of hours? Paris, Louvre, Rothschild 54. Photo: Kathryn M. Rudy.

Fig. 70
Christ in Judgment,
gilt engraving. Paris,
Louvre, Rothschild 55.
Paris, musée du Louvre,
collection Rothschild
Photo (C) RMN-Grand
Palais (musée du Louvre)/
Tony Querrec.

Fig. 71
Christ in Judgment, gilt
engraving. Paris, Louvre,
Rothschild 55.
Photo: Kathryn M. Rudy.

A highly crafted engraving depicting the Virgin and Child on a sliver of moon and surrounded by a rosary, Rothschild no. 69, may originally have had a place in Add. 24332 as folio *ccc xviii* (fig. 72). Although Lehrs had ascribed this print to the Master of the Housebook, no doubt because of its fine technique that resembles the drypoint for which that artist was famous, the print probably dates from the end of the fifteenth century. Again, one could imagine that a collector in the early nineteenth century would have passed through the beghards' manuscript and collected the most beautiful, exquisite, unusual prints, leaving the more mundane examples behind.

Fig. 72
Virgin and Child on a sliver of moon, surrounded by a rosary, originally in London, British Library, Add. Ms. 24332 as fol. ccc xviii? Paris, Louvre, Rothschild 69. Paris, musée du Louvre, collection Rothschild Photo (C) RMN-Grand Palais (musée du Louvre)/Tony Querrec.

For the most part, however, I concluded that the cache of prints removed from Add. 2432 had not entered the Rothschild collection *en masse*. My reason? In all, the fifteenth-century prints in the Rothschild collection are large. The baron was apparently not interested in small prints. Since the prints that came from Add. 24332 could not have been taller than

144 millimetres, I had to reject most of the Rothschild ones. Having not found what I was looking for at the Louvre, I returned to the BnF and tried a different tactic to find the missing prints.

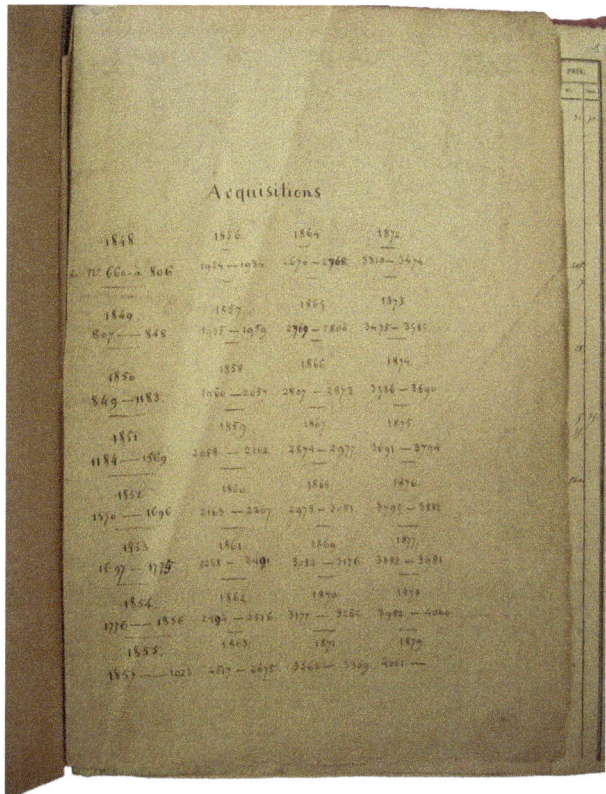

Fig. 73
Handwritten list of acquisitions from the nineteenth century, in Paris, BnF, Département des Estampes.

Tross, Again

Although going through all the fifteenth-century prints in the BnF systematically had allowed me to identify a few prints that may have come from Add. 24332, I could connect not a single one with certainty to the manuscript. Before abandoning Paris, I wanted to find out whether a group of prints had entered the BnF that might have been taken from the beghards' manuscript but then dispersed throughout the collection according to its own organisational demands. Philippe, who fetches prints in the reading room of the Réserve collection and has a long institutional memory, gave me a few more discovery aids. At a certain point, he brought me the Acquisitions Register. The BnF, like the British

Museum, has a handwritten list of acquisitions from the nineteenth century (fig. 73). Whereas the English curator at the BM gave a separate line to each item of acquisition, the French described an entire purchase of a group of items with a few descriptors. Because of this approach to record-keeping, the French Acquisitions Register divulges even less information than the English one. For example, it is nearly impossible to connect an item from the Acquisitions Register with an item currently in the collection.

One way to tackle this register was by looking for sellers' names. Tross, the dealer who had sold Add. 24332 to the BM, makes several appearances in this Acquisitions Register. For example, on 28 July 1859 he sold the BnF sixteen niellos from the twelfth century, which came from the Cathedral of Aix-la-Chapelle (Aachen) for 85 francs (fig. 74). And then on 28 March 1860, Tross sold them a cache of prints:

> Vingt-huit pièces du XVe siècle dont onze gravées au burin en manière criblée, quinze gravées au burin, une grave sur bois, et une pièce non décrite de maître au monogramme S. Ces vingt-huit pièces appartenants à l'époque dite des incunables décorent un manuscript enbas allemand qui porte la date de 1463.

For this the BnF had paid Tross 1250 francs (fig. 75). This description probably referred to a manuscript that Ursula Weekes has worked on (Paris, BnF, Rés Ea 6).[81] If so, Tross did not cut this up or try to sell the parts separately. It is difficult to deduce from this evidence whether he ever cut up items, or whether he just sold them as he had received them. He makes several other appearances in the Acquisitions Register for later prints of German origin. For example, on 11 August 1868, he sold the BnF: 'Deux pièces allemandes (non décrites) gravées en criblé par un maître anonyme de la première moitié du XVe siècle et servant d'ornement à un manuscrit. Les deux pièces représentent l'une *Le portement de Croix*, l'autre la Sainte Face' (fig. 76). Alas, I have not been able to connect these with a particular manuscript.

What can one deduce from these entries in the BnF's register? Tross did a swift trade in ecclesiastical objects by bringing items dislodged from the region around Aachen and Kleve to Paris. Prints formed only part of what he sold. He must have had many private clients, as well as the

---

81 For a description and discussion, see Weekes, *Early Engravers and Their Public*, pp. 294–301.

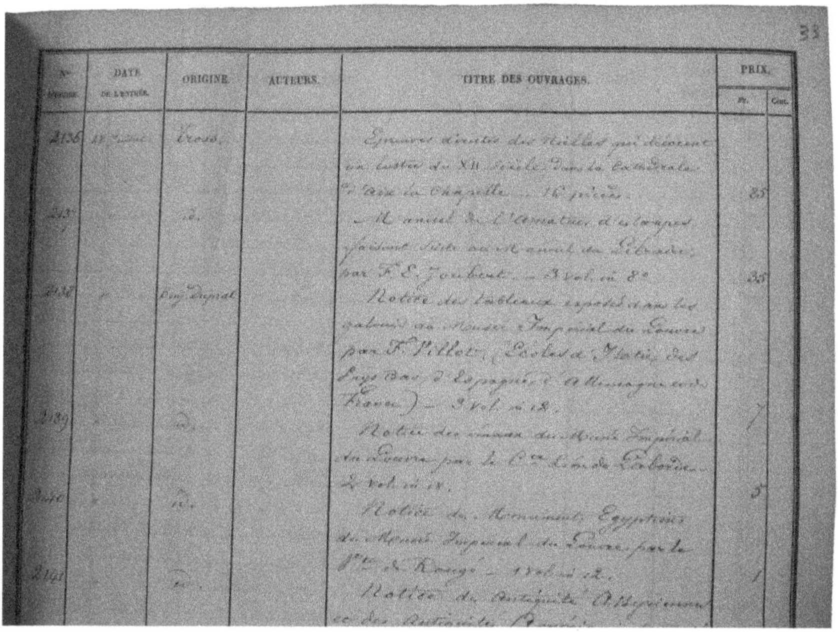

1. Cut, Pasted, and Cut Again 157

Fig. 74 Handwritten list of acquisitions from the nineteenth century, for 28 July 1859, BnF.

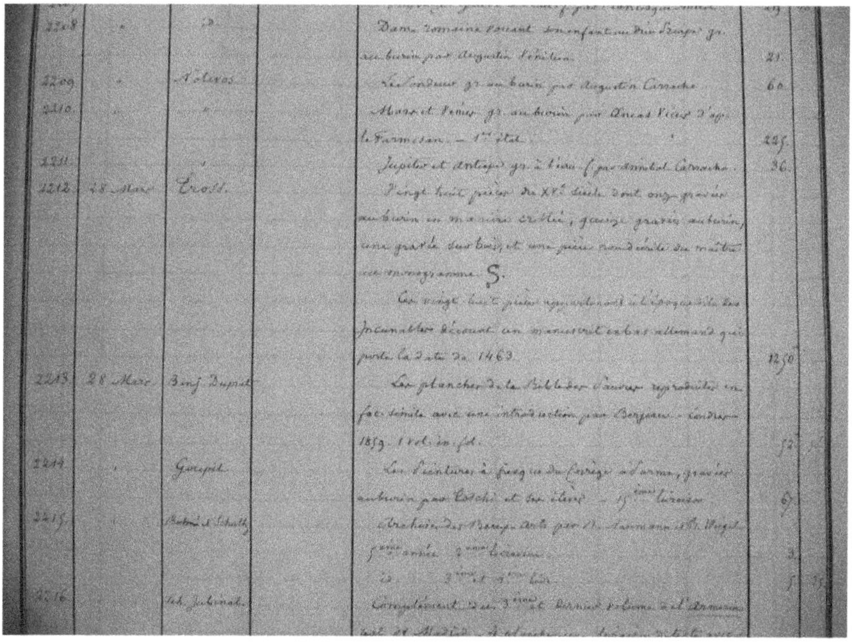

Fig. 75 Handwritten list of acquisitions from the nineteenth century, Vingt-huit pièces de XVe siècle, 28 March 1860, BnF.

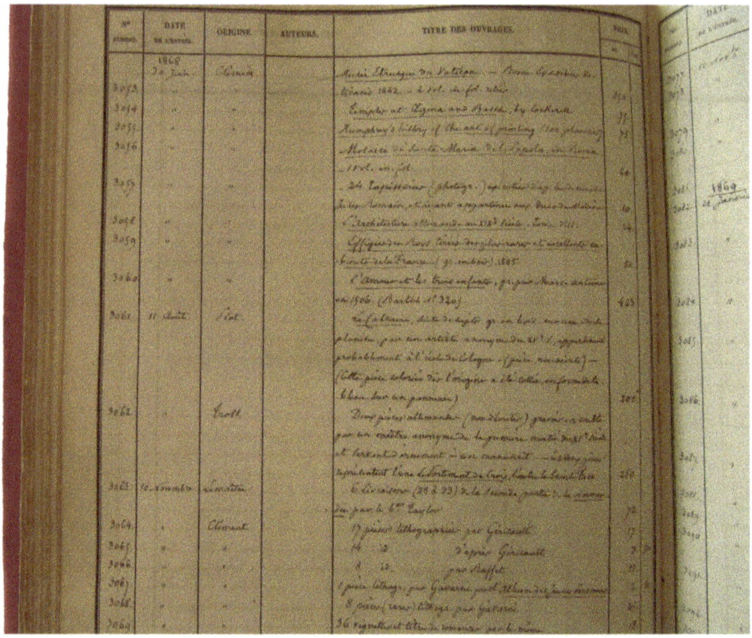

158   *Image, Knife, and Gluepot*

Fig. 76 Handwritten list of acquisitions from the nineteenth century, for 11 August 1868, in the BnF.

BnF, because his sporadic sales to the library would not have sustained his entire business. Indeed, he also sold items to London. However, I have no evidence that he broke up the beghards' manuscript and sold choice bits of it to the BnF. In fact, when he did sell manuscript-print hybrids, he left them intact. I could identify no other groups of prints in the acquisitions register that might have been candidates. In the end I had to conclude that the prints that had been cut out of the manuscript before Tross sold it to the English had not entered the BnF in one go, nor had they entered the Rothschild collection.

While in Paris, Séverine asked me to work on an exhibition at the Louvre with her; it was to be about the functions of early prints in Europe. I wrote two essays for her exhibition catalogue.[82] It was a satisfying way to redeem the time I had spent with the BnF and Rothschild collections, which had not divulged the items from Add. 24332. The University had declined my application for a promotion to Senior Lecturer, and

---

82   Séverine Lepape and Kathryn M. Rudy, *Les Origines de l'Estampe en Europe du Nord, 1400–1470*, Musée du Louvre (Paris: Le Passage: Louvre éditions, 2013).

I continued living paycheck to paycheck, because all of my salary, beyond food, rent, and petrol, was going into the 292 high-resolution digital images that were to be published in the other book I had been working on in this period, for Yale University Press. (Subventions from the Catherine Mackichan Trust, the Carnegie Trust of the Universities of Scotland and the Historians of Netherlandish Art, and the School of Art History, University of St Andrews had covered about £3000 of the £8700-worth of images.) My Head of School at the time, Brendan Cassidy, understood my financial distress and encouraged me to lift images from existing publications. One problem with that plan was that images I had studied were largely unpublished, so there were no publications to be ripped off in this way. Having to pay for new photography is the surcharge on doing original research on previously unstudied objects. I was so broke that I could not return to Paris to see the show when it eventually opened, but I hear it was a great success.

Working on this project in Paris in the summer of 2012, I had maximised the brief time allowed in the Réserve print room at the BnF and in the Rothschild collection. That week in Paris was still so expensive that when my time was up, I had only £4 in my bank account. After Paris, I was scheduled to give a lecture at the Herzog August Bibliotheek in Wolffenbüttel. I had purchased a cheap flight from Paris to Berlin months earlier but did not have enough money to take the train from Berlin to Wolffenbüttel. In the Berlin Hauptbahnhof I learned that I had run out of mobile phone credit. I talked some guy into letting me use his phone to call my bank (TSB) to ask them to give me some emergency cash. They would not. An eavesdropper bought me a sandwich. And in one of the most unexpected acts I have witnessed, a German train conductor recognised my urgency and desperation to get to Wolffenbüttel and let me ride the train for free by turning a blind eye to my ticket-less presence on the train.

Holes and Patterns

On 23 July 2013 — after pondering this for a year, and after poring over more than a thousand photographs from the Louvre and the BnF, and after studying and restudying the spreadsheet I had made of the contents of Add. 24332 — I saw something I had not seen before:

there was a pattern in the holes, the missing bits of the manuscript that corresponded to prints. In my spreadsheet, I had noted the dimensions of the missing prints. Nearly all the holes were rectangular. Because photographs from the British Library are expensive, I had not ordered photographs of all the folios with missing prints, but only of a few. I was visualising the missing prints as rectangular. However, studying one of the photographs I did have with a missing print — that with Add. 41338, folio 9v — allowed me see the situation in a new way (fig. 77). This folio has a diminutive image in pen and ink, which the scribe probably added, depicting a clerical figure in the lower margin, who is eagerly praying upward to what is now a piece of nineteenth-century blank white paper. The accompanying rubric announces that the prayer is dedicated to St Clare, who must also have been the subject of the print that had been cut out of the initial. I had noted that the hole is roughly rectangular, and I had been looking for a rectangular print to fill it. But then I had this realisation: when nineteenth-century cutters removed items, they did so with a knife that cut in straight lines. When they cut out round things, they left square holes. Therefore, I should also be looking for roundels. In my spreadsheet I looked for square holes and added notes to consider roundels in those cases.

This relic of the tool seems obvious now, especially because the print that came from Add. 41338, fol. 9v was a roundel that must have fitted the round letter *O*. In my estimation, this roundel must have had a diameter of about 42 millimetres. In going through thousands of fifteenth-century prints, the only image that meets that description is the roundel by Israhel van Meckenem depicting St Francis with St Clare, which the beghards could have cut from the engraver's larger sheets apparently meant for that purpose (e-fig. 65). A digital reconstruction provides an idea of what the folio originally looked like (fig. 78).

BM 1849,1208.739 — Six roundels depicting the infant Chris (e-fig. 65)

Six roundels depicting the infant Christ as Salvator Mundi and saints, signed by Israhel van Meckenem in the plate, intact. London, British Museum, Department of Prints & Drawings, inv. 1849,1208.739.

https://hdl.handle.net/20.500.12434/b2b2e1ee

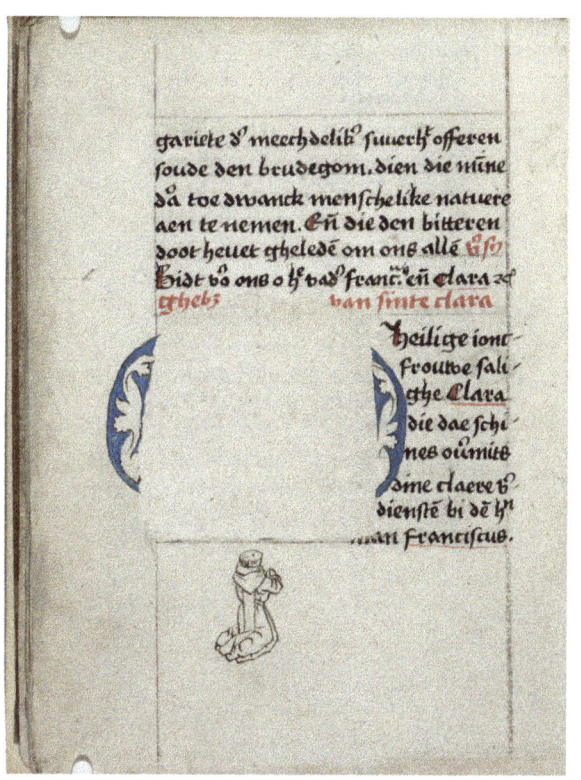

Fig. 77
Folio from the beghards' book of hours, with a pen drawing of a kneeling cleric, beneath an initial that probably once contained a print depicting St Clare. London, British Library, Add. Ms. 41338, fol. 9v.

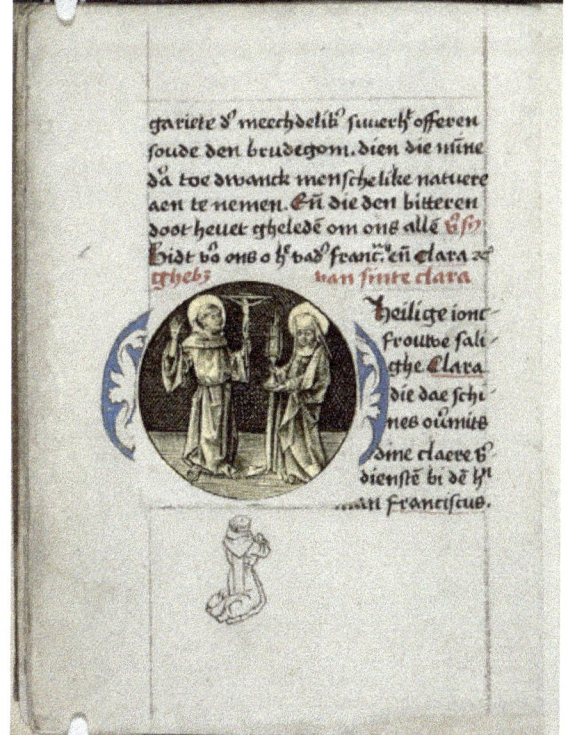

Fig. 78
Digital reconstruction: Israhel van Meckenem's roundel with SS Francis and Clare, superimposed on a leaf from what was the beghards' manuscript, now London, British Library, Add. Ms. 41338, fol. 9v.

Once I realised that square and rectangular holes could yield round prints, I knew that several of the other roundels on the same sheet by Israhel were probable candidates for the other missing prints. Israhel's sheet of six roundels, listed in Lehrs as 447, depicts the Infant Christ as Salvator Mundi; St Anne with Mary and the Christ Child; SS Cosmas and Damian; St Ursula with her maidens; SS Francis and Clare; and SS Dominic and Catherine of Siena.[83] Israhel designed them to be trimmed and deployed as roundels. A roundel with St Anne would fit on folio 351 (formerly folio *ccc xci*; fig. 79); one with St Ursula would fit on folio 396 (formerly folio *cccc xlij*). If I could find loose copies of these roundels (which are easy to recognise), they might lead me to a cache of other prints taken from Add. 24332, and I could complete the task of reconstructing the manuscript. According to Lehrs, copies of the roundels are housed in Berlin, Bologna, Brussels, London, Paris, Vienna, 'und andere'. Over the next several years, I visited all of these places and looked for the prints taken from Add. 24332. Several of these tantalize: the copies in London to which Lehrs refers include the roundel depicting Francis with Clare; however, as I will show in the next chapter, it was peeled from a different manuscript.

Conclusions

Books of hours, as a rule, were written on parchment, which conferred upon them a gravitas and longevity that were not characteristics of paper. Highly unusually, however, the beghards wrote their book of hours (Add. 24332) on paper. Does that fact indicate that they originally set out to make the book with prints glued in it? No. I have come to this conclusion because my reconstruction shows no evidence that the beginning of the manuscript had any foliated and inscribed prints, but only some that were added in a second wave; I therefore hypothesise that the beghards came up with the idea of affixing and integrating prints only part of the way through the making process. We are therefore witnessing their first, stumbling steps in applying the new technology.

The few prints near the beginning of the book did not include any at the major text divisions of the offices: this is precisely where one would

---

[83] Lehrs, vol. IX, p. 353, nr. 447.

1. Cut, Pasted, and Cut Again 163

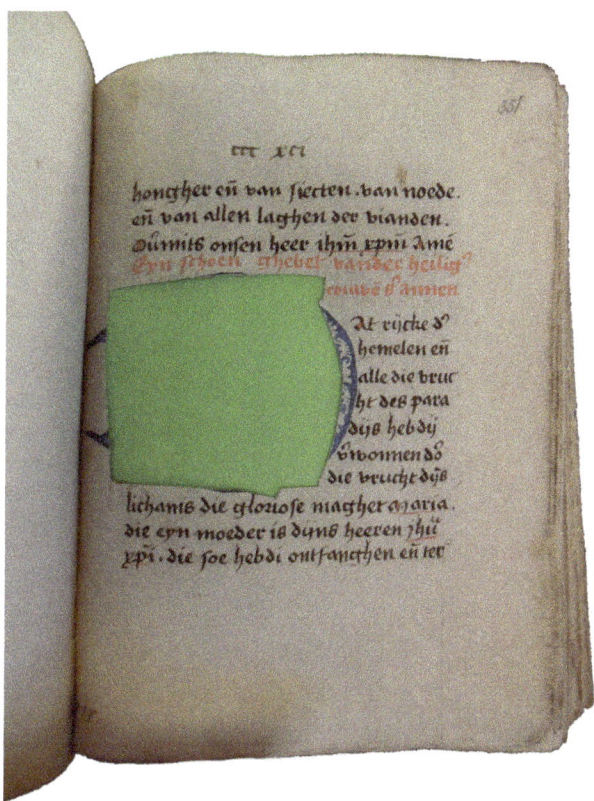

Fig. 79
Folio in the beghards' book of hours, with a prayer to St Anne, which has been partially mutilated. London, British Library, Add. Ms. 24332, fol. 351 (ccc xci).

expect to find imagery and embellishment, as nearly all illuminated books of hours have. It appears that the book's designer (Jan van Emmerick?) only thought of the idea of enhancing the book with prints when the copying was partly completed. But as the beghards progressed with the writing, they pasted in more and more prints, so that by folio *ccc xvii*, for example, there are (were!) prints pasted on both recto and verso (see fig. 4).

Not only that, but after the writing was completed, Jan van Emmerick could not stop adding images to the new book. Specifically, he must have added 632, 636, and 637. One of these is a Netherlandish engraving depicting the infant Christ seated on a pillow with the *Arma Christi* (632), which he added to preface the Seven Penitential Psalms, although this image does not relate to these prayers in an obvious way. In fact, all three of these prints have a less than obvious relationship with the texts in the prayerbook, whereas most of the other prints in the book depict, say, a saint mentioned in close proximity to where the image was glued; it is therefore plausible that Jan had these three prints in his possession before 1500, but that he found places for them in the manuscript only after a long think.

That he added these after the manuscript was foliated would explain why these prints were blank on the back: because they were not present when the writing began. I surmise that he wanted to populate the beginning of the manuscript with images because the first hundred-odd folios had a dearth of them. This was because the idea of integrating prints into the hand-written manuscript only occurred part-way through the writing. The earliest place in the book where I have evidence that the scribe was integrating prints during the writing process is fol. *c xlvi*, which was cut out. This folio would have prefaced the litany (fol. *c xlvii*; or 118). That the text is discontinuous from 116v-118r indicates that the folio that was removed — presumably for its print — also contained text, and that, therefore, image and text were integrated on this page.

Given the prints' origins in different sources, they are not of a standard size, and therefore the beghards had to handle them differently. Some rectangular prints were printed onto octavo-sized sheets, and the entire sheet inserted into the binding, so that the paper of the print itself became a page of the book. With the exceptions just mentioned, the verso sides of these sheets have been ruled to take the scribe's text. Small roundels were turned into instant historiated initials. Medium-sized images were integrated on text pages: sometimes the scribe pasted the image in such a way that it ran well into the border area so that it would not take up too much writing space. All this suggests that the people who assembled Add. 24332 (Jan van Emmerick and companions) had access to a large number of prints when writing the manuscript, but that these prints were not acquired specifically to be included in this manuscript. The haphazardness of the prints, their sizes and media, provides evidence that the beghards were not making prints themselves. If they were, they would have probably standardised the sheets, worked in a single technique, made the subjects that they needed, and emphasised local saints. By using the printed products of remote producers, they were at the mercy of what the market would provide, to some extent. Producers did not understand consumers' exact needs. When the beghards could not obtain what they wanted, they trimmed, scribbled, overpainted, relabelled, reframed, and reidentified printed subjects to make the prints fit their needs.

The beghards' assembly methods represent a particular category of hybrid book production. Before the fifteenth century, manuscripts had largely been bespoke; from the early fifteenth century, books were beginning to be made for a market, without a buyer in mind before construction started. Add. 24332 represents a third category: a manuscript made for one's own use. In fact, in the fifteenth century manuscripts at the highest end of the market (those made by the most skilled practitioners for elite recipients) and those at the lowest end (books made by amateurs for their own use) often contain some of the greatest innovations, while those made for the middle of the market (for example, books of hours with illuminations attributed to the Masters of the Gold Scrolls) often contain images and texts based on boilerplate models, with a division of labour and specialisation. The inclusion of printed images changed the books for these markets in different ways. For the beghards, prints represent the ultimate in the division of labour, since they make use of the labour of dozens of anonymous printmakers, whose skills could dazzle buyers, but from a distance of hundreds of miles away. Prints allowed amateur men in Maastricht to include many images, although their skill as draughtsmen was undeveloped.

Understanding what the beghards added involves examining the process of later removal. This is a kind of forensics that is continuous with ideas of book reconstruction and stratigraphy but goes beyond that to coordinate absences, rather than presences. When the French occupied Maastricht, closed the monasteries, and confiscated their property, they probably brought the manuscript to France, where many of the prints (now lost) must have been cut out. Although I have an idea about what these prints depicted, I have not been able to put my finger on them. From the size of the holes left in the manuscript, some of which would perfectly accommodate Israhel van Meckenem's roundels, I infer that the first wave of prints cut out by a nineteenth-century dealer included engravings by Israhel. This engraver embellished many of the prints he made with ornate display letters, much to the satisfaction of collectors, who often prefer objects with a nameable artist. Israhel's signatures made his work easily recognisable to early collectors of engravings. One of the prints the collector missed in his pass through the manuscript was the Virgin and Child, in which polychromy obscures the monogram of the artist (633, see fig. 34). After a collector had removed the choice prints, the British Museum bought the manuscript from the Parisian dealer Edwin Tross in 1861 and further disassembled it.

Although the manuscript-cum-print assemblage has been harvested at least twice, and its parts now scattered, putting the prints together with the manuscript — even partially — is extremely fruitful for its research results. For example, neither Lehrs nor Geisberg had described number 670 (e-fig. 32), so it escaped the wishful attribution of many of the other early engravings in the BM collection, and instead is simply listed as 'made by Anonymous.' It is probably Netherlandish. The museum's record notes that it is a 'Leaf to a prayerbook', but does not connect it to the other prints from the same source. Whereas the BM had dated it to the sixteenth century, probably because it is delicate and expressive, the manuscript evidence presented here shows that it predated 1500. Reconstructing this manuscript allows us to take fresh stock of the accomplishments of the fifteenth century. Paradoxically, my sharing my data with the museum has led them to update their records, meaning that information I in fact generated could appear belated by the time the current study is published.

Reconstructing this manuscript has permitted a hitherto unavailable snapshot of the prints that were available in Maastricht in 1500 and given the fullest possible picture of how prints were used as one of several systems for creating the richest book with minimal labour. Since the scribes and the monastic house to which they belonged were male, they demonstrate that men, not just women, 'illustrated' manuscripts with prints. One can also perceive the didactic role that the prints played in the manuscript, and one senses that the beghards as teachers were looking for multi-media ways to stimulate their students, to teach not just how to read, and the content of those readings, but also how to use a book, how to use images, how to organise and navigate through information. In short, the reconstructed book allows one to evaluate the history of books, information, and ideas in a way that its disparate parts cannot do. What this project has demonstrated is that the beghards were willing to treat prints interchangeably, and that at least one of the scribes possessed an extremely organised mind and expressed it by making important advances in the way in which he ordered and indexed information. In the following chapter I delve more deeply into these processes.

2. A Novel Function for the Calendar in Add. Ms. 24332

The broken manuscript, with its calendar, revealed something important about how the beghards organised information; specifically, it showed how they exploited fungibility. It took several months to crack the secrets of the beghards' calendar. Once I understood it, I realised that fungibility was a value that they applied in several areas of their book making, including how they used prints. They found new routes to efficiency by combining technologies (manuscript with print, as I showed in Chapter 1; and calendars with tables of contents, as I am about to discuss now). They invented new finding aids, which made it not only efficient to find prayers and texts in their manuscript in the early sixteenth century, but also possible for me to reconstruct the book in the twenty-first. The calendar yielded information that would help me piece together the broken manuscript.

This chapter about the table of contents forms a slight departure from the principal narrative in this book, about the cut-and-pasted print. It is particularly meant for those who are interested in information systems, the changing technologies of finding aids. As Mary Rouse and Richard Rouse have shown, finding aids and scholarly apparatus developed over the course of the twelfth century, with such tools as biblical concordances and alphabetical subject indexes.[1] The beghards exploited

---

1   The Rouses' fundamental studies of medieval finding aids are: Richard Rouse, 'Cistercian Aids to Study in the Thirteenth Century', in *Studies in Medieval Cistercian History II*, ed. J. R. Sommerfeldt (Kalamazoo, MI: Cistercian Publications, 1976),

a range of technologies to limit their labour, to avoid duplication, and to make prayers and information discoverable.

The calendar in Add. Ms. 24332, although admittedly an unlikely place to find clues about the beghards' mental habits, is highly unusual and deserves some analysis. Whereas all medieval calendars serve as perpetual calendars, based on the annual repeated veneration of certain saints on certain days, this calendar has an added feature: someone has devised an extra function for it, by adding folio numbers to the 365 days, thereby turning the calendar into a table of contents. The calendar was so innovative and unusual, that it took some time to figure out its intricacies.

Calendars and the Principle of Interchangeable Parts

All late medieval calendars give the dominical letter, *A–G*, for each day of the year (which correspond to the seven days of the week and are reassigned each year, rendering the calendar perpetual), and list saints' days, often with the most important local cults inscribed in red. What differentiates the calendar in Add. 24332 is that many of the saints' names are followed by a Roman numeral. My first thought

---

pp. 123–34; M. A. and R. H. Rouse, '*Statim invenire*: Schools, Preachers and New Attitudes to the Page', in *Renaissance and Renewal in the Twelfth Century*, ed. R. L. Benson and G. Constable (Cambridge, MA, 1982), pp. 201–25, repr. in their *Authentic Witnesses: Approaches to Medieval Texts and Manuscripts* (Notre Dame, Ind: University of Notre Dame Press, 1991), pp. 191–219; M. A. and R. H. Rouse, 'The Development of Research Tools in the Thirteenth Century' also reprinted in *Authentic Witnesses: Approaches to Medieval Texts and Manuscripts* (Notre Dame, Ind: University of Notre Dame Press, 1991), pp. 221–55; M. A. and R. H. Rouse, 'La naissance des index', in *Histoire de l'édition française, I: Le livre conquérant: Du Moyen Âge au milieu du XVIIe siècle* (Paris, Promodis, 1983), 77–85; M. A. and R. H. Rouse, 'Concordances et index', in *Mise en page et mise en texte de livre manuscrit*, ed. H.-J. Martin and J. Vezin (Paris, Éditions du Cercle de la Librairie. Promodis, 1990), pp. 219–28. Although alphabetization is older, scholars from the twelfth century onward had a particular passion for making alphabetized lists. For example, an Italian bat book of the thirteenth century lists medical recipes from 'Antidotum asclepiadeum' to 'Ziriofilos minus' for which see J. P. Gumbert, *Bat Books: A Catalogue of Folded Manuscripts Containing Almanacs or Other Texts*. Bibliologia: Elementa ad Librorum Studia Pertinentia, 41. (Turnhout: Brepols, 2016), p. 38. See also Lloyd W. Daly, *Contributions to a History of Alphabetization in Antiquity and the Middle Ages* (Brussels: Latomus, 1967).

was that these Roman numerals might indicate the phase of the moon or help calculate movable feast days, for this information sometimes appears in medieval calendars.[2] But that was not their function in this manuscript. Trying different angles of attack, I noted that saints listed in black have their Roman numerals in red, while saints in red have their Roman numerals in black, apparently for contrast. This suggested that the Roman numerals have something to do with the saints, rather than with celestial bodies. Furthermore, most of the numerals were between *ccc* and *cccc*: rather than serving any astrological function, they referred to folios. This concept made sense given that the manuscript was foliated at all, for the only reason to foliate a book would have been to key it to some indexing system, such as a contents table; otherwise, there would be no reason to impose such a reference system. This odd feature was one I had noted the very first time I had encountered a folio from the manuscript — the black and white photo representing the St Barbara roundel (discussed in Chapter 1), with its Roman numeral inscribed in the upper margin. The scribe, I speculated, had turned the calendar into a table of contents.

I tested the hypothesis. Under 17 September one finds an entry for St Lambert (*Lambertus buscop*), followed by the Roman numeral *cccc xxij*, and sure enough, there is a prayer to St Lambert on the verso of that folio (fig. 80). In the month of May, a Roman numeral corresponding to St Dymphna sends the reader to fol. *ccc lxv*, where the reader does indeed find a prayer and image for that saint on the verso (fig. 81). So far, so good. But then I tested my theory with 6 February, where one finds an entry for Amandus and Vedast, who were both bishops and confessors, followed by the Roman numeral *cccc xxiiii*. When I turned to that folio, I found a prayer to St Lambrecht on the recto, and the rubric for a prayer to SS Cosmas and Damian on the verso, with no mention of Amandus and Vedast whatsoever. Therefore, the system was more complicated that I had first thought, and I had yet to fully crack it.

---

2   For Netherlandish calendars, see Eef. A. Overgaauw, 'Saints in Medieval Calendars from the Diocese of Utrecht as Clues for the Localization of Manuscripts', *Codices Manuscripti* 16 (1992), pp. 81–97.

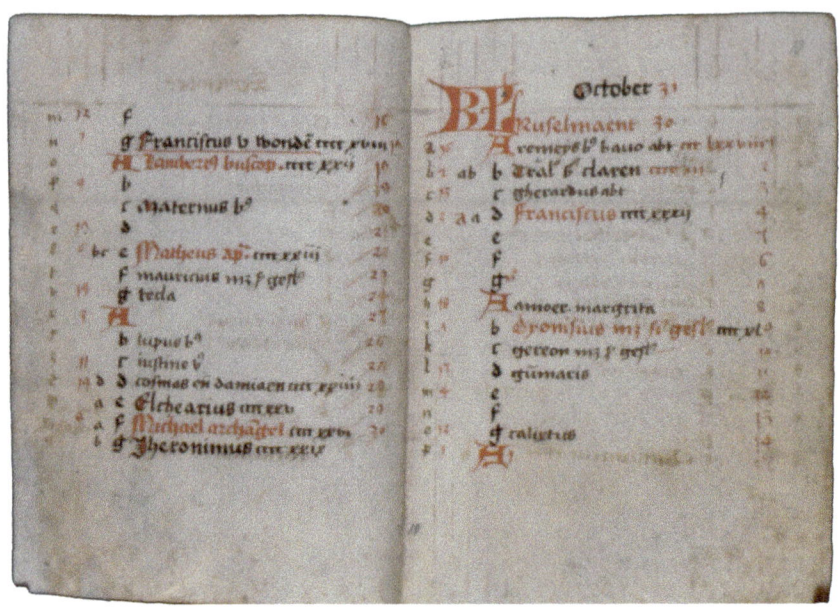

Fig. 80 Calendar in the beghards' book of hours for the end of September and beginning of October. London, British Library, Add. Ms. 24332, fol. 9v–10r.

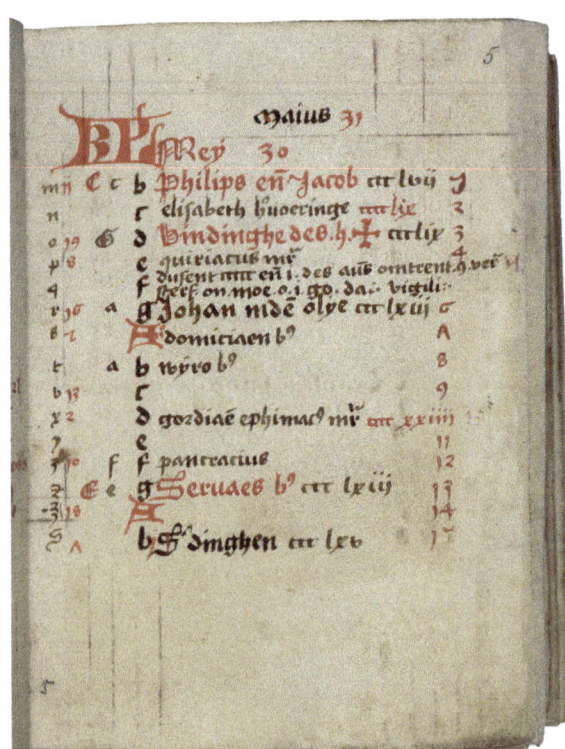

Fig. 81 Calendar in the beghards' book of hours for the beginning of May. London, British Library, Add. Ms. 24332, fol. 5r.

I transcribed the whole calendar, including the Roman numerals, into a spreadsheet (which I later integrated into the Appendix). Calendar entries for Gordian and Epimachus (martyrs); Peter and Marcellinus (martyrs); Primus and Felicianus (martyrs); Vitus and Modestus (martyrs); Quiricus and Julitta (martyrs); Gervasius and Protasius (martyrs); John and Paul (martyrs), and finally, Cosmas and Damian all directed the reader to the same folio: *cccc xxiiii*. What this list of saints all have in common, as you no doubt will have noticed, is that they are all pairs of martyred saints who are celebrated together. When the indexer added the contents table to the calendar, he was indicating that the manuscript specifically did *not* contain prayers dedicated to each of these saints in the calendar, but only to Cosmas and Damian. Anyone who wanted to recite a prayer to those other saints needed only replace the names of Cosmas and Damian with those of, say, Gordian and Epimachus, while reading the prayer on folio *cccc xxiiii*. Therefore, the calendar either directs the reader to the prayers to a specific saint or to the next best possible substitute. The foliation and the table of contents not only saved the user time (because he could more easily turn to the folio with the desired passage or prayer), but they also saved the producer time (because he had only to inscribe one prayer to Cosmas and Damian, omitting prayers to seven other pairs of saints).

Analogous logic is at work throughout the calendar/table of contents. For a prayer appropriate for a male saint who was martyred with a group of friends, the reader is directed to folio *cccc xlv*. Saints in that category include the 10,000 martyrs, the Seven Sleepers, the Seven Brothers, SS Cyriacus, Boniface, Kilian, and Ypolitus, each with his respective companions. This system therefore enabled the scribe to cut his labour considerably, inscribing one prayer instead of seven. Likewise, one finds on folio *ccc xlix* a prayer to the bishop St Ambrose, who provides the model for veneration of other sainted bishops — Valerius, Hilarius, Dierick, Blasius, and Gisbertus. The reader has only to change the names in his head while reading.

Anticipating the reader's lack of familiarity with this new-fangled system, the scribe provided instructions for this calendar in a discursive passage on fol. *ii* (fig. 82):

fol. *ii* (modern foliation 14r): Jheronimus seet in eynre epistolen die hi voer sijnen calendier scrivet dat ghein dach binnen den iaer is sonder iaersdach, daar en sijn vijfdusent martelaren in ghedoet	St Jerome says in one of his epistles that he wrote for his calendar that there is not a single day during the year that does not have an anniversary, in which five thousand martyrs have been killed
Daer om laetse ons eeren mit alre devoecien ende eynicheit, mit psalmen, mit ymmenen, antiffen, versenen, responsen, ende coelecten, ende dancbaerheiden, met vasten, waken, ende wieren, ende haer leven te overdencken, ende nae te volgen, etc.	Therefore, let us honour with all devotion and praise, with psalms, with hymns, antiphons, verses, responses, and collects, and tokens of gratitude, by fasting, keeping vigil, and incensing, and by thinking about the life [of the martyr] and by following him, etc.
Eyn wisinghe om te vinden dat hier nae volcht in deesen boek	*An index in order to find what follows in this book*
Om die devocie te vervecken tot onsen lieven heer ende tot Maria, ende tot allen lieven heilighen, santen ende santinnen ende sonderlinghe daer wi devosie toe hebben, om di te eren soe volghen hier ghetijden, ghebeden ende colecten. Ende dat soect al nae dat ghetael der blader ende die niet en hebben op hen selven, dat nemt int ghemeyn [14v] of van eynighen heilighen die hem ghelijct, verwanlende den naem nae dien heilighen dien ghi eeren wilt.	To awaken the devotion for our dear Lord and to Mary and to all of the dear holy male and female saints, and especially to those to whom we have devotion, to honour them, there follow hours, prayers and collects. And look for it according to the number on the folio and [for] those who do not have one for themselves, take a general [prayer] or take one from a saint that resembles him, and just change the name to the name of the saint you want to honour.

Within the logic of fungibility, if the reader wants to honour a saint who does not have a prayer in the book, he may simply read the prayer to a different saint with a similar set of credentials, and swap the name. This means that the beghards were living with an entire ethos of substitution. This is also, as I showed in the previous chapter, how they treated the prints they deployed in the book — with a practical sense of approximation plus fungibility.

The beghards' calendar demonstrates two things: that the manuscript was a space of technological experimentation (considering the calendar as technology), and that the beghards of Maastricht were not shy about altering the structure and contents of their prayerbooks in the name of efficiency, whether of manufacture or use. This calendar is not unlike the print itself: it is a time-saving technology introduced into an older type of book. On the one hand, the complexity of the calendar indicates the unwieldiness of late medieval devotions. But on the other hand, it shows that beghards were willing to create new adaptations to make their books more usable for prayer, among these the idea that, though saints' days were specific, prayers (and the components of the book in general) could be used interchangeably, within some simple parameters. In short, they turned one indexing system (the calendar, which lays out saints' feasts in twelve spreadsheets) into a different kind (a contents table).

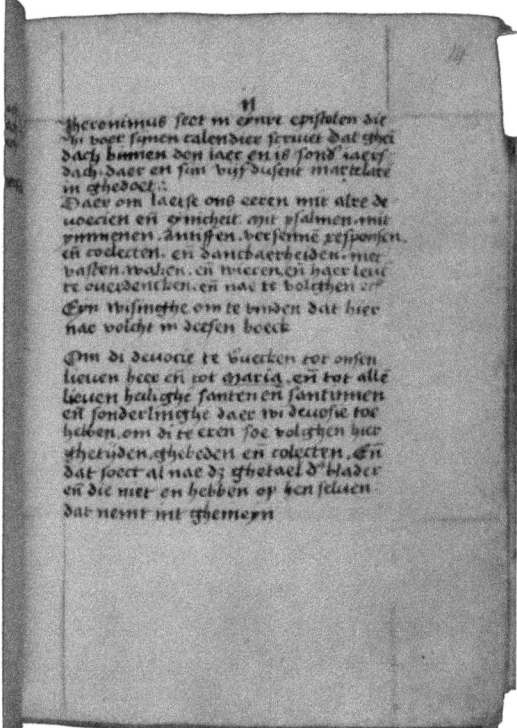

Fig. 82
Explanation of the Table of Contents in the beghards' book of hours. London, British Library, Add. Ms. 24332, fol. ii (modern foliation 14r).

Their newly deployed technology echoes one used elsewhere in the inchoate printing industry: a pair of prints now in Paris reveals that such interchangeability also took place at the level of the prints themselves.

Specifically, printmakers used the same principle to adapt print matrices by having some removable plugs within the block. Such is the case with a pair of prints depicting female saints, Catherine and Mary Magdalene (figs 83a and 83b).[3] The backgrounds of the two prints are identical. Close inspection reveals a disturbance around the torso of Mary Magdalene, which resulted from the unusual experiment in block-cutting represented here: the cutter must have made a background image with a recess where the virgins' upper torsos would go. He could then swap just this component, thereby changing the attribute of the saint, and therefore her identity. Just the section of the matrix with the name, face, and identifying object has changed. This also explains why Mary Magdalene's left hand appears in a strange position: it had to be worked into the matrix plug somehow. Polychromy has helped to distinguish the two images, so that their differences obfuscate their similarities.

Book Technologies and Social Networks

The beghards in Maastricht invented the systems of superimposing a table of contents over a calendar and using substitutions to reduce scribal labour. This is one event in a long development of information technologies belonging to the history of the book. Indeed, they may have learned about this system of organising information because, as I have discussed, they had a bindery, and therefore saw all kinds of book technologies passing through their studios. In particular, the beghards would have been part of several networks, including a network of other Franciscans who were also book producers and users. As with any social network, the beghards shared ideas over a wide geographical swathe, where the various houses (primarily in cities, since Franciscans are primarily urban) form the nodes. Along these network lines are traded ideas about book technology as well as books themselves; texts; prints; gifts; approaches to decorating books; leather, oak boards, and other supplies used in binding manuscripts; and services (including but not limited to copying, decorating, binding, teaching, correcting). Because the beghards in Maastricht had a bindery, they also must have been a large node in a network for bookish exchanges, as people sent them new books and old, falling-apart books for (re)binding. In using prints

---

3   Lepape and Rudy, *Les Origines de l'Estampe*, pp. 62, 66, cat. 28–29.

Fig. 83a
St Catherine, hand-coloured woodcut print, Southern Germany or Swabia. Paris, BnF, Rés. Ea-5 (8)-Boîte (Schreiber 1317/Bouchot 136). Published with kind permission from the Bibliothèque nationale de France.

Fig. 83b
St Mary Magdalene, hand-coloured woodcut print, Southern Germany or Swabia. Paris, BnF, Rés. Ea-5 (8)-Boîte (Schreiber 1594/Bouchot 139). Published with kind permission from the Bibliothèque nationale de France.

in manuscripts, and in using the calendar as a contents table, they were copying (and extending) ideas exploited by others Franciscans who must have been in their network.

Organising information has an intricate history that is bound up with the history of the book itself. The codex is a structure for holding information and making it retrievable. In these tasks the codex far outstrips the roll, as it allows the user to tabulate various kinds of information and to cross-index. Although early medieval secular administrators invented some structures for tabulating and retrieving information, the devices facilitating such finding functions were rather limited until the central Middle Ages, when finding aids became more numerous and varied.[4] Scholastic cultures of the twelfth and thirteenth centuries in particular prompted the advancement of finding aids.[5] For example, thirteenth-century Paris bibles have running headings indicating the book and chapter of the Bible, so that the reader may know where he is in the book and find any text easily.[6]

Early tables of contents in Netherlandish manuscript (with accompanying foliation) appear in books of sermons, as this would enable preachers to find material for sermons more easily. Such is the case of the *Limburg Sermons* (The Hague, KB, Ms. 70 E 5), composed around 1300, as Wybren Scheepsma has discussed.[7] This manuscript had been in the convent of Tertiaries of the Convent Maagdendriesch in Maastricht, and came to the Royal Library as part of the Maastricht Collectie.

---

[4] On early finding aids, see Adam Kosto, 'Statim invenire ante: finding aids and research tools in pre-scholastic legal and administrative manuscripts', *Scriptorium* 70 (2016), pp. 285–309.

[5] In addition to the items by the Rouses listed above in fn 96$, see M. B. Parkes, '"Folia librorum querere": Medieval Experience of the Problem of Hypertext and the Index', originally published in 1995, and republished in *Pages from the Past: Medieval Writing Skills and Manuscript Books*, ed. P. R. Robinson and R. Zim (Farnham: Ashgate, 2012), item X, pp. 23–50; Emily Steiner and Lynn Ransom, eds, *Taxonomies of Knowledge: Information and Order in Medieval Manuscripts* (Philadelphia, PA: The Schoenberg Institute for Manuscript Studies, University of Pennsylvania Libraries, 2015).

[6] Paul Saenger gave a series of three lectures presented on 14, 15, and 17 April, 2008 in the Rosenwald Gallery of the Van Pelt Library, University of Pennsylvania on 'The Latin Bible as Codex'.

[7] For many examples, see Wybren Scheepsma, *De Limburgse Sermoenen (ca. 1300): De Oudste Preken in het Nederlands*, Nederlandse Literatuur en Cultuur in de Middeleeuwen (Amsterdam: B. Bakker, 2005), translated as Wybren Scheepsma, *The Limburg Sermons: Preaching in the Medieval Low Countries at the Turn of the Fourteenth Century*, Brill's Series in Church History (Leiden; Boston: Brill, 2008).

One can easily see why someone would want to index sermons in this way: no one would read a book of sermons from cover to cover but, rather, to retrieve a particular sermon for a particular purpose. It is not coincidental that such book technologies as foliation accompany the rise of the preaching orders.

In a secular context, given the nature of their content, histories and chronicles were often given tables of contents. As with all reference works, a reader might dip into relevant sections. Jacob van Maerlaent, one of the first vernacular poets of Middle Dutch, even wrote a rhyming table of contents as a preface to his *Nature Bloemen*. One can imagine that a courtly audience would appreciate an aural performance of the new technology in advance of hearing particular sections read aloud.[8]

Jan van Emmerick embraced new forms of information organising, and he imposed such structures on several of the manuscripts he played a part in writing, such as the beghards' cartulary (Maastricht, RHCL, 14.D015, inv. no. 6). In 1500, only the first few folios of the book had been inscribed, and the rest of the 92-folio book was blank, but then Jan started working on it. He started a table of contents, and then foliated it with roman numerals, furnishing all of the blank pages — all 93 of them — with numbers, even though when he was using it, it was still close to an empty, blank book. He was foliating the future.

Contents tables are a rarity in books of hours because they were not part of the standard apparatus for this genre of book: people navigated their books of hours primarily through the hierarchy of decoration, and with spatial clues. It is doubly rare for an original table of contents to survive, because they are made separately; the few that were made were especially vulnerable during rebinding. Apart from Add. 24332 and one closely related example I shall discuss shortly, I know of no other books of hours with contents tables and only a few prayerbooks that are foliated but have lost their tables of contents.[9] An example of the latter is The Hague, KB, Ms. 135 E 36, a book of hours in Latin and Dutch assembled over the course of decades from c. 1400 until c. 1450 and now

---

8   Although Joyce Coleman writes about aurality in England and France, her conclusions are also valid for the Netherlands. See her *Public Reading and the Reading Public in Late Medieval England and France* (Cambridge: Cambridge University Press, 1996).

9   Another manuscript prayerbook with original foliation that emerged in the course of this study, is Add. 31002, for which see Chapter 3.

in a binding from c. 1500. Parts of the manuscript are in different styles, some from the Southern Netherlands or northern France, some from the Eastern Netherlands, and some miniatures probably from Utrecht.[10] One of the segments comprising this convolute bears original foliation in red ink (fig. 84).

Fig. 84 Book of hours with original foliation reading lvii (although it has lost its table of contents). The Hague, Koninklijke Bibliotheek, Ms. 135 E 36, fol. 45v–46r. http://manuscripts.kb.nl/zoom/BYVANCKB%3Amimi_135e36%3A045v_046r

It has been integrated into the dense marginal decoration of the recto side of each leaf. On fol. 46r, for example, a paraplegic beggar rests on a pair of makeshift wooden clogs while urgently ringing bells to get attention. Inadvertently, he calls attention to the number *lvii* just above his head. Unfortunately, parts of this manuscript have been lost, and the contents table that presumably once ordered these folio numbers has not survived.

As tables of contents do not usually appear in prayerbooks, the presence of one in Add. 24332 requires some explanation and

---

10 For a study of manuscripts assembled from components, sometimes from different times and places, see Kathryn M. Rudy, *Piety in Pieces: How Medieval Readers Customized Their Manuscripts* (Cambridge: Open Book Publishers, 2016), https://doi.org/10.11647/OBP.0094; https://www.openbookpublishers.com/product/477

contextualisation. It reveals something about the late medieval organisation of information, the spread of ideas, and the intellectual milieu of the book's makers. Although unprecedented for a book of hours, the concept of turning a calendar into a table of contents was also not new. Some other types of books — besides books of hours — contain perpetual calendars, and therefore provide opportunities for such tables. One example is the *Golden Legend*, Jacobus de Voragine's compilation of miracle stories, assembled in the thirteenth century and recopied throughout the late Middle Ages. Originally, the stories were arranged in order of the liturgical calendar, so that the book could be read from cover to cover and the readings would correspond to the sequence of the saints celebrated during the year. Therefore, copies of the manuscript were often made with a calendar preceding the text.

A Middle Dutch copy of the *Golden Legend*, made by a male Franciscan tertiary in Amsterdam, has a contents table layered over the calendar: The Hague, KB, Ms. 73 D 9 (fig. 85). Copies of the *Golden Legend* are usually so large that they are split into two halves, and the relevant halves of the calendar also distributed logically. This enormous copy contains only the second half of the year, the so-called 'summer part', with readings corresponding to saints' days from July to December. As one would expect, the calendar/contents has been made on a separate quire (folios IIr–IIIr), but written at the same time and by the same hand as the rest of the manuscript. Brother Peter, the scribe of this *Golden Legend*, signed his name in a colophon on folio *cclix*.[11] He notes that he was a member of the monastery of St Paul in Amsterdam (confusingly also called the Sint-Georgiusklooster), within the Third Order of St Francis, and he also dates his work 1450. He made the book for the female tertiaries of St Margaret either in Amsterdam or Haarlem. Brother Peter therefore may have first invented the use of the calendar as a table of contents; I know of no earlier examples.

---

11 Under the entry for August, the scribe has noted 'Int iaer ons heren m cccc ende lx starf Aed Dirc Claeser wijf'. The colophon on fol. *cclix* indicates that it was copied by Brother Peter from the Tertians of St Paul ('Dit boec heeft ghescreven broeder peter priester des convents st pouwels vander derder oerden st Franciscus. Ende tis gheeindet int iaer ons heren m cccc ende l in die maent augustus op st Bernaerts dach. Biddet om gods willen voir den scriver'. See Margriet Hülsmann, 'Gedecoreerde Handschriften uit Tertiarissenconventen in Amsterdam en Haarlem: Boekenbezit versus Boekproductie', *Ons geestelijk erf* 74, nos. 1-2 (2000), pp. 153–80.

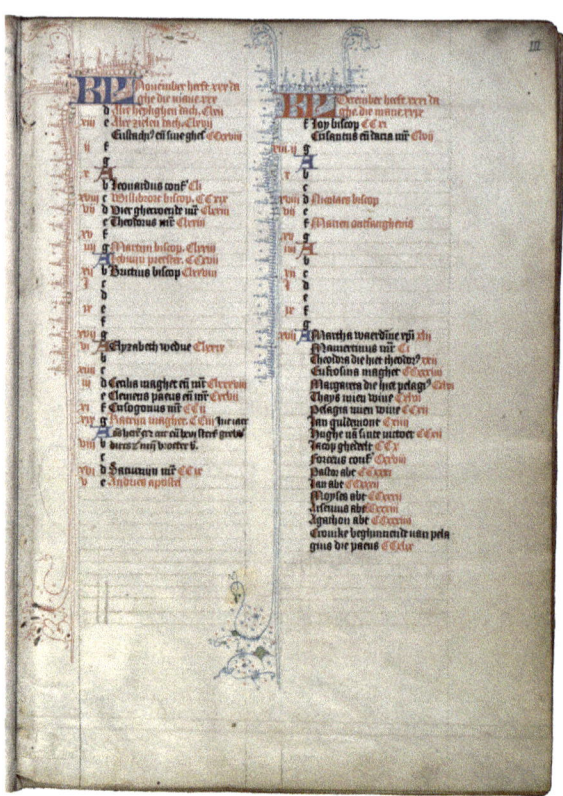

Fig. 85
Calendar in a Golden Legend turned into table of contents: months of November and December, Amsterdam, 1450. The Hague, Koninklijke Bibliotheek, Ms. 73 D 9, fol. IIIr.

Analysing the month of November reveals just why the contents table was useful. All Saints' Day (1 November), directs the reader to folio *clxii*, and All Souls' Day (2 November) follows logically on the next folio (*clxvii*), where the reader will find readings relevant to those feasts. But the feast day after that, celebrating *Eustachius ende sine ghesellen* (Eustace and his companions), directs its reader to folio *ccxxviii*, out of calendrical order. The reason for this concerns the text's distant origin. When the *Golden Legend* was compiled in France in around 1260, the individual stories were copied in the order that they would be celebrated in the calendar; however, the sequences of local saints changed per region and were different in other regions. For example, Willibrort (9 November) and Lebuin (13 November), two saints especially revered in the Northern Netherlands, were venerated on different days from those in the French prototype. In the calendar/table of contents in KB 73 D 9, the folio numbers corresponding to these saints are therefore out of sequence with the other saints venerated in November. Even more telling is the group of saints under 31 December, not because they were all to be fêted on New Year's Eve, but because these names corresponded to saints whose *Lives* were included in earlier (French) redactions of the *Golden Legend*: these saints were not especially venerated in the Northern Netherlands, and therefore did not have feast days in the Dutch calendar. These stragglers include 'Margaret who is called Pelagius' (*Margareta die hiet Pelagius*) and Hugh of St Victor. The latter was a twelfth-century theologian and writer but was never canonised or venerated in any way. He was the main proponent of the Victorines. This category of misfits also included one more entry that the copyist had to include somewhere: a chronicle beginning with Pope Pelagius (*Cronike beghinnende van Pelagius die paeus*), copied at the very end of the *Golden Legend*, on folio *ccxlix*. All these texts are relegated to 31 December, because there was no organic place for them in a Northern Netherlandish calendar, but they had to go somewhere.

Fig. 86
Folio in a Golden Legend showing original foliation in the upper border, Amsterdam, 1450. The Hague, Koninklijke Bibliotheek, Ms. 73 D 9, fol. 179r.

One more technical point illuminates how scribes produced contents tables. On folio 179r of the *Golden Legend*, the Roman numeral overlaps the penwork (fig. 86), which means that the foliation was done after the decoration. For the *Golden Legend*, foliation was the penultimate step and adding the folio numbers to the calendar was the final step. This fact is important for my interpretation of the Add. 24332.

Significantly, these ideas about organising and indexing information seem to have originated and been transmitted in Franciscan circles. This preaching order, after all, was working in cities among people who were merchants, who had a high degree of numeracy, and who were organising information to maximise profits. Beghards in Maastricht made Add. 24332 about 50 years after their Franciscan brethren copied the *Golden Legend* in Amsterdam; in Maastricht they applied the same thinking to their book of hours, when they superimposed a table of contents on the existing calendar. Despite the logic of combining these two different indexing systems, the idea never really took hold in other places, although the Franciscan beghards of Maastricht continued to use and develop these ideas into the sixteenth century.

These examples demonstrate that there were in fact manuscripts with original foliation and tables of contents before the beghards applied these ideas to Add. 24332 in 1500, but they applied them to a different kind of manuscript, the book of hours. In addition to the calendar, which indexes the folio numbers of the texts containing prayers to saints listed in the calendar, the beghards also wrote a separate table of contents. It appears on fol. 15r, after the calendar (fig. 87). The texts that the book contains, as well as its organisation, finding aids, and other meta-textual components, reveal much about the intended audience.

The Table of Contents in Add. 24332, Transcribed and Translated

Text	Original folio	Translation
Ten yersten dat pater noster, ende den Ave Maria ende den Credo	v	(First) Pater Noster, Ave Maria, Credo
Alsmen dat hl sacrament op heffet	vi, vcxii, vcxv	Prayers to say during the elevation of the host

2. A Novel Function for the Calendar in Add. Ms. 24332   183

Text	Original folio	Translation
Die benediste ende gracie	vi	Benediction and grace before meals
Den Confiteor	xii	The Confiteor
Den miserere, deprofondis, salve	xvi	Psalms 129 & 130, the Salve Regina
Ghebet totten hemelschen vader	xxii	Prayer to God
Ghebet tot Joachim ende Anna	xxiii, xxiiii, xxv	Prayer to Mary's parents
Eyn groet tot Maria	xxvi	Greeting to Mary
Dat roesenkrensken	xxvii	Rosary devotion
v grueten tot Maria x doechden	xxxviii, xliii	Five greetings to Mary's virtues
Eyn ander roesenkrensken	xliiii	Another rosary
v vervrouwen van Maria	lxv	Five Joys of Mary
v grueten totten v wonden ons heeren	lxvii	Five greetings to the Five Wounds of our Lord
Eyn offeringe op alle gebeden	lxxiii	An offering to all prayers
Die cruisgheteijden cort ende scoen	lxxv	The short and beautiful Hours of the Cross
Die vii ghetijden vanden hl gheist		The Seven Hours of the Holy Spirit
Metten	xci	Matins
Pr[ime]	cxxiii	Prime
T[erce]	clxiii [etc]	Terce
[Sext]	clxxi	Sext
[Nones]	clxxvii	Nones
[Vespers]	ccxxxviii	Vespers

Text	Original folio	Translation
[Compline]	cclii	Compline
Die vij ghetijden van onse vrouwen		The Seven Hours of Our Lady
Die metten	xcvij	Matins
Priem	cxxvij	Prime
Die vij salmen	cxxxiiij	The Seven Penitential Psalms
Letany	cxlvij	Litany of the Saints
Terce	clxvi	Terce
Sex	clxxiij	Sext
Noen	clxxix	Nones
Die vigili	clxxxiiij	Vigil for the Dead
Vesper	ccxliij	Vespers
compeleet	cclv	Compline
Eyn ghebet op di ghetiden	cclxij	A prayer to the hours
Van aeflaet te verdienen	cclxiij	On indulgences to earn
Bernardus gebet voerden hl +	cclxvij	Prayer of St Bernard before the Holy Cross
xiiij grueten tot onsen here	cclxxix	Fourteen greetings to Our Lord
Dri deprecor	cc lxxxi	Three Deprecors
Die vij ghetiden van Maria liden	cclxxxiiij	The Seven Hours of Mary's Suffering
Eng gebet tot onsen [heer]	cclxxxviij	A Prayer to our Lord
Dri pater noster	cclxxxix	Three Pater Nosters
noch dri	cc xc	Three more Pater Nosters
Hier volghen die ghebeden vanden heilighen ende sonderlinghe vanden heilighen diemen wiert ende sommige vernoemde heiligen		Here follow the prayers for the saints and especially for the saints that one venerates and some named saints.

As its contents table lays out, this book might be appropriate for a number of audiences, including children and those new to reading. Although tables of contents are rare in prayerbooks, one exception is The Hague, KB, Ms. 133 F 2, which is an instructional manual made for a child in Ghent in the mid-sixteenth century.[12] Such finding aids and didactic explanations ('how to use this book') are associated with materials made for children.

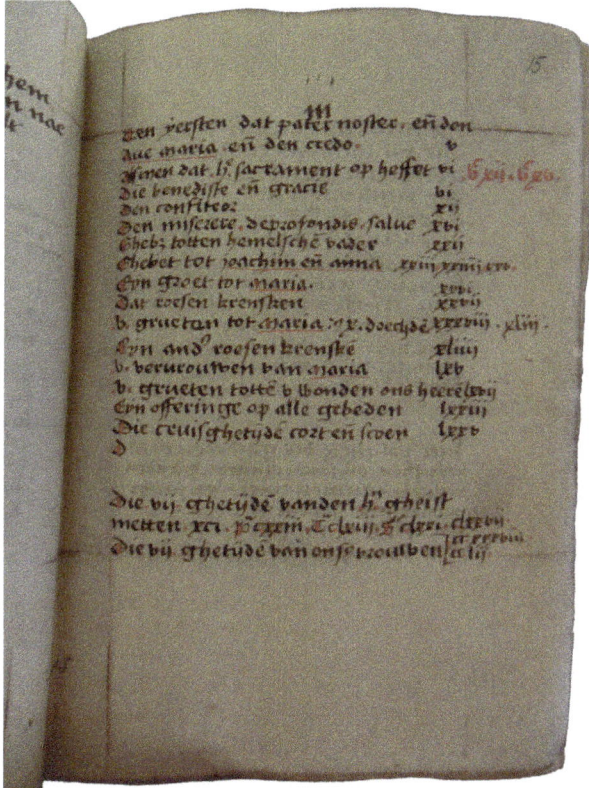

Fig. 87
Table of contents in the beghards' book of hours. London, British Library, Add. Ms. 24332, fol. 14v-15r.

---

12 M. H. Porck and H. J. Porck, 'Eight Guidelines on Book Preservation from 1527: How One Should Preserve All Books to Last Eternally', *Journal of Paper Conservation* 13:2 (2012), pp. 17–25.

A Book for Children

Several clues about the function and original audience of the manuscript are provided by its contents: it was a book for school children or young learners. The manuscript begins with the Pater Noster, Ave Maria, and Credo (formerly folio *v*, fol. 26r; fig. 88), along with the other items listed at the top of the Contents, all of which are texts that were used to teach reading and at the same time inculcate new learners with tenets of the faith.[13] A neophyte reader would have been able to parse the Latin texts without the hurdle of abbreviations, because the scribe wrote these texts in full, itself a further indication that they functioned here as teaching texts. They do have heavily abbreviated Middle Dutch rubrics, suggesting that they were geared towards readers who had already mastered some degree of vernacular literacy but did not yet know Latin.

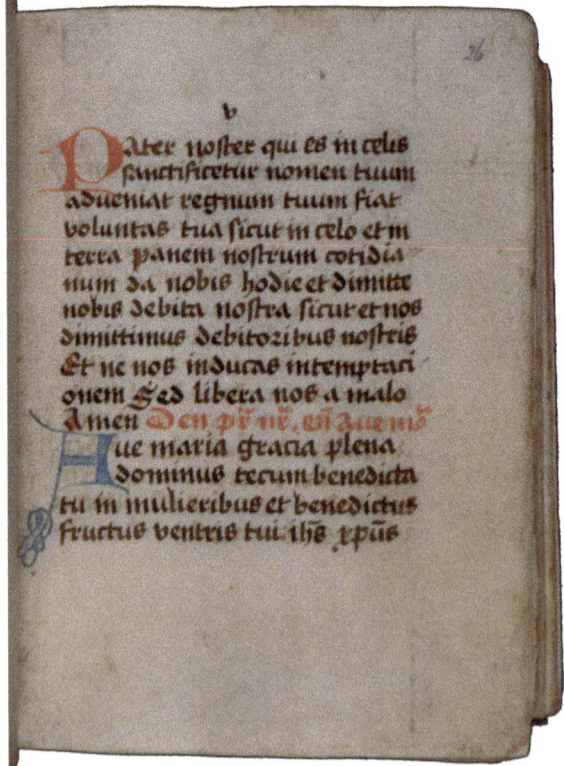

Fig. 88
Folio in the beghards' book of hours, with the Pater Noster, and beginning of Ave Maria. London, British Library, Add. Ms. 24332, fol. 26r.

---

13   For manuscripts made for children, see Kathryn A. Smith, 'The Neville of Hornby Hours and the Design of Literate Devotion', *The Art Bulletin* 81, no. 1 (1999), pp. 72–92;

To help the novice reader more, several of the texts near the beginning of Add. 24332 are given in bilingual editions. As the Contents indicates, the *Confiteor* begins on folio *xii* (fol. 33v). Remarkably, the Latin prayer text is interlineated with a rubricated Middle Dutch translation of the prayer.[14] These interlineated texts were probably used as teaching aids, and Franciscan ones at that: St Francis is mentioned in the *Confiteor*. Other bilingual texts that the Franciscan teachers deemed appropriate include 'Die benedicite' (The Benediction, fols 27v–28v), a prayer to the sacrament, 'Totten avontmael des ewichs' (To the eternal evening meal, fol. 28v), and a prayer to be read at collation, 'Alsmen colaci drinct' (fol. 33r). Here *colaci* (collation) may refer to a custom of reading in the refectory together with a *caritas* (drink) on Saturdays. These prayers appear on folios ruled so that Latin words appear in large black letters and vernacular words in smaller red ones. Finally, the *Pater Noster, Ave*, and *Credo* are then supplied in the vernacular, beginning on fol. 65r, as if providing a translation of the most basic prayers for the faith were an afterthought, and its inclusion necessary to ensure that learners got it right. These basic prayers and bilingual teaching texts are confined to quires near the beginning of the codex.

In fact, few bilingual instructional books survive from the late Middle Ages. One of these is a book of hours written in Latin in red, with phrase by phrase translations in English in black (Glasgow, Hunterian Museum, Ms. H512, fols 32v and 33r; fig. 89). This book likewise begins with the *Pater Noster, Ave Maria*, and *Credo*, which further mark its function as a book for teaching children the rudiments of reading and the faith. The Glasgow manuscript also contains vernacular religious poetry, on which the rubricator drew lines to connect the rhyming lines

---

Nicholas Orme, *Medieval Children* (New Haven, CT; London: Yale University Press, 2001); Roger S. Wieck, 'Special Children's Books of Hours in the Walters Art Museum', in *Als Ich Can: Liber Amicorum in Memory of Professor Dr. Maurits Smeyers*, ed. by Bert Cardon, Jan van der Stock, Dominique Vanwijnsberghe and Katharina Smeyers. Corpus of Illuminated Manuscripts = Corpus van Verluchte Handschriften, pp. 1629–39 (Leuven: Peeters, 2002); Kathryn A. Smith, *Art, Identity, and Devotion in Fourteenth-Century England: Three Women and Their Books of Hours* (London: British Library and University of Toronto Press, 2003); Kathryn M. Rudy, 'An Illustrated Mid-Fifteenth-Century Primer for a Flemish Girl: British Library, Harley Ms 3828', *Journal of the Warburg and Courtauld Institutes* 69 (2006), pp. 51–94.

14   For interlineal glosses, see Malcolm Beckwith Parkes, '*Folia librorum quaerere*: Medieval experience of the problem of hypertext and the index', originally published in 1995 and republished in his *Pages from the Past: Medieval Writing Skills and Manuscript Books*, ed. Pamela R. Robinson and Rivkah Zim (Farnham: Ashgate, 2012), Chapter X, pp. 23–50, and Plates I-VIII, esp. pp. 25–26, with further references.

in the stanzas, no doubt to make manifest the rhyming structure of the prayer. In a different, earlier manuscript, the Maastricht beghards had used a similar approach to teach: they copied two Lives of St Servatius (the patron of Maastricht) into a single manuscript now preserved in Leiden University Library (Ms. BPL 1215).[15] One copy is in Latin prose and the other in Middle Dutch verse. Although they do not present a line-by-line translation, the tandem set seems to form a study book for students, as the contents themselves, plus some circumstantial evidence, suggest. A note on the final flyleaf written in fifteenth-century script

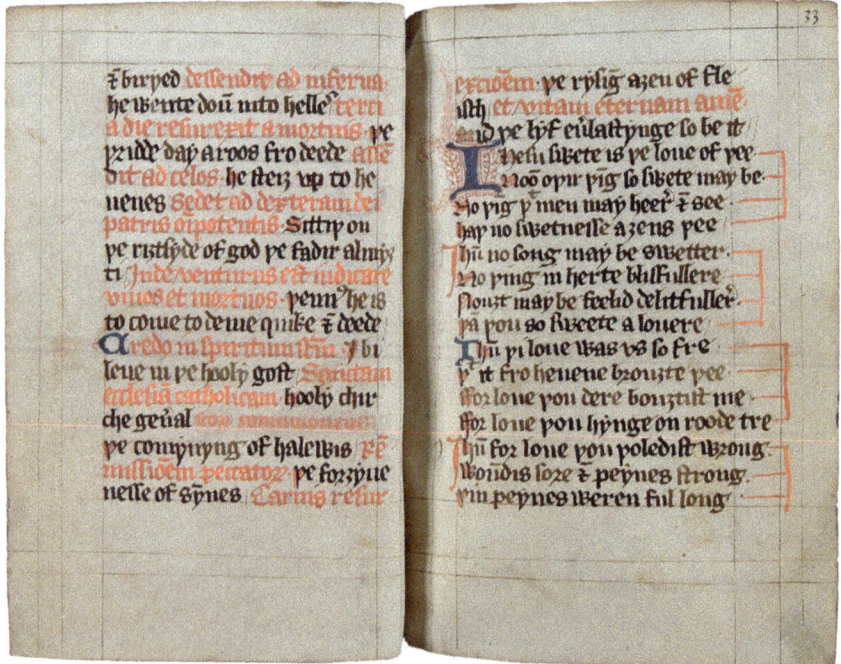

Fig. 89 Opening in an English book of hours, in English and Latin, and with red lines to mark rhyming lines of poetry. Glasgow, University Library, Ms. Hunter, H512, fol. 32v-33r.

indicates that Hendrick Lenssen owned the book; he was a teacher in the beghards' school. The beghards engaged in a variety of teaching practices and must have used various volumes to do so. Techniques

---

15   Geert Warnar, 'Servatius in School', *Omslag: Bulletin van de Universiteitsbibliotheek Leiden en het Scaliger Instituut* 3 (2010). For further bibliography, visit the Bibliotheca Neerlandica Manuscripta BNM website https://bnm-i.huygens.knaw.nl/ and search for 'BPL 1215'.

deployed in their books reveal, for example, that they wrote instructions to the users, provided simultaneous translations, and, in the case of Add. 24332, peppered their books with attractive printed images.

How to use a book is one of the lessons on offer. The scribe was apparently aware that tables of contents were a rarity in medieval books, and that the book's user might require instructions. Studying the unusual table of contents in Add. 24332 reveals the book to be the product of combining multiple innovations for a particular purpose.

If the contents table forms one new finding aid in prayerbooks, then the abundant prints are another. The Franciscans set out to make the most navigable manuscript they could. In Add. 24332 the prints, as all imagery and decoration in manuscripts, can be considered as finding aids, since the presence of a print signposts a text related to the figure or event depicted in the print. Prints are usually (but not always) pasted at the beginning of a section; in that way, they help the reader find the beginning of the passage and therefore enhance the function of the contents table by providing a second quick visual way of finding information within the dense manuscript. Prints were an adaptable and cheap way to make the book a more effective tool.

Jan van Emmerick

There is an especially organised mind behind the construction of Add. 24332, who guided several people that worked on it. One of these people appears in the section beginning on folio 27v, which is a peculiar bilingual text: it consists of common prayers written in Latin in black letters, with an interlineated translation in smaller red script (fig. 90). This section, which continues til fol. 37r, was designed for teaching students to read Latin, and consists of prayers to read before meals, in addition to the Confiteor.[16] Unusually, the Confiteor makes particular mention of St Francis: the beghards created opportunities to insinuate their patron into lessons and prayers. The same hand that made the interlineal translations also foliated the manuscript at the top recto of (nearly) every folio, partly wrote the table of contents, inscribed the

---

16   Anne Rudloff Stanton, 'The Psalter of Isabelle, Queen of England 1308–1330: Isabelle as the Audience', *Word & Image: A Journal of Verbal/Visual Enquiry* 18, no. 4 (2002), pp. 1–27. also discusses a bilingual manuscript that was clearly intended for learning Latin.

letters into the calendar and added many saints, either in red or in a slightly watery brownish ink. This scribe was not only involved in teaching students how to read, as evidenced by this bilingual text, but also how to use a book, if one is to judge by his adapted calendar. This is the hand of Jan van Emmerick, a Franciscan beghard first mentioned at the beginning of Chapter 1. Despite my best effort to resist this, I have fallen into the pit of the nineteenth-century cult of the genius by attributing greatness to one of the figures in this monastery whom I can identify.

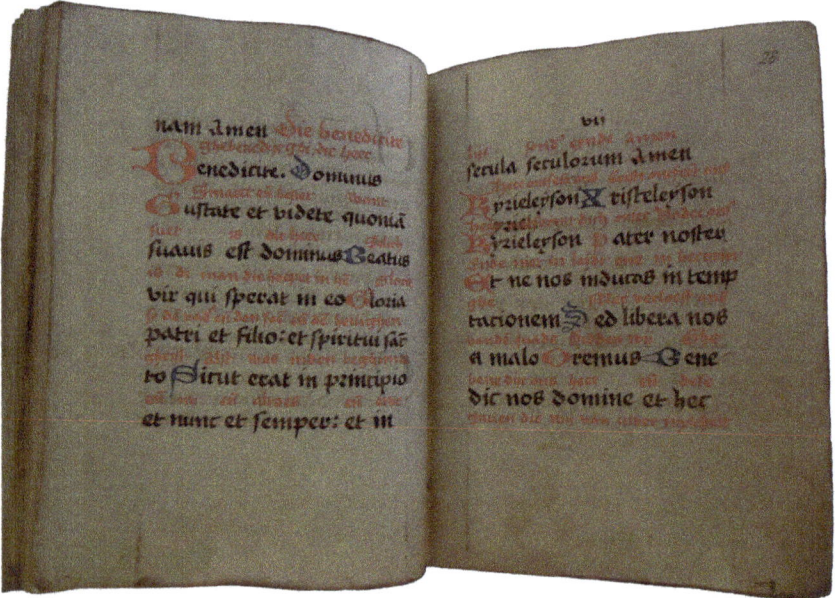

Fig. 90 Opening in the beghards' book of hours: the beginning of the benediction, with interlineal rubricated translation. London, British Library, Add. Ms. 24332, fol. 27v-28r (modern foliation).

A number of manuscripts from the Maastricht Franciscans ended up with the Minderbroeders in Weert in the heart of Limburg. After I left the Netherlands, my opportunities to visit out of the way museums dwindled, but eventually one did arrive. In June 2016 I delivered the keynote lecture at the Rijksmuseum in Amsterdam at a conference about the uses and transformations of early printing (fig. 91). There I presented this project and afterwards took a train to Weert to study the group of books given by the Franciscans to the Gemeentemuseum Jacob van

Horne. As the museum is not equipped for readers, the curator set me up in their main exhibition space, where, surrounded by manuscripts, I became part of the exhibition (fig. 92).

Fig. 91 Symposium at Rijksmuseum, Amsterdam, June 2016.

Fig. 92 Weert, Gemeentemuseum Jacob van Horne, Museum interior in 2016.

Jan van Emmerick signed his name in some of the manuscripts on which he worked. He was probably born around 1440, joined the beghards around 1460, and worked in the scriptorium of the beghards' house when he was in his twenties. He probably started out as a scribe, and copied many manuscripts in the 1460s and 70s, a few of which survive. One of his signed books is a copy in Middle Dutch of David van Augsburg's *Profectus religiosorum*, now in Cambridge.[17] Jan wrote part of this manuscript, and signed and dated it (1466) on folio 204r: 'Hier eyndet dat ander boeck van profecten. Ende is volscreven inden jaer ons heren doen men screef .M.CCCC ende lxvi, op sinte peters ende pouwels avont per manum fratris iohannis test natus de embrica presbiter'. That same year, 1466, he copied Hendrik Herp's *Spiegel der volcomenheit*.[18] Thus, he could copy both Latin and vernacular books. He also finished writing manuscripts that others had begun, such as a prayerbook with texts by Jordanus van Quedlinburg: in 1473 Jan van Emmerick wrote folios 113r–266v of that manuscript, then signed and dated the colophon on folio 266v: This book was finished in the year of our lord 1473 in the month of August on St Sixtus's day.[19] One of the most important manuscripts he copied in this period was a great Latin missal, now in Stonyhurst, Lancashire. He signed and dated this manuscript (1472) in a colophon on the final folio.[20]

There are no known manuscripts copied by his hand dating from the 1480s or 90s, when Jan van Emmerick was in his thirties and forties. Perhaps he worked as a corrector during this period. Perhaps he taught in the school that the beghards ran, teaching reading in Latin and the

---

17 Cambridge, HUL, Ms. Lat. 268. Manuscript on parchment, 223 ff, 205 x 145 (150 x 95) mm, 1 column with 27-29 lines. Seymour de Ricci, *Census of Medieval and Renaissance Manuscripts in the United States and Canada*, 3 vols. (New York: H. W. Wilson, 1935–1940), p. 1017; Jan Deschamps, *Middelnederlandse Handschriften uit Europese en Amerikaanse Bibliotheken: Tentoonstelling ter Gelegenheid van het Honderdjarig Bestaan van de Koninklijke Zuidnederlandse Maatschappij voor Taal- en Letterkunde en Geschiedenis, Brussel, Koninklijke Bibliotheek Albert I, 24 Okt.-24 Dec. 1970: Catalogus*, 2nd edn (Leiden: Brill, 1972), pp. 204, 214, 216; Stooker and Verbeij, no. 870.

18 Weert, *Minderbroeders*, p. 10.

19 'Dit boec waert gheeent inden Jaer ons heren Mcccc lxxiii inden maent augusti op sinte Sixtus dach'. Weert, Minderbroeders, Ms. 12.

20 Stonyhurst, Great College, Ms. 4, fol. 295v: 'Item Missale istud scriptum est in conventu fratrum tercii ordinis sancti Francisci opidi traiectensis per manus fratris iohannis presbiteri de embrica. ad summe individueque trinitatis honorem. Anno M° cccc° lxxii°'. See N. R. Ker et al, *Medieval Manuscripts in British Libraries*, 5 vols. (Oxford: Clarendon Press, 1969–2002), pp. 374–76.

vernacular to pupils, and perhaps he ran the bindery. As is evident from his distinctive handwriting, Jan corrected a Middle Dutch *Leven van Jezus* (Life of Christ) copied by him, the Servaas copyist, and Adam de Beecke in 1459 and 1466, as mentioned in Chapter 1.[21] He corrected other manuscripts copied by the Servaas copyist, such as one now in The Hague, KB, as well as an undated Middle Dutch translation of the *Letters of Jerome*[22] and an undated Middle Dutch translation of Cassianus's *Collationes patrum*.[23] He often worked in conjunction with the 'Servaas copyist', who was certainly also a beghard in Maastricht and who copied the Servaas codex now in Leiden, mentioned earlier. For example, Jan's hand can be seen at work in the margins of The Hague, KB, Ms. 133 D 29, folio 92r, a Middle Dutch translation of the Epistles of Paul. Assuming that Jan van Emmerick was born around 1440, he was about 60 years old at the time he participated in writing Add. 24332. What is extraordinary is that, even at this advanced age, he was willing to dive into the new technology of printmaking to enhance his manuscript.

The beghards were piling organisational and finding aids into this book. Some were material, some conceptual. Some involved glue, others involved complicated instructions. Finally, another set of residues points to another system for idea retrieval. Specifically, the page with St John on Patmos (e-fig. 32)[24] reveals yet another way in which the beghards enhanced the book's usability. They did not stop with the table of contents, the foliation, the extensive application of prints: this page originally had a tab for easy finding when the book was closed. Like the rest of the book, the tab was made of paper. Although it has not survived, its stain on the page in the outer margin are clear. Using any means possible, the book's scribes set out to make the textual contents attractive and easy to find. In fact, gluing in these tabs utilised some of the same materials and techniques that were used in combining manuscript and print: cutting specific shapes with a knife, and gluing them into a precise location. This finding aid made it possible to navigate the book with one's fingertips.

---

21 Weert, Minderbroeders, Ms. 9.
22 Brussels, Bollandists' Library, Ms. 494.
23 Weert, Minderbroeders, Ms. 11.
24 Leaf from the beghards' book of hours, with an engraving depicting St John on Patmos. London, British Museum, Department of Prints & Drawings, inv. 1861,1109.670. https://www.britishmuseum.org/research/collection_online/search.aspx?searchText=1861,1109.670

Conclusions

In addition to its emphatic use of prints, the manuscript is interesting because it has tools for organising and indexing the information found within the codex, namely, an unusual calendar with finding aids, a table of contents, and a list of activities for which indulgences are granted. The beghards who made the book were innovators not only in the sourcing and use of prints but also in the imposition of information retrieval systems. Some of these systems bear a structural resemblance to printing itself: performing an action once in order to produce multiple benefits. Just as a printer could cut one matrix of, say, St John the Evangelist, and yield 250–400 copies of that print, here the scribes were writing one prayer to, say, a female virgin with companions, which they could deploy for many different situations. Moreover, the beghards could use multiple copies of the same print, and make slight adjustments to it by trimming slightly here, or adding an attribute there, to change the identities of the pictured saint. All these examples explore ways to squeeze more efficiency out of a system.

By recognising these flexible systems, one can see that the manuscript reveals much about fifteenth-century category formation and classification systems, just as the contents of the BM boxes reveal something of the nineteenth-century mentality, and the current online catalogue of the BM is based on those nineteenth-century models of intellectual organisation that it inherited. But, in fact, the ingenious systems present in the codex only become visible when the entire codex is treated as a whole system, with its folios, foliation, prayers, (adjusted) prints, table of contents, and instructions. The whole is much greater than the sum of its parts.

Add. 24332 is a book of hours, nominally, with many other texts that seem to meet a specific pedagogic need: to teach a neophyte reader how to read (beginning with the *Pater Noster*), how to recognise saints and their attributes, how to appreciate the Franciscan saints in particular, and, more abstractly, how to use a book. All this learning would have taken place in the Franciscans' house on the Witmakersstraat. Connecting their house on their small street were rivers and roads that led to printmakers, who supplied the beghards with their new wares, and to other Franciscan houses. The beghards of Maastricht had access to this labour-saving system of information management, I believe, because they belonged to a network of Franciscans who traded books and ideas. And the brothers on the Witmakersstraat made themselves essential in these processes by offering their services as book makers and as bookbinders. Their importance continued in the sixteenth century, as the next chapter chronicles.

3. The Beghards in the Sixteenth Century

One day in 2006 when I had called up the print of St Mark (643, see fig. 37) in the BM's paper mine, another rich vein presented itself. I worked this vein in the same sessions as pursuing the mother lode of Add. 24332. In the nineteenth century, curators mounted duplicate prints from the same matrix onto the same matte, side by side, so that they could be compared. After all, Heinrich Wölfflin (1864–1945) — the art historian who had pioneered the use of dual projectors in classrooms, so that related images could mutually emphasise each other's similarities and differences — had shaped how the study of images would be taught. This had far-reaching consequences for how they would be stored and displayed, too. An example was the matte I had before me. Stuck to it was a print accessioned on 9 November 1861 from the beghards' manuscript. It depicted St Mark but contained signs that a beghard had tampered with it: he had added what looked like a red kiosk to the otherwise empty area on the horizon line. This refashioned print of St Mark appeared on the matte with its twin, a print made from the same plate. This other print, which had been accessioned on 14 November 1868, had been treated differently. It had no extra lion stuck to it, no red penwork frame, and was instead painted with colour washes.[1] What route had this print followed to land in the museum? It was time to return to the Register — the great handwritten ledger in which curators

---

1   As David S. Areford shows in *The Viewer and the Printed Image in Late Medieval Europe, Visual Culture in Early Modernity* (Farnham, England and Burlington, VT: Ashgate, 2010), such interventions turn mechanically reproduced images into unica.

had inscribed new acquisitions in the nineteenth century — this time for the volume dated 1868.

Tracing this print to its original manuscript took me on a journey that led back to Maastricht, once again. St Mark came from a manuscript that provides a snapshot of the beghards 25 years later and provides insights into how they changed over that period. The beghards' early experiment with prints around 1500 had blossomed into a mania by 1525. They also developed their initial calendar-cum-table of contents and systematized it in the later book. I argued earlier that the beghards were interested in prints because prints allowed them to produce highly illustrated manuscripts with little skill. But this later example demonstrates another reason why they were enamoured of prints: they allowed the beghards to keep up with a quickly changing, image-centred devotional culture.

Another Hoard of Prints From Maastricht

According to the Register, 231 early prints entered the collection on 14 November 1868, with the accession numbers 1868,1114.1–231.[2] They were all purchased in a single lot from a certain Mr Drugulin. In the Register, in another hand, a note was scrawled: 'See *Naumann's Archiv*, 1868.1'. When the British Library physically split off from the British Museum in 1997, most of the reference books went to the new building — the library — so it would be a while before I could figure out what *Naumann's Archiv* was and peruse it, but for the moment I studied the Register and started calling up groups of the 231 prints.

As I ordered about five prints at a time, dismembered manuscript pages glued to mattes emerged from boxes. Working through a few boxes of prints immediately revealed that the prints accessioned on 14 November 1868 had come from a single manuscript. About two thirds of the prints had been peeled off their manuscript supports, and the other third were still mounted on the folios of the manuscript. For example, a print depicting the Virgin of the Sun was mounted on a disgorged manuscript leaf as in e-fig. 67.

---

2   In fact there were more than 231 prints entered on this day; the conservators deliberately skipped several of the small ones and interpolated them later with an asterisk, so that they would correspond to the numbering in *Naumann's Archiv*, specifically, 20* (a Resurrection roundel), as well as 49*, 85*, 134*, and 210* have all been added later. Therefore, 236 prints were entered on 14 November 1868.

3. The Beghards in the Sixteenth Century

BM 1868,1114.196 — Virgin *in sole*, engraving pasted to the leaf of a prayerbook (e-fig. 67)

 Virgin *in sole*, engraving pasted to the leaf of a prayerbook. London, British Museum, Department of Prints & Drawings, inv. 1868,1114.196.

https://hdl.handle.net/20.500.12434/fc2487da

These folios once again had the strange and distinctive feature of being foliated. So overwhelmed was the person charged with mounting the prints in 1868 that he simply organized them thematically, by subject, not bothering to divide them by 'hand' or school. For example, one matte brandished a fistful of folios from the manuscript, all with Christological themes (fig. 93). Another matte turned up seventeen 'trimmed and silhouetted saints' from the manuscript (fig. 94).

Fig. 93
Matte from 1868, with Christological prints removed from Add. 31002. London, British Museum, Department of Prints & Drawings.

Fig. 94
'Trimmed and silhouetted saints' affixed to a matte assembled in 1868. London, British Museum, Department of Prints & Drawings.

As is clear from the designs made by gluing print fragments onto archival mattes, the motivations went beyond the desire to join like with like. Another urge was to create sympathetic, symmetrical designs by rearranging curios from the past, including manuscript illumination. For example, a nineteenth-century collector, possibly in England, applied knife and glue to several manuscripts, including a Bolognese liturgical manuscript from the early fourteenth century. She or he excised the Latin script from the page and reorganized the silhouetted miniatures and disembodied pieces of acanthus into surreal designs, pasting them onto the clean, inviting pages of a modern album (e-fig. 68).[3]

Devoid of walls of Latin script, initials, and frames, the figures have been reduced to abstract forms of painted parchment. A kneeling saint praying

---

3 The Koninklijke Bibliotheek — The National Library of The Netherlands — purchased the album in 1900 from antiquarian bookseller J. Tregaskis, London (cat. 463, no. 387). See http://manuscripts.kb.nl/show/manuscript/131+F+19

Folio from an album with manuscript cuttings (e-fig. 68)

 Folio from an album with manuscript cuttings. The Hague, Koninklijke Bibliotheek, Ms. 131 F 19, fol. 10r.

https://hdl.handle.net/20.500.12434/31a0dbf8

to a giant bird flying overhead typifies the absurdist compositions and the jolting variations in scale. The album maker exercised other principles: that the composition should be as symmetrical as the elements allowed, and that each element should have maximum space around it, with no overlapping. Another composition reveals that at least two manuscripts donated their vital organs to make this compilation (e-fig. 69).

Folio from an album with manuscript cuttings (e-fig. 69)

 Folio from an album with manuscript cuttings. The Hague, Koninklijke Bibliotheek, Ms. 131 F 19, fol. 12r.

https://hdl.handle.net/20.500.12434/b3b64d40

The composer has decided to top and tail the main narrative — about the massacre of a group of clerics — with acanthus clipped out of books from two periods. The page therefore reveals further principles of design: to cut down the illuminations to the quick, even when that means expelling visual data essential for meaning-making, and to offer visual variety. These practices were popular among collectors even before the nineteenth century. In 1769 James Granger started cutting up books to liberate images to paste in other books, a process later called Grangerization.[4] The practices of collectors reflected the practices of museum curators.

An enormous and densely illustrated prayerbook must have undergone extreme vivisection to yield this quantity of printed relics. All the prints in the group had been hand-coloured in the same palette, consisting of washes in muted red, green, and yellow. Typical are

---

4   On the topic of Grangerization, I have benefitted from conversations with my former undergraduate student, Vanessa Kroos, who wrote her honours dissertation titled 'Nostalgia and Disregard: The Hague, KB 131 F 19 and the Collection and Manipulation of the Medieval in Nineteenth-Century England' in 2014–2015 under my supervision at the University of St Andrews (unpublished).

the washes that appear on an engraving by the Monogrammist MB depicting the Nativity (e-fig. 70).

BM 1868,1114.210 — Folio of the beghards' later book of hours (e-fig. 70)

Folio of the beghards' later book of hours, with an engraving depicting the Nativity attributed to Monogrammist MB. London, British Museum, Department of Prints & Drawings, inv. 1868,1114.210.

https://hdl.handle.net/20.500.12434/73f718b0

Colours have been applied to the brick wall to give it a relentless pattern and dizzying recession. Moreover, the painter has added a decorative border to nearly all the prints. These borders consist of red-brown pen and ink and wash. Their chromatic consistency suggests that the person who applied the colour to the prints may have been the same person who added this decoration. It seemed likely, therefore, that the person or persons who wrote and decorated the manuscript purchased the prints in black and white and then coloured them systematically. This stands in contrast to the situation with Add. 24332, in which most of the prints were either left in black and white or purchased already coloured. This suggests that in the intervening 25 years printers had stopped marketing hand-coloured prints, or stopped trying to make them look like miniatures, or that the public had become used to black and white prints and were ready to accept them as they were, without the extra colouring. The owner of these prints was able to turn their dullness into a virtue by giving them a common look.

Like Add. 24332, the host manuscript for this new cache of prints was a prayerbook written in an eastern dialect of Middle Dutch. I wondered whether the parent manuscript was also in the British Library. Rather than using the Bibliotheca Neerlandica Manuscripta as a guide to continue to work through every Netherlandish manuscript in the BL in numerical order, a plan that I reckoned would take about ten years, I took a shortcut, namely, scouring Priebsch's catalogue of the Dutch- and German-language manuscripts of what had been the British Museum at the time when he was writing, in 1896–1901.[5] Priebsch notes the provenance of each manuscript and describes several as having been 'Transferred from

---

5   Robert Priebsch, *Deutsche Handschriften in England*, 2 vols (Erlangen: Fr. Junge, 1896–1901).

the Dept of Prints and Drawings'. I made a list of these transferred and called them all up the next time I could get to the British Library, which was 26 April 2006. One of those on my list was Add. Ms. 31002, a thin volume with the calendar and the ragged, mangled, stripped-down pages of a once richly decorated book of hours. The book was emaciated because much of its bulk had been sliced off and accessioned into the BM's Department of Prints and Drawings in November 1868.

Fig. 95
Folio in the beghards' later book of hours, with Virgin of the Sun standing on the moon (added engraving), c. 1525. London, British Library, Add. Ms. 31002, vol. I, fol. 138r.

There was a single print left in the volume, showing the Virgin of the Sun (fol. 138, fig. 95). It provided an indication of what at least half the incipits would have looked like. According to a note on the second paper flyleaf, the manuscript was 'Transferred from the Dept of Prints and Drawings 24 March 1879'. I had uprooted another broken manuscript and was already well on my way to reconstructing it. That first day I got a feel for the book and started transcribing the calendar.

Putting this book together would again be aided by a late medieval organisational system — foliation. Like the loose leaves preserved in the

British Museum, the leaves in this manuscript have the folio numbers written in large numerals at the top of every recto. The scribe who wrote them must have seen the advantages of Arabic numerals over Roman, cognitively, mathematically, and spatially. Not only did he inscribe them at a scale commensurate with the large letters in the text block, but he further called attention to their presence by decorating them: the numbers often appeared in a nest of penwork. Some numbers appeared in decorative frames, such as the number 235 (e-fig. 72), where the scribe/illuminator responded to the bulbous fruit form inside the frame and extended that shape with festooning penwork into the margin.

On other pages, ornate manicules point to the numbers. For their maker and early users, these numerals framed the modern system organising the book. For me, these numbers would help to connect the loose sheets to the body of the book in their original sequence. I realised very quickly that the prints' accession numbers corresponded to their position in the manuscript, Add. 31002. In other words, their accession numbers correspond to the order in which they were removed from the manuscript, which was systematic, from the beginning of the manuscript to its end. That is one reason I decided not to make a spreadsheet to reconstruct the manuscript, since to do so was uninteresting as a puzzle, but only a simple task and that requires zipping the removed prints and folios up with the bound folios in Add. 31002. Their accession numbers fall in the same sequence as the folio numbers of the manuscript.

Recontextualizing the prints reveals that the makers adjusted some of them before inserting them. For example, they silhouetted an engraving depicting a bishop wearing a mitre.

BM 1868,1114.115 — Bishop wearing a mitre (e-fig. 66)

Bishop wearing a mitre. Hand-painted engraving, trimmed and silhouetted. London, British Museum, Department of Prints & Drawings, inv. 1868,1114.115.

https://hdl.handle.net/20.500.12434/cc55a7af

This print was lifted from fol. 272 (now Add. 31002, Part 2, modern fol. 62) (fig. 96), a folio with an elaborate penwork frame that must have originally snuggled around the print, some red strokes of which are still visible on the fragment. The scribe was interpreting the print as a

St Lambert, because only the top of the print was used: the head and the attribute were cut off. This print may have originally depicted a different bishop, but, as the beghards did in 1500, they could creatively trim inconvenient details from prints in order to adjust their identities.

Fig. 96
Folio in the beghards' later book of hours, c. 1525, from which an engraving depicting a bishop's upper body was removed in 1868. London, British Library, Add. Ms. 31002, vol. II, 62r (original fol. 272).

The Calendar of Add. 31002

In 2006 I was not, in fact, seeing this manuscript for the first time; I had seen it a few years earlier, before I started systematically dating my notes. However, at that time, I had rejected it for the project I had been working on, but puzzled over its unusual calendar with its extra row of numbers. I had not suspected that the numbers referred to folios within that particular prayerbook, that it formed an internal indexing system. I did not have the lenses to see the extraordinary features in the manuscript until I saw it for the second time. That is typical of my experience with primary evidence. I need to study it, reflect on it, and return to it months or years later before I can grasp its working even partially. Funding councils never understand this: it takes multiple trips to Paris, London, Maastricht, and elsewhere to work out such relationships.

When I began working on Add. 31002 in earnest, in 2006, the prints in the BM with the accession numbers 1868,1114.1–231 had not yet been scanned. This made it extremely difficult to work on them since they were available for only a few hours a day, on the opposite side of the English Channel from where I lived. I directed my attention instead to the manuscript from which they had come, Add. 31002. But even that took a long time. Because professional photography was prohibitively expensive, and hand-held photography was not permitted in the manuscript reading room at the British Library then, I had to work on the manuscript in the flesh. A little more than a year passed before I could return to the BL to transcribe the whole calendar, on 17 May 2007. When I did so, I learned that the calendar has an extraordinary number of feasts for the translations of saints local to the eastern Netherlands, as well as many Franciscan feasts. Specifically:

April	28	Translation of St Lambert, bishop of Maastricht (272)
May	13	St Servaas, bishop of Tongeren, whose relics are in Maastricht (283)
	25	Translation of St Francis (285)
	30	Translation of St Hubert (287)
June	7	Translation of St Servaas (283)
	13	Translation of St Bartholomew (332)
	21	Martin, bishop of Tongeren
July	31	Translation of the 11,000 Virgins (360)
Aug.	5	Translation of St Ghielis [aka Gilles] (338)
	11	Translation of St Trudo (384)
	12	Clara virgin (323)
Sept.	1	Ghielis abbot (338) and Translation of St Mathias (258)
	9	Feast of the Dedication of the Church (no folio number)
	16	Five Wounds of St Francis (343)
	17	Lambert bishop and martyr (345)
	29	Michael archangel (350)
Oct.	3	Translation of St Clara (323)

	4	Francis confessor (355)
	11	Gummarus knight
		(venerated in Lier; no folio number)
	13	Lambrecht's victory
		(venerated only in the diocese of Luik; 345)
	22	Severus bishop (361)
Nov.	3	Hubert bishop (371)
	23	Trudo abbot and confessor (384)
Dec.	9	Translation of St Bartholomew (332)

As these feasts indicate, the calendar emphasises Franciscan saints (Francis, Clara, Trudo), saints venerated in the diocese of Liège and in Maastricht in particular (St Lambert was the bishop of Maastricht and St Servaas was the bishop of Tongeren and Maastricht; fig 97 and 98). I pored over lists of pre-Reformation monastic houses by region and by rule affiliation. Was it possible that Add. 31002, like Add. 24332, had been produced in Maastricht by the beghards of St Michael and St Bartholomew? Indeed, Michael and Bartholomew are also featured in the calendar; the problem was that these two were widely venerated and therefore featured in nearly every calendar. It is much easier to use calendrical data to localise a manuscript to a church dedicated to some obscure saint, venerated in only one minuscule church, and written in gold with maybe an extra prayer dedicated to that saint, which is also singled out with special decoration. The calendar in 31002 did not provide proof enough. And it differed significantly from that in 24332. I baulked at the thought that the two manuscripts had come from the same place because, frankly, they hardly resembled each other.

Moreover, the calendar of Add. 31002 has some entries that make it clear that the later manuscript was not a copy of the earlier one, and it may have been made for a different community. Firstly, whereas the earlier manuscript has some blanks in the calendar, there are none in the later manuscript. Secondly, Add. 31002 has the feast of the church consecration on 10 September, a feast which is lacking in Add. 24332. I wondered, therefore, whether the later manuscript could have been made by different male Franciscans in the diocese of Luik, who had borrowed Add. 24332 as a model. A further problem with the indexing system is that the folio numbers referred to items that were not actually

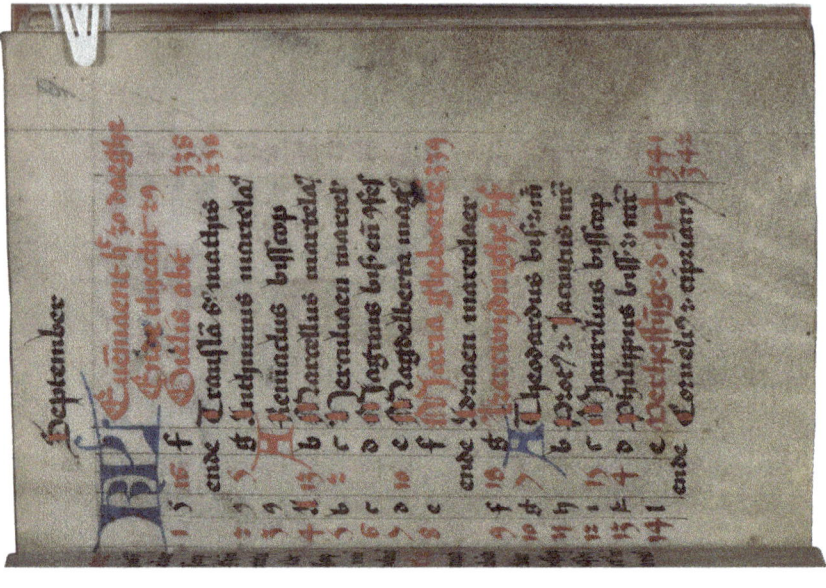

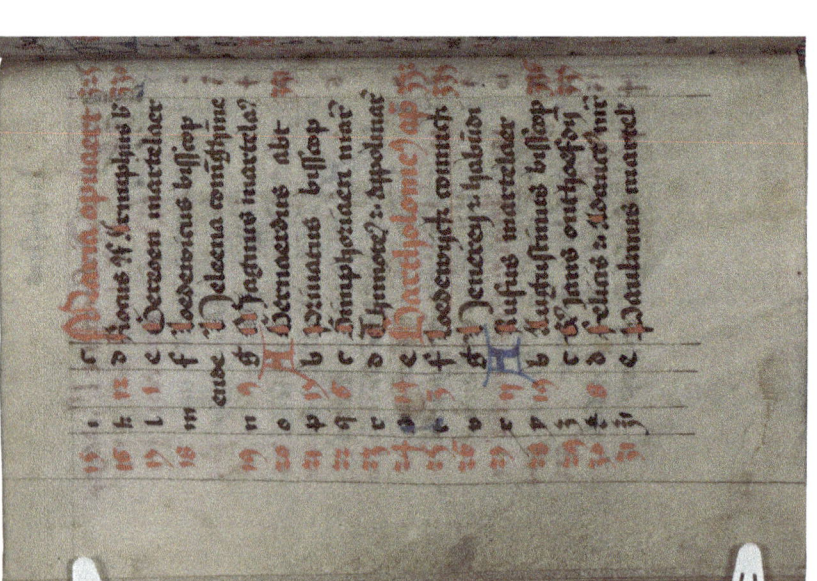

Fig. 97 Opening from the calendar of the beghards' later book of hours for August-September. London, British Library, Add. Ms. 31002, vol. I, fols 8v-9r.

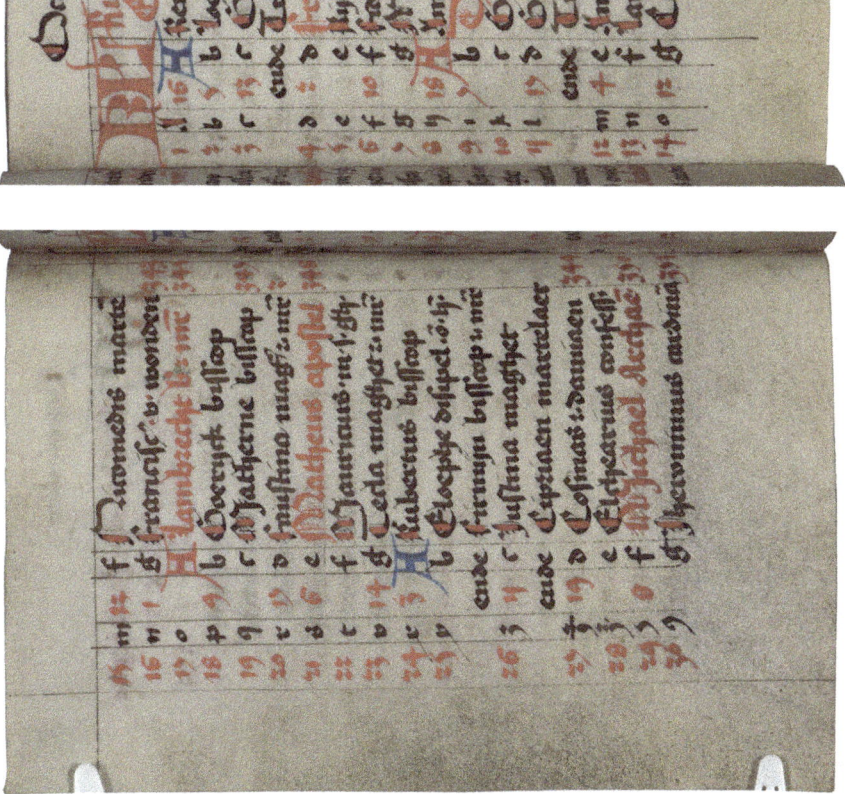

Fig. 98 Opening from the calendar of the beghards' later book of hours for September–October. London, British Library, Add. Ms. 31002, vol. I, fols 9v–10r.

in the book, which had only 197 folios. Could it be that the index pointed to another book altogether? If so, then the organisational system in Add. 31002 was even more complex than that in Add. 24332.

In the meantime, I finally tracked down an article by A. Andresen in the *Archiv für zeichnenden Künste*, edited by Robert Naumann and published in Leipzig in 1868. (Years later, it is now digitized and available online.) This volume is referred to as *Naumann's Archiv* in the literature, and abbreviated N. A. in the documents of the BM, including the mounts to which the prints with accession numbers 1868,1114.1–231 are pasted. The article begins (in my translation from the German):

> Mr Drugulin the art dealer has recently acquired a Low German prayerbook from the first half of the sixteenth century, which is rich with images and deserves its own study. Any friend of old copper engravings should be especially interested in the contents, because nearly all the leaves it contains are unknown and do not appear in Bartsch or Passavant.[6]

Andresen's article was published in 1868, the same year that the BM acquired the manuscript and accessioned the prints (on 14 November). Wilhelm Eduard Drugulin (d. 1879) was an art dealer in Leipzig who specialised in prints and drawings. When Andresen studied the manuscript shortly before 1868, the prints were still affixed to the leaves of the intact manuscript.

Attributing the manuscript to the convent at St Trond, Andresen writes:

> One can assume with great likelihood that this prayerbook originated with a monk in the monastery of St Trond in Liège. The library in Liège preserves a number of manuscripts from this above-named convent, and another from 'Frater Truda Gemblacensis' decorated with 58 prints belongs to T. O. Weigel in Leipzig. The same Meister M who is represented in this manuscript with 7 leaves, also appears in our prayerbook with a series of leaves.[7]

---

6 A. Andresen, 'Beiträge zur älteren Niederdeutschen Kupferstichkunde des 15. und 16. Jahrhunders', Archiv für die zeichnenden Künste mit besonderer Beziehung auf Kupferstecher- und Holzschneidekunst und ihre Geschichte im Vereine mit Künstlern und Kunstfreunden, herausgegeben von Dr. Robert Naumann 14, no. 1 (1868), p. 1. The volume is now available at https://books.google.co.uk/books?id=VNYXAQAAIAAJ

7 Ibid., p. 1.

St Trond or Truiden, established in 1226–1231, was the first Franciscan establishment in the Netherlands. If the manuscript were from St Trond, that would make sense: it would account for the fact that the Drugulin manuscript and Add. 24332 are conceptually similar yet stylistically diverse. Franciscans in St Truiden and those in Maastricht could have worked closely together, and they could have exchanged ideas about how to make and organise manuscripts, and how to tap into the new technology of printmaking. But was Andresen correct? Was Drugulin's manuscript made at St Trond/Truiden?

Tackling this question involved thinking about another clue in the calendar: 9 September is listed as the feast of the dedication of the church. But which church was this? Did it mark the date of the church consecration in Maastricht or St Truiden or some other Franciscan church? To find the answer to this question, I emailed Bert Roest, a scholar of Franciscans based in the Netherlands, who did not know but suggested I ask the Franciscan Study Center in St Truiden (the *Instituut voor Franciscaanse Geschiedenis*). I had visited them in 2000, when I studied and photographed a treasure in their collection, a manuscript that contained prints pasted in it. Back then I had shared the photographs with James Marrow, who rephotographed the book and gave the images to Ursula Weekes, who went on to write about the manuscript very intelligently.[8] Alas, the modern brothers in St Truiden did not know whose dedication feast took place on 9 September. Finding a match proved difficult. Few calendars list a feast for a church dedication, so I had to hunt around for several months. I was living in the Netherlands at this time, so had many relevant manuscripts — those from the eastern part of the Northern Netherlands — available to me. A new spreadsheet took form as I logged the contents of several calendars. Arrays of data help not only to organise information but also to generate new knowledge. From the spreadsheet, I learned that Leiden UB, Ltk 303, which had a similar eastern Netherlandish dialect to Drugulin's manuscript (Add. 31002), had an entry for 9 May which specified 'kerk wijnghe [sic] Tongeren' (church dedication in Tongeren). So I now knew that Andresen's proposal that Add. 31002 had been made for Tongeren was incorrect.

---

8   Ursula Weekes, *Early Engravers and Their Public*, pp. 121–43, 303–05.

Another manuscript provided a positive identification for the church dedication on 9 of September. For that date, Maastricht, RAL Ms. 462 announced the 'Kercwijnghe S Servaes' (church dedication of St Servatius). Now I had a match. St Servatius, of course, was the dedicatory saint of the main church in Maastricht, and RAL Ms. 462 was made in Maastricht for the female Franciscan convent, Maagdendriesch (mentioned earlier). I therefore had an answer: Add. 31002 must have been made for use in Maastricht. In other words, the calendar suggested that Add. 31002 was made by the same beghards who made Add. 24332, but a generation later, using a mishmash of manuscript exemplars. It testifies to a world changing rapidly under the beghards' feet. It is possible that the sisters of Maagdendriesch made Add. 31002, using prints and calendar/table of contents technology borrowed from the beghards, although there are no manuscripts from the female tertiaries in Maastricht that resemble it.

On another note, I did look through every paper and digital database of manuscripts in Liège to search for the other manuscripts with prints that Andresen mentioned. And I went there on 11 July 2009 to search in person: I found no manuscripts with prints, but many with fascinating illumination. My search for Weigel's manuscript with 58 prints stuck in it ended without satisfaction. Like much of the material culture of Europe, these manuscripts were probably disrupted by the First and Second World Wars. Maybe publishing this book will shake them out of hiding.

Similarities Between Add. 24332 and Add. 31002

On my next visit to the British Library, I went to study Add. 31002 and the attendant asked me which volume I wanted. This question caught me by surprise. Although Priebsch and the BNM had described Add. 31002 as a single volume, I now discovered that, in fact, the manuscript had been split into two. At some point during the ten years and four months between the accessioning of the individual prints and the transfer of the manuscript skeleton to the Manuscripts Department, the conservators at the BM must have rebound the manuscript. Rebinding was undoubtedly necessary after 200-odd leaves and prints were removed from the manuscript, which must have weakened it and made its covers fit too loosely. Rather than adding blank sheets to represent the missing folios (as the restorers had done with Add. 24332), they collected the folios into two thin volumes that mostly accounted for the text-only leaves and leaves that had blank, gluey rectangles where prints had formerly been pasted.[9] Seeing the two volumes together, along with the more than 200 prints, provides a much fuller picture of the original production.

Although Add. 31002 was made about 25 years later, it has conceptual similarities with Add. 24332. Like its predecessor, Add. 31002 has a calendar that also functions as a table of contents. The scribe of 31002 must have copied the concept from Add. 24332, for this is an extremely unusual feature, as I have shown above in Chapter 2. Objecting to the haphazard way in which the Roman numerals were listed in the earlier manuscript, the scribe of Add. 31002 ruled the calendar so that the foliation numbers occupy their own column (see fig 97 and 98). Furthermore, he standardised these numbers by making them all red, and he abandoned the confusing Roman numerals in favour of Arabic numerals, which are much easier to read, cause fewer errors, and take up less space on the line.

Another similarity was pedagogical. I have proposed that the brothers had used Add. 24332 as a prayerbook, but also as a book for teaching reading and the rudiments of the religion, which warranted the extensive instructions on how to use the book. Unlike Add. 24332, Add. 31002 does not contain the *Pater Noster* and the other texts for teaching new readers; however, it does have a multiplication table (fig. 99). Unfolded for use, it becomes larger than the book block. This table is spread over 3 folios, with the numerals 1–17 down the first column, and 1–32 across the top, so that the square at the lower right of the table contains the number 544, which equals 32 x 17. That someone overcame the challenge of creating a table outwith the normal size and had to prepare it separately from the other folios, suggests that its inclusion was highly desired. It also demonstrates a commitment to ordering information in tabular form, and an almost cultish zeal for numerical sequencing and mathematical

---

9   London, BL, Add. Ms. 31002, Part I contains the calendar plus the folios originally foliated 1–197 in pen; Part 2 contains the folios originally foliated 198–411. The original foliator did not foliate the last few folios of the manuscript (now in Part 2, modern foliation 148–54).

operations. The multiplication table may relate to one of the prayerbook's functions, to teach students (children?) mathematical basics. Although such operations are required for calculating Easter, the central feast of Christianity, this table is not contextualized as a tool for Christian utility, but rather as one for pure knowledge, which is indeed highly unusual in a prayerbook.

Like Add. 24332, the later manuscript also includes prints used as pages, as well as prints used as historiated initials, and prints mounted onto blank pages. Most of the prints fell into this third category — trimmed and pasted to the written page. Those who lifted them later did so cleanly most of the time, but occasionally peeled up only a layer of the printed paper, thereby damaging the image, as with an engraving depicting Mary Magdalene (e-fig. 71). But some prints became the page, as with an engraving depicting the Virgin of the Sun (e-fig. 72), which became folio 235.[10] The ink has severely bitten through the printed paper, but not through most of the text pages, which were made with thicker paper. One wonders how soon after its creation it began to autophage, and whether the printmakers envisioned their wares being put to such a purpose. If they had, perhaps they would have used tougher paper.

BM 1868,1114.221 — Mary Magdalene (e-fig. 71)

Mary Magdalene. Engraving removed from the beghards' later book of hours. London, British Museum, Department of Prints & Drawings, inv. 1868,1114.221.

https://hdl.handle.net/20.500.12434/82930606

BM 1868,1114.207 — Folio removed from the beghards' (e-fig. 72)

Folio removed from the beghards' later book of hours, formerly fol. 235, with a hand-coloured engraving depicting Virgin *in sole*. London, British Museum, Department of Prints & Drawings, inv. 1868,1114.207.

https://hdl.handle.net/20.500.12434/16858f27

---

10   The original foliator made some errors, so that there were two folios inscribed '235' in Add. 31002.

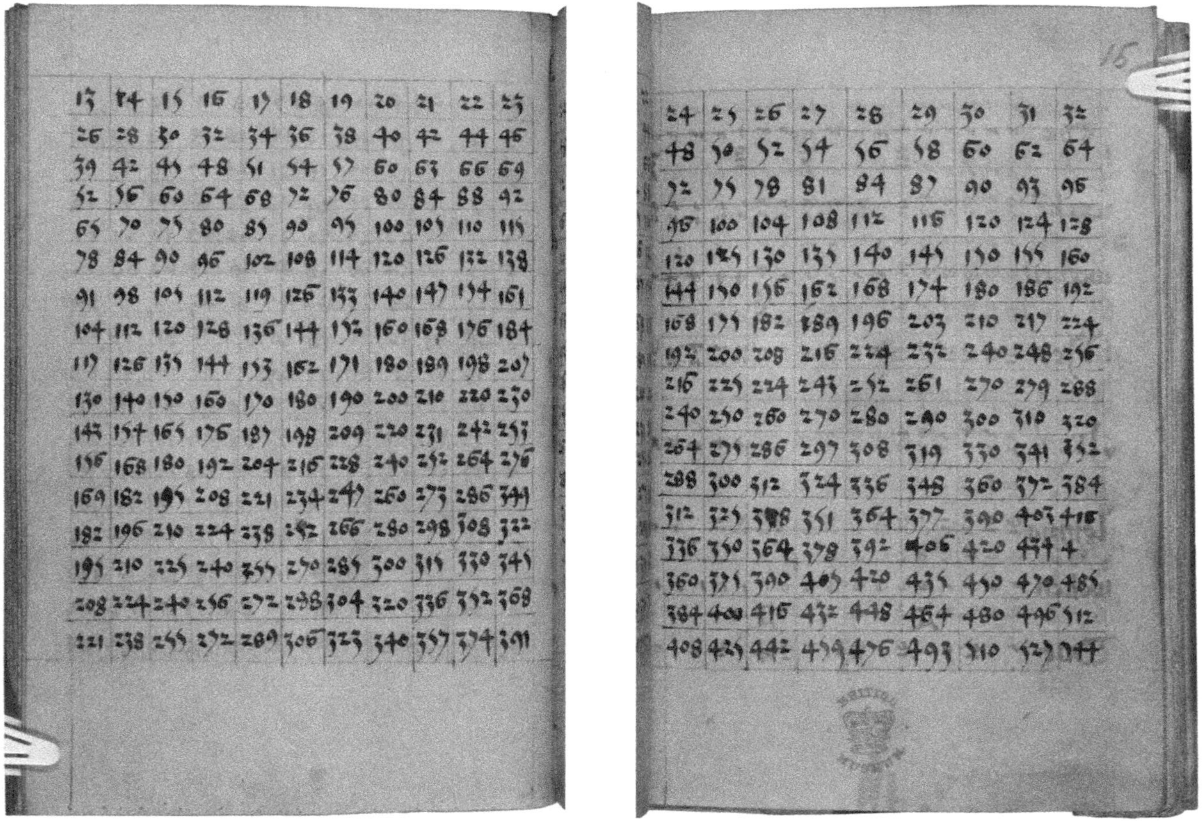

Fig. 99 Multiplication tables. London, British Library, Add. Ms. 31002, vol. I, fol. 14v-15r.

Like the earlier manuscript, Add. 31002 also contains coloured drawings, which depict saints unavailable as prints. Whoever cut up Add. 31002 in the nineteenth century must have had such a low opinion of these that he did not bother to cut them out, and three drawings therefore remain in the manuscript. One of these miniatures depicts St Lambert as a bishop with a bishop's crook, a sceptre, and a book, trampling a figure wearing a Jew's hat, indicating that Lambert converted the Jews by force (fig. 100). St Lambert was venerated in Maastricht.

Fig. 100
Folio in the beghards' later book of hours, with a coloured drawing depicting St Lambert. London, British Library, Add. Ms. 31002, vol. II, fol. 106r.

A second drawing still in the manuscript represents a small surprised-looking acolyte kneeling at the skirts of his patron, St Francis, whose bare beet and upraised hands reveal the stigmata (fig. 101). Possibly the drawing is meant to show St Francis receiving the stigmata in the presence of his acolyte Brother Leo; it has been greatly simplified, due to the artist's limited skills, and the draughtsman has omitted the usual flying Jesus and has represented the Leo figure as a beghard, comparable to the kneeling beghard figures drawn into the folios of Add. 24332. In this way, the drawing further connects Add. 31002 with a Franciscan community. It also suggests that the beghards themselves did not produce prints; if they did, they would certainly have mechanically produced numerous images of St Lambert, St Francis, and other saints of local importance, but the book's makers were apparently unable to obtain these as prints and instead had to create homespun versions of these locally important subjects.

Fig. 101
Folio in the beghards' later book of hours, with a coloured drawing depicting Brother Leo kneeling before St Francis. London, British Library, Add. Ms. 31002, vol. II, fol. 114v.

A third drawing in Add. 31002 depicts a church and accompanies 'a prayer for the dedication of the church' ('een ghebeet van der kerckwijdijnghe'; fig. 102). The prayer is a transcription of the prayer from Add. 24332, folio *ccc xcij*, and the church is positioned at the upper left-hand corner, much like the position of the print of a church in the earlier manuscript (686–687) (e-fig. 20). Clearly, the beghard did not have an appropriate print depicting a church; instead he drew this church simply with a ruler for the verticals and relying on the ruling of the page for the horizontals, and then gave his creation weathervanes in the form of pen flourishes. Although prints must have become increasingly available after the turn of the century, the subjects of those prints was determined by the producers, not the consumers.

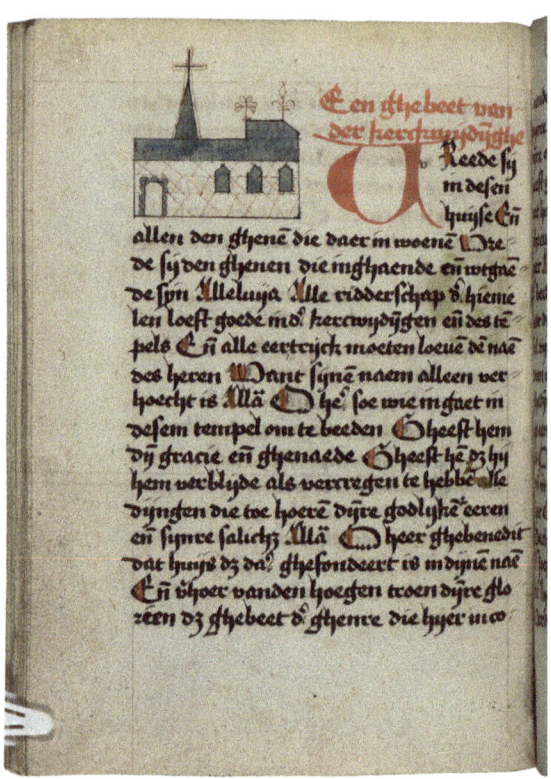

Fig. 102
Folio in the beghards' later book of hours, with a coloured drawing depicting a church. London, British Library, Add. Ms. 31002, vol. I, fol. 50v.

25 Years Later

I viewed Add. 31002 on 26 April 2006, again in December, and then on 17 May and 7 July 2007, revelling in the weirdness of the manuscript each time. When I had first looked at the manuscript, I had not suspected that it also came from the beghards of Maastricht because the style differs considerably from that of the earlier manuscript. Whereas the earlier calendar has many blank dates, the later one has a saint for every day of the year and has filled the blanks with such little-known saints as Zoe of Rome and Mary of Oignies. What confused me, and still confuses me in fact, is that the litany in Add. 31002 does not fully point to the beghards: Johannes, Trudo, Hubrecht, and Barbara are stroked in red. (My earlier hypothesis, that the manuscript may have originated with the tertiaries of Maagdendriesch, partially fits these observations, since they were dedicated to St Andrew & St Barbara; however, one would expect more fanfare than red stroking for Barbara's feast. As an apostle, St Andrew would be red in any calendar.) The beghards of Maastricht remained the most likely producers of the richly illustrated Add. 31002. It is possible that the beghards made this manuscript for consumption by another religious house, just as they bound manuscripts for other monastic houses.

Technology had shifted during the two-and-a-half decades since the beghards had made Add. 24332. Whereas the earlier manuscript constituted a group effort, a single hand wrote the later manuscript. Whereas the beghards had not come up with the idea of pasting in prints until they were part of the way through Add. 24332, they of course possessed the idea from the beginning of Add. 31002, and they had prints available from many more printmakers. Engraving had almost completely replaced woodcuts. If the beghards indeed made Add. 31002, they were now celebrating the dedication of the church of St Servatius, the main church of Maastricht.

Add. 31002 is extraordinary because it spans categories. It is a manuscript, yet was made deep within the printed book period (c. 1525). Instead of being made on paper, it is made on a combination of materials, with the calendar, the fold-out computational diagrams, and first and last folio of every quire made on parchment, so that the parchment falls on major text breaks, and the rest paper. This also allows the most decorated parts of the book to fall on parchment, which holds paint better than does paper. The folios have numerous places for prints, mostly roundels, throughout the book, and these are decorated with penwork. In some cases, one can see the planner's instructions for which image belongs where, such as 'Veronica' (fig. 103). Electronic reconstruction reveals what the page originally looked like (fig. 104).

From this example it is clear that the scribe had a stack of images before him and measured out the print onto the text box in order to inscribe around the empty rectangle. In other words, the prints were planned from the beginning and not an afterthought.

Earlier I mentioned another similarity: an engraving depicting St Mark appears in fine impressions in both manuscripts (1861,1109.643 and 1868,1114.114, e-fig. 12 and e-fig. 61). In the earlier manuscript, the designer has pasted an extra lion onto the page, and drawn a chapel around it with rubricator's ink, features that are lacking in the later manuscript. One narrative that could explain how these two impressions of the same print appear in the two manuscripts is this: the beghards acquired hundreds, if not thousands of prints, beginning in or before 1500, and used them to illuminate the manuscript prayerbooks that they manufactured in their monastery, an activity they concentrated on after several of their looms were removed by the Maastricht city council. Many of these prints they were able to acquire in multiple copies; they possessed so many of certain prints around 1500 that they were still using them in the 1520s.

Furthermore, the aesthetics of colouring had changed significantly in the intervening years. As I looked through these prints, I noted that they all had similar hand-colouring in light washes (with a few minor exceptions), presumably by the same person. This situation was quite different from that in Add. 24332, in which groups of related prints were hand-coloured the same. These observations suggested that in the earlier example, from 1500, the beghards bought groups of prints from various sources, and that some of them were delivered already hand-coloured, whereas the later beghards must have received unpainted prints, and applied washes to them themselves. It is possible that these two examples describe a larger trend: before 1500 or so, prints were more rapidly available pre-coloured, whereas a generation later, the standard had changed.

A handful of earlier prints used in Add. 31002 that were coloured in a different palette provide an exception. These, I suspected, had been in the beghards' possession for decades, and they had received them already coloured before 1500. Leaves in this category include 1868,1114.168, which showed St Bartholomew (e-fig. 73).

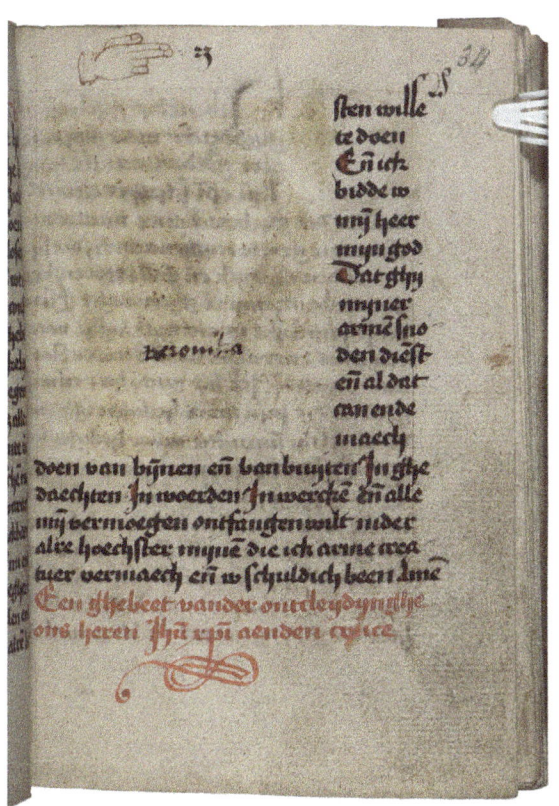

Fig. 103
Folio in the beghards' later manuscript with a space reserved for an image of Veronica. London, British Library, Add. Ms. 31002, vol. II, fol. 34r.

Fig. 104
Electronic reconstruction of Veronica page: superimposition of London, British Museum, Department of Prints & Drawings, inv. 1868,1114.24 onto London, British Library, Add. Ms. 31002, vol. II, fol. 34r.

BM 1868,1114.168 — St Bartholomew (e-fig. 73)

 St Bartholomew. Engraving removed from the beghards' later book of hours. London, British Museum, Department of Prints & Drawings, inv. 1868,1114.168.

https://hdl.handle.net/20.500.12434/c4171f63

Lehrs had attributed this image to Israhel, and then Hollstein dis-attributed it. Relevant here is that the print probably dates from the 1470s, and the beghards may have had it for more than 50 years before incorporating it in their book. I wondered whether they had another copy, which they had inserted into Add. 24332; however, my spreadsheet did not reveal an appropriate place for such a St Bartholomew print in that book. Nevertheless, this print, like many others, reveals layers of secrets: Lehrs had noted that the label 'Scs Bartholomeus' was engraved into the plate but that the letters had been added by a different hand. The text on the banderol ('Ascendit ad celos, sedet ad dexteram dei patris omnipotentis') is part of the Apostles' Creed.[11] Here is a scenario to explain this: by 1500 the beghards had realised how useful prints were for 'illuminating' manuscripts. They were frustrated that the available prints did not perfectly meet their needs, so they hand-drew a few essential images in their books or, in some cases, they adjusted existing images, for example changing an attribute or an inscription. In this case, a printmaker realised that an image of St Bartholomew, with his name in bold letters, would be much appreciated by the beghards of Maastricht. That printmaker had a plate with the apostle, but he recut the plate to add the name Bartholomew to the bottom. The image would have formed the corporate mascot for the beghards. To make any fewer than, say, 100 copies, would not have warranted re-cutting the plate. The beghards used them, and gave them, perhaps, to those who heard them preach. But this is the only one that survives. In other words, someone had underscored Bartholomew's identity so that it would be unmistakable, so that the print would become an appropriate calling card for the beghards of Maastricht.

---

11   Lehrs notes that this section of the Creed is usually brandished by St Simon, not Bartholomew; however, the Hungarian Franciscan Pelbartus Ladislaus de Temesvár (1430–1504), who had assigned each phrase of the Creed to one of the Apostles, had in fact matched 'ascendit ad coelos, sedet ad dexteram Dei Patris omnipotentis' with St Bartholomew.

Lehrs points out that this is a unique impression, so if the beghards did make or order numerous copies, they have now been lost. I could imagine, however, that the beghards, having learned about the use of prints 25 years earlier, were finding ever more applications for them, and that early on in their discovery of prints, they wanted to have a print depicting their dedicatory saint. As ever, the problem with prints is their fixedness. Mechanical reproduction comes at the cost of rigidity. Once an image was made, it could depict, say, St Wolfgang, until someone went to great lengths to scratch out that saint's attribute and transform him into St Servatius. But rather than change every finished print, one could also adjust the plate. Or take an old and somewhat worn-down plate, re-inscribe the lines, and take the opportunity to make other adjustments as well. It is difficult to know whether the beghards were dealing with the printers themselves, or whether they were buying the prints from middlemen on the river. Whatever the system was, it allowed for the consumer (the beghards) to get a message back to the producers that they wanted printed images depicting St Bartholomew.

Dating the Later Manuscript

Add. 31002 contains features that help to date it, or at least give it several 'earliest possible dates'. For example, there is a reference in Add. 31002 to Julius II (pope in 1503–1513),[12] which provides a *terminus post quem* for the writing of the manuscript, although the manuscript clearly is much later than 1503. Prints themselves also provide clues for dating the book. In particular, the youngest prints in the manuscript can help to date its production. Young, datable prints include a reverse copy of an engraving made c. 1519 by Albrecht Dürer (e-fig. 74).

BM 1868,1114.27 — After Albrecht Dürer, Crucifixion roundel (e-fig. 74)

After Albrecht Dürer, Crucifixion roundel. Engraving removed from the beghards' later book of hours. London, British Museum, Department of Prints & Drawings, inv. 1868,1114.27.

https://hdl.handle.net/20.500.12434/66ce57c7

---

12   London, BL, Add. Ms. 31002, vol. I, fol. 75v.

It depicts the Crucifixion with the Virgin Mary, St John, and the Magdalene embracing the bars of the Cross. As it is a copy of Dürer's work, it must therefore postdate c. 1519. Among the other young prints is an engraving representing St Helen made by an anonymous German artist who signed his print with the monogram 'IB' and dated it 1523 at the upper right (e-fig. 75).[13] Furthermore, the manuscript contains two prints by Jacob Binck (1494/1500–1569), a German artist who spent part of his career in the Netherlands and was especially active as an engraver in the late 1520s. Two engravings made by this artist are Christ as the Man of Sorrows (1868,1114.22) (e-fig. 76) and an *Ecce Homo* (1868,1114.69) (e-fig. 77).

BM 1868,1114.120 — St Helen (e-fig. 75)

St Helen, dated 1523, with the monogram 'IB'. Engraving removed from the beghards' later book of hours. London, British Museum, Department of Prints & Drawings, inv. 1868,1114.120.

https://hdl.handle.net/20.500.12434/e2a03a80

BM 1868,1114.122 — Christ as the Man of Sorrows (e-fig. 76)

Jacob Binck, Christ as the Man of Sorrows. Engraving removed from the beghards' later book of hours. London, British Museum, Department of Prints & Drawings, inv. 1868,1114.122.

https://hdl.handle.net/20.500.12434/046cf84f

BM 1868,1114.69 — *Ecce Homo* (e-fig. 77)

Jacob Binck, *Ecce Homo*. Engraving removed from the beghards' later book of hours. London, British Museum, Department of Prints & Drawings, inv. 1868,1114.69.

https://hdl.handle.net/20.500.12434/3b054c33

Many of these later prints make use of Italianizing decorations. For example, St Trudo (e-fig. 78), which is sometimes attributed to Jacob Binck but is not signed, shows the saint nestled in a series of frames:

---

13 Confusingly, this is not the same person as the 'Monogrammist IB'.

large drapery with intricate edges that frames his body and face, and architectural frames with compound columns and swags cram the available space full of elaborate detail. Another ornate border, around a St Christopher, shows a number of hybrid creatures, putti battling, and decorative arabesques (e-fig. 79). Printmakers must have realised that printing the frames — or even using interchangeable frames — would save their customers the labour of having to add their own. This could have been a selling point for the printers.

BM 1868,1114.199 — St Trudo (e-fig. 78)

St Trudo. Engraving removed from the beghards' later book of hours. London, British Museum, Department of Prints & Drawings, inv. 1868,1114.199.

https://hdl.handle.net/20.500.12434/b4d830d4

BM 1868,1114.150 — St Christopher (e-fig. 79)

St Christopher. Engraving used as a folio, removed from the beghards' later book of hours. London, British Museum, Department of Prints & Drawings, inv. 1868,1114.150.

https://hdl.handle.net/20.500.12434/c983aac2

Finally, from the same period, there is one print made by Allaert Claesz, a Dutch printmaker who was active in the 1520s. The image represents St Lucy (with a knife in her neck) and St Genevieve (holding a candle), with a strongly Italianizing aesthetic communicated by the elegant garb of the women and the decorative nested frames (e-fig. 80).

BM 1868,1114.86 — St Lucy and St Genevieve (e-fig. 80)

St Lucy and St Genevieve. Engraving used as a folio, removed from the beghards' later book of hours. London, British Museum, Department of Prints & Drawings, inv. 1868,1114.86.

https://hdl.handle.net/20.500.12434/e04ba44f

According to my analysis, the prints were not added later, but were part of the book from the beginning, and can therefore help establish a date for the production. In short, the dated and datable prints indicate that 1523 is the *terminus post quem* of Add. 31002. A date of c. 1525 (after 1523) therefore makes sense. This dating also reveals that even in the third decade of the sixteenth century the beghards were still obtaining prints from both Netherlandish and German printers.

Israhel van Meckenem

While the youngest prints in the manuscript helped to date the production, the oldest prints helped to establish a longer view of the beghards' activities. Israhel van Meckenem, who was active from c. 1465 until his death in 1503, made some of the earliest prints in Add. 31002. I suspected that these, and other early prints used in the book, had been stored in the monastery since the end of the fifteenth century. Although only these two books of hours from the beghards' workshop have come to light so far, one can imagine that the beghards were making similar books filled with prints continuously for several decades.

Israhel supplied the book's two grandest prints in the form of large roundels. One depicts the Annunciation (e-fig. 81) and the other depicts Christ with the *Arma Christi* with 'ecce homo' inscribed on the scroll (e-fig. 82).

BM 1868,1114.109 — Israhel van Meckenem (e-fig. 81)

Israhel van Meckenem, Annunciation. Engraving used as a folio, removed from the beghards' later book of hours. London, British Museum, Department of Prints & Drawings, inv. 1868,1114.109.

https://hdl.handle.net/20.500.12434/89d6e804

BM 1868,1114.28 — Israhel van Meckenem (e-fig. 82)

Israhel van Meckenem, Christ with the *Arma Christi*; on the scroll: 'ecce homo'; below the borderline, signed 'Israhel'. Engraving used as a folio, removed from the beghards' later book of hours. London, British Museum, Department of Prints & Drawings, inv. 1868,1114.28.

https://hdl.handle.net/20.500.12434/dce280fb

The beghards have taken the round prints and trimmed them to fit a rectangular page, thereby turning them into whole pages of a small manuscript rather than embellishments to a large one (probably the artist's intended purpose). One can imagine that the beghards had obtained these prints at the end of the fifteenth century, but had failed to find a place for them in Add. 24332, since they are large, round objects. In the 1520s the beghards found a way to put a round object in a rectangular frame: just trim it with a knife.

When viewing the image of the Annunciation in its uncut state, its original purpose becomes clear: the image functioned as a large letter *D*. Seen in relation to the Annunciation engraving, the image of Christ as Man of Sorrows also comes into focus as a letter *O*.[14] Both images are signed *Israhel* in the plate below the borderline, but it seems that the artist meant this to be trimmed off before use because the image was intended as an entire letter itself, not just an image to be stuck into a hand-rendered letter. It is possible that the Annunciation in the D could have been designed for a book of hours as the beginning of the Hours of the Virgin (*Domine labia mea aperies...*), and that the Christ as Man of Sorrows in the O could initiate the Gregorian verses (*O, Adoro te in cruce...*). However, the prints are really too large for a book of hours (which is why they were trimmed for use in Add. 31002: to fit into an octavo-sized book), and they would make much more sense in a larger book type. Israhel must have intended them to function as instant historiated initials for large manuscripts, perhaps folio-sized choir books, to mark the incipits of texts related to the Annunciation and Passion, respectively. For example, the D with the Annunciation could be for an Antiphonal to mark the first Sunday in Advent (*Dominica Prima Adventus*).[15] He was trying to exploit the market of manuscript-makers to create specific prints that would save them labour, providing the whole package, letter and image, which could be hand-coloured by someone

---

14   For both letters, including references for uncut versions, see Lehrs, vol. IX (https://digi.ub.uni-heidelberg.de/diglit/lehrs1934bd9text), cat. 12, p. 15; and cat. 162, p. 173. See also Achim Riether, Israhel Van Meckenem (um 1440/45-1503): *Kupferstiche - Der Münchner Bestand*; [Katalog zur Ausstellung der Staatlichen Graphischen Sammlung München, Pinakothek der Moderne, 14. September - 26. November 2006] (Munich: Staatliche Graphische Sammlung, 2006), pp. 192–93, 226–27, pl. 4, 62.

15   I thank Margaret Bent and John Harper for this suggestion.

of limited skill. I have found few examples in which manuscript-makers used Israhel's prints in the way that he had intended.[16]

Israhel van Meckenem was not the first to make prints for the manuscript industry, but he made the widest range, and his prints are the easiest to spot, since he mechanically repeated his signature on the uncut sheets. As with all new media, dispersing the media disperses not only the content (such as a saint, a miraculous image) but also the idea of the new medium (prints themselves as a replacement for illumination). It is not surprising, therefore, that other printmakers, such as an anonymous Netherlandish engraver, similarly made historiated letters that could simply be glued in place (e-fig. 83).

BM 1868,1114.32 — Christ as Man of Sorrows with the *Arma Christi* in a letter O (e-fig. 83)

Christ as Man of Sorrows with the *Arma Christi* in a letter O. Engraving removed from the beghards' later book of hours. London, BM, P&D, 1868,1114.32.

https://hdl.handle.net/20.500.12434/6d2fc836

It depicts Christ as Man of Sorrows amid the *Arma Christi* in a letter O. Unlike Israhel's enormous letter (92 millimetres high) brandishing the same subject, this one is made for an octavo-sized book, as a commanding and large historiated initial. With the print nearly the same width as the text block, the scribe has only been able to fit a thin column of text beside it. Undoubtedly, the engraver was responding to book makers' desiderata for this iconography, so that they could include images of this subject alongside a prayer beginning 'Adoro te', which carried a large indulgence. At the top of the sheet is the tail end of the rubricated indulgence, announcing 6666 (years') indulgence. The printmaker must have known that a scribe could adjust the prayer so that it began 'O' in either Dutch or Latin.

Beghards used prints by Israhel in their early and their late experiments. Were Israhel's prints simply cheap and available? Or did the beghards favour them and seek them out? Available evidence

---

16 London, BL, Add. Ms. 24332 uses Israhel's roundels in the prescribed manner. A hand-painted version of the Annunciation was pasted into an initial D[eus] in Mainz, Stadtbibliothek; and a copy of the Christ with Arma Christi appears in Munich, Stadtbibliothek, Clm. 386.

does not answer these questions. What it does tell us is that Add. 31002 contained prints from several different series that Israhel signed, including his 'Memento mori' series. Like his page of roundels with saints, discussed in the previous chapter, this sheet he apparently sold whole. Users, in this case the beghards, would cut the sheet apart and use the printed roundels separately. Several of these sheets of roundels are preserved intact, such as one in the British Museum (e-fig. 84). The beghards used at least one of these roundels in Add. 31002; it shows death visiting the Pope (e-fig. 85).

BM 1848,1125.19 — Israhel van Meckenem's roundels (e-fig. 84)

Israhel van Meckenem's roundels, intact, with death theme. London, British Museum, Department of Prints & Drawings, inv. 1848,1125.19.

https://hdl.handle.net/20.500.12434/73ad2a6f

BM 1868,1114.74 — Israhel van Meckenem (e-fig. 85)

Israhel van Meckenem, Death visiting the Pope, roundel from Memento mori series. Engraving removed from the beghards' later book of hours. London, British Museum, Department of Prints & Drawings, inv. 1868,1114.74.

https://hdl.handle.net/20.500.12434/960bc5aa

One might expect that the other roundels from the same sheet would appear in Add. 31002, but they do not. Perhaps the beghards had already used the other prints in previous projects, such as Add. 24332, their book of hours from 1500. Copies of the roundels on this sheet may have been removed from initials there, where square holes now remain.

The beghards had multiple sheets of Israhel's roundels available to them, and at least three other roundels within Add. 31002 come from another series he made: the Nativity (e-fig. 86); Presentation in the Temple; (e-fig. 87); Circumcision of Christ (e-fig. 88); and the Virgin of the Sun, half-length and cupped in a moon (e-fig. 89). These roundels were cut from a sheet bearing Israhel's name elaborately engraved in prominent letters at the bottom (e-fig. 90). That some of the sheets remain intact suggests that people kept them as collector's items from their inception, no doubt made more precious by the artist's audacious branding of the object.

BM 1868,1114.209 — Nativity (e-fig. 86)

Israhel van Meckenem, Nativity roundel. Engraving removed from the beghards' later book of hours. London, British Museum, Department of Prints & Drawings, inv. 1868,1114.209.

https://hdl.handle.net/20.500.12434/2a22e9e7

BM 1868,1114.96 — Presentation in the Temple (e-fig. 87)

Israhel van Meckenem, Presentation in the Temple roundel. Engraving removed from the beghards' later book of hours. London, British Museum, Department of Prints & Drawings, inv. 1868,1114.96.

https://hdl.handle.net/20.500.12434/abd2bdbf

BM 1868,1114.84 — Circumcision of Christ (e-fig. 88)

Israhel van Meckenem, Circumcision of Christ roundel. Engraving removed from the beghards' later book of hours. London, British Museum, Department of Prints & Drawings, inv. 1868,1114.84.

https://hdl.handle.net/20.500.12434/f2fd8c27

BM 1868,1114.43 — Virgin *in sole* (e-fig. 89)

Israhel van Meckenem, roundel. Engraving removed from the beghards' later book of hours. London, British Museum, Department of Prints & Drawings, inv. 1868,1114.43.

https://hdl.handle.net/20.500.12434/24c07a98

BM 1873,0809.641 — Sheet of 6 roundels (e-fig. 90)

Israhel van Meckenem, Sheet of 6 roundels depicting Christ as Man of Sorrows, the Virgin of the Sun, and 4 scenes from the Infancy of Christ. London, British Museum, Department of Prints & Drawings, inv. 1873,0809.641.

https://hdl.handle.net/20.500.12434/c49908ee

3. The Beghards in the Sixteenth Century

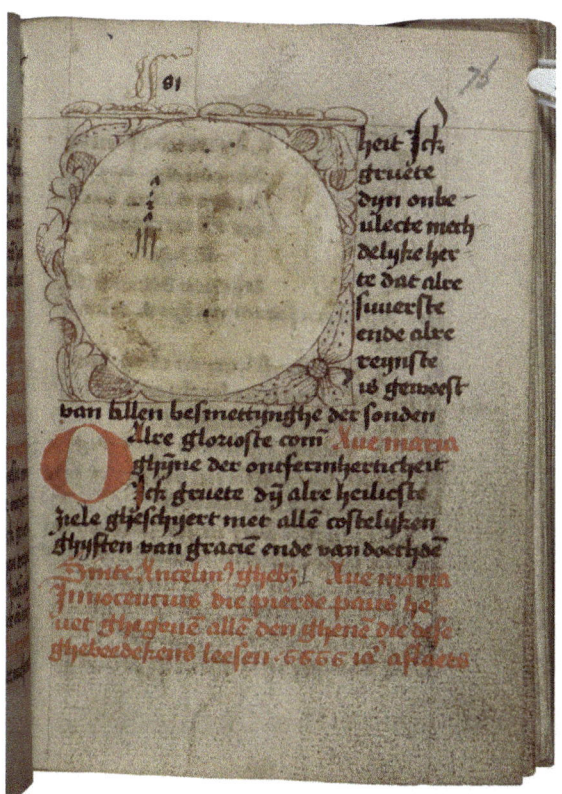

Fig. 105
Folio from the beghard's later manuscript with a prayer, an indulgence, and a blank area where a Marian roundel was formerly pasted. London, British Library, Add. Ms. 31002, vol. I, fol. 76r.

These and other roundels have been accessioned into the British Museum without their respective manuscript substrates. The folios from which small prints were steamed reveal something of the making process. For example, one emptied roundel has the letter M inside, to which someone has added 'Maria' (to be read vertically, from bottom to top) to clarify what was to be glued onto the blank (fig. 105). Other folios with prints that have been steamed off reveal that someone used this same technique of planning out the book, jotting down the name of the saint that should eventually be pasted in. For example, the preceding folio formerly bearing an image of the Virgin has a similar guide word (Add. 31002, Vol. I, fol. 75r; fig. 106). This suggests that the prints were measured and planned as the scribe was writing, but that they were glued in afterwards. Perhaps the beghards separated the operations of writing and gluing, because writing on a freshly glued page could be damp and lumpy. Separating the tasks, and dividing the labour, was part of the general trend towards efficiency. This is different from the process by which Add. 24332 was made, as described earlier, in which the scribe seems to have pasted in images as he went along.

Fig. 106
Folio from the beghard's later manuscript with a prayer and a blank area where a Marian print was formerly pasted. London, British Library, Add. Ms. 31002, vol. I, fol. 75r.

Apparently, the beghards bought several sheets of Israhel's printed roundels when they had the opportunity to do so. From such a sheet, they used in a manuscript his image of SS Cosmas and Damian (e-fig. 91); a SS Francis and Clare (e-fig. 92); and a SS Dominic and Catherine of Siena (e-fig. 93).

These have all been cut from a single sheet, signed by Israhel van Meckenem (e-fig. 65). It is possible that they used the other three for the earlier project. In fact, the roundel with St Ursula would fit perfectly in Add. 24332, on folio *cccc xlij* (396). A fuller picture of the beghards' access to and use of prints emerged not only when I

BM 1868,1114.178 — SS Cosmas and Damian (e-fig. 91)

Israhel van Meckenem, SS Cosmas and Damian roundel. Engraving removed from the beghards' later book of hours. London, British Museum, Department of Prints & Drawings, inv. 1868,1114.178.

https://hdl.handle.net/20.500.12434/b139197d

BM 1868,1114.158 — SS Francis and Clare (e-fig. 92)

Israhel van Meckenem, SS Francis and Clare roundel. Engraving removed from the beghards' later book of hours. London, British Museum, Department of Prints & Drawings, inv. 1868,1114.158.

https://hdl.handle.net/20.500.12434/3805277f

BM 1868,1114.117 — SS Dominic and Catherine of Siena (e-fig. 93)

Israhel van Meckenem, SS Dominic and Catherine of Siena roundel. Engraving removed from the beghards' later book of hours. London, British Museum, Department of Prints & Drawings, inv. 1868,1114.117.

https://hdl.handle.net/20.500.12434/cb7df4d6

reconstructed both manuscripts, but also when I considered the two manuscripts together. One scenario that fits the evidence is this: the beghards bought single sheets of several of Israhel's roundels, with six subjects to a page, in or shortly before 1500. They cut the roundels apart and then used several of them in Add. 24332. Most of these were recognised by a nineteenth-century collector and removed with a knife, leaving square holes in the page. Only three of these survived in the manuscript at the time it was sold to the British Museum. The BM removed these remaining three, and accessioned them in Prints and Drawings. In the 1520s in Maastricht, the beghards used more of the Israhel roundels in their subsequent experiments involving gluing prints to manuscripts. Many more of these roundels survived in Add. 31002, until 1868 when the BM steamed them all off and accessioned them.

In addition to the sheets by Israhel, the beghards had access to other sheets of roundels. In fact, they used another sheet of roundels intact and inserted the entire thing as folio 366 in the original Add. 31002 (e-fig. 94).

BM 1868,1114.188 — Five roundels depicting the most lucrative indulgenced images (e-fig. 94)

Five roundels depicting the most lucrative indulgenced images. Hand-coloured engraving used as manuscript page, removed from the beghards' later book of hours. London, British Museum, Department of Prints & Drawings, inv. 1868,1114.188.

https://hdl.handle.net/20.500.12434/4b46faac

The maker of this page of roundels, who signed the print '+ML', identified the most potent indulgenced images and printed them together as a single sheet, so that five circles each contain a devotional image: Christ as the Man of Sorrows standing in his tomb with the *Arma Christi* (the Gregorian vision); the Virgin and Child with St Anne; the Virgin of the Sun; St Veronica holding the sudarium; and the initials 'IHS' *in sole*. St Gregory's vision was well-known as an image that activated a prayer beginning 'Adoro te in cruce pendentem', which granted the votary thousands of years of purgatorial remission.[17] Likewise, the votaries had to view an image of the Virgin of the Sun in order to win an indulgence of 11,000 years.

This printed leaf has been used as a page in a prayerbook and therefore was inscribed on the back. While the printer probably conceived these five as separate images to be cut apart, possibly to create instant historiated initials, it is not clear why the book maker left the sheet intact: possibly it was to multiply the benefits of the images grouped together on the single page. Other, larger, full-page versions of each of these subjects appeared elsewhere in the manuscript, so perhaps here the book maker was simply experimenting with the form. This is yet another way that, by ca. 1525, the beghards were bending the prints to their own requirements, having had at least 25 years' experience making such manuscripts and wrestling the rigid objects into their new manuscript creations. Rather than cutting the

---

17   For the Mass of St Gregory and ideas about purgatory, see Rudy, *Rubrics, Images and Indulgences in Late Medieval Netherlandish Manuscripts*, pp. 101–36.

sheet apart, the beghards chose the path of least resistance and simply used the entire sheet as a page, foliating it '365' at the top. It is clear that the market was trying to supply book makers with new wares, but that sometimes the market misjudged its buyers' needs. Users adapted the prints accordingly.

The beghards had other prints that have been attributed to Israhel, including an engraving depicting St Quirinus that gives the saint the haughty look of a noble knight (e-fig. 95). This, like other engravings of saints, was cut from a larger sheet. It is possible that the beghards bought two or more copies of this print when they had the opportunity in or shortly before 1500. It would have fitted thematically on the now-missing fol. *ccc lv* of Add. 24332 (see the Appendix).

BM 1868,1114.116 — St George/Quirinus (e-fig. 95)

Israhel van Meckenem, St George/Quirinus. Engraving removed from the beghards' later book of hours. London, British Museum, Department of Prints & Drawings, inv. 1868,1114.116.

https://hdl.handle.net/20.500.12434/1fc325da

Whereas the nineteenth-century curators in London created mounts on which they juxtaposed related prints — often those they assigned to the same hand or 'school' — the curators in Paris went a step further and reconstructed sheets of prints. For example, they placed their copy of the St Quirinus alongside the three other prints from the same sheet (fig. 107). Whereas the SS Cornelius, Hubert, and Quirinus prints had apparently survived in someone's print collection where they remained quite clean, the fourth print in the group — of St Anthony — was gleaned from some other source (a prayerbook?) where it had been used and soiled. Parisian curators brought the four saints back together on the page, lining them up as if Israhel had just printed them there. Clearly, their first intention was to pay homage to the master, to reconstruct his oeuvre, at the expense of showing the prints' original context or function. By literally trimming off that context, they have made it especially difficult to reconstruct.

Fig. 107
Israhel van Meckenem, St Quirinus and three other saints, separate engravings mounted on one sheet. Paris, BnF, Département des Estampes, Ea48aRes(IvM). Published with kind permission from the Bibliothèque nationale de France.

This says much about nineteenth-century sensibilities. They valued the hand of the maker, in other words, genius. It also explains why so many engravings were attributed to Israhel. 'Genius magnetism' is especially prevalent in fifteenth-century art, when only a few makers signed their works. Meanwhile, the large anonymous remainder is more difficult to categorise, and somehow less satisfying, because it is easier psychologically to imagine the past if one can populate it with proper names. The nineteenth-century project of cataloguing required that objects be categorised by names, and that the genius's creations be reassembled chronologically into early, middle, and late periods. Many other prints were assigned to Israhel, making his output appear even larger than it was. Some of the unsigned objects, which were deemed lower in quality, could easily slide into his early period, or be deemed prints made from reworked plates.

Nineteenth-century cataloguers revelled in attributing other engravings from Add. 31002 to Israhel, including, for example, an engraving depicting Christ at Emmaus (e-fig. 96).

BM 1868,1114.37 — Christ at Emmaus (e-fig. 96)

Christ at Emmaus. Engraving removed from the beghards' later book of hours. London, British Museum, Department of Prints & Drawings, inv. 1868,1114.37.

https://hdl.handle.net/20.500.12434/b2b6888f

This engraving comes from a large suite comprehending 55 sheets in several variations. Lehrs attributed the series to Israhel, claiming that he copied it from the so-called Master of the Martyrdom of the Ten Thousand, which in turn, was largely copied from a series by the Master of the Berlin Passion. In other words, Lehrs constructed a complicated pedigree for this and a group of related prints.

Lehrs also attributed a group of apostles to Israhel. These early prints include the engravings depicting St Mark and St Bartholomew discussed earlier (e-fig. 73) and a closely related St Luke (e-fig. 97).

BM 1868,1114.184 — St Luke (e-fig. 97)

St Luke. Engraving removed from the beghards' later book of hours. London, British Museum, Department of Prints & Drawings, inv. 1868,1114.184.

https://hdl.handle.net/20.500.12434/5fc58440

Lehrs thought that these came from the same apostle series and were by Israhel, but Hollstein did not think the prints were by him. They are, however, from the late fifteenth century: this can be established because the St Mark also appears in Add. 24332, whose *terminus post quem* is 1500. From this one can deduce that the beghards had purchased a great number of prints before 1500 and still had not exhausted the supply in the 1520s, while at the same time replenishing the supply with new prints, made by both German and Dutch printmakers. These apostle prints are in a much older style than the other prints that the beghards added to Add. 31002; assuming that they purchased them before 1500, they therefore had them around for more than 20 years before inserting them into Add. 31002. Either they possessed a large supply of prints, or else they had a small, precious cache and used them slowly. Lehrs also assigned an engraving depicting the Circumcision of Christ to Israhel van Meckenem (e-fig. 98) asserting that he had copied it from the Master of the Berlin Passion.

BM 1868,1114.85 — Circumcision of Christ (e-fig. 98)

Circumcision of Christ, attributed to Israhel van Meckenem. Engraving removed from the beghards' later book of hours. London, British Museum, Department of Prints & Drawings, inv. 1868,1114.85.

https://hdl.handle.net/20.500.12434/91db362d

It is possible that the beghards obtained this print around 1500, together with others from this series, including that of Jairus's Daughter (1861,1109.636), to which it is closely related (e-fig. 55).

Some early prints simply did not fit into these neat categories, so the cataloguers grouped them and came up with new personalities for them, often with unfortunate names. One of these was the Master of the Martyrdom of the Ten Thousand. This artist became a catch-all for engravings of middling quality, which were not quite good enough to attribute to Israhel.[18] One of these, for example, represents the Virgin Mary as a child climbing the steps of the Temple (e-fig. 99).

BM 1868,1114.197 — Virgin Mary as a child climbing the steps of the Temple (e-fig. 99)

Virgin Mary as a child climbing the steps of the Temple. Engraving removed from the beghards' later book of hours. London, British Museum, Department of Prints & Drawings, inv. 1868,1114.197.

https://hdl.handle.net/20.500.12434/93ffcf6d

It was claimed that the Master of the Martyrdom of the Ten Thousand copied it after the Master of the Berlin Passion, one anonymous entity copying another.

---

18 For a discussion of attributions to this artist, see Weekes, *Early Engravers and Their Public*, pp. 60–65 and passim.

I am not interested here in arguing with, or refuting, the lineage of these prints according to Lehrs and Hollstein, but I want to make three points: first, that nineteenth-century cataloguers were quick to attribute prints to Israhel. Second, that in the late fifteenth century the market for prints was growing quickly enough to support several different printers in the Rhine basin making series of similar prints, depicting the lives of Jesus and Mary. They exploited the growing market by engraving their own sets of plates (or refreshing existing plates), making subtle changes. In the end, they made a living by copying the copies. And third, that regardless of whether Israhel made this particular print or not, he was particularly adept at scooping up prints, series, and ideas and remaking and rebranding them. Part of his innovation was to churn out prints, anticipating a large number of needs and potential uses, and to distribute them widely and aggressively.

Conclusion: Changes Over Three Decades

Because the beghards of Maastricht made at least two manuscripts with pasted prints, comparing the early one (Add. 24332) with the late one (Add. 31002) reveals changes in the types of prints available from 1500 to ca. 1525, in the subjects and media of those prints, and corresponding shifts in devotion. Beghards were obtaining prints from a variety of sources over the course of several decades. In Add. 24332 the earliest prints might date from the 1460s, and the latest prints in Add. 31002 from the 1520s. Thus, they were dealing with printmaking as it developed over 70 years. These prints were made with a variety of media, in different sizes, shapes, and dimensions. As this evidence has suggested, when the beghards wrote and assembled Add. 31002 ca.1525, they still had a number of early (that is, pre-1500) prints available to them.

The early and the late manuscript differ in their attention to saints. The calendar in Add. 31002, which has been turned into a table of contents, indicates that it originally had far fewer suffrages and individual prayers to saints than did Add. 24332. Whereas there is only one Rosary prayer in Add. 24332, Add. 31002 has several, with an entire bouquet of images of the Virgin of the Sun, the Virgin of the Rosary, the Apocalyptic Virgin, and related imagery that grew up to meet the demands of the Rosary devotion.[19] In the intervening years between 1500 and ca. 1525, many more prints relevant to these devotions became available. I suspect that they were even cheaper by ca. 1525, and they were quite commonplace.

One major difference was in the attitude towards colour. For the earlier manuscript, the beghards used the prints in the way they had received them, either coloured or not. In the later manuscript, Add. 31002, the prints arrived mostly uncoloured. But the beghards must have taught themselves to hand-colour the images, for hundreds of them receive a similar treatment and palette. It is possible that they wanted to use colour in order to impose an evenness, a unity, on the images, which otherwise presented a hodgepodge of sizes, styles, and shapes.[20] These prints bear coloured washes in characteristic tones, comprising a limited palette: yellow, orange-red (a colour often used for frames), and olive-green washes, maroon (which has often flaked off), grey (which may be watered-down ink, as on SS Dominic and Catherine of Siena (e-fig. 93)), and occasionally teal (as on the robe that Death wears in Israhel's Death visiting the pope, 1868,1114.74 (e-fig. 85), which the beghards applied to most of the prints in Add. 31002. Clearly, they had acquired the print in an uncoloured state, and then applied the colours themselves.

A second major difference relates to experimentation and confidence: whereas Add. 24332 is uneven, with several scribes, emendations, and long sections without any prints, Add. 31002 is remarkably even throughout. Add. 24332 may represent the beghards' first attempt at making a manuscript with prints; as I suggested in the previous chapter, the beghards began affixing the prints only after they had already begun copying the book, and they revised their methods as they went along. By the 1520s, they were thoroughly familiar with the technique and executed it evenly. Those later book makers were perfecting a system

---

19   For a detailed history, see Anne Winston-Allen, *Stories of the Rose: The Making of the Rosary in the Middle Ages* (University Park, PA: Pennsylvania State University Press, 1997).

20   A similar strategy is described in Kathryn M. Rudy, 'Reconstructing the Delbecq-Schreiber Passion (as part of the St Godeleva manuscript)', *Unter Druck. Mitteleuropäische Buchmalerei im 15. Jahrhundert. Akten der Tagung, Wien, Österreichische Akademie der Wissenschaften, 13.1.–17.1.2016*, herausgegeben von Jeffrey F. Hamburger und Maria Theisen. Buchmalerei des 15. Jahrhunderts in Mitteleuropa Herausgeben von Jeffrey F. Hamburger, Band 15 (Petersberg: Michael Imhoff Verlag, 2018), pp. 156–67.

that had been invented a generation earlier, and they figured out how to use penwork to fill in gaps for awkwardly-sized prints.

Another difference between the books concerns the content, both textual and visual. Add. 24332 contains numerous texts that offer indulgences, whereas the later book does not, with relatively few rubrics announcing them.[21] It is possible that the controversies around indulgences — which ultimately led to the Protestant Reformation — had already made their mark on the beghard community by 1525, and that they were steering their devotions in other directions. Instead of indulgences, Add. 31002 emphasises the Rosary, with multiple prints depicting the Virgin within a string of beads. In one of these, the painter has carefully coloured the beads yellow and red, possibly to suggest amber nuggets with coral beads after each decade (1868,1114.172, e-fig. 100). Another shows the Virgin of the Sun appearing to St Dominic, which refers to the origin myth of the Rosary devotion (1868,1114.211, e-fig. 101). A third print of the same subject treats the image more simply (1868,1114.51, e-fig. 102). A fourth depicts the dragon below the Virgin's feet, and emphasises the shape of the rosary with red roses (1868,1114.98, e-fig. 103). These closely related examples show the extent to which printmakers both responded to and also created a market for rosary paraphernalia.

BM 1868,1114.172 — Rosary print (e-fig. 100)

Rosary print. Engraving removed from the beghards' later book of hours. London, British Museum, Department of Prints & Drawings, inv. 1868,1114.172.

https://hdl.handle.net/20.500.12434/9d1ea162

BM 1868,1114.211 — Rosary image (e-fig. 101)

Rosary image, with the Virgin of the Sun appearing to St Dominic. Engraving removed from the beghards' later book of hours. London, British Museum, Department of Prints & Drawings, inv. 1868,1114.211.

https://hdl.handle.net/20.500.12434/e14aa8c6

---

21   That the beghards concerned themselves with indulgences is a topic I took up in a previous study: Kathryn M. Rudy, *Rubrics, Images and Indulgences in Late Medieval Netherlandish Manuscripts*, pp. 40–41.

BM 1868,1114.51 — Rosary image (e-fig. 102)

Rosary image, with the Virgin of the Sun. Engraving removed from the beghards' later book of hours. London, British Museum, Department of Prints & Drawings, inv. 1868,1114.51.

https://hdl.handle.net/20.500.12434/fe120a58

BM 1868,1114.98 — Rosary image (e-fig. 103)

Rosary image. Engraving removed from the beghards' later book of hours. London, British Museum, Department of Prints & Drawings, inv. 1868,1114.98.

https://hdl.handle.net/20.500.12434/ec7218ed

These rosary subjects did not appear in the beghards' earlier manuscript. But one might ask how much these changes reflect changing notions of devotion. Perhaps printers were foisting particular kinds of devotion onto the public, because certain practices could be summarized by and reliant upon a single-leaf print. But to what extent did printers' changing wares reflect the devotional tastes of the public, and to what extent did they shape those tastes? I shall argue that printmakers inflected the shape and content of manuscripts themselves. That they also encouraged the public to participate in an image-centred devotion (for which the printmakers could supply the images) seems entirely plausible.

The other set of changes concerns the prints themselves, which reveal dramatic changes in style and technique over the period under scrutiny. As I showed earlier, prints after c. 1520, such as those by Jacob Binck, were often made with borders, and those borders were often heavily Italianizing or contained secular features. Furthermore, the medium had shifted. Whereas the earlier period saw experiments with woodcut, metalcut, and engraving, by the later period, engraving stood out as the normal medium for the kinds of small prints that someone might glue into a book. (Of course, Dürer was still using woodcut as a technique, but he seems to have been exploiting it as a self-conscious artistic statement in images such as *Knight, Death and the Devil*. Dürer's speciality prints may have been destined for collectors, not for those who wanted to populate a prayerbook with saints.) What remained constant over the period in question was an interest in, and reliance on, prints by Israhel. His works remained topical and fashionable for half a century. Perhaps, too, he had flooded the market, or even created the market.

By the 1520s the beghards of Maastricht had acquired a number of income-generating skills. They ran a school, they wove linen, they operated a bindery, and obviously they made manuscripts. It is unlikely, however, that they made prints, and a few pieces of evidence support that conclusion: first, if they had an in-house engraver, why would they continue to buy numerous prints from other sources? Any engraver would, presumably, have a modicum of graphic skills, but the shoddy drawings left in Add. 31002 suggest that there was nobody with such skills in the house. Furthermore, while the beghards made a considerable number of un-illustrated manuscripts, I do not have any evidence that they made more books with prints than just these two. They may have made dozens, but I have no proof of this.

Of the vast number of prints that entered the BM on 14 November 1868, the final ten in the series were different from the rest. They did not have the same subdued washes, but were painted with thick gouache, finished with gold leaf. Furthermore, they were all from a generation earlier, several of them copies after the Master of the Berlin Passion. Was it possible that the beghards had stacks of prints that they used up over the course of decades? After all, they owned at least two copies of the St Mark, which they used with a twenty-five-year interval between them. A simpler answer, though, is far more likely: these ten prints had been removed from a different manuscript altogether. These, and other manuscripts formerly bearing prints, are the subjects of the next chapter.

4. Manuscripts with Prints: A Sticky Idea

As part of my regular job as curator of illuminated manuscripts at the Koninklijke Bibliotheek (from 2006–2009) I acquired a few items for the collection. A manuscript written in the vernacular from the Meuse valley, near Roermond or Venlo, with numerous prints pasted into it (and not ripped or cut out) came onto the market, and I wrote a proposal to purchase it. But my bosses wanted to know whether it was made in the Netherlands or Germany, which was a difficult question considering that these nations did not even exist when the manuscript was made around 1490, and no clear language barrier separated the regions; rather, Middle Dutch morphed into German as one travelled from west to east in the fifteenth century. They would only consider releasing the money if I could prove that the manuscript was made on 'our' side of the line. I began to realise the extent to which nationalism plays a role in museum and library acquisitions.

While working at the Koninklijke Bibliotheek in The Hague, my mental health started crumbling. I took a trip to Paris for a weekend with an old friend, shortly before a consultation with a doctor, who afterwards asked, 'Did you enjoy Paris?' I answered in the negative, and was diagnosed instantaneously as depressed. Failing to enjoy Paris is the clinical test in the Netherlands that determines whether or not they give you prescription drugs. During that period of 2006–2009, escaping to London was my greatest tonic. I would fly or take the Eurostar, go straight to the British Museum with my luggage, then work very slowly, immersing myself in a paper world free of meetings and managers. Under these conditions, leaves from Add. 24332 and Add. 31002 surfaced slowly. They were distributed across dozens of boxes and, of course, as I was going through them, I tried to fight the temptation not to look at other fascinating objects in those boxes, but I always succumbed. This added several years to the project. Matching up *membra* that had become *disjecta* across European collections was like playing the card game Memory, in a session that would last more than a decade. I began amassing a rather large collection of prints — or rather, digital pictures of prints — that had formerly been pasted into manuscripts.

For work-related travel, I often extended trips by a day or two to work in libraries and archives. I looked for orphaned prints and for manuscripts with holes and shadows. All these travels and plunges into the archival material revealed the extent of the intermarriages between script and print. I was able to go through the Netherlandish manuscripts in the British Library, the Morgan, the Staatliche Museen Preussischer Kulturbesitz in Berlin, the Germanisches Nationalmuseum in Nuremberg, the Koninklijke Bibliotheek van België in Brussels, the Bibliothèque Nationale in Paris, the Fitzwilliam Museum, the University Library, and Trinity College in Cambridge, and of course the Koninklijke Bibliotheek in The Hague, as well as approximately 80 other smaller libraries and private collections during the thirteen years I have been working on this and related projects.

In visiting these collections, I looked for fragments from print-manuscript hybrids, while also searching more specifically for the remaining prints taken from the beghards' early manuscript (Add. 24332). What other prints did the beghards collect around 1500? Which prints did the modern collectors remove first? I went through every one of the 100 enormous volumes *Einblattdrucke des Fünfzehnten Jahrhunderts*, edited by Paul Heitz and Wilhelm Ludwig Schreiber (Straßburg: Paul Heitz, 1899–2016). These volumes have facsimiles of the prints tipped onto their large album-like pages, so the books themselves resemble the collector's archive. The early collectors were the very people who were writing and publishing these volumes, including Wiegel, Schreiber, and Heitz; consequently, the ways in which early collectors mounted prints inflected the ways in which early scholars of the material published them. With the scholar, the collector, and the archivist barely distinguishable, their methods blended and reflected one another.

I looked for groups of prints that all entered a collection on a single day; prints with late medieval handwriting on them; prints with a distinctive kind of painting, even if they were not in the same collection. I travelled to Maastricht twice to poke around in the hope that the rest of the prints from Add. 24332 might have dropped close to the tree. Curators at the Ruusbroec Library in Antwerp showed me some previously uncatalogued early prints, but they had not come from the beghards' manuscript. I scoured the print collection at Amsterdam's Rijksmuseum, and spent several months going through the prints in the National Gallery of Art in Washington, as a fellow at the Center for Advanced Study in the Visual Arts.

During the years that I searched for prints and the manuscripts from which they had been removed, several things happened. Institutions loosened up their regulations about photography. For that I am immensely grateful. The BnF became more welcoming. More scholars (including David Areford and Suzanne Karr Schmidt) became interested in the early functions of prints. I made more than 10,000 pages of notes (not just for this project, but for the five books I worked on simultaneously during this period; serial book-writing seems to me completely inefficient). I scanned my early handwritten notes and ran them through Optical Character Recognition (OCR) software. A computer can read them better than I can. I made a multi-tiered relational database, fully illustrated. Technological advances in the twenty-first century helped to paint a picture of the great technological shift that was taking place from c. 1465 to c. 1525.

Patterns

Pattern recognition did not just mean sifting through large groups of prints to hunt for scraps of handwriting or paint: in some cases the pattern lay in the very shape of the print. For example, a ghostly void haunts the painted frame of a book of hours now preserved in the British Library, Add. Ms. 17524 (fig. 108).[1] This book of hours, written in Middle Dutch, has 'metallic borders' decoration typical of manuscripts made near Arnhem in the mid-fifteenth century. Such borders, with burnished gold leaf baguettes dominating the decorative programme,

---

1 Robert Priebsch, *Deutsche Handschriften in England*. 2 vols (Erlangen: Fr. Junge, 1896–1901), vol. II, no. 186; Ursula Weekes, *Early Engravers and Their Public*, pp. 145–50, 157, 159.

were produced by convent sisters in this region. They affixed prints alongside colourful decoration to mark the incipits of major text divisions. They used prints to take the place of miniatures and adopted the visual vocabulary of hand-crafted manuscript illumination layered upon the mechanically reproduced images. The sisters pasted the prints onto blank pages — almost always the left side of an opening, to face an incipit — and then painted the prints with body colour used for illuminating manuscripts, and added elaborate painted and gilt borders.

The opening at the Hours of Eternal Wisdom brandishes a parchment-coloured space within the image frame, made when its print was lifted. At some point the exact print removed from this folio revealed itself in a box at the British Museum: a Christ as Salvator Mundi (e-fig. 104).

BM 1848,0212.119 — Christ as Salvator Mundi (e-fig. 104)

Christ as Salvator Mundi, silhouetted. Engraving removed from what is now London, British Library, Add. Ms. 17524. London, British Museum, Department of Prints & Drawings, inv. 1848,0212.119.
https://hdl.handle.net/20.500.12434/6357207f

I would not have been able to connect this print and this manuscript had the print not first been silhouetted. The manuscript's makers had apparently cut the printed image down to the quick so that they could gild and burnish the background. Gold sticks to parchment better than it does to paper, and tough parchment can withstand the rigours of burnishing, whereas Western paper often cannot. Trimmed into a rectangle, the print would not have yielded a sufficiently distinctive shape to identify it with certainty. Perhaps what's extraordinary about this is that the person who constructed this book recognized the artistry of the engraving, did not try to apply paint to it, and found that an appropriate response to the flimsy paper image was to frame it in a thick layer of gold. She or he had ample resources at hand, including enough gold foil to fill in the entire area behind Christ and tool the surface with decorative punches. Virtually replacing the image in the gold recess feels like the resolution of a tense absence.

What the sisters in Arnhem were creating might be termed *skeumorphs*, which according to a dictionary definition are 'an object or feature which imitates the design of a similar artefact made from another

Fig. 108 Opening at the Hours of Eternal Wisdom, in a book of hours from the region of Arnhem. London, British Library, Add. Ms. 17524, fol. 109v-110r.

material'. Instead of hand-drawn lines and forms on parchment, they used printed lines on paper. In so doing, they produced books of hours that had traditional design features associated with luxury manuscripts: richly painted and gilt concoctions on parchment with a hierarchy of decoration that reiterated the structure of the book. Silhouetting the prints minimized the amount of exposed paper and simultaneously maximized the parchment. In addition to pages embellished with prints, they also created illuminations painted directly onto the parchment page, but these consisted of abstract shapes, simplified figures such as the abstracted Lamb of God, and devotional letters such as the IHS monogram.[2] In other words, the sisters avoided drawing human figures and relied instead on prints to provide them.

At the Hours of the Cross, there was probably a painted crucifixion, which has made an inroad into the decoration at the top of the frame (fig. 109). I have not identified the exact print that was lifted from this spot. Two hand-coloured engravings remain in Add. 17524: the Dormition (fol. 137v) to preface the Penitential Psalms; and Abraham sacrificing Isaac (fol. 157v) to preface the Office of the Dead. These are odd choices to face these texts, and they suggest that the sisters who made the manuscript had difficulty obtaining the prints they needed for the books of hours they were making, and they therefore made do with the motifs at hand. Such was a shortcoming of using engravings: printers produced their wares at some remove from the consumers, and the consumers only occasionally dictated the subjects of the prints.[3]

Both the manuscript (now Add. 17524) and the loose print (the engraving representing Christ as Salvator Mundi) entered the collection of the British Museum in 1848, but they arrived via different routes. The British Museum purchased the manuscript in 1848 from antiquarian

---

2   Kathryn M. Rudy, 'Manuscripts from Zutphen, Lamb of God roundels, and a new iconography of penance', special issue of *Quaerendo* 41 dedicated to Prof. Dr. Jos Hermans, ed. by Jos Biemans and Anne Korteweg (2011), pp. 360–72.

3   The three engravings depicting Our Lady of Einsiedeln, made by the Master ES in 1466, provide examples. The Swiss monastery commissioned the prints as part of their jubilee celebration. See Landau and Parshall, *The Renaissance Print*, p. 49. Convent sisters may have also commissioned prints with particular subjects, especially those communicating their corporate identity, for which see the various studies by Weekes. Margaret of Austria apparently commissioned a print on parchment depicting St Margaret as a shepherdess, for which see Rudy, *Postcards on Parchment*, pp. 91–98.

Figs. 109 Opening at the Hours of the Cross, in a book of hours from the region of Arnhem. London, British Library, Add. Ms. 17524, fol. 59v–60r.

bookseller Th. Rodd, London, and bought the print from the London art dealer Colnaghi on 12 February 1848. The print was one of 630 items that the Museum accessioned that day. Here is a case, therefore, where a dealer is probably the person who peeled the print from its manuscript substrate.

With the absence of important clues (script on the print that might help to anchor it to a particular language region, a distinctive shape, a paper trail, a provenance, some distinctive iconography), the task of reconstructing becomes much more difficult. Many manuscripts have 'holes' in them where prints or other images were formerly pasted. One of these is a book of hours probably made by Franciscan women in Zutphen, not far from Arnhem (fig. 110).[4] At each of the major text divisions, the manuscript has a large decorated initial, with painted and gilt border decoration on four sides, and a facing folio that would originally have contained an image. I have not tracked down all the prints that I presume went into these spaces, but propose that the opening at the incipit of the Hours of the Holy Spirit might have had an engraving of the Pentecost, which fits perfectly into the hole. An example survives in London, although this is unlikely to be the very print that originally filled the hole, as the colours clash like pickles and cream (e-fig. 105).

BM 1847,0318.128 — Pentecost (e-fig. 105)

Pentecost, engraving. London, British Museum, Department of Prints & Drawings, inv. 1847,0318.128.

https://hdl.handle.net/20.500.12434/d63bfd64

One always has the feeling that the staff who fetch the prints are slightly put out, so one does not want to vex them, but to request only as many boxes as can be worked through in a single day. Curators and reading room attendants have the institutional knowledge, expertise, and an overview of the collection to be able to recommend books, catalogues, other prints, and resources or, on a bad day, they can withhold all these things. I knew, from being on the other side, how close some overworked, underpaid cultural workers might be to snapping.

---

4   Rudy, 'Manuscripts from Zutphen'.

4. *Manuscripts with Prints: A Sticky Idea* 253

Fig. 110 Opening in a book of hours probably made by Franciscan women in Zutphen, with space left for prints to be pasted in. The Hague, Koninklijke Bibliotheek, Ms. 77 L 58, fol. 85v-86r.

Hiding in Plain Sight: Prints from Another Drugulin Manuscript

For the date 14 November 1868, none of the last ten items in the BM's Prints & Drawings Register (222–31) appears in *Naumann's Archiv* (discussed in Chapter 3). These ten are not flagged as being different or separate in the Register, where, for example, 231 is described as 'Christ on the cross in the middle of a sort of dial, with vignettes below of the Mass of St Gregory and the virgin with St Anne' (e-fig. 106). No. 229 is 'Seven medallions on a wheel, surmounted by a figure of the virgin with the child'. (e-fig. 107).

BM 1868,1114.231 — Christ on the cross on Earth (e-fig. 106)

Christ on the cross on Earth surrounded by the rings of the planets of the solar system, with the Mass of St Gregory, the Annunciation, and the Virgin *in sole* below. Hand-coloured engraving removed from what is now London, British Library, Ms. 31001. London, British Museum, Department of Prints & Drawings, inv. 1868,1114.231.

https://hdl.handle.net/20.500.12434/747401b8

BM 1868,1114.229 — Seven Joys of the Virgin (e-fig. 107)

Seven Joys of the Virgin. Hand-coloured engraving removed from what is now London, British Library, Ms. 31001. London, British Museum, Department of Prints & Drawings, inv. 1868,1114.229.

https://hdl.handle.net/20.500.12434/a6c77c4a

These descriptions are somewhat more convoluted than those in 1–221, but I was slow to realise that they comprised a separate group of prints, which came from a different manuscript entirely. Part of the reason for my slowness was that the nineteenth-century museum assistant had arranged them all together, intermingling the prints from Add. 31002 with those from another manuscript. This clustering had a powerful effect, and forged a relationship where none existed. The mounter had made a 'collection' simply by placing the prints together. For example, one matte (fig. 111) contains ten prints with devotional subjects that were entered on 14 November 1868. All share a similar scale, medium (hand-painted engraving), and palette, with red lake and a yellow wash familiar from many of the other prints lifted from Add. 31002. The print at the top centre has a large area of blue, otherwise not present in the Add. 31002 group, but I did not make anything of this the first few times I saw it. Only later did I realise that this print came from a different context, with a different palette, harvested from a different manuscript.

According to the Register for 14 November 1868, all the prints that were entered under the numbers 1–231[5] came from the Leipzig art dealer Wilhelm Eduard Drugulin. The Register gives the misleading impression that these prints all came from a single manuscript from Drugulin's collection. Rather, the 231 prints came from two manuscripts. As I have shown in the previous chapter, most of these prints were removed from the manuscript that became Add. 31002, volumes I and II, which was 'Transferred from the Dept of Prints and Drawings 24 March 1879', according to a note on the flyleaf of vol. I. The BM must have purchased the entire manuscript, prints and all, and removed the images systematically. After the print curators removed and accessioned the prints in 1868, they stored the manuscript in the Department of Prints and Drawings for eleven years, before transferring it to the Department of Manuscripts. As it turns

---

5   As explained earlier, there are 231+5 prints in this group, five of them denoted by an asterisk in order to correspond with Andersen's article.

Fig. 111
Matte from 1868, with prints taken from two manuscripts. London, British Museum, Department of Prints & Drawings.

out, a manuscript co-traveller embarked on this same journey: from the Netherlands, to Drugulin, to the British Museum's Department of Prints and Drawings, to the Department of Manuscripts. This manuscript now bears the adjacent shelf number, Add. 31001, and not only is its history entangled with that of Add. 31002 but so were its very prints. Add. 31001 bears a nearly identical note on its first flyleaf: 'Transferred from the Dept of Prints & Drawings, 24 March 1879'. Drugulin sold them to the British Museum at the same time; they were both stripped of their prints, and their prints were registered on 14 November 1868. The hulls of both books were then transferred to the Manuscripts Department on the same day together. Whoever mounted the prints made a collage with prints from both manuscripts together.

I wish I could say that I realised right away that the image at the top of the matte (see fig. 111), with Christ in half-length holding the orb, did not belong with the others. Someone had painted it with a different technique and palette from the rest of the prints stuck on the matte, but I wrote this difference off. And it is earlier than the other prints on the sheet, but again, I had begun to see these as a category and when that happens, one is predisposed to find similarities rather than differences. Only slowly did I realise that this print came from a different manuscript, by a different religious house; eventually I worked out that they had come from a prayerbook full of 'virtual' pilgrimages rather than a book of hours full of extra suffrages. When art historians write up their research, they usually just report on the solutions and conclusions, without revealing how they arrived there. They skip some steps, in which they look bumblingly stupid, and move directly to the climax. I'd wager that moments of epiphany occur only in the movies: the lightbulb goes on in the fantasy versions of our research, but rarely in reality. This set of discoveries I have been chronicling happened slowly: wrong ideas were eroded when they rubbed up against many small grains of evidence, until their shape changed into more correct notions. Events unfolded slowly. During the time it took me to finish the research for this book, I completed three others. In the down times, sometimes I connected pieces of information that led towards reconstruction. Sometimes I simply forgot things. And I had to stare at the evidence several times before accepting it, or even realising that it was evidence. Perhaps you, my reader, would have seen Christ with the orb pop out from the matte, spotted the difference straight away and known the solution. But I did not. I now see that this is the only print in the group that uses blue pigment. Once you conceptualise them as different, it is impossible to revert to seeing them as the same.

In both dismembered manuscripts — Add. 31001 and Add. 31002 — the prints were numbered in the same sequence that they had appeared in their respective manuscripts. Immediately after they were harvested, the prints from the beghards' manuscript (now Add. 31002) were given the BM accession numbers 1868,1114.1–221, as described earlier. Those prints that came from the other manuscript (Add. 31001) received the numbers 1868,1114.222–231. Seeing that these prints came from two manuscripts, not one, provides a fuller picture of the use of prints in manuscripts in the Low Countries at the end of the fifteenth and beginning of the sixteenth centuries.

Add. 31001 — a prayerbook — originally had ten distinctively painted prints glued to its paper folios, now 1868,1114.222-231 (fig. 112).⁶ When the conservator harvested the ten prints, he cut out not just the prints but the entire paper folio each was pasted to. These ten folios had text on one side and a print filling the other: indeed, the prints are only slightly smaller than the manuscript that contained them, the folios of which measure 136 x 96 millimetres. Then the conservator peeled the prints off the paper pages and accessioned them into the Department of Prints & Drawings as LBM 1868,1114.222–231. Instead of reattaching these ten folios, inscribed on one side but now blank and grubby on the other, at their correct locations within the manuscript, he simply pasted them together into a booklet and inserted this booklet at the end of the manuscript. It therefore came about that the verso sides of folios 197–206 (the last ten folios in the manuscript) are singletons stained with glue, revealing that they formerly had objects pasted to them.

Fig. 112 Ten hand-coloured engravings removed from what is now London, British Library, Ms. 31001. London, British Museum, Department of Prints & Drawings, inv. 1868,1114.222-231.

In this case, reconstructing the original order of the folios provides a clear sense of the role the images played in the maker's original plan.

---

6 I first wrote about these prints in Kathryn M. Rudy, *Virtual Pilgrimages in the Convent: Imagining Jerusalem in the Late Middle Ages* ed. Isabelle Cochelin and Susan Boynton, Disciplina Monastica, vol. 8 (Turnhout: Brepols, 2011), pp. 175–92; and 399–410, which includes a description of Add. 31001.

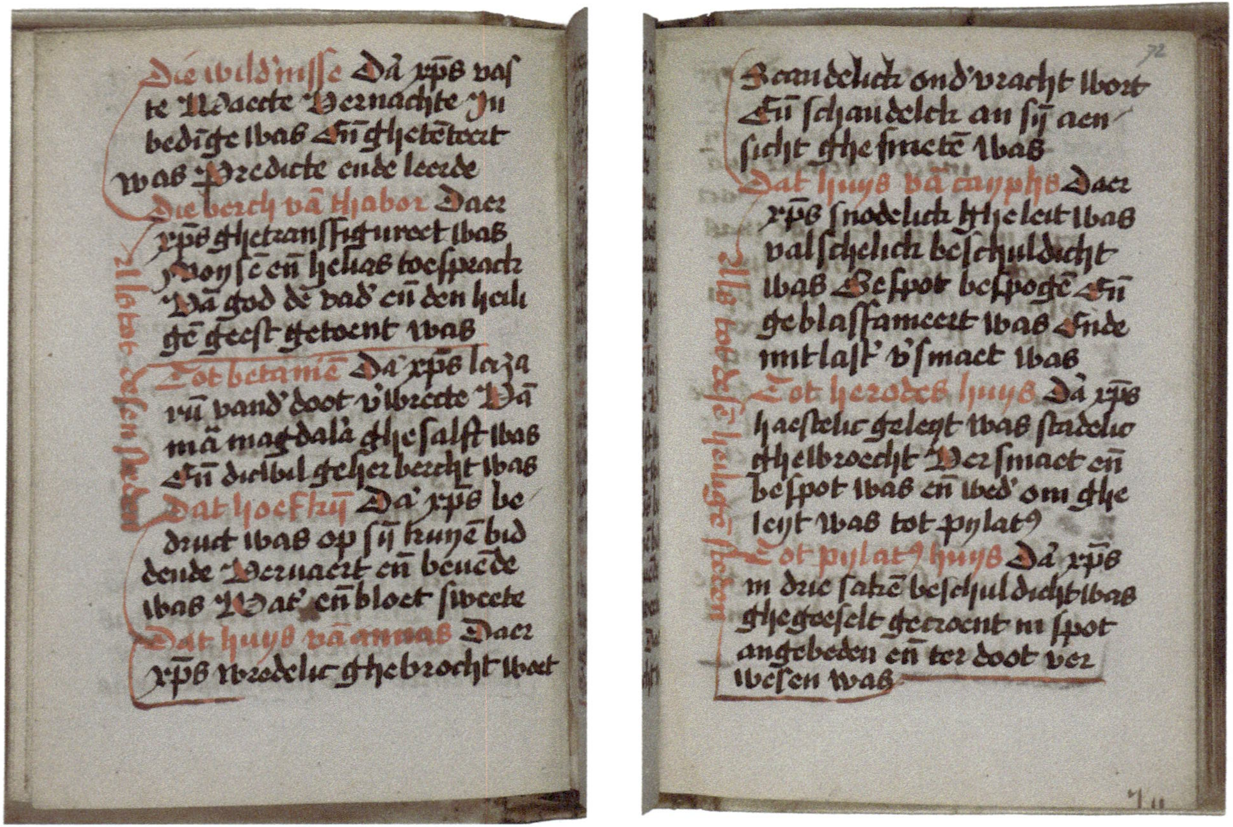

Figs. 113 Instructions for visiting sites around Jerusalem. Opening of a prayerbook with texts for conducting virtual pilgrimages. London, British Library, Ms. 31001, fols. 71v-72r.

The prints were originally used to mark the beginnings of text passages in a manuscript that contained a prayer for visiting places in the Holy Land, listing the major events that took place at each location (fig. 113). Seven of the prints were used to preface texts to the Seven Principal Churches, where each church is assigned a letter from A-G. This key is then used in a narrative calendar elsewhere in the manuscript, in which the reader virtually visits the churches according to a set sequence, earning indulgences signified by red and blue crosses (fig. 114). All this material I worked on assiduously, and the reconstructions formed the basis for analysis about how women religious used prints to aid devotions based around 'virtual' pilgrimage. These I published in a book called *Nuns' Virtual Pilgrimages*, which came out in 2011.

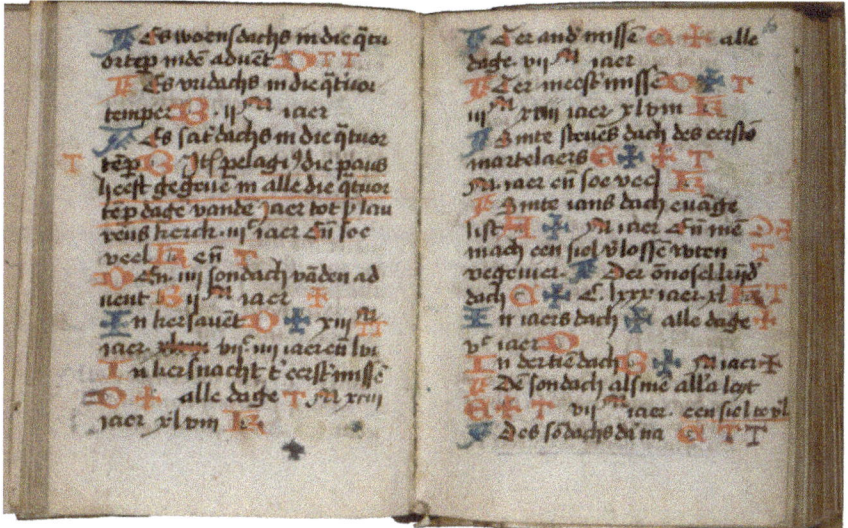

Figs. 114 Calendar with indulgences for virtual visiting the Seven Principal Churches of Rome. Opening of a prayerbook with texts for conducting virtual pilgrimages. London, British Library, Ms. 31001, fols. 59v-60r.

At that time, I followed Ulla Sander Olsen, who catalogued this manuscript as Birgittine, because on the first folio verso is this text, written in the same hand as the rest of the manuscript: 'Item, het is gemenlick in St Brigitten cloesteren, soe wie Marien eygen wil sijn, die sal op een dach van haer hoechtiden lesen vii .c. Ave Marien' (It is the usual practice in Birgittine convents, for those who want to imitate Mary herself, to read 700 Ave Marias on her feast days).[7] The most famous Birgittine manuscripts written in Dutch have been connected with the convent of Mariënwater in Rosmalen, which is where Sander Olsen localised this manuscript.[8] Stooker and Verbeij, who endeavoured to list every manuscript with an origin in a Netherlandish monastic context, repeated this assessment.[9] Although I thought that the manuscript was from Utrecht, not Rosmalen, I am guilty of following them in calling it a Birgittine manuscript without sufficient questioning. In October 2017, Clarck Drieshen at the British Library shared his analysis about this book with me and convinced me that the book was actually written in the context of a female Dominican convent.[10] For example, one prayer refers to 'our holy patron and father St Dominic, St Catherine of Siena' (fol. 185r: 'onsen heiligen potroen [sic] ende vader sint Dominicus sint Katryn vander seyn'). The litany also names St Catherine twice, one referring to St Catherine of Alexandria, the other to St Catherine of Siena, a Dominican tertiary. Catherine of Siena is also mentioned in the Golden Litany (fol. 174v). A text to earn the indulgences of the Seven Churches in Rome states that 'the brothers and sisters of the Order of Preachers must read the Seven [Penitential] psalms' (fol. 57v: 'die bruederen ende susteren vander predicaer orden moeten lesen eens een seven psalm'), whereas the text does not specify instructions for other religious orders.

Contextualising the manuscript in a Dominican rather than a Birgittine milieu changes the way in which one understands its image-text relationships. Most of the prints in the manuscript (seven out of ten, 222–228) were used to preface prayers to be read while visiting in imagination the Seven Principal Churches of Rome (fols 9r–33v, 198r–203r). These

---

7   Ulla Sander Olsen, 'Handschriften en Boeken uit het Birgittinessenklooster Maria Troon te Dendermonde', in *Spiritualia Neerlandica. Opstellen voor Dr. Albert Ampe S. J. hem door Vakgenoten en Vrienden Aangeboden uit Waardering voor zijn Wetenschappelijk Werk*, ed. E. Cockcx-Indestege, Ons Geestelijk Erf (Antwerp: Universitaire Faculteiten Sint-Ignatius te Antwerpen Ruusbroecgenotschap (Centrum voor Spiritualiteit), 1990), pp. 389–406.

8   Ulla Sander Olsen, 'Handschriften uit het Birgittinessenklooster Mariënwater te Rosmalen bij 's-Hertogenbosch,' in W. Verbeke, ed., *Serta devota in memoriam Guillelmi Lourdaux* (Leuven: Leuven University Press, 1992–1995 = Mediaevalia Lovaniensia, Series I, Studia 20–21), vol. II, pp. 225–54.

9   Stooker and Verbeij, vol. II, p. 358–59, no. 1069.

10   I am grateful to Clarck Drieshen, who generously shared his notes regarding the Dominican references in Add. 31001 when we met in London in October 2017.

churches are San Pietro, San Lorenzo, San Sebastiano, San Giovanni in Laterano, San Paolo, Sta Croce, and Sta Maria Maggiore. Each print marked a reading to one of the churches, which refers both to the church and to one of Christ's seven sheddings of blood. Most of these events belong to the Passion narrative. For example, the reader was directed to the Church of San Pietro while simultaneously addressing Jesus when he 'lay on the Mount of Olives sweating water and blood' (fol. 198r). In this way, the prayers embed the Seven Churches with the Passion narrative.[11]

Since Add. 31001 is Dominican, rather than Birgittine, it connects with a tradition of representing these Seven Principle Churches that one finds, inter alia, in the Dominican convent in Augsburg.[12] In 1496 sisters there commissioned a series of large oil paintings from Hans Holbein the Elder, Hans Burgkmair the Elder, and the artist now known as the Monogrammist LF. These paintings depict the Seven Principle Churches, but each also features an event from the Passion of Christ at the top. For example, the panel depicting the basilicas of San Lorenzo and San Sebastiano is surmounted by an image of Judas betraying Christ with a kiss (fig. 115).

A record of transaction indicates the function of these *Basilikenbilder*: the commission followed an indulgence privilege of 1487 by Pope Innocent VIII, which gave pilgrims to St Katherine's convent in Augsburg the same indulgence they would receive if they went to Rome

---

11   For a fuller discussion of this prayer and the images, see Rudy, *Virtual Pilgrimages in the Convent: Imagining Jerusalem in the Late Middle Ages*, pp. 177–83.

12   See E. Weis-Liebersdorf, *Das Jubeljahr 1500 in der Augsburger Kunst* (Munich: Algemeine Verlaggesellschaft, 1901), passim; and Gisela Goldberg, ed, *Altdeutsche Gemälde, Staatsgalerie Augsburg Städtische Kunstsammlungen, Bd. 1* (Munich: Bayerische Staatsgemäldesammlungen, 1988), 69–76 and 129–58, with further bibliography; and Gisela Goldberg, "Peregrinatio, quam vocant Romana': Miscellanea zu Stellvertreterstätten römischer Hauptkirchen', in *Wallfahrt kennt keine Grenzen*, ed. Lenz Kriss-Rettenbeck and Gerda Mohler, (exh. cat, Munich: Bayerisches Nationalmuseum) (Munich: Schnell & Steiner, 1984), pp. 346–51; Marie-Luise Ehrenschwendtner, 'Virtual Pilgrimages? Enclosure and the Practice of Piety at St Katherine's Convent, Augsburg', *Journal of Ecclesiastical History* 60, no. 1 (2009), pp. 45–73; Magdalene Gärtner, Römische Basiliken in Augsburg: Nonnenfrömmigkeit und Malerei um 1500 (Augsburg: Wissner, 2002). On virtual pilgrimage more generally, see Kathryne Beebe, 'The Jerusalem of the Mind's Eye: Imagined Pilgrimage in the Late Fifteenth Century', in *Visual Constructs of Jerusalem* ed. Bianca Kühnel, Galit Noga-Banai, and Hanna Vorholt (Turnhout: Brepols, 2014), pp. 409–20; Rudy, *Virtual Pilgrimages in the Convent: Imagining Jerusalem in the Late Middle Ages*.

Fig. 115 Attributed to the Monogrammist LF, Basilicas of San Lorenzo and San Sebastiano surmounted by an image of Judas betraying Christ with a kiss, painting on panel, 1502. Commissioned by Helena Rephonin for the Dominican convent of St Catherine in Augsburg.

during the Jubilee year of 1500.[13] The Sta Maria Maggiore is the only painting of the series to have been completed before the Jubilee. Thus, the paintings in Augsburg are contemporary with Add. 31001, and they promoted a related form of devotion: 'virtual' pilgrimage to the Seven Churches of Rome, rewarded with significant indulgences, and designed for Dominican women who may not have been able to travel. Both the series of panels and the array of prints in Add. 31001 map the Churches of Rome onto events of Christ's bloodshed, although they do not follow the same sequence and pairings. Although the panels were made in Augsburg and the manuscript in the Netherlands, they may have been informed by the same Dominican reformers.

Where was Add. 31001 made? There were only a few houses of female Dominicans in the Dutch-speaking regions:

---

13 For the indulgences available to pilgrims, real and virtual, see Nine Miedema, '"Geestelike rijckdom": over pelgrimsreizen en aflaten in de Middeleeuwen', *Een school spierinkjes: Kleine opstellen over middelnederlandse artes-literatuur*, ed. W. P. Gerritsen, Annelies van Gijsen, and Orlanda S. H. Lie (Hilversum: Verloren, 1991), pp. 123–26; and N. C. Kist, 'De aflaten der zeven kerken van Rome', *Archief voor kerkelijke Geschiedenis van Nederland* 6 (1835), pp. 303–18.

Assebroek near Bruges (Assebroek bij Brugge), called Valley of the Angels (Engelendale);

Leiden, Second Order Dominicans dedicated to Maria Magdalene, called the 'white nuns';

Westroyen near Tiel (Westroyen bij Tiel), Second Order Dominicans dedicated to Mary Magdalene;

Wijk near Duurstede (Wijk bij Duurstede), Second Order Dominicans dedicated to Mary Magdalene.

When I showed Peter Gumbert, the great codicologist, pictures of Add. 31001, he told me that it was made in the bishopric of Utrecht. With this in mind, the most likely candidates were Leiden, Westroyen, and Wijk. Given the affinities between the panels in Augsburg and the manuscript made near Utrecht, it makes sense that both their religious ideas — such as the particular approach to the Seven Churches of Rome — and engravings with religious subjects could have travelled along networks in which Dominican convents formed nodes.

The Dregs in Paris

In Paris no prints that were definitely from Add. 24332 had announced themselves. However, other fragments appeared, which revealed that other manuscripts-cum-prints had been broken down and their printed parts accessioned. A few prints in the BnF still have tattered fragments of their original context. For example, one collector apparently decided to salvage a metalcut print depicting a female saint for a print collection (fig. 116).[14] This fifteenth-century parchment leaf probably formed the final flyleaf in a manuscript prayerbook. It is clear that the leaf was cut from a manuscript, because there were at least three round badges also sewn to the page, and these were impressed into the parchment with a degree of pressure such as that exerted by a closed book. Some of the badges overlapped the print. Someone, perhaps the original owner, has also trimmed away part of the paper at the bottom, possibly so

---

14 François Courboin, *Catalogue Sommaire des Gravures et Lithogrphies composant la Réserve*, Bibliothèque Nationale, département des Estampes, 2 vols (Paris, 1900–01), no. 614; Bouchot 140; Schreiber 2716.

that she could attach a badge directly to the strong parchment rather than to the much weaker paper. On first inspection, one might think that the image represents St Dorothy, who carried a basket of flowers. Angels hold a cloth of honour behind the saint, as she carries a basket of flowers as well as a blossoming sprig. However, the inscription makes plain that the owner conceptualized the image as St Opportune, which is the name that the early owner has also written at the foot of the print in a competent fifteenth-century hand.[15] The book was later dismantled when a collector decided that the print had more value as an object in a frame. Fortunately, the dismantler realised that the substrate on which the print was attached also had some value, and therefore cut out the entire parchment leaf to which it was affixed.

Fig. 116
Folio removed from a manuscript, with a woodcut print depicting St Opportune. Paris, BnF, Département des Estampes. (Courboin 614; Bouchot 140; Schreiber 2716). Published with kind permission from the Bibliothèque nationale de France.

---

15   Lepape and Rudy, *Les Origines de l'Estampe*, p. 137.

As I have argued elsewhere, late medieval owners who affixed one thing into a book often affixed several: it was a matter of conceptualizing the book as a storage chest for small devotionalia.[16] In this case, the owner not only glued the print into the book but also attached several small round metal discs (either pilgrims' badges or tokens from having taken the Eucharist).[17] These have left an offset on the page. Apparently, the book's owner thought of this page as being the one on which he or she would collect various devotional items. The large badge may represent Mary Magdalene, whose shrine was at Ste Baume in Provence, where the saint was said to have lived as a hermit and ascended to heaven on the backs of angels to consume the Eucharist every day.

The production of prints on paper was not dissimilar from the production of badges in cheap lead-tin: both involved making small moulds for the mechanical reproduction of compact images, most of them religious (but the techniques were cheap and easy enough to experiment with non-religious images). With few exceptions (such as the Hours of Charles d'Angoulême, discussed below), only religious images ended up in manuscript prayerbooks. As far as I know, there are no occurrences of sexual imagery on badges affixed to religious manuscripts.

An image of the Descent of the Holy Spirit, engraved and then hand-painted, was used in the fifteenth century to historiate an initial in a large manuscript, possibly a choir book (fig. 117). This engraving is attributed to the Master of the Berlin Passion, who was active in the Middle and Lower Rhine regions around 1460. Abstract shapes painted around the print fill up the extra space. Later a collector cut out the colourful initial — print, frame, letter, and all — turning it into a decontextualized, independent image that would look pretty in a frame on the wall. The palette within the engraved image of the Pentecost, with strong red, blue, and green, plus purple reserved for the Virgin — is repeated in the geometric pattern framing the print. However, the large green initial and its framing red background are made in a different type of paint

---

16   Rudy, *Postcards on Parchment*, pp. 1–17 and passim.
17   See Aden Kumler, 'The Multiplication of the Species: Eucharistic Morphology in the Middle Ages', *Res* 59/60 (2011), pp. 179–91; and Kathryn Rudy, 'Sewing the Body of Christ: Eucharist Wafer Souvenirs Stitched into Fifteenth-century Manuscripts, Primarily in the Netherlands', *Journal of Historians of Netherlandish Art* 8, 1 (Winter 2016), Article 1 (48 pages).

with a slightly different palette. Whereas the print is hand-coloured in semi-transparent washes, the red and green of the frame are executed in opaque body colour, built up and modelled to depict acanthus. This suggests a division of labour. One painter made the initial, while another filled in the initial with a print and made a design to fill the otherwise awkward gap. Although some printers might have constructed prints especially for the purpose of using them as historiated initials, this rectangular one was probably not built for that purpose: roundels find a more comfortable home within letters. A fascinating element of early prints is their indeterminacy: we do not know the original intended destination for this print, nor the identity of the person who adapted it to become an initial.

Fig. 117 Pentecost engraving pasted into a painted initial removed from a manuscript. Paris, BnF, Département des Estampes, Ea 18 c Res (Lehrs 25). Published with kind permission from the Bibliothèque nationale de France.

Many of the early prints pasted into initials came from this region, as for example an engraving depicting the Virgin of the Sun, which has been carefully painted and then pasted into the letter H in a German prayerbook (fig. 61). The collector harvested the whole letter with some of the nearby script, which is rather shaky and distinctive enough to be easily recognisable. Nevertheless, I have not yet located the manuscript from which this was presumably cut. Many other prints in Paris were probably cut out of manuscripts, but they do not have any manuscript flesh hanging off their bones. Unlike London's, the collection in Paris did not, as far as I can tell, have the manuscript hulls in the manuscripts department. The Paris and London print rooms held in common the notion that prints should be filed and mounted separately in order to give them a certain curatorial or scholarly context. The archivists and librarians in the BnF of the nineteenth century used the same tools the beghards had used to assemble highly illustrated manuscripts in the first place, only they had different contextualizing priorities. This knife-and-glue approach to imposing order was a practice that stretched across post-Napoleonic Europe.

Berlin

In a formative summer in Berlin in 1990 after the Wall came down, I lived with a refugee from East Africa and a German lute-player who was into aromatherapy. It was my introduction to BBC radio, hand-whipped cream, and goat cooked with fruit. That summer I read Thomas Pynchon's *V*, and did performance art on the street in front of the British consulate, which had lent us a table for the endeavour. We were commenting on the commerce in the streets: Eastern Europeans were selling Russian underwear and discovering Nutella. When in 2015 I spent a week in Berlin to look for prints that might have come from the beghards' manuscript, the city had changed and become more generic. Fragments of wall were smashed up and offered for sale. There were no more throngs on the streets who looked like they had crawled out of a gulag. It felt more like Frankfurt and less like Kiev. There I made a last-ditch effort to find the missing cache of prints. I did not find them, but did of course find some other prints, which were at least as interesting, and told some other stories about the early attempts to move from manuscript to print in the fifteenth century.

One of these depicted St Augustine with his mitre, writing into a codex at a desk (fig. 118). This woodcut has several kinds of printed border decoration framing the saint. First, there are two boundary lines. Outside those is a layer of flower and leaf motifs. Surrounding those are two more boundary lines. In other words, the printer has added border decoration that resembles those found on illuminated manuscripts, trying to bring the visual aesthetic of printing in line with the technology it was slowly replacing. To enhance these, a decorator armed with several tools (a brush, a pen, and a metal-burnishing device) added a competing array of colour to the image. He (or she) added a metallic layer to the saint's halo and to the inner frame (most of which has flaked off), and painted the borders with washes, and then carefully painted in the figure with several intensities of red wash in order to heighten the illusionism of the drapery folds. But then the decorator (or another user) picked up a pen and dipped it in red ink and added an array of items that were not in the printed lines: the sun, moon and stars, the trajectory lines of a dove speeding into the saint's ear, a backrest for what would otherwise be an uncomfortable bench, and the saint's name, Sanctu Augustinus, by using a horizontal plank of the bench as if it were the top and bottom rulings on a manuscript page. Many of these rubricated interventions resemble those used by the beghards in Add. 24332, but here they are even more emphatic and insist on pulling the mechanically produced print back into the world of the manuscript. Here were two technologies, each fighting to occupy the top layer.

These values competed even more strongly in an unusual image in the Berlin collection, which shows the Stripping of Christ before the Crucifixion (fig. 119). Here the painter has begun with a German engraving from a Passion series and used that as a template, applying thick, opaque paints in bold colours over the printed lines. He or she has painted the landscape with an emphatic green, which is as bold in the foreground as in the background, and frames the grim events at the centre: Christ is having his purple robe pulled off his body by an armoured soldier, to which the painter has added an important detail with dabs of red paint: pulling off the garment yanked off the scabs that were covering the lacerations from the Flagellation, and reopened all the wounds. The painter has used the white paper with its delicate engraved lines to highlight the body of Christ at the centre of the image, silhouetting it against the green, so that the red-and-white body occupies

Fig. 118
St Augustine, woodcut print, hand-painted. Berlin, Kupferstichkabinett, Box 107 A3A. (Schreiber 1244 E).

the centre of attention. Brown purple has also been cleverly used for both the cross and the garment, so that these two objects isolate and frame the Corpus Christi. Moreover, the painter has modulated the colour applied to the other figures, reserving the most intense blue for the man raising his hand behind Jesus, so that his action draws the viewer's attention, but painted the figures to the right with either watered-down pigment or no pigment at all, so as to diminish their compositional importance. The thoughtful painter also produced the triple-layered frame, as well as the floral border decoration. This floriated border is unusual in that the four sides (including the left and right) are of equal width, and the overall shape of the sheet is square, not rectangular. This means that the object was not designed as a page in a manuscript, which nearly always has a thicker outer border than inner one.[18] It has traces of glue on all

---

18   I discuss this distinction in ibid, pp. 14–15 and passim.

four sides, especially at the top and bottom, which indicates that the sheet was mounted and framed, although the mounting and framing could have taken place at any point along the object's biography. Here print technology and manuscript techniques have come together to form something new: a colourful autonomous image designed to live outside a book or album, perhaps on a wall.

Fig. 119 Master the Berlin Passion, Stripping of Christ, hand-painted engraving. Berlin, Kupferstichkabinett, Inv. 2-56. (Lehrs 28 I).

Printers of single-leaf images, however, wanted to make their products competitive with the old hand-made kind, and they innovated ways to do this. A not entirely successful experiment appears in a print depicting the Virgin and Child (fig. 120).[19] Here the printer has co-opted

---

19 For a discussion of this print in the context of other engravings printed on parchment in the region of Cologne, see Weekes, *Early Engravers and Their Public*, pp. 67–69.

the material of manuscript illumination by printing the engraving on parchment. This was incorporated into a manuscript and inscribed on the back. Strangely, however, the medium of engraving calls attention to itself, because the book maker has allowed the printed lines to represent the Virgin and Child, without further hand-colouring. Studying the image reveals why. Just as the engraving of Christ formerly in Add. 17524 was silhouetted so that the parchment background could be gilded (e-fig. 104), so too this image of the Virgin and Child has been isolated and gilded. A crusty field appears behind them, consisting of a thin skin of chalk glue. This was the sticky white gesso that was applied in order to make the gold adhere. And this was the thinnest possible layer of gold leaf, most of which has launched itself from the page. Similarly, the floriated border was treated with this same mucilaginous skin. It is possible that the glue had also been applied with mechanical means by a plate, or more likely a stencil, prepared with the white sticky substance, so that the gilding process could likewise be semi-automated.[20] If this is the case, then only the tri-petalled flowers in the border would have been hand-painted, although they, too, have shed their paint, turning the sheet into a ghostly apparition of its formerly sparkly and colourful self. By printing the image, automating the gilding as far as possible, refraining from detailed penwork, and restricting the paint to the corralled areas in the gold recesses, the maker of this object found multiple ways to create something that smacked of luxury, while simultaneously reducing labour and skill.

Printers also used parchment regularly as a substrate for a particular application: making large Crucifixion prints (fig. 121). This reveals another way in which printers were trying to become involved in manuscript-making practices. They fell upon a niche in the market with large images of Christ crucified between Mary and John. A complete census of these is yet to be written. I suspect that they were made to be used in missals, which usually had one image only: the Crucifixion, to accompany the Canon of the Mass. These images wore out because they were kissed and handled during the regular course of the Mass, and book makers were sometimes employed to replace the crucifixion pages. Printers saw a gap in the market and attempted to fill it with sheets such as this one, which is printed on parchment. One can see

---

20 For this assessment, I am indebted to a conversation with Ad Stijnman.

Fig. 120
Master of the Dutuit Garden of Olives, Virgin and Child engraving, printed on parchment and gilt. Berlin, Kupferstichkabinett, Inv. 446-I (Lehrs 49).

Fig. 121
Monogrammist AG, Large Crucifixion, hand-painted engraving on parchment. Berlin, Kupferstichkabinett, Inv. 998-I (Lehrs 3b).

by the discolouration at the top, bottom, and left sides, but the clean right edge, that this sheet was cut out of a book. For collectors in areas that had become Protestant, the large printed image in a Catholic missal might have been the only part worth saving.

Bleeding into a Chalice

My slow, cheap travel around Europe had actually begun in March 1999, when I moved to Antwerp to do my dissertation research. One of my first trips had been to the Park Abbey in Heverlee, outside Leuven. It was before email was widely used, so I had written a letter to the Abbey to ask to see one of their manuscripts, which Maria Meertens had described.[21] I quickly received a note back, with an invitation to visit. Before moving to Belgium I had studied manuscripts in New York as a graduate student at Columbia. Going to the Pierpont Morgan Library involved complying with the institution's unspoken formal dress code. I did not know what one was supposed to wear to an abbey, so I put on the only skirt-suit and heels that I had schlepped across the Atlantic, and then faced down the public transport system in Belgium. (I had put an entire milk crate full of files into my bursting luggage, which did not leave much room for clothes. As a going-away present, my flatmates had given me a roll of duct tape and a bottle of aspirin, anticipating problems with my luggage and my head.)

From Antwerp, getting to the Park Abbey involved two trains, a bus, and then a long walk in heels down what seemed an interminable, rutted, muddy track, where there were exotic chickens and fowl of every variety filling the giant yard around the abbey. The Norbertine who opened the door towered above mud-splattered me and led me in, where I quickly sidestepped a hunk of plaster that nearly fell on my

---

21 For a full description of the contents, see Maria Meertens, *De Godsvrucht in De Nederlanden. naar Handschriften van Gebedenboeken der XVe Eeuw*, 6 vols. ([n.p.]: Standaard Boekhandel, 1930–1934), vol. VI, cat. 833bis. Meerten's foliation does not correspond to the current foliation. Although she recognised that the manuscript came from Augustinian nuns in North Brabant, she did not localise it to Geel. See also Kathryn Rudy, 'How to Prepare the Bedroom for the Bridegroom', in *Frauen--Kloster--Kunst: Neue Forschungen zur Kulturgeschichte des Mittelalters: Beiträge zum Internationalen Kolloquium vom 13. bis 16. Mai 2005 anlässlich der Ausstellung 'Krone und Schleier'*, ed. Jeffrey F. Hamburger, Carola Jaeggi, and Hedwig Röckelein (Turnhout: Brepols, 2007), pp. 369–75.

head, which only seconds earlier had formed part of a deep relief ceiling sculpture representing Saul falling off his horse and becoming St Paul. I had narrowly escaped a violent religious conversion. Sagging heavily, the baroque staircase resembled a tiered wedding cake that had shifted in transit. But we did not stay in there long. He quickly whisked me outside again to an outbuilding with a double door of the sort one finds in stables. Only the lower door opened; the upper door was stuck in place. I had to crawl through chicken manure to get to the other side.

When I opened my eyes inside the dark building, what came into focus was an aquarium filled with human femurs sticking up vertically. He must have registered my surprise. 'Those are the bones of our brothers we find when we're gardening.' Next to it was a table covered in a thick green velvet cloth, covered with stacks and stacks of dusty, handwritten account books. He then indicated where I should sit, as if I were to take up a position next to the phantom accountant and his abandoned task. Next the towering Norbertine presented the manuscript to me. The small window was so filthy that it hardly let in any light, so I sacrificed the elbow of my suit to clean it. He then left me alone, with the manuscript, the chicken excrement, the pre-Napoleonic ledgers, and the skeletons. I had a film camera with me, and only one roll of 36 frames, so every shot was precious. I had enough to document the manuscript, but not the surroundings. Before I sat down to begin studying it, I reached into my bag for my glasses, and realised that I had forgotten them. In the semi-darkness, glasses-less, I thought that the manuscript contained a series of engravings forming a Passion series, plus a series of roundels and various texts in Dutch. Photographing it was a disaster, in low light without being able to focus properly, using a fully manual, film camera.

It was not until July 2005 that I was able to see the manuscript again. This time I was living in Amsterdam, where I had been in tremendous abdominal pain and had to have an operation. It was a hot July. When I returned from the hospital, I was delirious and weak, and my artist friend Henriëtte decided I was good for not much else than serving as a life model and came over and photographed the surgical wound across my abdomen. I looked like a *vièrge ouvrant*. My mother flew over to help me, and I also hired a struggling immigrant to help with laundry and household tasks. Not realising it was not a cleaning product like the other bottles under the sink, he polished my entire kitchen with

WD40. The apartment was uninhabitable, so my mother and I taped up my abdomen and went to Belgium, and then hobbled to the abbey. The chickens had disappeared, and we photographed the manuscript together in a well-lit room with frothy Rococo paintings. The hands in the pictures of the manuscript are hers.

Now under decent lighting, the manuscript, I could see, contained a series of small, engraved roundels representing scenes from the Passion of Christ. I could confirm Maria Meertens's assessment: Heverlee, Abdij van Park, Ms. 18 was made near the end of the fifteenth century for Dutch-speaking Augustinian sisters in Brabant.[22] Several features of this manuscript are highly unusual. The manuscript contains a variety of texts written in the vernacular, that is, in Middle Dutch, many of which are for communal use, and several of which are for private meditation. One text offers detailed instructions for the young sister to prepare the bedroom inside her heart for her bridegroom. As such it toggles between the extended metaphor of the heart-as-house, and concrete instructions to prepare and furnish a physical space.[23] In addition to the spiritual bedroom text, the manuscript contains prayers to be read at selected feast dates throughout the liturgical year (fols 10v–85v). In structure and style, the feast day texts are related to the Spiritual Bedroom, as both texts comprise instructions written in the second person that ask the reader to prepare and decorate the trappings associated with the respective festivities, for example to make crowns, sew special clothes, or embellish objects with particular words. Furthermore, both texts provide a running interpretation of the rituals, as well as a running commentary about the objects used in those rituals.

Many of the feast-day prayers have been illustrated with historiated initials of the sort encountered in Chapter 1: small engraved roundels, hand-coloured and pasted into initials. In all, eleven small, round, hand-coloured engravings depicting scenes from the Passion have been pasted into some of the initials marking the beginnings of corresponding texts. These prints embellish the section of the book that provides readings for the Easter season of the liturgical year. They were made after a set by the Master ES (Lehrs 201) that contains twelve scenes from the Passion and six saints, all printed together on the same sheet. Master ES's plate

---

22   Meertens, *De godsvrucht in de Nederlanden*, cat. 833bis.
23   Rudy, 'How to Prepare the Bedroom for the Bridegroom'.

was probably reworked, and some of the resulting prints were pasted into a German prayerbook, a manuscript now in St Gallen.[24] Another engraver copied these re-worked images, thereby reversing them. The resulting roundels — but only the Passion cycle — appear pasted into initials of the Heverlee manuscript (fig. 122). All this suggests that several engravers were tapping the market of book makers who wanted instant historiated initials, to the degree that various engravers could make competing series; some even copied each other in order to gain a slice of this market. The surviving number of manuscripts with printed roundels pasted in, however, is small. Assuming that each engraver would have to make around 100–400 copies of a print to be able to turn a profit, then less than 1 per cent of this early printed material survives.

Fig. 122 Opening in a prayerbook, with prayers for the weeks of the liturgical year, each one beginning with an initial filled with a hand-painted engraving. Heverlee, Abdij van Park, Ms. 18, fols 27v-28r.

In the Heverlee manuscript, someone has coloured in the prints, largely with red and blue, which could be the same paints used for the red and

---

24 St Gallen, Stiftsbibliothek, Codex Sangallensis 479. German prayerbook, manuscript on paper, octavo, 227 folios. See Gustav Scherrer, *Verzeichniss der Handschriften der Stiftsbibliothek von St. Gallen* (Halle: Verlag der Buchhandlung des Waisenhauses, 1875; reissued Hildesheim; New York: Georg Olms Verlag, 1975), p. 154.

blue frames that define the letters around the roundels and provide a decorative armature. Indeed, the person who added colour to the black-and-white prints may also have made the decorative flourishes. In the background of the Flagellation, the colourist has added a red cross-hatched back wall, as if extending Christ's lacerated flesh to fill the room. These lines are not in the print, but were added by the colourist. What is striking is that the lines are thin, straight, and parallel, of the sort one might make with a pen, and they are executed in the same shade of red as the red penwork. This, in turn, appears to be the same red as the rubricated words. Meanwhile the blue area at the top of the roundel appears to be a watered-down wash of the same blue paint found in the letter O. It is not implausible that the scribe both executed the penwork and coloured in the engravings.

What is extraordinary is that the printed roundels have defined the illustrative programme for the entire highly decorated manuscript: whoever made the book copied the size and format of these engraved roundels to make painted historiated initials. In other words, the painter could have executed square miniatures, or marginal images, or historiated initials of any size, but chose to replicate the size and form of the round initials that measure eight lines high. Although there are many examples of illuminators using prints as models for their images, here the illuminator seems to have drawn on engraved roundels not for the subjects or compositions but for their size, shape, and graphic approach to representation. Consequently, the historiated initials look like line drawings filled with light wash, and therefore resemble the prints, which are black ink printed on paper filled in with light wash.

The prints, it would seem, formed the organizing principle for the pictorial elements in the book, which the book maker, possibly an Augustinian sister, extended with twenty-four of her own small, round images. This includes images relevant to other feasts, which have all been painted as roundels, eight lines high. For example, for the 'glorious feast of the Holy Sacrament' ('Op die gloriose feeste des heilighen sacraments', fol. 49v; fig. 123), the book maker has drawn an image of Jesus opening his side wound into a chalice. Like the background behind the Flagellation, this one has also been cross-hatched, this time with a drop of red 'blood' in every chamber, thereby exploiting a metaphor that Marlene Hennessy has elucidated: that of Christ's blood as ink.[25] The roundel follows certain other conventions of the engravings, such as the low horizon line, the outlined approach to figural representation, and the clumsy use of space. Likewise, for a prayer to be read on the feast day of the translation of the Cross ('Vander verheffinghen des heilig cruys', fol. 54v; fig. 124), the format remains the same, with an eight-line roundel. This time the colours make plain that whoever painted the image was using the same palette as the person inscribing the initial O and decorating it, as the same red, blue, and green reappear in the historiated initial. It therefore seems likely that the person who executed the roundels was also the person who added the decoration to the pages.

Fig. 123
Folio in a prayerbook, with prayers for the feast of the Sacrament. Heverlee, Abdij van Park, Ms. 18, fol. 49v.

---

25   Marlene Villalobos Hennessy. 'The Social Life of a Manuscript Metaphor: Christ's Blood as Ink'. In *The Social Life of Illumination: Manuscripts, Images, and Communities in the Late Middle Ages*, ed. by Joyce Coleman, Mark Cruse and Kathryn A. Smith. Medieval Texts and Cultures of Northern Europe (Turnhout: Brepols, 2013), pp. 17–52, Pl. xvii.

Fig. 124 Folio in a prayerbook, with prayers for the feast of the Holy Cross. Heverlee, Abdij van Park, Ms. 18, fol. 54v.

Several more of these images populate the section of prayers for feast days honouring particular saints: John the Baptist, John the Evangelist, Peter, Lawrence, Augustine, Jerome, Mary Magdalene, and Barbara. Among the feast day texts are those for St Augustine, who is called 'our holy father and worthy patron' ('Onsen heilighen vader ende werdighen patronen sinte Augustinus', fol. 79v). The accompanying historiated initial depicts a woman in a white habit and a black veil kneeling at the feet of the saint (fig. 125). This confirms that the book was made for an Augustinian nun.

Another historiated initial features St Elizabeth, who administered to the sick and hungry and was selected as the patron saint of most medieval hospitals of the region (fol. 85r, fig. 126).[26] Elizabeth, the daughter of the King of Hungary, the least common of the three female saints with a specially celebrated feast day, is depicted in a historiated initial clothing a naked man who hobbles on crutches. After the death

---

26 Gasthuiszusters Augustinessen, also called Zwartzusters, operated hospitals in Leuven, Antwerp, and Mechelen, and in many other towns in the Low Countries. Their libraries and visual culture (except for the *besloten hofjes*, or enclosed gardens, made in Mechelen) have not been studied.

of her husband, Ludwig IV of Thuringia, Elizabeth of Hungary (1207–1231) founded a hospital in Marburg where she also worked. She was celebrated for having administered to the sick, naked, and hungry, and as such was the patron saint of most, if not all, of the Augustinian hospitals from the late Middle Ages.[27] Near the end of the manuscript is a single prayer to St Dymphna. These facts suggest that the convent for which the Heverlee manuscript was made had Augustinian sisters and held SS Elizabeth and Dymphna in especial esteem. The dialect points to north Brabant, an area that covers the central swathe of what is now Dutch-speaking Belgium. A few convents are possible, one being that of the Augustinian canonesses dedicated to St Elizabeth in Brussels. These sisters had taken the rule of St Augustine and Elizabeth as their patron saint. Many manuscripts from fifteenth-century canonesses survive, as they were particularly productive book makers. Heverlee 18, however, does not resemble any of the many surviving manuscript from canonesses, either in textual content or decorative style.

Fig. 125 Folio in a prayerbook, with prayers to 'our holy father' St Augustine, with an Augustinian sister kneeling before him. Heverlee, Abdij van Park, Ms. 18, fol. 79v.

---

27 In addition to acting as patron of most hospitals, St Elizabeth was also the patron saint of the Franciscan Tertiaries. See a leaf depicting her among the Tertiaries, *Krone und Schleier: Kunst aus mittelalterlichen Frauenklöstern*. Exh. cat, Essen, Ruhrlandmuseum: Die frühen Klöster und Stifte 500-1200/Bonn, Kunst- und Ausstellungshalle: Die Zeit der Orden 1200–1500, ed. Jeffrey Hamburger, Robert Suckale, et al. (Essen; Bonn, 2005), cat. 250.

4. Manuscripts with Prints: A Sticky Idea

Fig. 126 Folio in a prayerbook, with prayers to St Elisabeth. Heverlee, Abdij van Park, Ms. 18, fol. 85r.

A more likely origin of the manuscript was among the *gasthuiszusters*, who, like the canonesses, took a vow of the Augustinian order. Unlike the canonesses, they were a working order: 'gasthuis' still means hospital in current Dutch, and nurses are still called 'zusters'. Many towns and cities in the Low Countries had a hospital staffed by *gasthuiszusters*, including Antwerp, Mechelen, and Geel, which all possessed convents of Augustinians connected to hospitals that took St Elizabeth as their patron. These facts accord with the contents of the Heverlee manuscript, as noted: it is written in a Brabant dialect, calls Augustine 'our patron', and possesses a full-length prayer and historiated initial dedicated to Elizabeth. Moreover, the suffrage addressed to St Dymphna makes Geel a likely possibility, since she is the patron saint of Geel and her relics are kept at the church connected with the *gasthuiszusters*' convent and hospital in Geel. It is plausible that the manuscript came from this convent, although the Augustinian hospital in Lier is also a possible origin.

If I cautiously accept that the manuscript was made for the Augustinian *gasthuiszusters*, probably those at Geel, this would shed light on the texts and images in the manuscript. Rather than being a contemplative praying order, as were the Augustinian canonesses who sang the Divine Office daily, the *gasthuiszusters* were a working order who rolled up their sleeves and worked with the poor, sick, and dying, so it is no surprise that the manuscript also contains instructions to be carried out 'if one of us sisters dies', followed by prayers to be read 'when anyone dies'.[28] Certainly, the *gasthuiszusters* would have to deal on a regular basis with patients who died. Secondly, the manuscript emphasises devotion to the Holy Sacrament, which is not unusual for fifteenth-century manuscripts made for women religious, but here one wonders whether it took on the urgency of spiritual medicine delivered to the sick. The prayer for 'the glorious feast of the Holy Sacrament' depicts Christ nearly naked, with his left arm outstretched as if he were still on the Cross (see fig. 123). Whereas the borders of most of the folios are blank, the folio here is decorated with exuberant penwork on all four sides, indicating that this feast day was held in special esteem. Such attention and embellishment may indicate that the Host took on the urgency of spiritual medicine delivered to the sick. Thirdly, several of the historiated initials in the manuscript show a generalised sister who is interacting with an extremely bloodied and wounded Jesus and, by extension, illustrate a high degree of propinquity with the sick, dying, and wounded. One, for example, depicts Jesus releasing his arms from the Cross in order to embrace the woman (fig. 127); this motif puts her in the role of St Gregory, who envisioned Jesus loosening himself from the Cross to embrace him.[29] In another image, Christ stands before the sister as he opens his side wound, draining his blood into a chalice that stands on the ground before him (fig. 128). The accompanying prayer begins, 'Come to me, all of you who labour' ('Comt tot mij, alle die daer arbeydende sijt'). The sister, who counts herself among the labourers — those who work with the sick — has indeed come to Jesus in the initial, and kneels before his five open wounds.

---

28   Compare the *Agenda mortuorum* from the late fifteenth century and the mid-sixteenth century, written at the Mariënpoel Convent outside Leiden, described in Truus van Bueren, with W. C. M. Wüstefeld, *Leven na de dood. Gedenken in de late Middeleeuwen*, [exh. cat, Utrecht, Museum het Catharijneconvent] (Turnhout: Brepols, 1999), 189, cat. 54, and 50–51, where the ceremonies surrounding the death of a convent sister are discussed. Namely, all the members in the convent, as well as a priest, became involved in the ritual surrounding a sick sister's passing.

29   Caroline Walker Bynum, 'Formen weiblicher Frömmigkeit im späteren Mittelalter', in *Krone und Schleier: Kunst aus mittelalterlichen Frauenklöstern* (exh. cat, Ruhrlandmuseum, Essen; and Kunst- und Ausstellungshalle, Bonn, 2005), pp. 118–29.

Fig. 127 Opening in a prayerbook, with an initial depicting Christ releasing his arms from the cross in order to embrace an Augustinian sister. Heverlee, Abdij van Park, Ms. 18, fol. 137v-138r.

Fig. 128 Folio in a prayerbook, with an initial depicting Christ opening his side wound in the presence of an Augustinian sister. Heverlee, Abdij van Park, Ms. 18, fol. 109r.

The texts in the Heverlee manuscript suggest that it served as a book to which members of the community referred on feast days, when someone died, or when a new woman entered the community. Several texts stress the physicality of Christ and of his presence to the reader, including the Spiritual Bedroom, which addresses a young nun or a prepostulant as she is entering the convent. These *Gasthuiszusters Augustinessen* may have owned the small manuscript and used it in conjunction with their role as hospital sisters. A nun who appears in it several times probably does not represent a particular nun, but rather 'everynun', a generic figure in the garb of the sisters who ran most of the clinics in the Low Countries. The engraved roundels would have saved the book's maker some time in constructing the pictorial programme. He, or more likely she, was able to assemble some fixed motifs — the Passion sequence — and would undoubtedly have used more of such roundels if they had been available with different images. But the engravers must have been cautious at the end of the fifteenth century, and were more willing to copy existing motifs that they thought would sell, than to forge new motifs at higher risk. The very existence of the engraved roundels changed the way that the book maker executed the painted roundels. Those prints functioned as a motivating design element for the rest of the pictorial programme, as the drawings follow the prints in size, shape, and to some extent their graphic design. The technology of the printed image was adapting to the way people made manuscripts. It is also possible that viewing this manuscript during my own acute medical situation — post-surgical and bandaged — inflected my interpretation of it.

Manuscripts Still Intact

Although the manuscript in Heverlee is a rarity, it demonstrates that not all the late medieval manuscripts containing prints have been dismembered.[30] A few examples in collections around Europe, including the British Museum, have made it to our century intact, or nearly intact.

---

30 Jan van der Stock's catalogue of early prints in Brussels is unique in that he combined prints preserved in the Department of Prints, with those still in manuscripts and preserved in the Department of Manuscripts. Essentially, he was erasing a false distinction between these categories. Jan van der Stock, *Early Prints: The Print Collection of the Royal Library of Belgium. Print Collection of the Royal Library of Belgium* (London: Harvey Miller Publishers, 2002).

One of the most richly illustrated was made in the monastery of St Catherine's in Nuremberg (London, BM, PD, 1890,1013.54.1–35)[31] (e-fig. 108).

BM 1890,1013.54.1–35 — Manuscript from St Catherine's (e-fig. 108)

Manuscript from St Catherine's, Nuremberg.
London, British Museum, Department of Prints & Drawings, inv. 1890,1013.54.1–35.

https://hdl.handle.net/20.500.12434/c2c5e6d4

Perhaps this managed to escape dismantlement because it entered the collection not in the 1860s but in 1890, after a change of regime and when there was a new ethos about keeping artefacts intact; or possibly it was spared because it was made on parchment, a higher-status material than paper, and the curators were loathe to cut into it. Or perhaps it was spared because it is still in its fifteenth-century binding, although this concern did not stop the knife-wielders from taking Add. 24332 apart.

This manuscript from Nuremberg is fascinating because the parchment sheets have been printed on both sides. That is yet another way in which the technology of single-leaf printing was inflecting the trajectory of the book making process: with no skill in draughtsmanship, someone could produce an image-centred devotional book, which was relentless in its presentation of images. In fact, the images were conceptualized first, and the text had to be fitted around them. Consequently, the scribe had to make adjustments along the way so that the text roughly coordinates with the images. Doing this, however, created many blank pages. An early owner has gone through the book and filled many of these blanks with more texts (what I call quire fillers) so as to make better use of the available space.[32] She has also added some more images and notes. Book owners either considered their books precious objects to handle as gingerly as possible, or else they considered them to be repositories for all kinds of devotional detritus. Someone who adds one kind of thing to a book (for example, more prayers) is

---

31 In addition to the BM accession numbers assigned to the prints, this manuscript as a whole also has a shelf number: London, BM, 158* b.3. See Schmidt, *Gedruckte Bilder*, pp. 66–69, with further examples of related books.

32 I discuss quire fillers in *Piety in Pieces*.

also likely to add other kinds of things (curtains, more images, objects such as badges, or souvenirs from having taken the Eucharist). The nun owner from Nuremberg of the manuscript now in London was of this second variety.

Other manuscripts in the BM also afford one an opportunity to study prints in their original contexts. One of these is a tiny book made from paper, which has been used so much that the edges of the paper have been eaten away (BM P&D, 158* b 32; fig. 129). This manuscript was probably made in Cologne but, unfortunately, it is too fragile to be photographed further. The one image I shot of it in 2008 shows a roundel depicting St George killing a dragon. Its early user has painted a bold frame around it in red and white, the colours of St George's banner that crystallised into the English flag, as if to heighten the drama of George's act while at the same time communicating his national identity. This roundel may have been created as an image for a historiated initial, but this book is so small that it functions as a full-page 'miniature' instead.

Fig. 129 Opening in a prayerbook with an added engraving depicting St George. London, British Museum, Department of Prints & Drawings, inv. 158* b 32.

Fitting round images into square frames was a challenge for scribes, who were making use of generic printed products that often fitted their particular circumstances rather poorly. That had been the case with the beghards in the mid-1520s, who trimmed Israhel's D and O initials — apparently intended for use in a large liturgical manuscript — into rectangular pages. Such ill-fitting images would vex other book makers as well.

The owner of a well-worn prayerbook from the Southern Netherlands clipped out a roundel from the apostles series and pasted it into a section of suffrages (Cambridge, Gonville and Caius College, Ms. 718/253; fig. 130).[33] Specifically, he or she pasted a roundel into the blank space of folio 366v so that it falls opposite the rubric and prayer to St Matthias. The pasting operation was apparently an afterthought, as the print overlaps the final line of script. However, the rubricator has framed the roundel with the same red as the textual rubrics, suggesting that the print was added between the time the book was copied and when it was rubricated. In some ways, the print serves a similar function as rubrication: they both bring visual interest to the beginnings of texts and underscore the saints to whom the prayers are dedicated.

Fig. 130 Opening in a prayerbook with an added roundel by Israhel van Meckenem. Cambridge, Gonville and Caius College, Ms. 718/253, fols 366v-367r.

---

33 Nigel J. Morgan, and Stella Panayotova, eds., *Illuminated Manuscripts in Cambridge: A Catalogue of Western Book Illumination in the Fitzwilliam Museum and the Cambridge Colleges. Part One: The Frankish Kingdoms, the Netherlands, Germany, Bohemia, Hungary and Austria*, 2 vols (London: Harvey Miller, in conjunction with the Modern Humanities Research Association, 2009), cat. 188, pp. 122–23.

Likewise, the Augustinian canonesses from Soeterbeeck in Deursen near Ravenstein applied Israhel van Meckenem's prints to unintended functions, in a music manuscript written in shaky, sixteenth-century script. To the lower margin, they have added roundels cut out from Israhel's 'Memento mori' series (fig. 131). (As I mentioned previously, an intact sheet of these survives in the British Library, see e-fig. 84.) Their manuscript was not the right scale to have such large roundels populating historiated initials. To use them as intended would have required that the canonesses rethink the entire layout of their book. However, it appears that they pasted the roundels in as part of the original campaign of work, that they were not an afterthought, for the scribe deliberately left room for them at the bottom of the red-ruled music staves.

Fig. 131
Music manuscript with pasted-in roundels made by Israhel van Meckenem, from Soeterbeeck in Deursen near Ravenstein, a convent of Augustinian canonesses. Nijmegen, Radboud Universiteit, Soeterbeeck Coll. Ms IV 136.

Just as the beghards had, the makers of Caius 718/253 also had a variety of images available, all from disparate sources. This manuscript was made in the Southern Netherlands and is in Latin (unlike the manuscripts in the vernacular Dutch more common in the northern Netherlands). Although the manuscript contains instructions for a priest (pp. 65–70), it may not have been made for a priest, as it also contains prayers more closely associated with lay piety, such a prayer to one's guardian angel (pp. 363–65). That it lists St Anne first among the virgins in the litany suggests that the manuscript was inscribed around 1500, when veneration of that saint reached a pinnacle. Whereas the beghards wrote their book in 1500 on paper, the makers of this manuscript chose the more traditional material of parchment, which clashed with the pasted-in prints on paper. The person who removed the prints peeled the paper from the parchment, thereby dividing the book up by material.

Among the images still in the Caius manuscript, one depicts the Virgin of the Sun, which the scribe inserted to fall opposite an indulgenced prayer to the Virgin (fig. 132). This image was made on parchment, which has been inserted into the book block as a page. Although it resembles a hand-coloured print, it is in fact a drawing. Not surprisingly, it has been painted in a completely different palette from the Israhel roundel, because the two types of images had a separate genesis. Perhaps the prints arrived already hand-coloured. It is clear that the scribe had a stack of images — some prints, some drawings — available from the outset and deployed them as she went along.

Fig. 132 Opening in a prayerbook with an added engraving depicting the Virgin of the Sun. Cambridge, Gonville and Caius College, Ms. 718/253, fols 280v-281r.

When it was time to copy a prayer to one's personal angel, the scribe skipped an entire verso folio for the relevant image (fig. 133). Although someone later tried to remove the image, thereby destroying it, the residue on the page provides some more clues about the design process. This time the print did not fill the entire page but, rather than rule around it, the scribe pasted the image so that it aligned with the top left corner of the frame and treated it as a 'full-page miniature', rather than an embedded miniature. Like many solutions that save time or require less skill, this one also wasted more material.

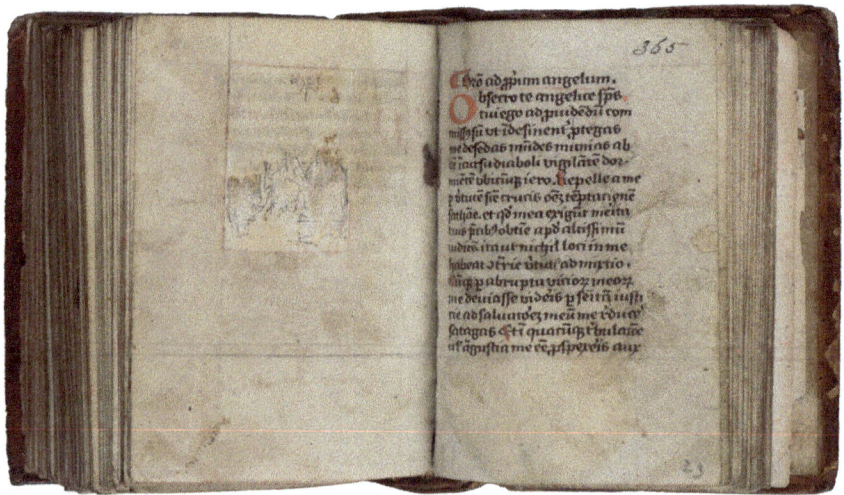

Fig. 133 Opening in a prayerbook with the remains of added engraving, opposite a prayer to a personal angel. Cambridge, Gonville and Caius College, Ms. 718/253, fols 364v-365r.

A different scribe wrote the text that accompanies a small woodcut depicting St Barbara (fig. 134). In terms of layout and coherence, this experiment might also be deemed a failure. The prayer, added by a scribe using a thick nib and a slight backslant, addresses the Virgin, but the image embedded in the text presents St Barbara. This is yet another case of a scribe using prints that were not perfectly coordinated to the texts. In many of these experiments, the primacy of the two media — script or print — was at odds. Since the scribe apparently did not have another image of the Virgin Mary, she used an image of any virgin, in this case, St Barbara. As with the image presumably depicting an angel (see fig. 133), this one has been partly destroyed by a souvenir-seeker. Like the beghards of 1500, the scribe here has used rubrication as a decorative feature, but has left a wide gap between the image and the text, so that the *mise-en-page* includes a redundant area of white space.

Fig. 134 Opening in a prayerbook with the remains of added woodcut depicting St Barbara. Cambridge, Gonville and Caius College, Ms. 718/253, fol. 384v-385r.

More images seem to have arrived throughout the attenuated production process, so that one of the users pasted in another print to preface a prayer, the Ave Maria of flowers, at the very end of the Caius book (fig. 135). He or she added this to what was a blank page; although it has since been removed, it left telling traces. The print was silhouetted before it was pasted in, and we can still read the ghostly form as a Virgin and Child, whose head forms an extra blob of clean parchment below her halo.[34] It must have been pasted in early in the book's history, so that it was frequently exposed to heavy handling by one or more users, who left a thick veil of grime across the well-loved opening. In fact, the user may have venerated the Virgin by repeatedly touching the (presumably printed) face, and making a stroking gesture into the textual frame; that would explain why the ghostly image is so clearly defined: because the grime of handling has delimited the edge of the now-absent object. The user has also marked the space beyond the silhouette as venerable by filling it with a prayer to the Virgin, so that the words hug the image and

---

34 For related examples, see Peter Schmidt, *Gedruckte Bilder in handgeschriebenen Büchern* 2003, figs. 136–39.

then spill into the opposite opening. He or she has written the text so that it touched the edges of the image, forming a textual aspic around it.

Fig. 135 Opening in a prayerbook with the ghost image of a print probably depicting the Virgin and Child. Cambridge, Gonville and Caius College, Ms. 718/253, fol. 406v-407r.

Inscribed around the absent Virgin, the prayer text bears conceptual similarities to the mixed and matched images. I have not been able to find the entire prayer text in one place, and it may be a *cento*, a text comprising quotations from other sources. For example, the first two and the last two lines come from a rosary devotion, but not in consecutive order:

Pia christifera, mea mater, virgo Maria,

Celi regina, radians dietatis alumna.

Nam tibi nil negitat, qui matrem semper honorat,

Alma valeto parens, michi crebra charismata mittens.[35]

The two central lines, written near the hem of the Virgin's dress, come from a different source. It is as if the writer had cut and pasted a favourite

---

35 Guido Maria Dreves, ed., *Analecta Hymnica Medii Aevi*, 54 vols. (Leipzig: Fues's Verlag, 1854–1932), vol. 48 (1905), pp. 533–34, nr. 503 (10). I am indebted to Jan Waszink for identifying this text and for noticing how its compiled nature conceptually mirrors the approach to selecting and gluing images into the book.

image, but also favourite lines of text, so that the entire devotion consists of pre-existing parts re-arranged on the page.

Examining Caius 718/253 reveals that its construction had been a group effort; that the makers had a variety of prints available; and that they made do with the prints they had, but that their placement sometimes defied logic or resulted in an awkward composition. They may not have had much agency in selecting which images they wanted, but may instead have received images as gifts, which would explain the variety of subjects, origins, and scales. It is also clear that they acquired at least one engraving by Israhel and incorporated this as best they could. With his enormous output, and his obvious attempts to target book makers as buyers for his wares, it is not surprising that many manuscripts do indeed contain engravings by this maker.

Israhel van Meckenem as a Master of Self-Promotion

Israhel was marketing prints along trade routes that other printmakers were also traversing, and there was much cross-fertilisation between makers. Israhel successfully created a new kind of object — the instant historiated initial and instant miniature — and then set about creating a new market for that object. In the process, he promoted himself so successfully that his brand was still in demand in the nineteenth century. I proposed earlier that his prints filled many of the now-empty roundels in the beghards' manuscript of 1500. They apparently bought so many of his prints that they were still using them thirty years later. He made sheets that could specifically be cut apart. To deploy them as instant initials, one had to dismember them. That is how the beghards used the Israhel roundels in 1500 and again in the mid-1520s.

Israhel must have had a second function for the sheets of roundels in mind from the beginning (see e-figs. 6, 7, 65, 84, 90). He signed them, but only in the blank space between the roundels, which suggests that he made the sheets as collectors' items: their authorship is only documented when the sheet is left intact. They retain a function as collector's items as long as they are not cut apart and used, a process that means discarding the signature. And that signature is so ornate! Unlike some of his contemporaries who sign their prints in the plate with a letter or monogram in a simple serif initial, Israhel extends the finials top and bottom, looping them into a frame of liquid lines. He also uses a letter variety that imitates a courtly display script, with a strong differentiation between thick and thin, and letters built from compound 'strokes', although of course the lines have been made with a burin, not a pen nib. His signature, on a sheet with roundels, for example, could be characterised as a skeuomorph (e-fig. 65). Here, engraving imitates courtly display script. That Israhel purposely promoted himself is also clear from the volume of his signatures, plastering his entire name or his initials on hundreds of his productions. An extension of this is the putative self-portrait he made, which he also signed.[36] A virtuoso rendering of curling beard, tightly bound turban, sagging, veined skin; this image projects a man desperately serious about his craft, and purposeful about guaranteeing his fame.

And make his mark he did. In addition to giving the world what is essentially clip art, Israhel helped to shift how manuscripts were made. Much of what I have discussed in this book has involved low-end production, manuscripts made by and for cloistered religious. But Israhel also changed how a luxury manuscript might be made.

Sloane Ms. 3981 in the British Museum is a manuscript book of hours with prints made by Israhel pasted into it, but it shows an entirely different conceptualization of manuscript and print from the other examples featured so far.[37] When I first viewed this manuscript on 6 July 2007, I realised that neither the manuscript nor the prints it contains are ordinary. The modern binding encloses a slim volume of 71 folios on parchment measuring 166 x 241 millimetres (with a text block of 158 x 99), which means that it is much larger than most books of hours. Its images were planned into this project from the beginning: the book

---

36 The signed self-portrait of Israhel van Meckenem is one of the most frequently reproduced images by the engraver. It appears, for example, on the front cover of Achim Riether, *Israhel Van Meckenem (um 1440/45-1503): Kupferstiche - Der Münchner Bestand* [Katalog zur Ausstellung der Staatlichen Graphischen Sammlung München, Pinakothek der Moderne, 14. September - 26. November 2006] (Munich: Staatliche Graphische Sammlung, 2006).

37 Before it came into the Sloane collection, the manuscript was owned by P. Giffart (whose coat of arms is three naked female busts) and was sold in Paris in 1746. The manuscript, confusingly, has several signatures. Besides being called Sloane Ms. 3981, it is also has the BM P&D signature 158 b 1* or B.vi.206.10–21. Furthermore, the BM P&D assigned each of the prints of the Large Passion (1897.0103.1–12) a separate number.

maker had created a large book in order to accommodate the twelve engravings by Israhel in his Large Passion series (1897.0103.1–12). The manuscript contains the following texts and images:

- 1r–3v: full calendar inscribed in two columns, in red, black, with blue titles;
- 4r–10v: Gospel readings, beginning with *In principio*, and followed by two prayers;
- 10v–12r: verses of St Gregory, rubric in French, seven-verse version, followed by forms of confession (in French);
- 12v: blank, ruled;
- 13r: **full-page, pasted-in print:** Christ washing the feet of the Apostles (1897,0103.1);
- 13v: Hours of the Cross, abbreviated (only the beginning of Matins and the end of Compline), no rubric;
- **14r: full-page, pasted-in print:** Arrest of Christ (1897.0103.2);
- 14v: Hours of the Holy Spirit, abbreviated;
- 15r: **full-page, pasted-in print:** Christ before Annas (1897,0103.3; fig. 136);
- 15v: Hours of the Virgin, for the use of Rome, Matins;
- 19r: **full-page, pasted-in print:** The Crowning with Thorns (1897,0103.4);
- 19v–23r: Lauds;
- 23v: **full-page, pasted-in print:** Flagellation (1897,0103.5);
- 24r–25v: Prime;
- 26r: **full-page, pasted-in print:** Ecce Homo (1897,0103.6);
- 26v–28r: Terce;
- 28v: **full-page, pasted-in print:** Christ before Pilate, and Pilate washing his hands (1897,0103.7);
- 29r–30v: Sext;
- 31r: **full-page, pasted-in print:** Christ carrying the Cross (1897,0103.8);

31v–33r:	Nones;
33v:	**full-page, pasted-in print:** Christ awaiting crucifixion in the foreground, with the Crucifixion in the background (1897,0103.9; fig. 137);
34r–36v:	Vespers;
37r:	**full-page, pasted-in print:** Lamentation (1897,0103,10);
37v–42r:	Compline;
42r–44v:	Variations for the Office of the Virgin, to be said during Advent at Vespers and at other times of the liturgical year;
45r:	**full-page, pasted-in print:** Resurrection (1897,0103,11);
45v–51r:	Seven Penitential Psalms and Litany;
51v:	**full-page, pasted-in print:** Christ at Emmaus (1897,0103,12);
52r–68v:	Vigil of the Dead;
69r/v:	blank, ruled;
70:	former paste-down.

Studying this list of contents reveals several things. First, its maker conceptualized the whole book as an album to showcase the twelve prints by Israhel. One can perceive that the scribe worked out which texts to use according to how many images were available. He or she started by organising them around the text central to the book, the Hours of the Virgin. It has eight canonical hours, and the scribe has used one print to preface each. This left four prints. One was used to mark the Penitential Psalms and one to mark the Vigil of the Dead, leaving two prints. In order to absorb these into the book's design without expanding its contents too much, the scribe wrote extremely short editions of the Hours of the Cross and the Hours of the Holy Spirit, each reduced to less than a page in length. One print prefaces each, meaning that all twelve prints have been deployed. The scribe has used the prints so that the twelve scenes unfold in chronological order through the book, even though the scenes are not those that usually preface their respective texts. It is as if the scribe were building an appropriate showcase for the twelve prints by giving them a contemplative religious framework. Some of these appear on the left side of the opening — the side that nearly all full-page miniatures were designed to fall on — but others were placed on the right side of the opening. In the case of Christ before Annas, the scribe has left nine lines of the previous folio blank, in his ultra-short version of the Hours of the Holy Spirit, in order to provide a text for the image, if not one that is immediately related. In the logic of this organisation, the image prefaces the Hours of the Virgin rather than the Hours of the Holy Spirit. The copyist has struggled to make the organisation logical because the texts are so short and the images so large, yielding a book that falls out of normal proportions for an illustrated book of hours. It is clear that the size of the prints — the largest Passion that Israhel made — has determined the scale of the entire project.[38]

Fig. 136 Opening in a book of hours, featuring a mounted engraving by Israhel van Meckenem depicting Christ before Annas. London, British Museum, Department of Prints & Drawings, inv. 1897,0103.3, also known as London, British Library, Sloane Ms. 3981, fols 14v-15r.

---

38 Alan Shestack, *Fifteenth Century Engravings of Northern Europe from the National Gallery of Art* (Washington, D.C.: National Gallery of Art, 1967), cat. 182–94.

Fig. 137 Opening in a book of hours, featuring a mounted engraving by Israhel van Meckenem depicting Christ awaiting crucifixion. London, British Museum, Department of Prints & Drawings, inv. 1897,0103.9, also known as London, British Library, Sloane Ms. 3981, fols 33v-34r.

In this series Israhel used the large surface area to multiply the points of interest. He has saturated the foreground, middle ground, and background of the images with commotion. Human activities occur inside and out, framed by doors and passageways, perceived as near and far. They divide up the composition into different temporal moments.[39] In so designing them, Israhel has ensured that the images are worthy of sustained absorption. He has also signed each of these engravings at front centre, in some cases showing the letters IM as if they were embedded in the floor tiles and receding.

Whereas in most books of hours, the images form colourful splashes to break up a black-and-white expanse of text, in this book, the images are left monochrome. The book maker seems to have realised that the busy engravings were best left in a naked state, and that painting them

---

39 For an intriguing approach to understanding relationships between depicted space and time, see Alfred Acres, 'The Columba Altarpiece and the Time of the World', *The Art Bulletin* 80, no. 3 (1998), pp. 422–51.

would only obscure the myriad printed lines. Instead, colour dances through the borders, first with a gold 'frame', which is then outlined with blue, brown, or green. These elaborate frames resemble polished marble, thereby introducing another precious substance into the book that causes one to question the material.

Inscribed with an even script, leaning towards a courtly bâtarde, the book has been carefully executed. Given that the rubrics are in French, the project was probably carried out for a French speaker who had come into possession of the entire large Passion series in the 1470s. Multiply produced, in black and white, on inexpensive paper, the engravings have motivated the construction of this entire exquisite object, buttressed with parchment and gold and high-quality hand-crafted labour. The book of hours has bent to the design of the prints.

The most astonishing of the manuscripts that use Israhel's prints as an underlying layer is BnF, Ms. Lat. 1173, known as the Hours of Charles d'Angoulême. It not only contains hand-coloured prints by Israhel but also drawings or miniatures made after prints by him.[40] Duplessis, in his *Essais sur la gravure dans les livres* (Paris, 1879), saw Lat. 1173 as a collaboration between engravers and miniaturists. When the manuscript was shown in the *Exposition des Primitifs Français* of 1904, it was dated 1464 on the basis of computational tables on folio 52v.[41] While the manuscript is a prodigy, it is not as early as that, but was made around 1480. It is enhanced with miniatures, including Pentecost (fol. 17v), a *danse champêtre* (fol. 20v), the Judgement of Solomon (fo. 34v), and a fight between the Centaures and the Lapiths at the beginning of the office of the dead (fol. 41v). This highly unusual imagery can be explained by the fact that the illuminator was copying motifs by Israhel.

---

40   Anne Matthews, 'The Use of Prints in the Hours of Charles d'Angoulême', *Print Quarterly* 3, no. 1 (1986), pp. 4–18. Earlier in the twentieth century, André Blum, 'Des Rapports de Miniaturistes Français du XVe Siècle avec les Premiers Artistes Graveurs', *Revue de l'Art Chrétien* LXI (1911), pp. 357–69, discussed this manuscript and reproduced some of its imagery.

41   André Malraux, Jean Porcher, and Sheila Browne, *Les Manuscrits à Peintures en France du XIIIe au XVIe Siècle* [Catalogue d'une Exposition à Paris en 1955–1956] (Paris: Bibliothèque Nationale, 1955), p. 162, no. 343; Victor Leroquais, *Les Livres d'Heures Manuscrits de la Bibliothèque Nationale*, 2 vols, plus a supplement (Paris: Bibliothèque Nationale, 1927–1929, suppl. Mâcon: Protat, 1943), vol. I, pp. 104–08, no. 38, Pl. XCII-XCV. Paris, BnF, Ms. lat. 1173, manuscript on parchment, 115 fol, 215x155 mm. Hours for the Use of Paris, made for Charles de Valois, comte d'Angoulême, father of François Ier. His name is given in an acrostic on fol. 53.

Additionally, the book contains seventeen engravings by Israhel van Meckenem, which have been carefully painted over. Three additional images have been attributed to Jean Bourdichon: the Nativity (fol. 9v), the Adoration (fol. 22v), and the Purification (fol. 24v). Thus, even though the book's imagery has its roots in a mechanically reproduced genre associated with low-skilled practitioners, it is in fact a virtuoso performance.

Conclusions: Some Assembly Required

The media historian Friedrich Kittler said something important about new technology: it is not technology that bends and adapts to human needs, but rather humans that bend to conform to new technology.[42] Once the typewriter had been invented, for example, people simply had to use it. Now there are no writers I know who have not adjusted their writing style to meet the needs of the computer. Likewise, once the printed image was available, it was impossible to ignore. Book makers took it up as a way to 'save labour', which is nearly always synonymous with saving money. A consequence of printing is that it concentrated craft skill in the hands of a few, such as Israhel, and led to the mass redundancy of scribes and miniaturists.

Prints changed the very processes and order of operations of book making. In one scenario, a printmaker could produce a series of prints, which would yield images in sequence to form a booklet, which would provide the structure around which text could be added.[43] In a quite different scenario, someone could glue a loose print into a finished manuscript. In the first example, the images are primary, and the text is fitted around a series of matched prints. In the second situation, a manuscript is written and completed, and prints added as an embellishment, as an afterthought.

Add. 24332 presents a third situation: someone who has access to a wide variety of prints, is purchasing them in groups that are pre-coloured, and fitting them into a manuscript as the writing progresses,

---

42 Friedrich Kittler, Dorothea von Mücke, and Philippe L. Similon, 'Gramophone, Film, Typewriter', *October* 41, (1987), pp. 101–18.

43 Ursula Weekes has done detective work to show how such booklets were manufactured, in *Early Engravers and their Public*, pp. 88–93, as has Peter Schmidt, *Gedruckte Bilder in handgeschriebenen Büchern*, pp. 66–69 and passim.

sometimes silhouetting the prints, sometimes cutting out roundels to form historiated initials, sometimes trimming rectangular prints to form column miniatures, and sometimes incorporating the entire printed sheet into the binding and writing on the other side. A picture could dominate an entire page or occupy only a corner of it, and the text would have to fill in the gaps. In this situation the copyist adjusts the images to meet the needs of the text, and adjusts the layout of the text in response to the available images. This option had not yet been fully analysed in the scholarship. It is only close observation of entire books — handwritten texts next to printed images — that reveals it.

According to this third scenario, manuscript books accommodated the new technology of single-leaf prints by inverting the normal primacy of the word in manuscript production. When manuscripts were made in the old way (say, before 1390, when the Masters of the Pink Canopies began creating single-leaf miniatures to be inserted into books of hours), there was a division of labour, but generally a copyist would write the words on a page and leave spaces so that an illuminator could add the images. The text and its placement dictated page design, so that new texts would be signalled by large initials. Previously, all decoration emanated from initials, but in manuscripts with pasted-in prints, the printed images dictated the design, and the words had to be fitted in around the fixed pictures.

In the decades following 1390, the work of the copyist became further separated (in terms of labour, skills, materials) from that of the illuminator, and books of hours (a driving force in innovating ever cheaper and ever more elaborately illuminated books) were increasingly written in such a way that the labour of image-making was separate from word-writing, and that pictures could be added to books later, and then continually, in stages.[44] Using a version of this new model around 1500, the beghard copyist might have been both writing the book and also 'illustrating' it by selecting and placing the images. In some ways, the roles of the copyist had expanded: she or he would now be a writer, designer, and illuminator. This also meant that the role of the manuscript illuminator was shrinking, or changing. The act of making and illuminating a manuscript was an act in the service of God, and paying for the same was also performing such service. But was pasting

---

44   This is the argument in Rudy, *Piety in Pieces*.

prints into a book as sacred an act, even if the goal were similar (an illuminated book)? One wonders.

Following a significant rise from 1440–1465 in the number of manuscripts written, there was a sharp and steady fall in manuscript production. It is likely that the surge in books available — printed books made in the era of movable type — briefly stimulated the production of manuscripts, so that for a short period after the printing press was introduced around 1450 more, not fewer manuscripts were made. In fact, the largest number of surviving manuscripts was made in the fifteenth century, many of them after 1450. But then the number of manuscripts quickly dropped as the number of prints soared.[45] Scribes and miniaturists simply became obsolete. The expanding number of readers instigated the invention of the printing press, just as much as the press multiplied the number of potential readers. Readers and printers formed a spiral of self-reinforcing genesis that implicated manuscript makers in the early years of its maelstrom. A second implication of this new technology was that some copyists were as likely to have a printed as a manuscript exemplar to copy out by hand. For example, a manuscript in Ghent made at St Luciendaal was copied in 1500 from a printed exemplar and then (probably) bound by the beghards.[46] That printing (meaning movable-type printing of entire books) stimulated the technology that it was simultaneously displacing is certainly a

---

45 Several scholars have recently measured the rise of print and its effect on the demise of manuscript, including Uwe Neddermeyer, 'Why Were There no Riots of the Scribes? First Results of a Quantitative Analysis of the Book Production in the Century of Gutenberg,' *Gazette du livre médiéval* 31 (1997), 1–8; Hanno Wijsman, 'Handschriften und gedruckte Bücher: der Wandel der Europäischen Buchkultur im 15. Jahrhundert', in: Christine Beier (ed.), *Geschichte der Buchkultur 5.1: Gotik*, Graz: Akademische Druck- und Verlagsanstalt/ADEVA, 2016, pp. 97–114; Hanno Wijsman, 'Une bataille perdue d'avance? Les manuscrits après l'introduction de l'imprimerie dans les anciens Pays-Bas', in *Books in Transition at the Time of Philip the Fair: Manuscripts and Printed Books in the Late Fifteenth and Early Sixteenth Century Low Countries*, ed. by Hanno Wijsman, with the collaboration of Ann Kelders and Susie Speakman Sutch. Burgundica, 15 (Turnhout: Brepols, 2010), pp. 257–72; Eltjo Buringh, *Medieval Manuscript Production in the Latin West: Explorations with a Global Database* (Leiden: Brill, 2011); Bühler, *The Fifteenth-Century Book*, p. 19.

46 Ghent, UB, Ms. 895, contains inter alia *Dietse Historie van Sint Anna*, by Pieter Dorlant, which was also published in Antwerp in 1501 by Govert Back. The manuscript comes from the convent of 'Sinte Luyciendaele gheleghen buyten der der goeder stadt van sintruden'. A colophon on fol. 250r reads: 'Ghescreven inden jaer XV^c van eender religioeser wies naeme geset moet wesen inden boeke des levens J H rusten moet sy inden ewigen vrede'. The binding is blind-stamped leather over boards, with a 'MATIAS' stamp.

weird twist of history.⁴⁷ A third implication was that the production of single-leaf prints also facilitated the illustration of manuscripts that a few decades earlier might have been unembellished.

As this study has shown, the trend from script to print is neither simple nor linear. The beghards' bindery and library were destroyed after the Napoleonic invasion, and the books dispersed before a catalogue was drawn up, so their holdings cannot be fully reconstructed. In one of the many antiquarian publications about the archives of Maastricht, there is a reference to a book that had gone missing shortly before 1893. It refers to 'een ritual van het klooster der Begaarden te Maastricht. Handschrift in folio, in drukletters geschreven, in het laatste der vorige eeuw. Het bevat onder meer, het ceremonieel der inkleeding' (a ritual from the convent of the beghards in Maastricht. Manuscript in folio, written in block letters, at the end of the previous century. It contains, among other things, the ceremony of taking the habit).⁴⁸ As the book is now missing, one can only rely on this brief notice for proof of its existence, which describes a manuscript copy of a ritual from the end of the seventeenth century. As for the beghards, it is not clear that they ever switched entirely to printed books, at least for ceremonial volumes such as this one. Although they were early adopters of print technology, they apparently continued to create manuscripts until the very last, defying Kittler's claim. At some level, the manuscript must have fulfilled ritual functions that print could not. In the period of print, manuscripts continued to be made but took on more specific cultural functions.

Reconstructing the beghards' first manuscript with prints (Add. 24332) reveals one of the most highly illustrated books of hours made around 1500, and provides insight into the organisation of information at that time, since the manuscript – originally comprehending more than 500 folios – is unusual for its table of contents as well as its elaborate calendar with finding aids. Although pasting prints into manuscripts was clearly a widespread practice, we have sparse evidence for exactly how prints were incorporated into pre-1500 manuscripts, since collectors in the nineteenth century commonly removed them; however, most of the

---

47   For more on this topic, see Gerd Dicke and Klaus Grubmüller, eds. *Die Gleichzeitigkeit von Handschrift und Buchdruck*, Wolfenbütteler Mittelalter-Studien, vol. 16 (Wiesbaden: Harrassowitz, 2003).
48   A. I. Flament, 'Het Rijks-archief in Limburg', *Verslagen omtrent 's Rijks Oude Archieven* (VROA), XVI (1893), p. 421 (Rituale van de Bogarden).

early prints that have survived into the twenty-first century have done so precisely because they were protected among the leaves of manuscripts. Ironically, the practice that allowed the prints to be preserved in the first place is so little understood because the prints were stripped of this context by eager collectors, private and institutional alike.

In the process of reassembling Add. 24332, Add. 41338, Add. 31001, and Add. 31002, I realised that the British Museum had bought several manuscripts in the nineteenth century that contained prints. As I have explained, some of those prints ended up in the prints department, and the protective manuscript in the manuscripts department, which was later transferred to the British Library. Having built a database to help with the process of reconstruction, I was able to apply it to several other manuscripts. The curators suggested that I do an exhibition on the fourth-floor prints gallery at the British Museum. I secured funding for the catalogue, talked to the curators at the British Library about lending the manuscripts so that they could be shown alongside the vast number of prints that had been removed from them, and selected 24 mattes that would enable me to tell this story. Anthony Griffiths, then Head of the Department of Prints and Drawings, rejected the proposal. Off the record, other insiders told me that if I rewrote it to gloss over the fact that the British Museum had cut up their own manuscripts, I might be able to do the exhibition elsewhere.

In the decade I spent writing this book, technology was changing under my feet, faster than it had during the nineteenth century when the second wave of knifework began. Whereas the amateur gentlemen German scholars of yesteryear had trust funds, index cards, and a wife, I have immigrant grit, an electronic spreadsheet, and a microwave, and, during my thirteen years of work, the digital camera became an increasingly important research tool. In effect, I am recreating objects with digital means, which allows me to make interpretations about the manufacturing of early modern books. To reconstruct these books is its own research problem, and tells one about the books' origins and functions. These pages address two sets of questions, one about undertaking research, the other about close noticing: one about methodology and the other about content.

When I started, the BL did not permit hand-held photography in the reading rooms. I wasted hundreds of hours returning to the British

Library to study Add. 24332, Add. 31001, Add. 31002, and Add. 41338 all before the managers changed the rules and allowed photography. Complete snapshots of these manuscripts would have saved me months of time and thousands of pounds in travel, and I would have burned considerably less aviation fuel. Add. 31002, and Add. 41338 are 'select' manuscripts and still may not be photographed in the reading room, even with the new rules. The professional images I had made of Add. 41338 cost hundreds of pounds. I simply could not afford to order extensive images from Add. 31002 to build a database to show exactly which images had been removed from which folios, and furthermore, as I said, the puzzle of reconstructing it is not difficult enough to hold my interest, since their accession numbers match their original sequence in the manuscript. I leave that project to a wealthy MA/MLitt student who needs a circumscribed thesis subject.

Although this study has been qualitative, one can imagine the benefits of assembling all of the pre-1500 prints into a single database, including those that are loose and those still in manuscripts, to assemble the most complete possible record of single-leaf prints in Western Europe. Computers would certainly extend the relational possibilities among and between prints, makers, collectors, manuscript projects, and albums, and may allow some statistical analyses to be carried out, despite the risk that the static caused by the gaps in the record might overwhelm the signal. However, for this project I focussed on the research unit defined as the 'individual manuscript with its prints pasted into it', as well as 'the journey that a large, open-ended research project entails'. Perhaps a quantitative study will be appropriate in about ten years.

This project took me a decade and cost me thousands of dollars, euros, and pounds, mostly in travel. I hope these results can show us something about how innovation took place in the late fifteenth and early sixteenth century. In writing it this way, I endeavoured to show what archive-intensive art history research looks like now. Here is one conclusion: there is a big disjunction between how art-historical research is funded and how that research really takes place. You cannot ask a funding body to give you 35 plane tickets to London so that you can work in your spare time. I would have had to sell an organ to pay for the digitization of the prints at the BM, and the project would therefore have been impossible had the BM not undertaken a mass digitization project. Most funding is intended for projects that are easily contained (a monograph about a particular manuscript, or a catalogue raisonné about an identifiable artist whose works are all held in three collections). In reality, most available funding for projects comes only at the very end, when you already know what the results will be, and after you have already invested countless hours in it. By the time the funding comes, you need it to maintain your car and pay your council tax bill, and it is hardly a drop in the bucket. Nonetheless, the funding is important, because it is the imprimatur of your council of peers before publication. It is one of the few forms of validation in academia.

My entire journey was set in motion by a photograph in a cabinet at the Warburg. Finding the documentary photograph of St Barbara was a clue to new processes, where I undid the work of the nineteenth-century collectors to reveal manuscripts and to show why those collectors wanted Israhel van Meckenem, whose work was widely circulated, branded, and so well-known that his fame has lasted for five centuries, even though his entire output was made on flimsy paper. In addition to printing his fame, Israhel, together with collaborators across Northern Europe, had created clip art, which beghards in Maastricht used to great profit. It gave the beghards the sense that they could 'create' imagery far beyond their ability to draw it. Their books anticipate Synthetic Cubism and even the Readymade. To create was to select and place objects, to make small changes where necessary, with red or black ink or even with a knife.

List of Illustrations

Chapter 1

1. Manuscript leaf written in Middle Dutch, with an engraved roundel by Israhel van Meckenem representing St Barbara, standing with her attribute. Unlabelled documentary photograph housed at the Warburg Institute, London.   16

2a; 2b. Manuscript binding, binding front and back, blind stamped leather over boards, made by the beghards of Maastricht c. 1500 (rebacked after 1861). London, British Library, Add. Ms. 24332.   17

3. Opening from the beghards' book of hours, Maastricht, c. 1500. London, British Library, Add. Ms. 24332, fols 311v–312r (modern foliation) or *ccc xlv* (original foliation).   19

4. Folio from the beghards' book of hours with part of a hand-painted woodcut depicting the Annunciation, Maastricht, c. 1500. London, British Library, Add. Ms. 24332, fol. 283v (modern foliation).   20

5. Folio from the beghards' book of hours with a printed rosette pasted into the initial. London, British Library, Add. Ms. 24332, fol. 254r (modern foliation).   21

6. Folio from the beghards' book of hours with a silhouetted engraving depicting Mary and John, Maastricht, c. 1500. London, British Library, Add. Ms. 24332, fol. 307v (modern foliation).   21

7   Calendar page for the first half of May. London, British Library, Add. Ms. 24332, fol. 5r (modern foliation). 22

8   Rubric revealing Franciscan affinities. London, British Library, Add. Ms. 24332, fol. 250r (modern foliation). 23

9   Manuscript binding, blind stamped leather over boards, made by the beghards of Maastricht c. 1500. Maastricht, Regionaal Historisch Centrum Limburg, 22.001A Handschriften GAM, inv.nr. 462. 28

10 Clock folio, facing January calendar page. Opening folios in a prayerbook made in Maastricht c. 1500. Maastricht, Regionaal Historisch Centrum Limburg, 22.001A Handschriften GAM, inv.nr. 462. 28

11 Franciscan church, Sint Pieterstraat, Maastricht (now the Regionaal Historisch Centrum Limburg). Photo: Kathryn M. Rudy. 30

12 Manuscript binding, blind stamped leather over boards, made by the beghards of Maastricht c. 1500. Amsterdam University Library, Ms. I G 12. 33

13 Opening in a prayerbook made in Maastricht, with computational circles dated 1500. Maastricht, Regionaal Historisch Centrum Limburg, 22.001A Handschriften GAM, inv.nr. 462, fol. 15v-16r. 35

14 Diagram for calculating the length of Advent, copied by Jan van Emmerick. Maastricht, Regionaal Historisch Centrum Limburg, 22.001A Handschriften GAM, inv.nr. 462, fol. 16v-17r. 36

15 Table with offset from now-missing leaf. Maastricht, Regionaal Historisch Centrum Limburg, 22.001A Handschriften GAM, inv.nr. 462, fol. 17v-18r. 36

16 The River Maas, photographed from the bridge, with a view of the medieval Marian church. Photo: Kathryn M. Rudy. 37

17 Manuscript leaf written in Middle Dutch, with an engraved roundel by Israhel van Meckenem representing SS Peter and Paul, standing with their attributes. Unlabelled documentary photograph, housed at the Warburg Institute, London. 40

18	Manuscript leaf written in Middle Dutch, with an engraved roundel by Israhel van Meckenem representing St Wolfgang, who has been transformed into St Servatius. Unlabelled documentary photograph, housed at the Warburg Institute, London.	41
19	The interior of the Prints & Drawings Study Room at the British Museum, London. Photo: Kathryn M. Rudy.	42
20	Page from Register for 9 November 1861. London, British Museum, Department of Prints & Drawings. Photo: Kathryn M. Rudy.	48
21	Letter from Mr Carpenter, dated 6 November 1861. London, British Museum, Department of Prints & Drawings. Photo: Kathryn M. Rudy.	50
22	Engraved roundels representing virgins, some used as initials in the beghards' book of hours. London, British Museum, Department of Prints & Drawings, inv. 1861,1109.659, 662, 663, 664, 673, 674.	56
23	Folio from a prayerbook with three engravings by the Master of the Flower Borders glued to it and one sewn to it. Vienna, Österreichische Nationalbibliothek, ser. Nova 12715, fol. 29r.	57
24	Folio from a prayerbook with three engravings by the Master of the Flower Borders glued to it and one sewn to it. Vienna, Österreichische Nationalbibliothek, ser. Nova 12715, fols 29v-30r.	58
25	Matte with manuscript leaves from Add. 24332 glued to it, with engravings representing St Francis and others. London, British Museum, Department of Prints & Drawings.	66
26	Matte with manuscript leaves from Add. 24332 glued to it, with small engravings. London, British Museum, Department of Prints & Drawings.	66
27	Matte with manuscript leaves from Add. 24332 glued to it, with small engravings. London, British Museum, Department of Prints & Drawings.	67
28	Israhel van Meckenem, *Christ as Man of Sorrows*, engraving. Paris, BnF, Département des Estampes, Ea 48Res.	76

29	Mosaic icon with the *Akra Tapeinosis* (Utmost Humiliation), or Man of Sorrows, in a series of frames. Mosaic icon, Byzantine, late 13th–early 14th century. Basilica di Sta Croce in Gerusalemme, Rome.	76
30	Detail of the Mosaic icon from the previous figure.	77
31	Detail of London, British Museum, Department of Prints & Drawings, inv. 1861,1109.637, flipped to reveal the offset inscription.	80
32	Digital reconstruction to show the proposed original state of the opening of the Seven Penitential Psalms (Add. 24332, fol. 104v and Add. 41338, fol. 6r).	82
33	Digital reconstruction to show the proposed third state of the opening of the Seven Penitential Psalms (London, British Museum, Department of Prints & Drawings, inv. 1861,1109.632 and Add. 41338, fol. 6r).	83
34	Leaf from the beghards' book of hours, with an engraving depicting the Virgin and Child, by Israhel van Meckenem. London, British Museum, Department of Prints & Drawings, inv. 1861,1109.633.	92
35	Leaf from the beghards' book of hours, reverse of London, British Museum, Department of Prints & Drawings, inv. 1861,1109.633.	95
36	Two leaves mounted onto a single matte. London, British Museum, Department of Prints & Drawings, inv. 1861,1109.638 and 639.	97
37	Two impressions of an engraving depicting St Mark, mounted onto a single matte. London, British Museum, Department of Prints & Drawings, inv. 1861,1109.643 and 1868,1114.114.	101
38	London, British Museum, Department of Prints & Drawings, inv. 1861,1109.634 (St Anne, Mary, and Jesus) and three other manuscript leaves, including two from the St Godeleva manuscript.	103
39	Folio in the beghards' book of hours, which has been partially cut off. Maastricht, c. 1500. London, British Library, Add. Ms. 24332, fol. 271v (modern foliation).	105

List of Illustrations 311

40 Folio in the beghards' book of hours, which has been partially cut off. Maastricht, c. 1500. London, British Library, Add. Ms. 24332, fol. 309v (modern foliation). — 106

41 Zodiac man, from the beghards' manuscript. London, British Library, Add. Ms. 41338, fol. 1r. — 114

42 Leaf formerly belonging to the beghards' manuscript. London, British Library, Add. Ms. 41338, fol. 1v. — 114

43 Unfoliated front matter, formerly belonging to the beghards' manuscript. London, British Library, Add. Ms. 41338, fol. 2r. — 115

44 Leaf from the beghards' manuscript. London, British Library, Add. Ms. 41338, fol. 2v. — 116

45 Folio in the beghards' book of hours, showing the offset of a now-missing image. Maastricht, c. 1500. London, British Library, Add. Ms. 24332, fol. 19r (modern foliation). — 117

46 Incipit of the Hours of the Cross, formerly belonging to the beghards' manuscript. London, British Library, Add. Ms. 41338, fol. 3r. — 120

47 Incipit of the Hours of the Holy Spirit, formerly fol. *xci* in the beghards' manuscript. London, British Library, Add. Ms. 41338, fol. 4r. — 121

48 Incipit of the Seven Penitential Psalms, formerly fol. *cxxxiiij* in the beghards' manuscript. London, British Library, Add. Ms. 41338, fol. 6r. — 121

49 Skeleton incipit prefacing the Vigil of the Dead, formerly fol. *c lxxxiiij* in the beghards' manuscript. London, British Library, Add. Ms. 41338, fol. 7r. — 122

50 London, British Library, Add. Ms. 41338, fol. 11v. — 122

51 Folio from the beghards' book of hours, with a marginal pen drawing depicting a kneeling cleric at the foot of the Cross. London, British Library, Add. Ms. 41338, fol. 13r. — 123

52 Folio from the beghards' book of hours, with a pen drawing depicting St Gertrude with mice. London, British Library, Add. Ms. 41338, fol. 8v = fol. *ccc xiii*. — 125

53   Folio from the beghards' book of hours, with a pen drawing depicting the Virgin of the Sun, with a kneeling portrait of a male cleric and a frame filled with inscribed prayers. London, British Library, Add. Ms. 41338, fol. 5r.   127

54   Virgin of the Sun, parchment painting, inserted to face a prayer to the Body Parts of the Virgin. The Hague, Koninklijke Bibliotheek, Ms. 75 G 2, fol. 196v-197r.   129

55   Folio from the beghards' book of hours, with a coloured drawing depicting St Lambert. The frame measures 123 x 68 mm. London, British Library, Add. Ms. 41338, fol. 10r, formerly folio *cccc xxiii*, BM 696.   131

56   Folio from the beghards' book of hours, with a coloured drawing depicting St Trudo. The frame measures 114 x 62 mm. London, British Library, Add. Ms. 41338, fol. 12v.   131

57   Folio from the beghards' book of hours, with an engraving depicting St Matthew. London, British Library, Add. Ms. 41338, fol. 10v.   132

58   Folio from the beghards' book of hours. London, British Library, Add. Ms. 41338, fol. 12r.   133

59   Title page from 1868 catalogue of the Bibliothèque Imperiale.   136

60   Album from Paris, BnF, Département des Estampes, with three engravings by Israhel van Meckenem representing Christ as the Man of Sorrows. Published with kind permission from the Bibliothèque nationale de France.   142

61   Virgin of the Sun engraving, hand-coloured and pasted into the letter H in a German prayerbook. Paris, BnF, Département des Estampes, Ea20aRes. Published with kind permission from the Bibliothèque nationale de France.   143

62   Crucifixion, hand-coloured engraving, with a red penwork frame. Paris, BnF, Département des Estampes, Ea18cRes 28. Published with kind permission from the Bibliothèque nationale de France.   144

63   Israhel van Meckenem, Christ as Man of Sorrows, engraving. Paris, BnF, Département des Estampes, Ea48Res. Published with kind permission from the Bibliothèque nationale de France.   146

64 Adoration of the Christ Child by the Magi, painted metalcut. Paris, BnF, Département des Estampes. Published with kind permission from the Bibliothèque nationale de France. 147

65 Reverse of the previous image. Paris, BnF, Département des Estampes. Published with kind permission from the Bibliothèque nationale de France. 147

66 Adoration of the Christ Child by the Magi, engraving. Paris, Louvre, Rothschild 57. Paris, musée du Louvre, collection Rothschild Photo (C) RMN-Grand Palais (musée du Louvre)/Tony Querrec 149

67 St Augustine encountering the infant Jesus on a riverbank, engraving. Paris, Louvre, Rothschild 56. Paris, musée du Louvre, collection Rothschild Photo (C) RMN-Grand Palais (musée du Louvre)/Tony Querrec 150

68 Pentecost, gilt engraving, formerly pasted to fol. *cccc xcvii* of the beghards' book of hours? Paris, Louvre, Rothschild 54. Paris, musée du Louvre, collection Rothschild Photo (C) RMN-Grand Palais (musée du Louvre)/Tony Querrec 152

69 Pentecost, gilt engraving, formerly pasted to fol. *cccc xcvii* of the beghards' book of hours? Paris, Louvre, Rothschild 54. Photo: Kathryn M. Rudy 152

70 Christ in Judgment, gilt engraving. Paris, Louvre, Rothschild 55. Paris, musée du Louvre, collection Rothschild Photo (C) RMN-Grand Palais (musée du Louvre)/Tony Querrec 153

71 Christ in Judgment, gilt engraving. Paris, Louvre, Rothschild 55. Photo: Kathryn M. Rudy 153

72 Virgin and Child on a sliver of moon, surrounded by a rosary, originally in London, British Library, Add. Ms. 24332 as fol. *ccc xviii*? Paris, Louvre, Rothschild 69. Paris, musée du Louvre, collection Rothschild Photo (C) RMN-Grand Palais (musée du Louvre)/Tony Querrec 154

73 Handwritten list of acquisitions from the nineteenth century, in Paris, BnF, Département des Estampes. 155

74 Handwritten list of acquisitions from the nineteenth century, for 28 July 1859, BnF. 157

75	Handwritten list of acquisitions from the nineteenth century, Vingt-huit pièces de XVe siècle, 28 March 1860, BnF.	157
76	Handwritten list of acquisitions from the nineteenth century, for 11 August 1868, in the BnF.	158
77	Folio from the beghards' book of hours, with a pen drawing of a kneeling cleric, beneath an initial that probably once contained a print depicting St Clare. London, British Library, Add. Ms. 41338, fol. 9v.	161
78	Digital reconstruction: Israhel van Meckenem's roundel with SS Francis and Clare, superimposed on a leaf from what was the beghards' manuscript, now London, British Library, Add. Ms. 41338, fol. 9v.	161
79	Folio in the beghards' book of hours, with a prayer to St Anne, which has been partially mutilated. London, British Library, Add. Ms. 24332, fol. 351 (*ccc xci*).	163

Chapter 2

80	Calendar in the beghards' book of hours for the end of September and beginning of October. London, British Library, Add. Ms. 24332, fol. 9v–10r.	170
81	Calendar in the beghards' book of hours for the beginning of May. London, British Library, Add. Ms. 24332, fol. 5r.	170
82	Explanation of the Table of Contents in the beghards' book of hours. London, British Library, Add. Ms. 24332, fol. *ii* (modern foliation 14r).	173
83a	St Catherine, hand-coloured woodcut print, Southern Germany or Swabia. Paris, BnF, Rés. Ea-5 (8)-Boîte (Schreiber 1317/Bouchot 136). Published with kind permission from the Bibliothèque nationale de France.	175
83b	St Mary Magdalene, hand-coloured woodcut print, Southern Germany or Swabia. Paris, BnF, Rés. Ea-5 (8)-Boîte (Schreiber 1594/ Bouchot 139). Published with kind permission from the Bibliothèque nationale de France.	175

List of Illustrations

84 Book of hours with original foliation reading lvii (although it has lost its table of contents). The Hague, Koninklijke Bibliotheek, Ms. 135 E 36, fol. 45v–46r. http://manuscripts.kb.nl/zoom/BYVANCKB%3Amimi_135e36%3A045v_046r — 178

85 Calendar in a Golden Legend turned into table of contents: months of November and December, Amsterdam, 1450. The Hague, Koninklijke Bibliotheek, Ms. 73 D 9, fol. IIIr. — 180

86 Folio in a Golden Legend showing original foliation in the upper border, Amsterdam, 1450. The Hague, Koninklijke Bibliotheek, Ms. 73 D 9, fol. 179r. — 181

87 Table of contents in the beghards' book of hours. London, British Library, Add. Ms. 24332, fol. 14v-15r. — 185

88 Folio in the beghards' book of hours, with the Pater Noster, and beginning of Ave Maria. London, British Library, Add. Ms. 24332, fol. 26r. — 186

89 Opening in an English book of hours, in English and Latin, and with red lines to mark rhyming lines of poetry. Glasgow, University Library, Ms. Hunter, H512, fol. 32v-33r. — 188

90 Opening in the beghards' book of hours: the beginning of the benediction, with interlineal rubricated translation. London, British Library, Add. Ms. 24332, fol. 27v-28r (modern foliation). — 190

91 Symposium at Rijksmuseum, Amsterdam, June 2016. — 191

92 Weert, Gemeentemuseum Jacob van Horne, Museum interior in 2016. — 191

Chapter 3

93 Matte from 1868, with Christological prints removed from Add. 31002. London, British Museum, Department of Prints & Drawings. — 199

94 'Trimmed and silhouetted saints' affixed to a matte assembled in 1868. London, British Museum, Department of Prints & Drawings. — 200

95	Folio in the beghards' later book of hours, with Virgin of the Sun standing on the moon (added engraving), c. 1525. London, British Library, Add. Ms. 31002, vol. I, fol. 138r.	203
96	Folio in the beghards' later book of hours, c. 1525, from which an engraving depicting a bishop's upper body was removed in 1868. London, British Library, Add. Ms. 31002, vol. II, 62r (original fol. 272).	205
97	Opening from the calendar of the beghards' later book of hours for August-September. London, British Library, Add. Ms. 31002, vol. I, fols 8v-9r.	208
98	Opening from the calendar of the beghards' later book of hours for September-October. London, British Library, Add. Ms. 31002, vol. I, fols 9v-10r.	209
99	Multiplication tables. London, British Library, Add. Ms. 31002, vol. I, fol. 14v-15r.	215
100	Folio in the beghards' later book of hours, with a coloured drawing depicting St Lambert. London, British Library, Add. Ms. 31002, vol. II, fol. 106r.	216
101	Folio in the beghards' later book of hours, with a coloured drawing depicting Brother Leo kneeling before St Francis. London, British Library, Add. Ms. 31002, vol. II, fol. 114v.	217
102	Folio in the beghards' later book of hours, with a coloured drawing depicting a church. London, British Library, Add. Ms. 31002, vol. I, fol. 50v.	218
103	Folio in the beghards' later manuscript with a space reserved for an image of Veronica. London, British Library, Add. Ms. 31002, vol. II, fol. 34r.	221
104	Electronic reconstruction of Veronica page: superimposition of London, British Museum, Department of Prints & Drawings, inv. 1868,1114.24 onto London, British Library, Add. Ms. 31002, vol. II, fol. 34r.	221
105	Folio from the beghard's later manuscript with a prayer, an indulgence, and a blank area where a Marian roundel was formerly pasted. London, British Library, Add. Ms. 31002, vol. I, fol. 76r.	231

List of Illustrations

106 Folio from the beghard's later manuscript with a prayer and a blank area where a Marian print was formerly pasted. London, British Library, Add. Ms. 31002, vol. I, fol. 75r. 232

107 Israhel van Meckenem, St Quirinus and three other saints, separate engravings mounted on one sheet. Paris, BnF, Département des Estampes, Ea48aRes(IvM). Published with kind permission from the Bibliothèque nationale de France. 236

Chapter 4

108 Opening at the Hours of Eternal Wisdom, in a book of hours from the region of Arnhem. London, British Library, Add. Ms. 17524, fol. 109v-110r. 249

109 Opening at the Hours of the Cross, in a book of hours from the region of Arnhem. London, British Library, Add. Ms. 17524, fol. 59v–60r. 251

110 Opening in a book of hours probably made by Franciscan women in Zutphen, with space left for prints to be pasted in. The Hague, Koninklijke Bibliotheek, Ms. 77 L 58, fol. 85v-86r. 253

111 Matte from 1868, with prints taken from two manuscripts. London, British Museum, Department of Prints & Drawings. 255

112 Ten hand-coloured engravings removed from what is now London, British Library, Ms. 31001. London, British Museum, Department of Prints & Drawings, inv. 1868,1114.222-231. 257

113 Instructions for visiting sites around Jerusalem. Opening of a prayerbook with texts for conducting virtual pilgrimages. London, British Library, Ms. 31001, fols. 71v-72r. 258

114 Calendar with indulgences for virtual visiting the Seven Principal Churches of Rome. Opening of a prayerbook with texts for conducting virtual pilgrimages. London, British Library, Ms. 31001, fols. 59v-60r. 259

115 Attributed to the Monogrammist LF, Basilicas of San Lorenzo and San Sebastiano surmounted by an image of Judas betraying Christ with a kiss, painting on panel, 1502. Commissioned by Helena Rephonin for the Dominican convent of St Catherine in Augsburg. 262

116 Folio removed from a manuscript, with a woodcut print depicting St Opportune. Paris, BnF, Département des Estampes. (Courboin 614; Bouchot 140; Schreiber 2716). Published with kind permission from the Bibliothèque nationale de France. 264

117 Pentecost engraving pasted into a painted initial removed from a manuscript. Paris, BnF, Département des Estampes, Ea 18 c Res (Lehrs 25). Published with kind permission from the Bibliothèque nationale de France. 266

118 St Augustine, woodcut print, hand-painted. Berlin, Kupferstichkabinett, Box 107 A3A. (Schreiber 1244 E). 269

119 Master the Berlin Passion, Stripping of Christ, hand-painted engraving. Berlin, Kupferstichkabinett, Inv. 2-56. (Lehrs 28 I). 270

120 Master of the Dutuit Garden of Olives, Virgin and Child engraving, printed on parchment and gilt. Berlin, Kupferstichkabinett, Inv. 446-I (Lehrs 49). 272

121 Monogrammist AG, Large Crucifixion, hand-painted engraving on parchment. Berlin, Kupferstichkabinett, nr 998-I (Lehrs 3b). 272

122 Opening in a prayerbook, with prayers for the weeks of the liturgical year, each one beginning with an initial filled with a hand-painted engraving. Heverlee, Abdij van Park, Ms. 18, fols 27v-28r. 276

123 Folio in a prayerbook, with prayers for the feast of the Sacrament. Heverlee, Abdij van Park, Ms. 18, fol. 49v. 278

124 Folio in a prayerbook, with prayers for the feast of the Holy Cross. Heverlee, Abdij van Park, Ms. 18, fol. 54v. 279

125 Folio in a prayerbook, with prayers to 'our holy father' St Augustine, with an Augustinian sister kneeling before him. Heverlee, Abdij van Park, Ms. 18, fol. 79v. 280

126 Folio in a prayerbook, with prayers to St Elisabeth. Heverlee, Abdij van Park, Ms. 18, fol. 85r. 281

127	Opening in a prayerbook, with an initial depicting Christ releasing his arms from the cross in order to embrace an Augustinian sister. Heverlee, Abdij van Park, Ms. 18, fol. 137v-138r.	283
128	Folio in a prayerbook, with an initial depicting Christ opening his side wound in the presence of an Augustinian sister. Heverlee, Abdij van Park, Ms. 18, fol. 109r.	283
129	Opening in a prayerbook with an added engraving depicting St George. London, British Museum, Department of Prints & Drawings, inv. 158* b 32.	286
130	Opening in a prayerbook with an added roundel by Israhel van Meckenem. Cambridge, Gonville and Caius College, Ms. 718/253, fols 366v-367r.	287
131	Music manuscript with pasted-in roundels made by Israhel van Meckenem, from Soeterbeeck in Deursen near Ravenstein, a convent of Augustinian canonesses. Soeterbeeck, IV 136.	288
132	Opening in a prayerbook with an added engraving depicting the Virgin of the Sun. Cambridge, Gonville and Caius College, Ms. 718/253, fols 280v-281r.	289
133	Opening in a prayerbook with the remains of added engraving, opposite a prayer to a personal angel. Cambridge, Gonville and Caius College, Ms. 718/253, fols 364v-365r.	290
134	Opening in a prayerbook with the remains of added woodcut depicting St Barbara. Cambridge, Gonville and Caius College, Ms. 718/253, fol. 384v-385r.	291
135	Opening in a prayerbook with the ghost image of a print probably depicting the Virgin and Child. Cambridge, Gonville and Caius College, Ms. 718/253, fol. 406v-407r.	292
136	Opening in a book of hours, featuring a mounted engraving by Israhel van Meckenem depicting Christ before Annas. London, British Museum, Department of Prints & Drawings, inv. 1897,0103.3, also known as London, British Library, Sloane Ms. 3981, fols 14v-15r.	297
137	Opening in a book of hours, featuring a mounted engraving by Israhel van Meckenem depicting Christ awaiting crucifixion. London, British Museum, Department of Prints & Drawings, inv. 1897,0103.9, also known as London, British Library, Sloane Ms. 3981, fols 33v-34r.	298

E-figures

Chapter 1

1. Joan Blaeu, Map of Maastricht, from the *Toonneel der Steeden* (Views of Netherlandish Cities), 1650. This page includes a number of details from the map. — 29

   https://hdl.handle.net/20.500.12434/6f08104e

2. IHS monogram, as a full-page image. Netherlandish engraving. London, British Museum, Department of Prints & Drawings, inv. 1861,1109.645. — 38

   https://hdl.handle.net/20.500.12434/6d0f3ffb

3. Manuscript leaf written in Middle Dutch, with an engraved roundel by Israhel van Meckenem representing St Barbara, standing with her attribute, formerly part of Add. 24332. London, British Museum, Department of Prints & Drawings, inv. 1861,1109.660. — 43

   https://hdl.handle.net/20.500.12434/bfade03b

4. Manuscript leaf written in Middle Dutch, with an engraved roundel by Israhel van Meckenem representing SS Peter and Paul, formerly part of Add. 24332. London, British Museum, Department of Prints & Drawings, inv. 1861,1109.679. — 43

   https://hdl.handle.net/20.500.12434/500265f2

5   Israhel van Meckenem, printed roundel with St Wolfgang, who has been transformed into St Servatius, pasted into the initial of manuscript folio, formerly fol. *ccc lxiii* of London, British Library, Add. Ms. 24332. London, British Museum, Department of Prints & Drawings, inv. 1861,1109.680.   43

https://hdl.handle.net/20.500.12434/1ac4bd1d

6   Israhel van Meckenem, sheet of six roundels depicting Christ as Salvator Mundi and five standing saints. London, British Museum, Department of Prints & Drawings, inv. 1873,0809.642.   44

https://hdl.handle.net/20.500.12434/db692147

7   Israhel van Meckenem, sheet of six roundels depicting pairs of standing apostles. London, British Museum, Department of Prints & Drawings, inv. 1873,0809.643.   44

https://hdl.handle.net/20.500.12434/92140750

8   Detached folio *cccc lxxij* with an engraving depicting St Barbara made by Israhel van Meckenem. London, British Museum, Department of Prints & Drawings, inv. 1861,1109.660.   45

https://hdl.handle.net/20.500.12434/67d4934e

9   Israhel van Meckenem, sheet of six roundels depicting Christ as Salvator Mundi and five standing saints. London, British Museum, Department of Prints & Drawings, inv. 1873,0809.642.   45

https://hdl.handle.net/20.500.12434/8f0229e3

10 Detached folio *ccc lxiii*, verso side. London, British Museum, Department of Prints & Drawings, inv. 1861,1109.680.   46

https://hdl.handle.net/20.500.12434/64120d59

11 Manuscript leaf written in Middle Dutch, with an engraved roundel by Israhel van Meckenem representing SS Peter and Paul, formerly part of Add. 24332. London, British Museum, Department of Prints & Drawings, inv. 1861,1109.679.   47

https://hdl.handle.net/20.500.12434/8d621959

12	Leaf from the beghards' manuscript with an engraving depicting St Mark, sometimes attributed to Israhel van Meckenem, and another smaller engraving depicting a winged lion. London, British Museum, Department of Prints & Drawings, inv. 1861,1109.643. https://hdl.handle.net/20.500.12434/dcfa6c6d	54
13	St Apollonia roundel (engraving), pasted into initial before a prayer to that saint. London, British Museum, Department of Prints & Drawings, inv. 1861,1109.659. https://hdl.handle.net/20.500.12434/8142772d	55
14	St Catherine roundel (engraving), pasted into initial before a prayer to that saint. London, British Museum, Department of Prints & Drawings, inv. 1861,1109.662. https://hdl.handle.net/20.500.12434/53765d41	55
15	St Cecilia? roundel (engraving), pasted into initial before a prayer to that saint. London, British Museum, Department of Prints & Drawings, inv. 1861,1109.663. https://hdl.handle.net/20.500.12434/0d62a32c	55
16	St Columba? roundel (engraving), pasted into initial before a prayer to that saint. London, British Museum, Department of Prints & Drawings, inv. 1861,1109.664. https://hdl.handle.net/20.500.12434/78e8d1bd	55
17	Mary Magdalene roundel (engraving), pasted into initial before a prayer to that saint. London, British Museum, Department of Prints & Drawings, inv. 1861,1109.673. https://hdl.handle.net/20.500.12434/6d0f15f6	56
18	St Margaret roundel (engraving), pasted into initial before a prayer to St Dymphna. London, British Museum, Department of Prints & Drawings, inv. 1861,1109.674. https://hdl.handle.net/20.500.12434/795948e7	56

19 Engraving depicting a generic figure, trimmed and used to represent St Elzéar. London, British Museum, Department of Prints & Drawings, inv. 1861,1109.665.   60
https://hdl.handle.net/20.500.12434/e378b127

20 Prayer for the consecration of a Franciscan church with two prints, one representing a Franciscan, the other a church. London, British Museum, Department of Prints & Drawings, inv. 1861,1109.686 and 687.   60
https://hdl.handle.net/20.500.12434/86e3ffd8

21 Jan van Eyck, *St Francis receiving the Stigmata*, ca. 1430-32. Oil on parchment on panel. Philadelphia.   61
https://hdl.handle.net/20.500.12434/add8a667

22 St Benedict, engraving. London, British Museum, Department of Prints & Drawings, inv. 1861,1109.641.   61
https://hdl.handle.net/20.500.12434/9d67d830

23 St Benedict, engraving. London, British Museum, Department of Prints & Drawings, inv. 1861,1109.640.   63
https://hdl.handle.net/20.500.12434/23281d22

24 St Anne with Virgin and Child, engraving. London, British Museum, Department of Prints & Drawings, inv. 1861,1109.634.   64
https://hdl.handle.net/20.500.12434/2efe8653

25 St Anne with Virgin and Child, engraving. London, British Museum, Department of Prints & Drawings, inv. 1861,1109.635.   64
https://hdl.handle.net/20.500.12434/b1721240

26 Manuscript leaf with a prayer to St Francis and an engraving. London, British Museum, Department of Prints & Drawings, inv. 1861,1109.666.   67
https://hdl.handle.net/20.500.12434/acbebc80

27	Manuscript leaf with a prayer to St Quentin and an engraving. London, British Museum, Department of Prints & Drawings, inv. 1861,1109.676.	68
	https://hdl.handle.net/20.500.12434/4d93048f	
28	Manuscript leaf from Add. 24332 with a prayer to St Peter and an engraving. London, British Museum, Department of Prints & Drawings, inv. 1861,1109.692.	68
	https://hdl.handle.net/20.500.12434/7c16bdd0	
29	Manuscript leaf from Add. 24332 with an engraving depicting St Matthias.	68
	https://hdl.handle.net/20.500.12434/29a6855a	
30	Manuscript leaf with a prayer to St Francis and an engraving. London, British Museum, Department of Prints & Drawings, inv. 1861,1109.667.	69
	https://hdl.handle.net/20.500.12434/72e479af	
31	Leaf from the beghards' book of hours, with three engravings glued to it. London, British Museum, Department of Prints & Drawings, inv. 1861,1109.668, 677, 678, and 669.	70
	https://hdl.handle.net/20.500.12434/a11440fb	
32	Leaf from the beghards' book of hours, with an engraving depicting St John on Patmos. London, British Museum, Department of Prints & Drawings, inv. 1861,1109.670.	70
	https://hdl.handle.net/20.500.12434/31e5559d	
33	Top half of a leaf from the beghards' book of hours, with an engraving representing the Virgin of the Sun. London, British Museum, Department of Prints & Drawings, inv. 1861,1109.657.	72
	https://hdl.handle.net/20.500.12434/6da68562	
34	Leaf from the beghards' book of hours, with an engraving depicting a winged ox. London, British Museum, Department of Prints & Drawings, inv. 1861,1109.685.	72
	https://hdl.handle.net/20.500.12434/8e6d1ef9	

35 Leaf from the beghards' book of hours, with an engraving depicting St Lawrence. London, British Museum, Department of Prints & Drawings, inv. 1861,1109.672.   73
https://hdl.handle.net/20.500.12434/0e573e54

36 Partial leaf from the beghards' book of hours, with an engraving depicting St Lawrence used to represent St Vincent. London, British Museum, Department of Prints & Drawings, inv. 1861,1109.682.   73
https://hdl.handle.net/20.500.12434/79a323c9

37 Leaf from the beghards' book of hours, with an engraving depicting St Lawrence, used to represent St Stephen. London, British Museum, Department of Prints & Drawings, inv. 1861,1109.671.   73
https://hdl.handle.net/20.500.12434/fe140795

38 Leaf from the beghards' book of hours, with an engraving depicting St Paul, used as St James. London, British Museum, Department of Prints & Drawings, inv. 1861,1109.690.   74
https://hdl.handle.net/20.500.12434/e9f19c47

39 Leaf from the beghards' book of hours, with an engraving depicting St Agatha. London, British Museum, Department of Prints & Drawings, inv. 1861,1109.693.   74
https://hdl.handle.net/20.500.12434/a8cfa393

40 Leaf from the beghards' book of hours, with an engraved roundel depicting Christ as Man of Sorrows used as a historiated initial. London, British Museum, Department of Prints & Drawings, inv. 1861,1109.658.   75
https://hdl.handle.net/20.500.12434/8ae40eb5

41 Jesus as an infant holding the *Arma Christi*, Netherlandish engraving. London, British Museum, Department of Prints & Drawings, inv. 1861,1109.632.   78
https://hdl.handle.net/20.500.12434/4389fc3b

42 Leaf from the beghards' book of hours, with an engraving depicting the dead Christ being supported by his standing mother, with the *Arma Christi* displayed as two coats of arms above. Netherlandish, engraving, attributed to Monogrammist F. London, British Museum, Department of Prints & Drawings, inv. 1861,1109.637.   78

https://hdl.handle.net/20.500.12434/a87353b9

43 Leaf from the beghards' book of hours, with a woodcut depicting St Nicholas. London, British Museum, Department of Prints & Drawings, inv. 1861,1109.646.   84

https://hdl.handle.net/20.500.12434/75a4b1c2

44 Leaf from the beghards' book of hours, with a woodcut depicting St Anthony. London, British Museum, Department of Prints & Drawings, inv. 1861,1109.647.   84

https://hdl.handle.net/20.500.12434/761ffcf0

45 Leaf from the beghards' book of hours, with a woodcut depicting St Barbara. London, British Museum, Department of Prints & Drawings, inv. 1861,1109.648.   84

https://hdl.handle.net/20.500.12434/8b52f262

46 Leaf from the beghards' book of hours, with a woodcut depicting St Catherine. London, British Museum, Department of Prints & Drawings, inv. 1861,1109.649.   85

https://hdl.handle.net/20.500.12434/b75dc987

47 Leaf from the beghards' book of hours, with a woodcut depicting St Erasmus. London, British Museum, Department of Prints & Drawings, inv. 1861,1109.650.   85

https://hdl.handle.net/20.500.12434/dea0315d

48 Leaf from the beghards' book of hours, with a woodcut depicting St Macarius, used as St Paul. London, British Museum, Department of Prints & Drawings, inv. 1861,1109.651.   85

https://hdl.handle.net/20.500.12434/a6f85a7f

49	Leaf from the beghards' book of hours, with a metalcut depicting St Margaret. London, British Museum, Department of Prints & Drawings, inv. 1861,1109.652. https://hdl.handle.net/20.500.12434/528638af	85
50	Leaf from the beghards' book of hours, with a woodcut depicting St Martin. London, British Museum, Department of Prints & Drawings, inv. 1861,1109.653. https://hdl.handle.net/20.500.12434/088e2934	85
51	Leaf from the beghards' book of hours, with a woodcut depicting St Sebastian. London, British Museum, Department of Prints & Drawings, inv. 1861,1109.654. https://hdl.handle.net/20.500.12434/5292976a	86
52	Leaf from the beghards' book of hours, with a woodcut depicting St Roch. London, British Museum, Department of Prints & Drawings, inv. 1861,1109.655. https://hdl.handle.net/20.500.12434/0cb2bc9d	86
53	Leaf from the beghards' book of hours, with an engraving depicting Bernard interacting with an image of Christ that comes alive. London, British Museum, Department of Prints & Drawings, inv. 1861,1109.688. https://hdl.handle.net/20.500.12434/23d63d3e	89
54	Leaf from the beghards' book of hours, with an engraving depicting St Christopher, attributed to the Master of the Martyrdom of the Ten Thousand. London, British Museum, Department of Prints & Drawings, inv. 1861,1109.689. https://hdl.handle.net/20.500.12434/fb8fbeb0	91
55	Leaf from the beghards' book of hours, with an engraving depicting Christ raising Jairus's Daughter, attributed to Israhel van Meckenem. London, British Museum, Department of Prints & Drawings, inv. 1861,1109.636. https://hdl.handle.net/20.500.12434/c521155b	92

56	Engraving depicting the Virgin and Child, by Israhel van Meckenem, signed 'IM'. Uncoloured version. London, British Museum, Department of Prints & Drawings, inv. 1851,1213.864. https://hdl.handle.net/20.500.12434/7b9c7c52	93
57	Leaf from the beghards' book of hours, with an engraving depicting the Virgin and Child, by Israhel van Meckenem. London, British Museum, Department of Prints & Drawings, inv. 1861,1109.633. https://hdl.handle.net/20.500.12434/a5c471dc	95
58	Leaf from the beghards' book of hours, with an engraving depicting St Cecilia. London, British Museum, Department of Prints & Drawings, inv. 1861,1109.638. https://hdl.handle.net/20.500.12434/885dfcd7	96
59	Leaf from the beghards' book of hours, with an engraving depicting St Catherine, used as Lucia. London, British Museum, Department of Prints & Drawings, inv. 1861,1109.639. https://hdl.handle.net/20.500.12434/cc830276	97
60	Leaf from the beghards' book of hours, with an engraving depicting St Michael, sometimes attributed to Israhel van Meckenem. London, British Museum, Department of Prints & Drawings, inv. 1861,1109.644. https://hdl.handle.net/20.500.12434/6c739957	99
61	St Mark, engraving. London, British Museum, Department of Prints & Drawings, inv. 1868,1114.114. https://hdl.handle.net/20.500.12434/d4915dff	101
62	Leaf from the beghards' book of hours, with an engraving representing St Bartholomew. London, British Museum, Department of Prints & Drawings, inv. 1861,1109.661. https://hdl.handle.net/20.500.12434/ed3dc20b	119

63 Manuscript leaf with a prayer to one's personal angel and an engraving representing an angel. London, British Museum, Department of Prints & Drawings, inv. 1861,1109.683.   119
https://hdl.handle.net/20.500.12434/219b6850

64 Master IAM of Zwolle, Virgin *in sole*, engraving. London, British Museum, Department of Prints & Drawings, inv. 1845,0809.95.   126
https://hdl.handle.net/20.500.12434/b558356e

65 Six roundels depicting the infant Christ as Salvator Mundi and saints, signed by Israhel van Meckenem in the plate, intact. London, British Museum, Department of Prints & Drawings, inv. 1849,1208.739.   160
https://hdl.handle.net/20.500.12434/b2b2e1ee

Chapter 3

66 Bishop wearing a mitre. Hand-painted engraving, trimmed and silhouetted. London, British Museum, Department of Prints & Drawings, inv. 1868,1114.115   204
https://hdl.handle.net/20.500.12434/cc55a7af

67 Virgin *in sole*, engraving pasted to the leaf of a prayerbook. London, British Museum, Department of Prints & Drawings, inv. 1868,1114.196.   199
https://hdl.handle.net/20.500.12434/fc2487da

68 Folio from an album with manuscript cuttings. The Hague, Koninklijke Bibliotheek, Ms. 131 F 19, fol. 10r.   201
https://hdl.handle.net/20.500.12434/31a0dbf8

69 Folio from an album with manuscript cuttings. The Hague, Koninklijke Bibliotheek, Ms. 131 F 19, fol. 12r.   201
https://hdl.handle.net/20.500.12434/b3b64d40

70 Folio of the beghards' later book of hours, with an engraving depicting the Nativity attributed to Monogrammist MB. London, British Museum, Department of Prints & Drawings, inv. 1868,1114.210.   202
https://hdl.handle.net/20.500.12434/73f718b0

71 Mary Magdalene. Engraving removed from the beghards' later book of hours. London, British Museum, Department of Prints & Drawings, inv. 1868,1114.221.   214
https://hdl.handle.net/20.500.12434/82930606

72 Folio removed from the beghards' later book of hours, formerly fol. 235, with a hand-coloured engraving depicting Virgin *in sole*. London, British Museum, Department of Prints & Drawings, inv. 1868,1114.207.   214
https://hdl.handle.net/20.500.12434/16858f27

73 St Bartholomew. Engraving removed from the beghards' later book of hours. London, British Museum, Department of Prints & Drawings, inv. 1868,1114.168.   222
https://hdl.handle.net/20.500.12434/c4171f63

74 After Albrecht Dürer, Crucifixion roundel. Engraving removed from the beghards' later book of hours. London, British Museum, Department of Prints & Drawings, inv. 1868,1114.27.   223
https://hdl.handle.net/20.500.12434/66ce57c7

75 St Helen, dated 1523, with the monogram 'IB'. Engraving removed from the beghards' later book of hours. London, British Museum, Department of Prints & Drawings, inv. 1868,1114.120.   224
https://hdl.handle.net/20.500.12434/e2a03a80

76 Jacob Binck, Christ as the Man of Sorrows. Engraving removed from the beghards' later book of hours. London, British Museum, Department of Prints & Drawings, inv. 1868,1114.122.   224
https://hdl.handle.net/20.500.12434/046cf84f

77　Jacob Binck, *Ecce Homo*. Engraving removed from the beghards' later book of hours. London, British Museum, Department of Prints & Drawings, inv. 1868,1114.69.   224
https://hdl.handle.net/20.500.12434/3b054c33

78　St Trudo. Engraving removed from the beghards' later book of hours. London, British Museum, Department of Prints & Drawings, inv. 1868,1114.199.   225
https://hdl.handle.net/20.500.12434/b4d830d4

79　St Christopher. Engraving used as a folio, removed from the beghards' later book of hours. London, British Museum, Department of Prints & Drawings, inv. 1868,1114.150.   225
https://hdl.handle.net/20.500.12434/c983aac2

80　St Lucy and St Genevieve. Engraving used as a folio, removed from the beghards' later book of hours. London, British Museum, Department of Prints & Drawings, inv. 1868,1114.86.   225
https://hdl.handle.net/20.500.12434/e04ba44f

81　Israhel van Meckenem, Annunciation. Engraving used as a folio, removed from the beghards' later book of hours. London, British Museum, Department of Prints & Drawings, inv. 1868,1114.109.   226
https://hdl.handle.net/20.500.12434/89d6e804

82　Israhel van Meckenem, Christ with the *Arma Christi*; on the scroll: 'ecce homo'; below the borderline, signed 'Israhel'. Engraving used as a folio, removed from the beghards' later book of hours. London, British Museum, Department of Prints & Drawings, inv. 1868,1114.28.   226
https://hdl.handle.net/20.500.12434/dce280fb

83　Christ as Man of Sorrows with the *Arma Christi* in a letter O. Engraving removed from the beghards' later book of hours. London, BM, P&D, 1868,1114.32.   228
https://hdl.handle.net/20.500.12434/6d2fc836

84 Israhel van Meckenem's roundels, intact, with death theme. London, British Museum, Department of Prints & Drawings, inv. 1848,1125.19.   229
https://hdl.handle.net/20.500.12434/73ad2a6f

85 Israhel van Meckenem, Death visiting the Pope, roundel from Memento mori series. Engraving removed from the beghards' later book of hours. London, British Museum, Department of Prints & Drawings, inv. 1868,1114.74.   229
https://hdl.handle.net/20.500.12434/960bc5aa

86 Israhel van Meckenem, Nativity roundel. Engraving removed from the beghards' later book of hours. London, British Museum, Department of Prints & Drawings, inv. 1868,1114.209.   230
https://hdl.handle.net/20.500.12434/2a22e9e7

87 Israhel van Meckenem, Presentation in the Temple roundel. Engraving removed from the beghards' later book of hours. London, British Museum, Department of Prints & Drawings, inv. 1868,1114.96.   230
https://hdl.handle.net/20.500.12434/abd2bdbf

88 Israhel van Meckenem, Circumcision of Christ roundel. Engraving removed from the beghards' later book of hours. London, British Museum, Department of Prints & Drawings, inv. 1868,1114.84.   230
https://hdl.handle.net/20.500.12434/f2fd8c27

89 Israhel van Meckenem, Virgin *in sole* roundel. Engraving removed from the beghards' later book of hours. London, British Museum, Department of Prints & Drawings, inv. 1868,1114.43.   230
https://hdl.handle.net/20.500.12434/24c07a98

90 Israhel van Meckenem, Sheet of 6 roundels depicting Christ as Man of Sorrows, the Virgin of the Sun, and 4 scenes from the Infancy of Christ. London, British Museum, Department of Prints & Drawings, inv. 1873,0809.641.   230
https://hdl.handle.net/20.500.12434/c49908ee

91 Israhel van Meckenem, SS Cosmas and Damian roundel. Engraving removed from the beghards' later book of hours. London, British Museum, Department of Prints & Drawings, inv. 1868,1114.178. 233

https://hdl.handle.net/20.500.12434/b139197d

92 Israhel van Meckenem, SS Francis and Clare roundel. Engraving removed from the beghards' later book of hours. London, British Museum, Department of Prints & Drawings, inv. 1868,1114.158. 233

https://hdl.handle.net/20.500.12434/3805277f

93 Israhel van Meckenem, SS Dominic and Catherine of Siena roundel. Engraving removed from the beghards' later book of hours. London, British Museum, Department of Prints & Drawings, inv. 1868,1114.117. 233

https://hdl.handle.net/20.500.12434/cb7df4d6

94 Five roundels depicting the most lucrative indulgenced images. Hand-coloured engraving used as manuscript page, removed from the beghards' later book of hours. London, British Museum, Department of Prints & Drawings, inv. 1868,1114.188. 234

https://hdl.handle.net/20.500.12434/4b46faac

95 Israhel van Meckenem, St George/Quirinus. Engraving removed from the beghards' later book of hours. London, British Museum, Department of Prints & Drawings, inv. 1868,1114.116. 235

https://hdl.handle.net/20.500.12434/1fc325da

96 Christ at Emmaus. Engraving removed from the beghards' later book of hours. London, British Museum, Department of Prints & Drawings, inv. 1868,1114.37. 237

https://hdl.handle.net/20.500.12434/b2b6888f

97 St Luke. Engraving removed from the beghards' later book of hours. London, British Museum, Department of Prints & Drawings, inv. 1868,1114.184. 237

https://hdl.handle.net/20.500.12434/5fc58440

98	Circumcision of Christ, attributed to Israhel van Meckenem. Engraving removed from the beghards' later book of hours. London, British Museum, Department of Prints & Drawings, inv. 1868,1114.85. https://hdl.handle.net/20.500.12434/91db362d	238
99	Virgin Mary as a child climbing the steps of the Temple. Engraving removed from the beghards' later book of hours. London, British Museum, Department of Prints & Drawings, inv. 1868,1114.197. https://hdl.handle.net/20.500.12434/93ffcf6d	238
100	Rosary print. Engraving removed from the beghards' later book of hours. London, British Museum, Department of Prints & Drawings, inv. 1868,1114.172. https://hdl.handle.net/20.500.12434/9d1ea162	241
101	Rosary image, with the Virgin of the Sun appearing to St Dominic. Engraving removed from the beghards' later book of hours. London, British Museum, Department of Prints & Drawings, inv. 1868,1114.211. https://hdl.handle.net/20.500.12434/e14aa8c6	241
102	Rosary image, with the Virgin of the Sun. Engraving removed from the beghards' later book of hours. London, British Museum, Department of Prints & Drawings, inv. 1868,1114.51. https://hdl.handle.net/20.500.12434/fe120a58	242
103	Rosary image. Engraving removed from the beghards' later book of hours. London, British Museum, Department of Prints & Drawings, inv. 1868,1114.98. https://hdl.handle.net/20.500.12434/ec7218ed	242

Chapter 4

104   Christ as Salvator Mundi, silhouetted. Engraving removed from what is now London, British Library, Add. Ms. 17524. London, British Museum, Department of Prints & Drawings, inv. 1848,0212.119.   248

https://hdl.handle.net/20.500.12434/6357207f

105   Pentecost, engraving. London, British Museum, Department of Prints & Drawings, inv. 1847,0318.128.   252

https://hdl.handle.net/20.500.12434/d63bfd64

106   Christ on the cross on Earth surrounded by the rings of the planets of the solar system, with the Mass of St Gregory, the Annunciation, and the Virgin *in sole* below. Hand-coloured engraving removed from what is now London, British Library, Ms. 31001. London, British Museum, Department of Prints & Drawings, inv. 1868,1114.231.   253

https://hdl.handle.net/20.500.12434/747401b8

107   Seven Joys of the Virgin. Hand-coloured engraving removed from what is now London, British Library, Ms. 31001. London, British Museum, Department of Prints & Drawings, inv. 1868,1114.229.   254

https://hdl.handle.net/20.500.12434/a6c77c4a

108   Manuscript from St Catherine's, Nuremberg. London, British Museum, Department of Prints & Drawings, inv. 1890,1013.54.1–35.   285

https://hdl.handle.net/20.500.12434/c2c5e6d4

Bibliography

Acres, Alfred. 'The Columba Altarpiece and the Time of the World.' *The Art Bulletin* 80, no. 3 (1998), pp. 422–51.

Andresen, A. 'Beiträge zur Älteren Niederdeutschen Kupferstichkunde des 15. und 16. Jahrhunders.' *Archiv für die zeichnenden Künste mit besonderer Beziehung auf Kupferstecher- und Holzschneidekunst und ihre Geschichte im Vereine mit Künstlern und Kunstfreunden, herausgegeben von Dr. Robert Naumann* 14, no. 1 (1868), pp. 1–56.

Areford, David S. *The Viewer and the Printed Image in Late Medieval Europe*, Visual Culture in Early Modernity. Farnham, England; Burlington, VT: Ashgate, 2010. https://doi.org/10.4324/9781315084961

Asperen de Boer, J. R. J. van. *Jan Van Eyck: Two Paintings of Saint Francis Receiving the Stigmata*. Philadelphia, PA: Philadelphia Museum of Art, 1997.

Bagnoli, Martina, ed. *Treasures of Heaven: Saints, Relics, and Devotion in Medieval Europe*, Exh. Cat., Cleveland Museum of Art, Walters Art Museum, British Museum. New Haven, CT: Yale University Press, 2010.

Beebe, Kathryne. 'The Jerusalem of the Mind's Eye: Imagined Pilgrimage in the Late Fifteenth Century.' In *Visual Constructs of Jerusalem*, ed. by Bianca Kühnel, Galit Noga-Banai and Hanna Vorholt, pp. 409–20. Turnhout: Brepols, 2014. https://doi.org/10.1484/m.celama-eb.5.103095

Blum, André. 'Des Rapports de Miniaturistes Français du XVe Siècle avec les Premiers Artistes Graveurs.' *Revue de l'Art Chrétien* LXI (1911), pp. 357–69.

Bober, Harry, 'The Zodiacal Miniature of the *Très Riches Heures* of the Duke of Berry-Its Sources and Meaning', *Journal of the Warburg and Courtauld Institutes* 11 (1948), pp. 1–34.

Bouchot, Henri. *Les Deux Cents Incunables Xylographiques du Département des Estampes: Origines de la Gravure sur Bois—Les Précurseurs—Les Papiers—Les Indulgences—Les 'Grandes Pièces' des Cabinets d'Europe—Catalogue Raisonné des Estampes sur Bois et sur Métal du Cabinet de Paris*. Paris: Librairie centrale des beaux-arts, 1903.

Broeckhuysen, Adam van. 'Het klooster der Bijgaarden in de Witmakersstraat gelegen', *Publications de la Société Historique et Archéologique dans le Duché de Limbourg = Jaarboek van Limburgs Geschied- en Oudheidkundig Genootschap*, XLII (1906), p. 38.

Bühler, Curt F. *The Fifteenth-Century Book*: *The Scribes, the Printers, the Decorators*. Philadelphia, PA: University of Pennsylvania Press, 2016, originally published 1960.

Buren, Anne H. van and Sheila Edmunds. 'Playing Cards and Manuscripts: Some Widely Disseminated Fifteenth-Century Model Sheets.' *The Art Bulletin* 56, no. 1 (1974), pp. 12–30.

Buringh, Eltjo. *Medieval Manuscript Production in the Latin West*: *Explorations with a Global Database*. Leiden: Brill, 2011. https://doi.org/10.1163/9789047428640

Carey, Frances. *Campbell Dodgson*: *Scholar and Collector, 1867–1948*. London: British Museum in association with the Parnassus Foundation, 1998.

Cobianchi, Roberto. 'Printing a New Saint: Woodcut Production and the Canonization of Saints in Late Medieval Italy.' In *The Saint between Manuscript and Print*: *Italy 1400–1600*, ed. by Alison Knowles Frazier, pp. 73–98. Toronto: Centre for Reformation and Renaissance Studies, 2015.

Coleman, Joyce. *Public Reading and the Reading Public in Late Medieval England and France*. Cambridge: Cambridge University Press, 1996.

Courboin, François. *Catalogue Sommaire des Gravures et Lithogrphies composant la Réserve*. Bibliothèque Nationale, département des Estampes. 2 vols. Paris, 1900–1901.

Crawford, Matthew B. *Shop Class as Soulcraft*: *An Inquiry into the Value of Work*. New York: Penguin Press, 2009.

Dackerman, Susan. *Painted Prints*: *The Revelation of Color in Northern Renaissance & Baroque Engravings, Etchings & Woodcuts*. University Park, PA: Pennsylvania State University Press, 2002.

Daly, Lloyd W. *Contributions to a History of Alphabetization in Antiquity and the Middle Ages*. Brussels: Latomus, 1967.

De Flou, Karel and Edward Gailliard. *Beschrijving van Middelnederlandsche en andere Handschriften, die in Engeland bewaard worden*: *Verslag ingediend bij het Belgisch Staatsbestuur en de Koninklijke Vlaamsche Academie*. 2 vols. Ghent: Siffer, 1895–1897.

De Hamel, Christopher, *The Rothschilds and Their Collections of Illuminated Manuscripts* London: The British Library, 2005.

de Ricci, Seymour. *Census of Medieval and Renaissance Manuscripts in the United States and Canada*. 3 vols. New York: H. W. Wilson, 1935–1940.

Delaissé, L. M. J., James H. Marrow and John De Wit (eds.). *Illuminated Manuscripts*. Fribourg: Published for the National Trust by Office du livre, 1977.

Deschamps, Jan. 'De Herkomst van het Leidse Handschrift van de Sint-Servatiuslegende van Hendrik van Veldeke.' *Handelingen van de Koninklijke Zuidnederlandse Maatschappij voor Taal- en Letterkunde en Geschiedenis* 12 (1958), pp. 53–78.

Deschamps, Jan. *Middelnederlandse Handschriften uit Europese en Amerikaanse Bibliotheken: Tentoonstelling ter Gelegenheid van het Honderdjarig Bestaan van de Koninklijke Zuidnederlandse Maatschappij voor Taal- en Letterkunde en Geschiedenis, Brussel, Koninklijke Bibliotheek Albert I, 24 Okt.-24 Dec. 1970: Catalogus*. 2nd edn Leiden: Brill, 1972.

Dicke, Gerd, and Klaus Grubmüller, eds. *Die Gleichzeitigkeit von Handschrift und Buchdruck*, Wolfenbütteler Mittelalter-Studien, vol. 16. Wiesbaden: Harrassowitz, 2003.

Dodgson, Campbell, *Catalogue of Early German and Flemish Woodcuts in the British Museum*, 2 vols. London: British Museum Trustees, 1903.

Dreves, Guido Maria, 1854–1909, Clemens Blume, 1862–1932, and Henry Marriott Bannister, 1854–1919, eds. *Analecta Hymnica Medii Aevi*. 54 vols. Leipzig: Fues's Verlag, 1854–1932.

Ehrenschwendtner, Marie-Luise. 'Virtual Pilgrimages? Enclosure and the Practice of Piety at St Katherine's Convent, Augsburg.' *Journal of Ecclesiastical History* 60, no. 1 (2009), pp. 45–73. https://doi.org/10.1017/s0022046908006027

Einblattdrucke des Fünfzehnten Jahrhunderts, ed. by Paul Heitz and Wilhelm Ludwig Schreiber. 100 vols. Straßburg: Paul Heitz, 1899–2016.

Eisenstein, Elizabeth L. *The Printing Revolution in Early Modern Europe*. Cambridge: Cambridge University Press, 1983.

Engen, Hildo van, *De derde orde van Sint-Franciscus in het middeleeuwse bisdom Utrecht*, Hilversum: Verloren, 2006.

Erler, Mary. 'Pasted-in Embellishments in English Manuscripts and Printed Books c. 1480–1533', *The Library*, 6th ser., no. 14 (1992), pp. 185–206.

Farquhar, James Douglas. 'The Manuscript as a Book.' In *Pen to Press: Illustrated Manuscripts and Printed Books in the First Century of Printing*, ed. by Sandra Hindman and James Douglas Farquhar, 11–99. College Park, MA: Art Dept., University of Maryland, 1977.

Gärtner, Magdalene. Römische Basiliken in Augsburg: Nonnenfrömmigkeit und Malerei um 1500. Augsburg: Wissner, 2002.

Geusau, Baron von. 'Korte Geschiedenis der Kloosters te Maastricht.' *Publications de la Société Historique et Archéologique dans le Duché de Limbourg = Jaarboek van Limburgs Geschied- en Oudheidkundig Genootschap XXXI*, nouvelle série, XI (1894), pp. 3–131.

Gould, Cecil Hilton Monk. *Trophy of Conquest: The Musée Napoléon and the Creation of the Louvre*. London: Faber & Faber, 1965.

Gumbert, J. P. *Bat Books*: *A Catalogue of Folded Manuscripts Containing Almanacs or Other Texts*. Bibliologia: Elementa ad Librorum Studia Pertinentia, 41. Turnhout: Brepols, 2016.

Gumbert, Peter. 'Fifty Years of Codicology', *Archiv für Diplomatik*: *Schriftgeschichte, Siegel- und Wappenkunde*, 50 (2004), pp. 505–26. https://doi.org/10.7788/afd.2004.50.jg.505

Hanno Wijsman, 'Handschriften und gedruckte Bücher: der Wandel der Europäischen Buchkultur im 15. Jahrhundert.' In Christine Beier (ed.), *Geschichte der Buchkultur 5.1*: *Gotik*, Graz: Akademische Druck- und Verlagsanstalt/ADEVA, 2016, pp. 97–114.

Hauwaerts, Evelien, Evelien de Wilde, and Ludo Vandamme. *Colard Mansion*: *Incunabula, Prints and Manuscripts in Medieval Bruges*. Exh. Cat., Groeningemuseum, Brugge. Ghent: Snoeck Publishers, 2018.

Hayles, Katherine and Jessica Pressman, eds., *Comparative Textual Media. Transforming the Humanities in the Postprint Era*. Minneapolis, MN: University of Minnesota Press, 2013. https://doi.org/10.5749/minnesota/9780816680030.001.0001

Hébert, Michèle. *Bibliothèque Nationale, Cabinet des Estampes. Inventaire des Gravures des Écoles du Nord*: *1440–1550*. 2 vols. Paris: Bibliothèque nationale, 1982.

Hennessy, Marlene Villalobos. 'The Social Life of a Manuscript Metaphor: Christ's Blood as Ink'. In *The Social Life of Illumination*: *Manuscripts, Images, and Communities in the Late Middle Ages*, ed. by Joyce Coleman, Mark Cruse and Kathryn A. Smith. Medieval Texts and Cultures of Northern Europe. Turnhout: Brepols, vol. 21, 2013, pp. 17–52, pl. xvii.

Hermans, Jos M. M. 'Elf Kisten Boeken uit het Gouvernementsgebouw te Maastricht: Lotgevallen van de Limburgse Handschriften en Oude Drukken, Gevonden in 1839.' In *Miscellanea Neerlandica. Opstellen voor Dr. Jan Deschamps ter Gelegenheid van Zijn Zeventigste Verjaardag*, ed. by Elly Cockx-Indestege and Frans Hendrickx, I, pp. 105–43. Leuven: Peeters, 1987.

Hindman, Sandra, and James Douglas Farquhar. *Pen to Press*: *Illustrated Manuscripts and Printed Books in the First Century of Printing*. College Park, MD: Art Dept., University of Maryland, 1977.

Hindman, Sandra. *The Robert Lehman Collection. IV*: *Illuminations*. New York and Princeton: Metropolitan Museum of Art in association with Princeton University Press, 1997.

Hollstein, F. W. H. *Dutch and Flemish Etchings, Engravings, and Woodcuts, ca. 1450–1700*. Amsterdam: M. Hertzberger, 1949.

Hülsmann, Margriet. 'Gedecoreerde Handschriften uit Tertiarissenconventen in Amsterdam en Haarlem: Boekenbezit Versus Boekproductie.' *Ons geestelijk erf* 74, no. 1–2 (2000), pp. 153–80. https://doi.org/10.2143/oge.74.1.616449

Ker, N. R., A. J. Piper, Andrew G. Watson and Ian Campbell Cunningham. *Medieval Manuscripts in British Libraries*. 5 vols. Oxford: Clarendon Press, 1969–2002.

Kittler, Friedrich, Dorothea von Mücke and Philippe L. Similon. 'Gramophone, Film, Typewriter.' *October* 41 (1987), pp. 101–18.

Klein, Jan Willem. 'Pragmatische Procesveranderingen in de Boekverluchting', in Manuscripten en Miniaturen: Studies Aangeboden aan Anne S. Korteweg bij haar Afscheid van de Koninklijke Bibliotheek, ed. J. A. A. M. Biemans, Klaas van der Hoek, Kathryn Rudy and Ed van der Vlist. Zutphen: Walburg Pers, 2007, pp. 217–29.

Kosto, Adam. 'Statim invenire ante: finding aids and research tools in pre-scholastic legal and administrative manuscripts', *Scriptorium* 70 (2016), pp. 285–309.

Kumler, Aden, 'Canonizing a Catastrophe: The Curious Case of the Carmelite Missal', lecture at the conference Canons & Contingence: Art Histories of the Book in England and America, University of Massachusetts, Amherst, 2017 (unpublished).

Kumler, Aden, 'The Multiplication of the Species: Eucharistic Morphology in the Middle Ages', *Res* 59/60 (2011), pp. 179–91. https://doi.org/10.1086/resvn1ms23647789

Landau, David and Peter W. Parshall. *The Renaissance Print: 1470–1550*. New Haven, CT; London: Yale University Press, 1994.

Lavin, Maud. *Cut with the Kitchen Knife: The Weimar Photomontages of Hannah Höch*. New Haven, CT: Yale University Press, 1993.

Lehrs, Max. *Geschichte und Kritischer Katalog des Deutschen, Niederländischen und Französischen Kupferstichs im XV. Jahrhundert*. 9 vols. Vienna: Gesellschaft für vervielfältigende Kunst, 1908.

Lepape, Séverine and Kathryn M. Rudy. *Les Origines de l'Estampe en Europe du Nord, 1400–1470*, ed. by host institution Musée du Louvre. Paris: Le Passage; Louvre éditions, 2013.

Leroquais, Victor. *Les Livres d'Heures Manuscrits de la Bibliothèque Nationale*. 2, plus a supplement vols. Paris: Bibliothèque Nationale, 1927–1929, suppl. Mâcon: Protat, 1943.

Mainardi, Patricia. 'Assuring the Empire of the Future: The 1798 Fête de la Liberté.' *Art Journal* 48, no. 2 (1989), pp. 155–63.

Malraux, André, Jean Porcher and Sheila Browne. *Les Manuscrits à Peintures en France du XIIIe au XVIe Siècle* [*Catalogue d'une Exposition à Paris en 1955–1956*]. Paris: Bibliothèque Nationale, 1955.

Marrow, James. 'A Book of Hours from the Circle of the Master of the Berlin Passion: Notes on the Relationship between Fifteenth-Century Manuscript

Illumination and Printmaking in the Rhenish Lowlands.' *The Art Bulletin* 60, no. 4 (1978), pp. 590–616.

Matthews, Anne. 'The Use of Prints in the Hours of Charles d'Angoulême.' *Print Quarterly* 3, no. 1 (1986), pp. 4–18.

Meertens, Maria. *De Godsvrucht in de Nederlanden. naar Handschriften van Gebedenboeken der XVe Eeuw.* 6 vols. [n.p.]: Standaard Boekhandel, 1930–1934.

Nagel, Alexander. *Medieval Modern: Art out of Time*. London: Thames & Hudson, 2012.

Neddermeyer, Uwe. 'Why Were There no Riots of the Scribes? First Results of a Quantitative Analysis of the Book Production in the Century of Gutenberg.' *Gazette du livre médiéval* 31 (1997), pp. 1–8.

Oliver, Judith. 'Je Pecherise Renc Grasces a Vos: Some French Devotional Texts in Beguine Psalters'. In *Medieval Codicology, Iconography, Literature, and Translation: Studies for Keith Val Sinclair*, ed. by Peter Rolfe Monks and D. D. R. Owen. Litterae Textuales. Leiden: E. J. Brill, 1994, pp. 248–66.

Oliver, Judith. 'Medieval Alphabet Soup: Reconstruction of a Mosan Psalter-Hours in Philadelphia and Oxford and the Cult of St. Catherine'. *Gesta* 24, no. 2 (1985), pp. 129–40.

Olsen, Ulla Sander. 'Handschriften en Boeken uit het Birgittinessenklooster Maria Troon te Dendermonde.' In *Spiritualia Neerlandica. Opstellen voor Dr. Albert Ampe S. J. hem door Vakgenoten en Vrienden Aangeboden uit Waardering voor zijn Wetenschappelijk Werk*, ed. by E. Cockcx-Indestege, 389–406. Antwerp: Universitaire Faculteiten Sint-Ignatius te Antwerpen Ruusbroecgenotschap (Centrum voor Spiritualiteit), 1990.

——. 'Handschriften uit het Birgittinessenklooster Mariënwater te Rosmalen bij 's-Hertogenbosch.' In W. Verbeke, ed., *Serta devota in memoriam Guillelmi Lourdaux.* vol. II, pp. 225–54. Leuven: Leuven University Press, 1992–1995 = Mediaevalia Lovaniensia, Series I, Studia 20–21.

Orme, Nicholas. *Medieval Children*. New Haven and London: Yale University Press, 2001.

Overgaauw, Eef. A. 'Saints in Medieval Calendars from the Diocese of Utrecht as Clues for the Localization of Manuscripts.' *Codices Manuscripti* 16 (1992), pp. 81–97.

Parkes, Malcolm Beckwith, '*Folia librorum quaerere*: Medieval experience of the problem of hypertext and the index', originally published in 1995 and republished in his *Pages from the Past: Medieval Writing Skills and Manuscript Books*, ed. Pamela R. Robinson and Rivkah Zim. Chapter X, pp. 23–50, and Plates I-VIII. Farnham: Ashgate, 2012.

Petev, Todor. 'A Group of Hybrid Books of Hours Illustrated with Woodcuts.' In *Books of Hours Reconsidered*, ed. by Sandra Hindman and James H. Marrow, pp. 391–408. London: Harvey Miller Publishers, 2013.

Pleij, Herman and J. Reynaert, eds. *Geschreven en Gedrukt: Boekproductie van Handschrift naar Druk in de Overgang van Middeleeuwen naar Moderne Tijd*. Ghent: Academia Press, 2004.

Pleij, Herman. 'Printing as a Long-Term Revolution', in *Books in Transition at the Time of Philip the Fair: Manuscripts and Printed Books in the Late Fifteenth and Early Sixteenth Century Low Countries*, ed. by Hanno Wijsman, with the collaboration of Ann Kelders and Susie Speakman Sutch. pp. 287–307. Burgundica, 15. Turnhout: Brepols, 2010. https://doi.org/10.1484/m.burg-eb.6.09070802050003050209080404

Porck, M. H. and H. J. Porck. 'Eight Guidelines on Book Preservation from 1527: How One Should Preserve All Books to Last Eternally.' *Journal of Paper Conservation* 13, no. 2 (2012), pp. 17–25.

Powell, Amy Knight. *Depositions: Scenes from the Late Medieval Church and the Modern Museum*. New York: Zone Books, 2012.

Priebsch, Robert. *Deutsche Handschriften in England*. 2 vols. Erlangen: Fr. Junge, 1896–1901.

Ringbom, Sixten. 'Some Pictorial Conventions for the Recounting of Thoughts and Experiences in Late Medieval Art.' In *Medieval Iconography and Narrative: A Symposium*, ed. by Flemming Gotthelf Andersen, 38–69. Odense: Odense University Press, 1980.

Roest, Bert. *A History of Franciscan Education (c. 1210–1517)*. Leiden; Boston: Brill, 2000.

——. *Franciscan Learning, Preaching and Mission c. 1220–1650: Cum Scientia Sit Donum Dei, Armatura ad Defendendam Sanctam Fidem Catholicam*. Leiden: Brill, 2015. https://doi.org/10.1163/9789004280731

——. *Franciscan Literature of Religious Instruction before the Council of Trent*. Studies in the History of Christian Traditions, 117 Leiden: Brill, 2004.

Rosenberg, Martin. 'Raphael's Transfiguration and Napoleon's Cultural Politics.' *Eighteenth-Century Studies* 19, no. 2 (1985), pp. 180–205.

Rouse, Richard H. 'Cistercian Aids to Study in the Thirteenth Century', in *Studies in Medieval Cistercian History II*, ed. by J. R. Sommerfeldt. pp. 123–34. Kalamazoo, MI: Cistercian Publications, 1976.

Rouse, Richard H. and Mary A. Rouse. 'Concordances et index', in *Mise en page et mise en texte du livre manuscrit*, ed. by H.-J. Martin and J. Vezin. pp. 219–28. Paris, Éditions du Cercle de la Librairie. Promodis, 1990.

——. 'La naissance des index', in *Histoire de l'édition française, I: Le livre conquérant: Du Moyen Âge au milieu du XVIIe siècle*, eds Henri-Jean Martin, Roger Chartier, Jean-Pierre Vivet. pp. 77–85. Paris, Promodis, 1983.

——. '*Statim invenire*: Schools, Preachers and New Attitudes to the Page', in *Renaissance and Renewal in the Twelfth Century*, ed. R. L. Benson and G. Constable. pp. 201–25. Cambridge, MA, 1982; repr. in their *Authentic*

Witnesses: Approaches to Medieval Texts and Manuscripts. pp. 191–219. Notre Dame, Ind: University of Notre Dame Press, 1991.

——. 'The Development of Research Tools in the Thirteenth Century' in their Authentic Witnesses: Approaches to Medieval Texts and Manuscripts. pp. 221–55. Notre Dame, Ind: University of Notre Dame Press, 1991.

Rudy, Kathryn M. 'An Illustrated Mid-Fifteenth-Century Primer for a Flemish Girl: British Library, Harley Ms 3828', *Journal of the Warburg and Courtauld Institutes* 69 (2006), pp. 51–94.

——. 'Dirty Books: Quantifying Patterns of Use in Medieval Manuscripts Using a Densitometer.' *Journal of Historians of Netherlandish Art* 2, no. 1, (2010) [n.p.]. https://doi.org/10.5092/jhna.2010.2.1.1

——. 'Manuscripts from Zutphen, Lamb of God Roundels, and a New Iconography of Penance', special issue of *Quaerendo* 41 dedicated to Prof. Dr. Jos Hermans, ed. by Jos Biemans and Anne Korteweg (2011), pp. 360–72. https://doi.org/10.1163/157006911x597441

——. 'Reconstructing the Delbecq-Schreiber Passion (as part of the St Godeleva manuscript)', *Unter Druck. Mitteleuropäische Buchmalerei im 15. Jahrhundert. Akten der Tagung, Wien, Österreichische Akademie der Wissenschaften, 13.1.– 17.1.2016*, herausgegeben von Jeffrey F. Hamburger und Maria Theisen. Buchmalerei des 15. Jahrhunderts in Mitteleuropa Herausgeben von Jeffrey F. Hamburger, Band 15, pp. 156–67. Petersberg: Michael Imhoff Verlag, 2018.

——. *Piety in Pieces: How Medieval Readers Customized their Manuscripts.* Cambridge: Open Book Publishers, 2016, https://doi.org/10.11647/OBP.0094; https://www.openbookpublishers.com/product/477

——. *Rubrics, Images and Indulgences in Late Medieval Netherlandish Manuscripts.* Vol. 55 Library of the Written World. Leiden: Brill, 2017. https://doi.org/10.1163/9789004326965

——. *Virtual Pilgrimages in the Convent: Imagining Jerusalem in the Late Middle Ages* Vol. 8 Disciplina Monastica, ed. by Isabelle Cochelin and Susan Boynton. Turnhout: Brepols, 2011. https://doi.org/10.1484/m.dm-eb.5.108575

——. 'A Play Built for One: The Passion of St. Barbara.' In *The Sides of the North: An Anthology in Honor of Professor Yona Pinson*, ed. by Tamar Cholcman and Assaf Pinkus, 56–82. Newcastle: Cambridge Scholars, 2015.

——. 'How to Prepare the Bedroom for the Bridegroom.' In *Frauen—Kloster— Kunst: Neue Forschungen zur Kulturgeschichte des Mittelalters: Beiträge zum Internationalen Kolloquium vom 13. bis 16. Mai 2005 Anlässlich der Ausstellung 'Krone und Schleier'*, ed. by Jeffrey F. Hamburger, Carola Jaeggi and Hedwig Röckelein, 369–75. Turnhout, Belgium: Brepols, 2007.

——. 'Sewing the Body of Christ: Eucharist Wafer Souvenirs Stitched into Fifteenth-century Manuscripts, Primarily in the Netherlands', *Journal of Historians of Netherlandish Art*, 8, no. 1 (Winter 2016), Article 1 (48 pages, [n.p.]). https://doi.org/10.5092/jhna.2016.8.1.1

———. *Postcards on Parchment: The Social Lives of Medieval Books*. New Haven and London: Yale University Press, 2015.

Scheepsma, Wybren. *De Limburgse Sermoenen (ca. 1300): De Oudste Preken in het Nederlands* Nederlandse Literatuur en Cultuur in de Middeleeuwen. Amsterdam: B. Bakker, 2005.

Scheepsma, Wybren. *The Limburg Sermons: Preaching in the Medieval Low Countries at the Turn of the Fourteenth Century* Brill's Series in Church History. Leiden; Boston: Brill, 2008. https://doi.org/10.1163/ej.9789004169692.i-488

Schmidt, Peter. 'Bildgebrauch und Frömmigkeitspraxis: Bemerkungen zur Benutzung früher Druckgraphik.' In *Spiegel der Seligkeit: Privates Bild und Frömmigkeit im Spätmittelalter*, ed. by Frank Matthias Kammel and Andreas Curtius, 69–83. Nürnberg: Verlag des Germanischen Nationalmuseums, 2000.

———. 'The Early Print and the Origins of the Picture Postcard.' In *The Woodcut in Fifteenth-Century Europe*, ed. by Peter W. Parshall, pp. 239–57. Washington, D.C.: National Gallery of Art, 2009.

———. 'The Use of Prints in German Convents of the Fifteenth Century: The Example of Nuremberg.' *Studies in Iconography* 24 (2003), pp. 43–69.

———. *Gedruckte Bilder in handgeschriebenen Büchern: Zum Gebrauch von Druckgraphik im 15. Jahrhundert* Pictura et Poesis: Interdisziplinäre Studien zum Verhältnis von Literatur und Kunst. Cologne: Böhlau, 2003. https://doi.org/10.7788/9783412324889

Schmidt, Suzanne Kathleen Karr and Kimberly Nichols. *Altered and Adorned: Using Renaissance Prints in Daily Life*. 1st ed. Chicago: Art Institute of Chicago; New Haven: Distributed by Yale University Press, 2011.

Schoëngen, M. and P. C. Boeren. *Monasticon Batavum*. 3 vols. Amsterdam: Noord-Hollandsche Uitg. Maatschappij, 1942.

Schreiber, Wilhelm Ludwig. *Manuel de l'Amateur de la Gravure sur Bois et sur Métal au XVe Siècle*. 8 vols. Berlin: A. Cohn, 1891–1911.

Schuppisser, Frizt Oskar. 'Copper Engravings of the "Mass Production" Illustration Netherlandish Prayer Manuscripts.' In *Masters and Miniatures: Proceedings of the Congress on Medieval Manuscript Illumination in the Northern Netherlands* (Utrecht, 10–13 December 1989), ed. by K. van der Horst and Johann-Christian Klamt, 3, pp. 389–400. Doornspijk: Davaco, 1991.

Shestack, Alan. *Fifteenth Century Engravings of Northern Europe from the National Gallery of Art*, 2 vols. Washington: National Gallery of Art, 1967.

Simons, Walter. 'Reading a Saint's Body: Rapture and Bodily Movement in the 'Vitae' of Thirteenth-Century Beguines'. In *Framing Medieval Bodies*, ed. by Sarah Kay and Miri Rubin, pp. 10–23. Manchester; New York: Manchester University Press, distributed by St. Martin's Press, 1994.

Smentek, Kristel. 'The Collector's Cut: Why Pierre-Jean Mariette Tore up His Drawings and Put Them Back Together Again', *Master Drawings* 46, no. 1 (2008), pp. 36–60.

Smeyers, Maurits. *Vlaamse Miniaturen Voor Van Eyck, ca. 1380-ca. 1420*: Catalogus: Cultureel Centrum Romaanse Poort, Leuven, 7 September-7 November 1993. Corpus of Illuminated Manuscripts = Corpus van Verluchte Handschriften, 6. Leuven: Peeters, 1993.

Smith, Kathryn A. 'The Neville of Hornby Hours and the Design of Literate Devotion', *The Art Bulletin* 81, no. 1 (1999), pp. 72–92.

Smith, Kathryn A. Art, *Identity, and Devotion in Fourteenth-Century England*: *Three Women and Their Books of Hours.* London: British Library and University of Toronto Press, 2003.

Smyth, Adam. *Material Texts in Early Modern England*. Cambridge: Cambridge University Press, 2018. https://doi.org/10.1017/9781108367868

Stanton, Anne Rudloff. 'The Psalter of Isabelle, Queen of England 1308–1330: Isabelle as the Audience.' *Word & Image: A Journal of Verbal/Visual Enquiry* 18, no. 4 (2002), pp. 1–27. https://doi.org/10.1080/02666286.2002.10404973

Steiner, Emily and Lynn Ransom, eds. *Taxonomies of Knowledge: Information and Order in Medieval Manuscripts*. Philadelphia: The Schoenberg Institute for Manuscript Studies, University of Pennsylvania Libraries, 2015.

Stock, Jan van der. *Early Prints: The Print Collection of the Royal Library of Belgium*. London: Harvey Miller Publishers, 2002.

Stooker, Karl and Theo Verbeij. *Collecties op Orde: Middelnederlandse Handschriften uit Kloosters en Semi-Religieuze Gemeenschappen in De Nederlanden*. 2 vols. Miscellanea Neerlandica. Leuven: Peeters, 1997.

Voigts, Linda E. and Michael R. McVaugh, 'A Latin Technical Phlebotomy and Its Middle English Translation', *Transactions of the American Philosophical Society* 74, no. 2 (1984), pp. 1–69.

Voragine, Jacobus de. *The Golden Legend: Readings on the Saints*. Translated by William Granger Ryan. 2 vols. Princeton, N.J.: Princeton University Press, 1993.

Warnar, Geert. 'Servatius in School.' *Omslag: Bulletin van de Universiteitsbibliotheek Leiden en het Scaliger Instituut* 3 (2010) [n.p.].

Weekes, Ursula. 'Convents as Patrons and Producers of Woodcuts in the Low Countries around 1500.' In *The Woodcut in Fifteenth-Century Europe*, ed. by Peter W. Parshall, 75, 258–75. Washington, D.C.: National Gallery of Art, 2009.

——. *Early Engravers and Their Public: The Master of the Berlin Passion and Manuscripts from Convents in the Rhine-Maas Region, Ca. 1450–1500*. London: Harvey Miller, 2004.

Weigel, Theodor Oskar. *Katalog frühester Erzeugnisse der Druckerkunst der T. O. Weigel'schen Sammlung*: *Zeugdrucke, Metallschnitte, Holzschnitte ... Versteigerung 27.(-29.) Mai 1872*. Leipzig: Weigel, 1872.

Wieck, Roger S. 'Special Children's Books of Hours in the Walters Art Museum', in *Als Ich Can*: *Liber Amicorum in Memory of Professor Dr. Maurits Smeyers*, ed. by Bert Cardon, Jan van der Stock, Dominique Vanwijnsberghe and Katharina Smeyers. Corpus of Illuminated Manuscripts = Corpus van Verluchte Handschriften, pp. 1629–39. Leuven: Peeters, 2002.

Wijsman, Hanno, with the collaboration of Ann Kelders and Susie Speakman Sutch, eds. *Books in Transition at the Time of Philip the Fair*: *Manuscripts and Printed Books in the Late Fifteenth and Early Sixteenth Century Low Countries*. Burgundica, 15. Turnhout: Brepols, 2010. https://doi.org/10.1484/m.burg-eb.6.09070802050003050209080404

Winston-Allen, Anne. *Stories of the Rose*: *The Making of the Rosary in the Middle Ages*. University Park, PA: Pennsylvania State University Press, 1997.

Ziegler, Joanna E. *Sculpture of Compassion*: *The Pietà and the Beguines in the Southern Low Countries, C.1300-C.1600*. Etudes d'Histoire de l'Art, 6. Brussels; Turnhout: Institut Historique Belge de Rome; Brepols, 1992.

General Index

Aachen 156
Adoration of the Magi 145–146
Advent 36, 112, 227, 296, 308
Agatha, St 74, 107, 326
Ambrose, St 116
Amsterdam 32–33, 63, 179–182, 190–191, 247, 274, 308, 315
Andreas, St 32
Andresen, A. 210–212
Andrew, St 70, 119, 219
Anna-te-drieën 65
Anne, St 63–65, 103, 118, 162–163, 234, 253, 289, 310, 314, 324
Annunciation, the 19–20, 88, 144, 226–227, 253, 307, 332, 336
Anthony, St 23, 84, 235, 327
Antwerp 247, 273, 281
Apocalypse 70, 119
Apollonia, St 55, 59, 323
Areford, David 12, 247
Arma Christi 77–78, 163, 226, 228, 234, 326–327, 332
Arnhem 247–249, 251–252, 317
Augsburg, David van 192, 261–263, 318
Augustine, St 116, 149–151, 268–269, 279–281, 313, 318
Augustinian 275, 277, 279–281, 283, 288, 318–319
Ave Maria 64, 182, 186–187, 291, 315

badges added to manuscripts 263–265, 286

Barbara, St 5, 15–16, 18, 39, 43, 45, 49, 55, 84, 169, 219, 279, 290–291, 306–307, 319, 321–322, 327
Bartholomew, St 15, 24, 31, 39, 69, 118–119, 206–207, 220, 222–223, 237, 329, 331
Beecke, Adam de 34, 193
beghards 8–9, 11, 13, 15, 17, 19–21, 24–35, 37–39, 44–45, 53–54, 56–57, 59–63, 65, 68–75, 77–78, 80–82, 84–100, 102–107, 109–110, 112–117, 119–125, 127–128, 131–134, 137, 142, 145–148, 151–152, 154–155, 158, 160–168, 170, 172–174, 177, 182, 185–186, 188–190, 192–195, 197–198, 202–203, 205, 207–209, 212, 214, 216–235, 237–243, 246–247, 256, 267–268, 287–290, 293, 301–303, 306–317, 323, 325–329, 331–335
beguines 30
Belgium 24, 111, 124, 137, 273, 275, 280
Benedict, St 61–63, 65, 324
Berlin 101, 159, 162, 237–238, 243, 246, 265, 267–270, 272, 318
Bernardino, St 38
Bernard, St 89–91, 107, 184
Binck, Jacob 224, 242, 331–332
bindery 26–27, 32, 174, 193, 243, 303
binding 17–18, 25–26, 28, 32–33, 35, 37, 49–51, 98, 102, 112, 164, 174, 178, 285, 294, 301, 307–308
Birgittine 259–261

Blaeu, Joan 29, 321
booklets 257, 300
books of hours 11, 13–14, 18–21, 39, 56, 70, 72–75, 78–79, 84–86, 89, 91–92, 95–97, 99, 103, 105–106, 109, 111, 117, 119, 123, 125, 127–128, 130–133, 137, 151–152, 161–163, 165, 170, 173, 177, 179, 182, 185–188, 190, 194, 202–203, 205, 208–209, 214, 216–218, 222–230, 233–235, 237–238, 241–242, 247, 249–253, 256, 294, 297–299, 301, 303, 307, 309–317, 319, 325–329, 331–335
Bouchot, Henri 139, 175, 264, 314, 318
Bourdichon, Jean 300
Brabant 26, 275, 280–281
Braque, Georges 1–2
British Academy 95, 140
Brussels 26, 138, 162, 246, 280

calendar 8, 22, 24–28, 34, 69, 81, 86, 115, 133, 167–169, 171–174, 176, 179–182, 190, 194, 198, 203, 205–209, 211–213, 219, 239, 259, 295, 303, 308, 316
Cambridge 4, 192, 246, 287, 289–292, 319
Cartesian 13–14
Catherine of Siena, St 162, 232–233, 240, 260, 334
Catherine, St 55, 58–59, 85, 96–98, 107, 174–175, 260, 262, 285, 314, 318, 323, 327, 329, 336
Cecilia, St 55, 59, 96–98, 106–107, 323, 329
Chapter of Our Dear Lady 31
children, books for 185–187
Christ 27, 34, 44–45, 63, 75–78, 80–82, 89–93, 109, 118, 120, 123, 135, 142, 145–149, 151, 153, 160, 162–163, 193, 224, 226–230, 234, 237–238, 248, 250, 253, 255–256, 261–262, 268, 270–271, 275, 277–278, 282–284, 295–298, 309, 312–313, 318–319, 322, 326–328, 330–336

Christ as Man of Sorrows 75–76, 118, 142, 145–146, 224, 227–228, 230, 234, 309–310, 312, 326, 331–333
Christianity 5, 27, 214
Christological 78, 199, 315
Christopher, St 91, 107, 225, 328, 332
Church of Our Lady 29
Claesz, Allaert 225
Clara, St 207
Clare, St 113, 128, 160–162, 232–233, 314
Columba, St 55, 59, 323
Confiteor 183, 187, 189
copying 9, 44, 100, 102, 110, 124, 129, 163, 174, 176, 238–240, 299
Cornelius, St 116, 235
Cosmas, St 162, 169, 171, 232–233, 334
Credo 182, 186–187
Cross 119–120, 123, 183–184, 224, 250–251, 278–279, 282, 295–296, 311, 317–318
Crucifixion 59–60, 144–145, 223–224, 268, 271–272, 296, 312, 318, 331
Cubists 2, 54
cutting 1, 3, 6, 11, 13, 19–20, 39, 44–46, 49, 51, 53–54, 56–57, 59–61, 64, 70–71, 88, 105–106, 112, 126, 132, 137–138, 141–142, 144–145, 149, 151, 156, 158, 160, 164–165, 167, 171, 174, 193–194, 201, 205, 216, 222, 229, 232–235, 245, 248, 257, 263–265, 267, 273, 285, 288, 292–293, 301, 304, 310–311

Damian, St 162, 169, 171, 232–233, 334
Deschamps, Jan 24
Dierick, St 63
Dodgson, Campbell 87, 108, 111–112
Dominican 25, 260–263, 318
Dominic, St 162, 232–233, 240–241, 260, 335
Dorothy, St 264
Drieshen, Clarck 260
Drugulin, Wilhelm Eduard 198, 210–211, 253–255

Duplessis, Maurice 299
Dürer, Albrecht 3, 9, 223–224, 242, 331
Dutch 15–16, 18, 24, 29, 37–38, 40–41, 43, 47, 58, 62, 78, 80–81, 96, 111, 130, 135–137, 141, 143, 177, 179, 181, 186–188, 192–193, 202, 225, 228, 237, 245, 247, 260, 262, 274–275, 280–281, 289, 307–309, 321–322
Dymphna, St 56, 58–59, 169, 280–281, 323

Easter 117, 214, 275
Elizabeth, St 279–281
Elzéar, St 60, 118, 324
Emmaus 237, 296, 334
Emmerick, Jan van 15, 24–25, 34–36, 46, 80, 94, 102, 128–129, 163–164, 177, 189–190, 192–193, 308
English 53, 58, 156, 158, 187–188, 206, 286, 315
engraver 16, 53, 55, 57, 62–64, 74–75, 91, 96, 99–100, 125–126, 160, 165, 224, 228, 243, 276
Erasmus, St 85, 88, 327
Eucharist 265, 286
Europe 6, 14, 25, 105, 138–140, 158, 212, 246, 267, 273, 284, 305–306
Eyck, Jan van 61, 324

First World War 54, 212
Five Wounds of St Francis 23, 206
Flagellation 268, 277, 295
Flemish 49, 62, 86, 106–108
France, French 105, 130, 132–139, 141–147, 151, 156, 165, 175, 178, 180–181, 236, 264, 266, 295, 299, 312–314, 317–318
Franciscan 8, 11, 23, 25–27, 29–30, 33, 60–61, 79, 113, 118, 124, 130, 174, 176, 179, 182, 187, 189–190, 194–195, 206–207, 211–212, 217, 252–253, 308, 317, 324
Francis, St 8, 23, 25–26, 30–32, 60–61, 66–67, 69, 113, 118, 160, 162, 179, 187, 189, 206–207, 216–217, 232–233, 309, 316, 324–325

Gabriel, angel 88
Geel 281
Gemeentemuseum 190–191, 315
Genevieve, St 225, 332
George, St 99, 235, 286, 319, 334
Germany, German 11, 16, 24, 37–38, 49, 53, 55, 62–63, 68, 73, 79, 89, 91, 98, 106–107, 136–137, 139, 141, 143, 156, 159, 175, 202, 210, 224, 226, 237, 245, 267–268, 276, 304, 312, 314
Gertrude, St 124–125, 311
Gerusalemme 75–76, 310
Ghent 86, 185, 302
Ghielis, St 116, 206
gluing 65, 110, 193, 200, 231, 233
God 2, 27, 58–59, 123, 183, 250, 301
Godeleva, St 103, 310
Golden Legend 150, 179–182, 315
Gospel 70, 295
Gothic 65, 69
Granger, James 201
  Grangerization 201
Gregorian 227, 234
Gregory, St 75, 116, 145, 234, 253, 282, 295, 336

Hague, The 79, 137, 193, 245–246
Harley, Edward 51
Harley, Robert 51
Hébert, Michèle 139
Heitz, Paul 135, 138–139, 246
Helen, St 224, 331
Holbein the Elder, Hans 261
Hollstein, Friedrich Wilhelm 63, 79, 83, 99–100, 222, 237, 239
Holy Sacrament 277, 282
Honorius III, Pope 26
Horne, Jacob van 191, 315
Hours of Charles d'Angoulême 265, 299
Hours of the Cross 119–120, 183, 250–251, 295–296, 311, 317

Hours of the Holy Spirit 120–121, 183, 252, 295–297, 311
Hours of the Virgin 129, 227, 295–297
Hubert, St 22, 116, 206, 235
Hubrecht, St 219
Hugh of St Victor 181

indulgences 23, 75, 94, 184, 194, 241, 259–260, 262, 317
Innocent III, Pope 26
Innocent VIII, Pope 261
Israhel van Meckenem 9, 16, 39–41, 43–47, 49, 53–54, 62–63, 75, 91–95, 99–102, 144–146, 160, 162, 165, 222, 226–230, 232–233, 235–240, 243, 287–289, 293–300, 306–310, 312, 314, 317, 319, 321–323, 328–330, 332–335
Italy 26, 134

Jairus's Daughter 92–93, 101, 238, 328
James, St 70, 73–74, 118, 326
Jerome, St 116, 172, 279
Jesus 38, 78, 89–92, 103, 150–151, 217, 239, 261, 269, 277, 282, 310, 313, 326
Jews 27, 216
Joest, St 64
Johannes, St 219
Johannes XXII 94
John the Baptist 116, 279
John the Evangelist 70, 118, 194, 279
Judas 261–262, 318
Julius II, Pope 223
Junius Brutus 134

Kittler, Friedrich 300, 303
knife 2–3, 19, 39, 54, 59, 62, 71, 73, 132, 141, 146, 160, 193, 200, 225, 227, 233, 267, 285, 306

Lambert, St 27, 130–132, 169, 205–207, 216–217, 312, 316
Last Judgement 81, 151
Latin 177, 186–189, 192, 200, 228, 289, 315
Lawrence, St 72–73, 119, 279, 326

Lebuin, St 180
Lehrs, Max 13, 52, 62–63, 79, 83, 90, 96–97, 99, 101–102, 106–107, 154, 162, 166, 222–223, 237–239, 266, 270, 272, 275, 318
Leiden 34, 137, 188, 193, 211, 263
Leipzig 210, 254
Leuven 26, 273
Liège 22, 32, 207, 210, 212
Limburg 11, 26–30, 35–36, 124, 176, 190, 308
London Review Bookshop 52
Low Countries 24, 37, 96, 100, 139, 256, 281, 284
Lower German 62, 106–107
Lower Rhine 16, 37, 100, 107–108, 265
Lucy, St 96, 98, 107, 225, 332
Luke, St 72, 119, 237, 334

Maagdendriesch 32, 176, 212, 219
Maas, river 29, 37, 39, 308
Maastricht 8, 11, 13, 15, 22, 24–27, 29–30, 32–34, 37, 39, 46, 60–61, 86, 105, 130, 133–134, 137, 145, 165–166, 173–174, 176, 182, 188, 190, 193, 195, 198, 206–207, 211–212, 216, 218–220, 222, 233, 239, 243, 247, 303, 306
Macarius, St 85–87, 327
Madden, Frederic 51
Magdalene, Mary 56, 58, 73, 174–175, 214, 224, 263, 265, 279, 314, 323, 331
Margaret, St 56, 85, 87–88, 179, 323, 328
Mark, St 54, 99–101, 197–198, 220, 237, 243, 310, 323, 329
Marrow, James 44, 211
Martin, St 85, 88, 328
Mary, Virgin 18–21, 29, 38, 58–60, 63–65, 72–73, 81, 91–95, 103, 118, 125–129, 143, 154, 162, 165, 172, 183–184, 198–199, 203, 214, 224, 227, 229–231, 234, 238–239, 241–242, 253–254, 259, 263, 265, 267, 270–272, 289–292, 295–297,

307, 310, 312–314, 316, 318–319, 323–325, 329–331, 333, 335–336
Mass of St Gregory 75, 145, 253, 336
Master ES 3, 44, 145, 275
Master IAM of Zwolle 125–126, 330
Master of the Berlin Passion 101, 237–238, 243, 265
Master of the Flower Borders 55, 57–58, 98, 107, 309
Master of the Housebook 154
Master of the Martyrdom of the Ten Thousand 79, 91, 237–238, 328
Masters of the Gold Scrolls 165
Masters of the Pink Canopies 109, 301
Master with the Banderols 79
Matthew, St 15, 130, 132, 312
Matthias, St 68–69, 287, 325
Mechelen 26, 281
Meertens, Maria 273, 275
Michael, archangel 24
Michael, St 24, 31, 99, 207, 329
Middle Ages 113, 141, 176, 179, 187, 280
Middle Dutch 16, 18, 40–41, 43, 47, 62, 96, 111, 137, 143, 177, 179, 186–188, 192–193, 202, 245, 247, 275, 307–309, 321–322
Middle Rhine 15–16, 100
Molder, Jan de 135
Monogrammist A 96–98
Monogrammist F 77–78, 327
Monogrammist LF 261–262, 318
Monogrammist MB 202, 331

Napoleon 134–135, 137–138
Napoleonic 27, 135, 267, 274, 303
Napoleon III 136
Nativity 202, 229–230, 300, 331, 333
Naumann, Robert 198, 210, 253
Netherlands, the 24–26, 34, 40, 47, 78, 124, 130, 135, 137, 140, 178, 180–181, 190, 206, 211, 224, 245, 255, 262, 287, 289
Nicholas, St 84, 88, 327

Norbertine 273–274
Nuremberg 246, 285–286, 336

O'Connell, Sheila 48, 53
Olsen, Ulla Sander 259–260
Opportune, St 264, 318

Paris 49, 51, 76, 90, 105–108, 134–135, 137, 139–150, 152–156, 158–159, 162, 173, 175–176, 206, 235–236, 245–246, 263–264, 266–267, 299, 309, 312–314, 317–318
Passion 25, 78, 81, 101, 109, 227, 237–238, 243, 261, 265, 268, 270, 274–276, 284, 295, 297, 299, 318
Pater Noster 182, 186–187, 194, 213, 315
Patmos 70, 119, 193, 325
Paul, St 40, 43, 55, 63, 70, 74, 85–87, 119, 145, 179, 274, 308, 326–327
Pelagius, Margaret 181
Pelagius, Pope 181
Pentecost 151–152, 252, 265–266, 299, 313, 318, 336
Peter, St 40, 43, 55, 68–70, 107, 145, 279, 308, 325
photography 37, 39, 43, 95, 148, 151, 159–160, 206, 211, 247, 274–275, 286, 304–305, 308
Picasso, Pablo 1–2
Pierpont Morgan Library 246, 273
Pius VI, Pope 134
prayerbooks 88, 173, 177–178, 185, 189, 220, 265
Priebsch, Robert 202, 212
Priebsch's catalogue 202
print, printing 2–6, 8–16, 18–20, 23, 25, 35, 37–65, 67–75, 77–84, 86–94, 96–113, 115, 118, 120, 123–126, 128–130, 132, 134–135, 137–146, 148–151, 154–156, 158–167, 172–175, 189–190, 193–194, 197–206, 210–214, 216–229, 231–243, 245–248, 250, 252–257, 259–271, 275–277, 284–297, 299–306, 314–315, 317–319, 324, 335

Procrustes 14
Protestant 241, 273

Quentin, St 68–69, 119, 325
Quirinus, St 235–236, 317

rebinding 177, 212
Register, the 48–49, 62, 84, 92, 101, 137, 155–156, 197–198, 253–254, 309
Rijksmuseum 190–191, 247, 315
Roch, St 86, 328
Roest, Bert 211
Rome 75–76, 90, 134, 219, 259–263, 295, 310, 317
Rosmalen 260
roundels 5, 16, 39–41, 43–47, 49, 54–59, 70–71, 75, 106, 145, 160–162, 164–165, 169, 219, 223, 226, 229–234, 266, 274–278, 284, 286–289, 293–294, 301, 307–309, 314, 316, 319, 321–323, 326, 330–331, 333–334
Rouse, Mary 167
Rouse, Richard 167

Salvator Mundi 44–45, 120, 160, 162, 248, 250, 322, 330, 336
Scheepsma, Wybren 176
Schmidt, Peter 12, 100, 247
Schofield, B. 111–113
Schreiber, Wilhelm Ludwig 13, 52, 83–84, 86–88, 106–108, 135, 175, 246, 264, 269, 314, 318
Schwitters, Kurt 54
Scotland 29, 140, 159
Sebastian, St 86, 328
Second World War 54, 212
Servaas copyist 193
Servatius, St 22, 27, 34, 41, 43, 46, 55, 98, 188, 206–207, 212, 219, 223, 309, 322
Seven Penitential Psalms 81–83, 120–121, 124, 151, 163, 184, 296, 310–311
Sixtus, St 192
Sta Croce 75–76, 261, 310

St Andrews, University of 140, 159
Stephen, St 73, 119, 326
Stooker, Karl 24, 260
St Trond 111, 210–211
Synthetic Cubism 1, 306

table of contents, calendar as 15, 25, 167–169, 171, 174, 177–180, 182, 189, 193–194, 198, 212–213, 239, 303, 315
Taylor, Paul 39, 43
Third Rule of St Francis 31–32
Tongeren 128, 206–207, 211
Trinity, the 27, 149–150, 246
Tross, Edwin 49, 51, 90, 106–108, 110, 137, 155–156, 158, 166
Trudo, St 26, 111, 113, 130–131, 206–207, 211, 219, 224–225, 312, 332

Ursula, St 162, 232
Utrecht 137, 178, 260, 263

Venray, Henrich van 130
Verbeij, Theo 24, 260
Veronica, St 234
Victorines 181
Vigil of the Dead 120, 122, 296, 311
Vincent, St 72–73, 119, 326
Virgin and Child 64, 91–95, 118, 127, 154, 165, 234, 270–272, 291–292, 310, 313, 318–319, 324, 329
Virgin of the Sun 18–19, 72, 125, 127–129, 143, 198, 203, 214, 229–230, 234, 239, 241–242, 267, 289, 312, 316, 319, 325, 333, 335

Warburg Institute 15–16, 18, 39–41, 52, 306–309
Weekes, Ursula 12, 23, 156, 211
Weert 34, 190–191, 315
Weigel, Theodor Oskar 135, 210, 212
West Flanders 86, 89
Wolffenbüttel 159
Wolfgang, St 41, 43, 46, 55, 98, 144, 223, 309, 322

Zodiac 111, 113–114, 311

Index of Manuscripts and Prints

Amsterdam, UB, Ms. I G 12 32–33, 308

Berlin, Kupferstichkabinett, Box 107 A3A 269, 318

Berlin, Kupferstichkabinett, Inv. 2-56 270, 318

Berlin, Kupferstichkabinett, Inv. 446-I 272, 318

Berlin, Kupferstichkabinett, Inv. 998-I 272

Brussels, Bollandists' Library, Ms. 494 193

Cambridge, Gonville and Caius College, Ms. 718/253 287–293, 319

Cambridge, Massachusetts, Harvard University Library, Ms. Lat. 268 192

Glasgow, Hunterian Museum, Ms. H512 187–188, 315

Hague, The, Koninklijke Bibliotheek, Ms. 70 E 5 176

Hague, The, Koninklijke Bibliotheek, Ms. 73 D 9 179–181, 315

Hague, The, Koninklijke Bibliotheek, Ms. 75 G 2 129, 312

Hague, The, Koninklijke Bibliotheek, Ms. 77 L 58 253, 317

Hague, The, Koninklijke Bibliotheek, Ms. 131 F 19 200–201, 330

Hague, The, Koninklijke Bibliotheek, Ms. 133 D 29 193

Hague, The, Koninklijke Bibliotheek, Ms. 133 F 2 185

Hague, The, Koninklijke Bibliotheek, Ms. 135 E 36 177–178, 315

Heverlee, Abdij van Park, Ms. 18 275–276, 278–281, 283–284, 318–319

Leiden, Universiteitsbibliotheek, Ms. Ltk 303 211

London, British Library, Add. Ms. 17524 250, 271

London, British Library, Add. Ms. 24332 11, 14–15, 17–24, 26, 32–35, 38–40, 43–44, 46–51, 53, 58–59, 66–68, 82, 86, 101, 105–106, 109–110, 112–113, 115, 117, 132, 134, 137, 139, 142–143, 145, 148–149, 151, 154–156, 158–159, 162–165, 167–168, 170, 173, 177–178, 182, 185–187, 189–190, 193–194, 197, 202, 207, 210–214, 217, 219–220, 222, 227, 229, 232–233, 235, 237, 239–241, 245–247, 263, 268, 285, 300, 303–305, 307–311, 313–315, 321–322, 325

London, British Library, Add. Ms. 31001 255–257, 261–263, 304–305

London, British Library, Add. Ms. 31002 199, 204–207, 210–213, 216–220, 223, 226–227, 229, 231,

233–234, 237–241, 243, 245, 254–256, 304–305, 315
London, British Library, Add. Ms. 41338 82–83, 111–116, 119–123, 125, 127–128, 131–134, 160–161, 304–305, 310–312, 314
London, British Museum, Department of Prints & Drawings, inv. 158* b 32 286, 319
London, British Museum, Department of Prints & Drawings, inv. 1847,0318.128 252, 336
London, British Museum, Department of Prints & Drawings, inv. 1848,0212.119 248, 336
London, British Museum, Department of Prints & Drawings, inv. 1848,1125.19 229, 333
London, British Museum, Department of Prints & Drawings, inv. 1851,1213.864 93, 329
London, British Museum, Department of Prints & Drawings, inv. 1861,1109 series 38, 43–47, 49, 54–56, 60–61, 63–64, 67–70, 72–75, 78, 80, 83–86, 89, 91–97, 99, 101, 103, 106–108, 119–120, 123, 193, 220, 238, 309–310, 321–330
London, British Museum, Department of Prints & Drawings, inv. 1868,1114 series 101, 198–199, 202, 204, 206, 210, 214, 220–226, 228–230, 233–235, 237–238, 240–242, 253–254, 256–257, 310, 316–317, 329–336
London, British Museum, Department of Prints & Drawings, inv. 1873,0809.641 230, 333
London, British Museum, Department of Prints & Drawings, inv. 1890,1013.54.1-35 285, 336
London, British Museum, Department of Prints & Drawings, inv. 1897.0103 series 294–295
London, British Museum, Sloane Ms. 3981 294, 297–298, 319

Maastricht, Regionaal Historisch Centrum Limburg, 14.D015, inv. no. 6 37, 177
Maastricht, Regionaal Historisch Centrum Limburg, 22.001A Handschriften GAM, inv.nr. 462 28, 35–36, 308
Munich, Stadtbibliothek, Clm. 386 228
Nijmegen, Radboud Universiteit, Soeterbeeck Coll. Ms IV 136 288
Paris, Bibliothèque Nationale de France, Département des Estampes, Ea 18 c Res 266, 318
Paris, Bibliothèque Nationale de France, Département des Estampes, Ea20aRes 143, 312
Paris, Bibliothèque nationale de France, Département des Estampes, Ea48Res 146, 312
Paris, Bibliothèque Nationale de France, Département des Estampes, Ea48Res 145–146, 312
Paris, Bibliothèque Nationale de France, Ms. Lat. 1173 299

Paris, Louvre, Rothschild Collection 134, 148–155, 158–159, 313

Stonyhurst, Great College, Ms. 4 192

Vienna, Österreichische Nationalbibliothek, ser. Nova 12715 57–58, 309

Weert, Gemeentemuseum Jacob van Horne, Minderbroeders, Ms. 9 193
Weert, Gemeentemuseum Jacob van Horne, Minderbroeders, Ms. 11 193
Weert, Gemeentemuseum Jacob van Horne, Minderbroeders, Ms. 12 192
Weert, Gemeentemuseum Jacob van Horne, Ms. CMW 41 34

This book need not end here...

Share

All our books — including the one you have just read — are free to access online so that students, researchers and members of the public who can't afford a printed edition will have access to the same ideas. This title will be accessed online by hundreds of readers each month across the globe: why not share the link so that someone you know is one of them?

This book and additional content is available at:
https://doi.org/10.11647/OBP.0145

Customise

Personalise your copy of this book or design new books using OBP and third-party material. Take chapters or whole books from our published list and make a special edition, a new anthology or an illuminating coursepack. Each customised edition will be produced as a paperback and a downloadable PDF.

Find out more at:
https://www.openbookpublishers.com/section/59/1

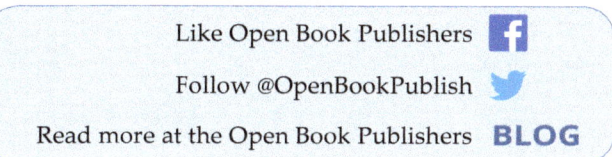

You may also be interested in:

Piety in Pieces
How Medieval Readers Customized their Manuscripts
By Kathryn M. Rudy

https://doi.org/10.11647/OBP.0094

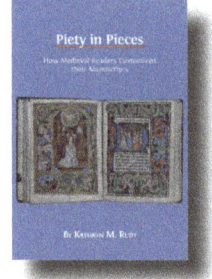

The Sword of Judith
Judith Studies Across the Disciplines
Edited by Kevin R. Brine, Elena Ciletti and Henrike Lähnemann

https://doi.org/10.11647/OBP.0009

From Dust to Digital
Ten Years of the Endangered Archives Programme
Edited by Maja Kominko

https://doi.org/10.11647/OBP.0052

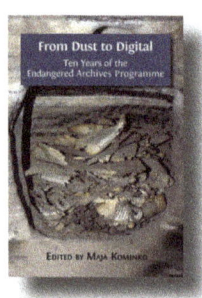